The Dawning of American Keyboard Music

Recent Titles in
Contributions to the Study of Music and Dance

THE DAWNING OF
AMERICAN KEYBOARD MUSIC

J. Bunker Clark

Contributions to the Study of Music and Dance,
Number 12

Greenwood Press
New York • Westport, Connecticut • London

786.4
C59d

Library of Congress Cataloging-in-Publication Data

Clark, J. Bunker.
  The dawning of American keyboard music / J. Bunker Clark.
    p. cm. — (Contributions to the study of music and dance,
  ISSN 0193-9041 ; no. 12)
    Bibliography: p.
    Includes index.
    ISBN 0-313-25581-4 (lib. bdg. : alk. paper)
    1. Piano music—History and criticism. 2. Music—United States—
History and criticism. I. Title. II. Series.
ML711.C6 1988
786.4'0973—dc19   88-3095

British Library Cataloguing in Publication Data is available.

Library of Congress Catalog Card Number: 88-3095
ISBN: 0-313-25581-4
ISSN: 0193-9041

First published in 1988

Greenwood Press, Inc.
88 Post Road West, Westport, Connecticut 06881

Printed in the United States of America

The paper used in this book complies with the
Permanent Paper Standard issued by the National
Information Standards Organization (Z39.48-1984).

10 9 8 7 6 5 4 3 2 1

Contents

Musical Examples

PREFACE

The original title of this book was to have been "Early American Keyboard Music, 1787-1830: A Descriptive and Critical Survey," but in the final stages of preparation I decided it would be more stylish to paraphrase the title of Anthony Philip Heinrich's opus 1, *The Dawning of Music in Kentucky* (1820). The more one investigates a subject, the more one discovers; in my case, American keyboard music in manuscript predating the first American keyboard publications of 1787. Nonetheless, the intent remains: to provide a comprehensive and thorough account of this country's initial keyboard creations in order to foster greater interest and more performances.

I began collecting photocopies of early American keyboard music in 1972 to choose representative works for an anthology, because of the scarcity of such works in reprint or in reliable modern edition. Whereas scores by European composers and studies of European music were available in abundance, the United States was not comparably blessed. There were important exceptions, however: notably, the writings of Oscar Sonneck (whose initial study was rejected by American publishers and appeared instead in Leipzig); the general surveys by John Tasker Howard (1931), Gilbert Chase (1955, 2nd ed. 1966, 3rd ed. 1987), Wilfrid Mellers (1964), and H. Wiley Hitchcock (1969, 2nd ed. 1974, 3rd ed. 1988); the important collection of essays on 17-19th century topics by Irving Lowens (1964); and the general anthology of music through the 19th century by W. Thomas Marrocco and Harold Gleason (1964).

Since 1972, the situation has noticeably improved, partially from events associated with the Bicentennial of 1976. Under the leadership of Irving Lowens, the Sonneck Society--named for the pioneer researcher on American music--was organized in 1974 and its quarterly journal *American Music* begun in 1983. Several editions of early keyboard music, including my own, were published, and some new recordings issued. Additional general surveys by Daniel Kingman (1979) and Charles Hamm (1983) appeared. American music is gaining respectability with musical scholars, symbolized by the election in 1981 of Americanist Richard Crawford as the president of the American Musicological Society.

In the specific field of early American keyboard music, the first study completed was the 1966 dissertation by Byron A. Wolverton, which is invaluable, especially in the identification, with library locations, of original editions of piano music published until 1830, after Richard J. Wolfe's bibliographical cutoff date of 1825. Wolverton's approach is somewhat different from mine: he discusses the works of each composer together, and these musicians are grouped geographically. My organization is primarily by genre. The dissertation of the same year by Charles A. Horton is less useful because of the lack of depth--his time-span stretches to 100 years. Important dissertations on individual composers are by John W. Wagner on James Hewitt (1966), by Ronald D. Stetzel on John Christopher Moller (1965), and by Neely Bruce (1971) on the 1820 piano works by Anthony Philip Heinrich.

The basic bibliographies used for the identification of published secular music of the period are Oscar Sonneck's *A Bibliography of Early Secular American Music (18th Century)*, as revised by William Treat Upton (1945), and Richard J. Wolfe's *Secular Music in America, 1801-1825: A Bibliography* (1964). (The first is abbreviated throughout this book with the relevant page number, such as "Sonneck-Upton, 393," and Wolfe with item number, such as "Wolfe 4594.") In the later stages of my work the catalog of the Newberry Library's sheet music appeared, although by that time (1983) I was already familiar with the collection. The following year (1984) John and Anna Gillespie's *Bibliography of Nineteenth-Century American Piano Music* was published, and I was glad to see that they chose some of my favorites.

Beginning in 1972, I visited these libraries to identify printed sheet music and to acquire copies: Duke University, University of North Carolina at Chapel Hill, College of William and Mary, Library of Congress, Free Library of Philadelphia, New York Public Library, Brown University, Boston Public Library, Harvard University, American Antiquarian Society, Eastman School of Music, Clements Library at the University of Michigan, Lilly Library at Indiana University, Baylor University, University of Missouri-Kansas City, and I even found a few originals at my own university. Abroad, I visited the British Library, the Cambridge University Library, and the important Harding collection at the Bodleian Library, Oxford. Further copies were acquired by the University of Kansas interlibrary loan services. For sheet-music bibliographers, detailed information on those items not included in the Sonneck-Upton or Wolfe bibliographies is here included in footnotes.

Although the growth of keyboard music is paralleled by that of other vocal, choral, chamber, and orchestral music in public concerts and in the parlor, social and cultural implications are left for other scholars to determine. My purpose is an examination of the music itself, sometimes in comparison with obvious European models but more especially in comparison with other American compositions of the same time and period. The reader should be cautioned, however, that the pieces discussed here do not represent the totality of published keyboard music composed by Americans to 1830. I have restricted myself, with few exceptions, to the more artistic forms.[1] Within this framework, my intent is to include all keyboard music, although some has escaped my grasp.

Simpler teaching exercises, and the functional genres of dances (waltzes, cotillions, quadrilles, and the like) and marches (composed for ensemble performance, but almost always published in reductions for piano) clearly predominate, but the sheer number prevents their inclusion. Nevertheless, the sonata, rondo, and variation set, by being based on tunes widely known at the time, such as traditional Scotch or Irish melodies or airs sung in the theater, were much more closely allied with the middle classes than is our "classical" music today.

Early publications of keyboard music were almost entirely intended for students. Not only is the style simple but the scores are often carefully fingered. There were apparently not sufficient numbers of accomplished amateurs in the late 18th and early 19th centuries to provide a sufficient market for more ambitious music. But the situation changed noticeably in the second decade of the new century, as seen in some of the pianistically demanding pieces by such composers as Gilfert, Hupfeld, and Moran. The works of Clifton, Meineke, Thibault, and Metz in the 1820s represent a high level of keyboard technique often bordering on virtuosity. The advance is represented by Benjamin Carr, whose teaching collection *Applicazione addolcita* of 1809, with easy rondos and sets of variations on popular tunes for the student, is matched by his difficult fantasia on "Gramachree," written as early as 1806 but not published until 1826. The height of complexity, both musically and for the performer, is attained in the music of Anthony Philip Heinrich. He, however, apparently reached too far; his collections of 1820 and 1823-26 had few--if any--sales. Yet his inventiveness and enthusiastic American nationalism are unmatched until Gottschalk and Ives.

Selected examples are included in order to provide the flavor of the music. For the most part, however, access to certain anthologies and editions is necessary for the reader to take full advantage of this book. They are:

Carr, Benjamin, ed. *Musical Journal for the Piano Forte*. Philadelphia: Carr & Schetky, 1800-04. Reprint in 2 vols. Wilmington, Del.: Scholarly Resources, 1972.

---

1. Exceptions prove the rule, and one is the pair of marches by Charles Thibault, "Greek March of Liberty," op. 10 [1824] (Wolfe 9332-33), the style of which is clearly intended for pianoforte and the parlor, not the band and public occasion. No. 1 lacks the clear formal divisions, or trio, of the usual march; its form approximates ABAB-CABD coda. Whereas No. 2 has the march form of AA | BA ‖ CC (trio) | DCC ‖ da capo, as well as a "trumpet" introduction, scale flourishes and brief motivic imitation align it more with the concert or operatic march. These marches represent the American concern for the struggle by Greece for independence from Turkey.

Carr, Benjamin, ed., *Carr's Musical Miscellany in Occasional Numbers.*
Baltimore and Philadelphia: Carr, 1812-25. Reprint, with intro-
duction by Eve R. Meyer. Earlier American Music, 21. New
York: Da Capo, 1982.

Clark, J. Bunker, ed. *Anthology of Early American Keyboard Music,*
1787-1830. Recent Researches in American Music, 1-2.
Madison: A-R Editions, 1977. Abbreviated throughout this book
as **EAKM**.

Gillespie, John, comp. *Nineteenth-Century American Piano Music.*
New York: Dover, 1978.

Gold, Edward, ed. *The Bicentennial Collection of American Keyboard*
Music (1790-1900). Dayton: McAfee, 1975.

Heinrich, Anthony Philip. *The Dawning of Music in Kentucky*, op. 1,
and *The Western Minstrel*, op. 2. Philadelphia, 1820. Reprint,
Earlier American Music, 10. New York: Da Capo, 1972.

Heinrich, Anthony Philip. *The Sylviad, or Minstrelsy of Nature in the*
Wilds of N. America, op. 3. Boston, 1823 and 1825-26. Reprint,
with introduction by J. Bunker Clark. Earlier American Music,
28. New York: Da Capo, forthcoming.

Hewitt, James. *Selected Compositions.* Ed. John W. Wagner. Recent
Researches in American Music, 7. Madison: A-R Editions, 1980.
Abbreviated as **Wagner ed**.

McClenny, Anne, and Maurice Hinson, eds. *A Collection of Early*
American Keyboard Music. Cincinnati: Willis, 1971. Abbreviated
as **McClenny-Hinson**.

Owen, Barbara, ed. *A Century of American Organ Music.* 3 vols.
Dayton: McAfee, 1975-76; Melville, N.Y.: Belwin-Mills, 1983.

Reinagle, Alexander. *The Philadelphia Sonatas.* Ed. Robert Hopkins.
Recent Researches in American Music, 5. Madison: A-R Editions, 1978.

A complete list of modern editions is in the bibliography.

As this book goes to press, I have been asked to begin the com-
pilation of another anthology of American keyboard music, from its
beginnings through the Civil War, for the series *Three Centuries of*
American Music. The general editor is Sam Dennison (Free Library of
Philadelphia), and the publisher is G. K. Hall of Boston. Obviously
some of the pieces given favorable treatment here will be included, as
well as others from the period 1830-65.

The earliest surviving keyboard compositions by Americans are
contained in Francis Hopkinson's manuscript book at the University of

Pennsylvania, now available in a facsimile edition.[2] Hopkinson probably copied the book about 1764, the impetus provided by his teacher James Bremner (d. 1780), who had immigrated to Philadelphia from England the previous year. Bremner was the composer of four pieces in the book, including a 3-staff (short band score?) March in D major (p. 117), a "Trumpet Air," probably for organ (p. 119; see chapter 6), a Lesson in B-flat in simple rondo form (pp. 114-15; see chapter 2), and "Lady Coventry's Minuet with Variations" (pp. 12-13; see chapter 3). All are charming and quite simple, suitable for the "gentleman amateur,"[3] as is the unimposing two-part piece "Lesson del Sigr. [John] Palma" (p. 39),[4] by a Philadelphia resident of the time who, by this title and his name, may have immigrated from Italy.

"American" here means "North America," since two sets of variations with Canadian associations were published before 1830: one, variations on a "Canadian Dance" by George Pfeiffer of Philadelphia, and the other by Theodore F. Molt of Quebec City. Both are included in *The Canadian Musical Heritage* 1: *Piano Music I*, edited by Elaine Keillor (1983), and are briefly described here in chapter 3.

The early drafts were written on the University of Kansas mainframe computer, then transferred to my personal computer (program: Nota Bene). Thanks are due to Kaia Skaggs at the Computer Center for help in transferring bytes and for other technical assistance. Camera-ready pages were printed at the word processing center in the College of Liberal Arts, where Nancy Kreighbaum (whose early death prevented her seeing the final version) and Paula Malone have been superb guides in the intricacies of computerized wordchewing for some eight years, and who have generously allowed me to operate the laser printers innumerable times for this project.

An earlier version of the chapter on the sonata was published in the journal *American Music* (fall 1984), and the chapter on organ music in *Diapason*, November 1981. I should like to thank H. Earle Johnson, Daniel T. Politoske, Carol MacClintock, John Gillespie, and Raoul Camus for reading various drafts. My wife, Marilyn S. Clark, patiently provided a final reading and caught some rough places and mistakes; the responsibility for any errors that remain, of course, is hers. I am also grateful to the University of Kansas, which provided general research grants to aid this project in the summers of 1977, 1979-83, and another in 1987 for musicology doctoral student Colin Holman to enter the musical examples (program: Professional Composer). Patrick Emerson, at the printing lab, Basic Studies, School of Fine Arts, was most kind to run interference in the operation of this

---

2. *Francis Hopkinson's Lessons: A Facsimile Edition of Hopkinson's Personal Keyboard Book: An Anthology of Keyboard Compositions & Arrangements Copied in Hopkinson's Own Hand*, notes by David P. McKay (Washington: C. T. Wagner, 1979).

3. The title of chapter 6 in Gilbert Chase's *America's Music*.

4. Also in John Tasker Howard, ed., *A Program of Early American Piano Pieces* (New York; J. Fischer & Bro., 1931), 22-23.

program--and even for the weeklong loan of a Macintosh for me to revise the examples and prepare them for printing. I combined text and music with the advanced technology of scissors and tape.

In the text, specific pitches are in italics, using the standard Helmholtz system: *C'*, *C*, *c*, *c'* (= middle C), *c''*, *c'''*, *c''''*. For analytical diagrams and some of the descriptions, uppercase denotes major keys, lowercase minor keys; e.g.: D is D major and d is D minor. In the musical examples, dotted barlines are editorial.

My overriding wish is that some of this music will be played and heard again in concert halls and parlors. It represents our musical beginnings and can still entertain--the basic purpose of the art.

J. Bunker Clark
Professor of Music History
University of Kansas
June 1988

THE DAWNING OF
AMERICAN KEYBOARD MUSIC

1

Sonatas, Rausch to Heinrich

The piano sonata was an important musical genre in Europe in the late 18th and early 19th centuries, as exemplified in the works of Haydn, Mozart, Beethoven, Clementi, and Schubert. This circumstance was reflected in American concerts of the late 18th century, in which piano sonatas were often played--although the identification of the work, or even composer, is not always clear.[1] One prominent pianist in Philadelphia, John Christopher Moller, played six sonatas in various concerts, 1790-95, and his daughter Lucy (at the ages of 9-14) some seventeen more.[2]

Later European composers, such as Schumann, Chopin, and Brahms, continued to write piano sonatas, of course, but these were increasingly overshadowed by one-movement pieces. The trend away from sonatas occurred much earlier in the United States. Solo sonatas by Hewitt, Carr, Taylor, and Moller were printed in the 1790s up to 1809, but American publishers issued only one new solo sonata by an American, Heinrich's *La Buona Mattina* sonata, in the following twenty years.[3] Only three sonatas each by Mozart and Haydn, and one

---

1. See Oscar Sonneck, *Early Concert-Life in America* (Leipzig: Breitkopf und Härtel, 1907; reprint, New York: Da Capo, 1978).

2. Ronald D. Stetzel, "John Christopher Moller (1755-1803) and His Role in Early American Music," 2 vols. (Ph.D. dissertation, University of Iowa, 1965), 1:137-38.

3. One exception is a two-movement "Le Retour de Braddock's: Sonata" by William R. Coppock, no. 2 of the series: Le Tout ensemble, a series of beautiful extracts original & selected, the whole arranged for the piano forte and inscribed to Columbia's fair daughters, by an eminent professor. New York, published by Firth & Hall, 358, Pearl Street [1827-31]. Title-page + pp. 2-3. Copy at the New York Public Library. As indicated in the series title, the sonata consists, however, only of two short, simple pieces, the first apparently a waltz, the second a rondo-arrangement of an unidentified popular tune.

by Beethoven (a duet, op. 6), were published in the United States before 1825.[4] The first public performance of a Beethoven piano sonata took place on 27 February 1819, when Sophia Hewitt, daughter of James, played the Sonata in A flat, op. 26, in a concert sponsored by Boston's Phil-Harmonic Society.[5]

The promise of a major source in *Twenty Four Sonatas for the Piano Forte, or Elegant Extracts from Mozart, Haydn, Beethoven, Steibelt, Kozeluch, Pleyel and other esteemed Authors with Preludes by N. B. Challoner*, published in Philadelphia about 1818 (Wolfe 1758-59), is disappointing: each extract is reduced to less than a page, the largest "lesson" being only 54 measures long. There were, however, simple sonatinas suitable for use by amateurs and piano students, such as those of the still-popular Clementi and the now-forgotten Colizzi.[6] Other sonatas by Europeans, such as Cramer, Nicolai, Pleyel, and Steibelt, were also published in the United States. Steibelt's Sonata op. 81, published in 1810-15 (Wolfe 8562), for example, is of a length and serious intent parallel to those from Beethoven's middle period. Of the sonatas by American composers, only those by Alexander Reinagle are comparable, and these have remained in manuscript until only recently. Sonatas were clearly overshadowed by the greater abundance of more popular genres such as dances, marches, and rondos and variations based on well-known tunes. Like most of this music, the few sonatas issued by American publishers were directed at the widest possible market--students and amateurs with modest keyboard ability.

Several sonatas were published in England before their composers emigrated to the United States, but, with one exception, they were not reprinted here. *A Favorite Sonata for the Piano Forte or Harpsichord, Composed in a Familiar Style for Young Practitioners* by Joseph Willson, published in London about 1798,[7] has a first move-

---

4. Sonneck-Upton, 391; Wolfe 500, 3543-44, and 6299-6302. As indicated in the Preface, throughout this book the first is a page-reference to Oscar George Theodore Sonneck, *A Bibliography of Early Secular American Music (18th Century)*, revised and enlarged by William Treat Upton (Washington: Library of Congress Music Division, 1945; reprint, with preface by Irving Lowens, New York: Da Capo, 1964). The second is an item-reference to Richard J. Wolfe, *Secular Music in America, 1801-1825: A Bibliography*, 3 vols. (New York Public Library, 1964).

5. H. Earle Johnson, *Musical Interludes in Boston, 1795-1830* (New York: Columbia University Press, 1943; reprint, New York: AMS Press, 1967), 107, 144.

6. Wolfe 1887; Sonneck-Upton, 396. Robert Hopkins, in the preface of his edition of the Reinagle sonatas (see below), note 20, seems to think Colizzi was an American composer; I can find no such evidence (e.g., see Wolfe, p. 204).

7. London: W. Cope; copy at the Bodleian Library.

ment not even long enough to be considered in sonatina form, but the second movement is a five-part rondo. When Willson came to America about 1800-01, he may have been associated with Dr. George K. Jackson (1757-1822), who had immigrated in 1796-97. Jackson's *A Favorite Sonata for the Harpsichord or Piano Forte*, op. 4, was issued in London by the composer about 1780.[8] It is more ambitious, definitely not for the "young practitioner." The 182-measure first movement is long enough for three themes, plus closing material, in the exposition; the other movements are a contrasting Air (Andante) in three-part form, and a lively rondo in 6/8.

Similar in scope are Francis Linley's *Three Sonatas for the Harpsichord or Piano Forte*, op. 3, published in London about 1795.[9] Each contains three movements. One characteristic of all three first movements is the introduction of a new theme in the development section. Linley was in the United States only in 1796-99, but several of his works were published here. It was probably the London publication, and not an American edition, of these three sonatas that was advertised for sale in Massachusetts in 1800.[10]

The divertimentos by P. Antony Corri, although in several movements, do not exhibit the formal characteristics of the sonata. The first movement of the divertimento *Halcyon Days*,[11] however, is labeled "sonata," which accurately describes its form. Otherwise, Corri wrote three piano sonatas, *La Eliza*,[12] *L'Augurio felice*,[13] and *La morte di Dussek*,[14] the last with obbligato accompaniment for violin with cello ad libitum. Corri changed his name to Arthur Clifton when he settled in Baltimore. He did not republish these sonatas or write new ones--unfortunately, because they are the finest by any English-born American composer published at the time.

---

8. Facsimile reprint in *The London Pianoforte School, 1766-1860*, ed. Nicholas Temperley, vol. 7 (New York: Garland, 1985), 7-20. The date in *The New Grove Dictionary of American Music* is given as ca. 1795.

9. Three Sonatas for the Harpsichord or Piano Forte, most respectfully dedicated (by permission) to John Carr, Esqr., of York, by F. Linley, organist of Pentonville Chapel. Op. 3. Price 6s/. London: Fentam. Title-page + pp. 4-27. British Library copy.

10. *Salem Gazette*, 21 November 1800; see Sonneck-Upton, 395.

11. London: Chappell & Co., [1816]; copy in British Library.

12. London: L. Lavenue, [1805-11]; copy in British Library.

13. London: Wilkinson & Compy., [1808]; facsimile reprint in *The London Pianoforte School, 1766-1860*, 7:249-62.

14. London: Chappell & Co., [1816]; copy at British Library.

Friedrich Rausch

The first published American sonata is a duet: "Sonatina a quatre mains, par Fr. Rausch," published in New York in 1794-95 (Sonneck-Upton, 396). This is an inauspicious beginning--which is surprising considering the background of the composer. The German-born Friedrich Rausch (1755-1823) had been a musician at the Russian court in St. Petersburg, and was also in London before his emigration to New York about 1793. This sonatina, however, could almost be retitled "sonatinissimo." Consisting of a single movement on two facing pages, there is only a succession of four themes, with no opportunity for thematic returns or even change of key from C major.

James Hewitt

Much better are the solo sonatas by the English-born James Hewitt (1770-1827). He came to the United States in 1792, pursued a successful musical career in New York and Boston, and was one of the most important musical figures in the young country. Although an exact contemporary of Beethoven, his keyboard works are much like those by Willson, Jackson, and Linley published in London in the 1790s. In contrast to many of the sonatas for professional pianists by the London residents Dussek and Clementi, Hewitt's were written for the amateur. His three piano sonatas, op. 5, published in 1795-96 (Sonneck-Upton, 395), each consists of only two movements. The openings of all three are short and unpretentious. The first sonata in D (Wagner ed., no. 30)[15] begins with introductory material for seven measures, then a regular 8-measure theme is stated twice. A 13-measure transition leads from the tonic D major to the dominant key for the 8-measure second theme (with an extension of four measures), in turn being succeeded by six measures of closing material (see Ex. 1-1). The style of the second theme is notably the same as that of the first. After the introduction, the left hand consists entirely of Alberti bass patterns, except in the transition which has the so-called Murky bass (alternating octaves).

Ex. 1-1.   Hewitt, Sonata 1 in D, op. 5, 1st movement:

a. Theme 1, meas. 8-15.

15. Two corrections in the first movement in Wagner's edition: the grace-note in meas. 10 should be *a'*; *c c* in the left hand of meas. 22 should both be *A*.

b. Theme 2, meas. 36-43.

Following the customary repeat mark, a 20-measure development leads through the keys of A minor, E minor, and D minor. The first theme does not return after the development, but the second theme and new closing material are presented in the tonic key, expanded from 18 to 22 measures. Hewitt's harmonic language is simple. In the development, however, the keyboard tremolos suggest a touch of the *Sturm und Drang* (see Ex. 1-2).

The first movements of the other two sonatas are similar in form and style. Sonata 2 in C major begins with triadic material. The two principal themes and closing theme are all accompanied with Alberti basses. Again, the recapitulation contains material from the second theme onwards, in the tonic key. The same procedure is followed in the third sonata in F major, except that there is no introductory section, and the three themes have different accompaniments. The last theme (Ex. 1-3) uses the keyboard equivalent of the string tremolo, and this figure is a regular feature of the development.

Ex. 1-2.   Hewitt, Sonata 1 in D, op. 5, 1st movement, development, meas. 58–65.

Ex. 1-3.   Hewitt, Sonata 3 in F, op. 5, 1st movement, closing theme, meas. 34–38.

Hewitt uses the ABACA rondo scheme for the second movement of both Sonatas 1 and 3--the last based on the popular tune "Malbrook" ("For he's a jolly good fellow"). Another popular melody, "Plough Boy" from William Shield's *The Farmer*, is given with three variations for the second movement of Sonata 2.

Hewitt also published a C-major sonata in 1809, dedicated to "Miss M. Mount" (Wagner ed., no. 29).[16] The second (and last) movement is a similar version of the "Plough Boy" variations that appeared as the second movement of op. 5, no. 2. The exposition in the first movement includes an arresting two-octave descending C-major scale as introductory material, and two distinct themes in C and G, both with triplet Alberti basses in the left hand. The closing material bears a striking resemblance to a similar place in the familiar C-major sonata by Haydn, H. 35 (see Ex. 1-4).

Ex. 1-4.   Hewitt, "Mount" Sonata in C, 1st movement, end of exposition, meas. 32-36.

In the development, Hewitt adheres to the key of E minor, but upon returning to C major, instead of presenting the first theme he substitutes another theme of similar character. The closing material is altered to include some chromaticism and secondary-dominant chords. The movement ends with the same Haydnesque music.

---

16. The following differences in the Wagner edition are in the copy (Wolfe 3781) at the Library of Congress. Movement 1, meas. 2, last beat: add 8ve *g"*; meas. 10: add dynamic *f*; meas. 21-22, 32-33, 74-75: accent marks are probably intended for the right hand. Movement 2, meas. 10: *f' e'* slurred; meas. 23, 39: left hand should have the arpeggio sign; meas. 41, last beat: take out *e"*; meas. 42: accent mark probably intended for the right hand; meas. 46, right hand, 1st beat: *e" c" d"*; meas. 58, right hand: last note *c"*. The original spelling of the second movement title is "The Plough Boy with Vareations."

These two works of Hewitt represent the beginning and end of published classical sonatas in the United States. He also published six sonatinas about 1799 (Wolfe 10244), which exhibit a smaller frame. There is no standard movement plan. The first movements of only nos. 1, 3, and 5 exhibit the binary aspect that is the backbone of sonata-allegro structure; they lack a return to the initial material in the second half to form an element of recapitulation. The first movement of the third sonatina (EAKM no. 7) is the longest; its 35 measures contain as many as four thematic ideas, each eight or four measures long.[17] The middle movement consists of a simple three-part form, and is characterized by a soft descending "sigh" figure in the right hand, answered by *forte* octaves in the bass. The last movement is a fast ABACA rondo in the style of Haydn, with the C section in the minor mode.

Sonatinas 2 and 5 also have slow second movements; fast ABACA rondos likewise end nos. 4, 5, and 6. The rondo which forms the second (and last) movement of no. 1 follows the pattern |: A :| B A codetta. This is a rondo in character only, and does not conform to today's textbook definition of rondo form in that there is only one digression. However, the short dictionary included in John Christopher Moller's *A Sett of Progressive Lessons for the Piano-Forte or Harpsichord*, op. 6 (London, 1785),[18] reprinted about 1801 as *A Compleat Book of Instructions for the Piano Forte, Harpsichord, or Organ*, op. 6, defines the rondo as "a Name applied to all Airs that end with the first Strain." By this definition, "rondo" also applies to the three-part form.[19]

John Christopher Moller

John Christopher Moller (1755-1803) was probably born Johann Christoph Möller in Germany; he arrived in England about 1780 and in the United States about 1790. By June 1791 he was active in

---

17. The themes are at meas. 1, 9, 21, 28. In the edition, perhaps the last movement should not have the "[D.C. al Fine]" at the end, but the "Fin[e]" at the end of meas. 8 is correct.

18. London: for the author by Longman and Broderip. The Library of Congress dates it 1792, the British Library and Bodleian Library ca. 1795. Stetzel, 1:251-52, found a 3 January 1785 advertisement for the publication. Contents: pp. 1-33, Lessons I-X; pp. 34-37, "Short and easy Instructions for playing the harpsichord or piano forte"; pp. 38-39, "An Explanation of the Italian Terms used in Music."

19. The tempos and forms of the other Hewitt sonatinas: I Allegro moderato (binary); Rondo (described above). II Moderato (a b c b' c'); Andante (binary); Minuetto (a b a, with no repeats indicated). IV Andante (a b a coda); Rondo-Allegretto. V Moderato; Andante (binary); Rondo (a b c d a b). VI Andantino (theme and two variations); Chasse (on the theme of the first movement).

Philadelphia's German society, as well as organist for the Zion Lutheran Church, where services were held in German.[20] The progressive "lessons" appearing in both of Moller's instruction books actually consist of ten short sonatas, all of two or three movements except Lesson VII, a Ground. Indeed, they become progressively longer and more difficult, as do the works actually labeled "sonata" in the *Eight Easy Lessons for the Piano Forte or Harpsicord* [sic] *for Young Practioners* [sic], op. 5, published in London about 1784.[21] Whereas the first sonata contains four short movements, as each sonata becomes longer the number is reduced to two, beginning with the third sonata.

The first movement of the last one, Sonata VIII (McClenny-Hinson, 6-8), was also published as a one-movement sonata by Moller, with the same title, in Philadelphia in 1793-94,[22] after he had immigrated. This movement is longer than the American sonata movements discussed thus far. The exposition and recapitulation are both 62 measures long, complete with first and second themes and closing material. The development, only eleven measures in length, is more modest. Many late 18th-century style traits are apparent: clear-cut phrase structures, a rest before the second theme and development to clarify the form, frequent use of Alberti and Murky bass accompaniments, and a thin texture of only two or three voices. Moller should have included in the American imprint his second movement, a delightful five-part rondo, which would at least have helped the reputation of early American keyboard music. Its style and form are very much like William Brown's three rondos of 1787, the first keyboard publication to originate in the United States.

Benjamin Carr

Foremost among musical figures in the United States in the late 18th and early 19th centuries was the composer and publisher Benjamin Carr (1768-1831). Born in London, he already had credentials

---

20. Stetzel, 1:66-67.

21. (London: J. Bland, [ca. 1784]); Stetzel, 1:352-53. Copy at the British Library: g.441.t.(15); another copy, ca. 1790, lacking title-page and p. 19: G.297.(7.).

22. Sonneck-Upton, 392; facsimile in Byron A. Wolverton, "Keyboard Music and Musicians in the Colonies and United States of America before 1830" (Ph.D. dissertation, Indiana University, 1966), 479-80; recorded in E. Power Biggs, *The Organ in America* (Columbia MS 6161, ca. 1960). The publication date of 1793-94 is explained in Stetzel, 1:382; an edition of the whole work, both movements, is in 2:70-78. Moller also wrote a three-movement Sinfonia which he and Henri Capron published as the first of *Moller & Capron's Monthly Numbers* in 1793. The Sinfonia is available in W. Thomas Marrocco and Harold Gleason, eds., *Music in America* (New York: Norton, 1964), 218-21, but it is a keyboard transcription of orchestral music.

as a composer before coming to the United States, in 1793, at the same time as his father Joseph and his brother Thomas. Joseph and Thomas established a music business in Baltimore, and Benjamin the same in Philadelphia. Among his many activities as pianist, organist, singer, concert entrepreneur, and music teacher, editor, and publisher, Benjamin was also an important composer of his time. He contributed six sonatas and three divertimentos to the published repertory. A separate manuscript list of Carr's own compositions includes the anonymous sonatas numbered 1, 4, 5, 6 printed in Francis Linley's *A New Assistant for the Piano-Forte or Harpsichord* (Baltimore: Joseph Carr, 1796), but all six are probably Carr's.[23] Again, each is different in scheme. Two consist only of a single movement; of these, no. 2 is a five-part rondo. Sonata 5, Rondo-Allegro, is a simplified one-page ABA version of Carr's three-page ABACA *Rondo from the Overture to the Opera of the Archers* (1813?;[24] modern reprint in *Carr's Musical Miscellany in Occasional Numbers*, no. 7). Sonata 4 is a duet. Only the first movement of no. 6 (EAKM no. 4) is long enough to have two complete themes, a development (only eight measures long), and a complete recapitulation of the two themes. The music throughout the publication, including the sonatas, is carefully fingered in keeping with its function as an instruction book for beginning keyboard students.[25]

Carr's *3 Divertimentos*, printed in his series *The Musical Journal for the Piano Forte*, also available in modern reprint (vol. 1 [1800], no. 18, pp. 34-36), should be included in the category of sonatas, as are a number of early Haydn keyboard divertimentos. All first movements are in rounded binary form (in which initial material returns in the second half). The first movement of the last divertimento has a B section which is developmental in character and overall length. It might be considered a sonata-allegro movement even though there is no clear

---

23. See Virginia Larkin Redway, "The Carrs, American Music Publishers," *Musical Quarterly* 18, no. 1 (January 1932): 175. Nos. 2 and 3 are not dissimilar in style; Sonneck-Upton, 289, describes all six as by Carr.

24. (Baltimore: Joseph Carr, [1813?]); Wolfe 1643.

25. The tempos and forms of the other sonata movements: I Tempo di Minuetto (rounded binary or |: a :|: b a :|); Allegro (a a' b a). III Allegro moderato (rounded binary); Rondo (5-part). IV Moderato (rounded binary); Allegro (rounded binary with no repeat of the second half). VI Spiritoso (described above); Andantino (5-part rondo). Also completely fingered are Carr's *Six Progressive Sonatinas for the Piano Forte*, op. 9 (Baltimore: J. Carr, [1812?], Wolfe 1657; modern reprint in Carr's *Musical Miscellany*, no. 2). Even though stating on the title-page "which may be played either with or without an Accompanyment for the Flute or Violin," the absence of the accompanying instrument makes the sonatinas even more threadbare, so as to become the ultimate in simplicity. But see the more sympathetic description in Eve R. Meyer, "Benjamin Carr's *Musical Miscellany*," *Notes* 33, no. 2 (December 1976): 264-65.

second theme. The final movements are rondos. The rondo form of the last divertimento, however, has the atypical scheme with alternating tempos |: a b :|: a b :| D.C. The first theme is marked adagio, the second theme allegro. The second section is entirely in the dominant key.

A "Duett for Two Harpsichord[s]," included in an undated manuscript in Carr's hand, is perhaps his first sonata--if indeed he composed it.[26] The work can be performed on a single instrument, in spite of its title, since the players alternate a great deal, and when both play together the primo part is located in a range higher than the secondo. Although harpsichords are specified, several indications of dynamics, including crescendo, imply the pianoforte. The first movement, Allegro moderato e cantabile, is not miniature--no fewer than 197 measures long, it contains at least three themes in the exposition, and the recapitulation matches the exposition in length. The quality of the writing is immediately apparent in the first theme (Ex. 1-5). Some of the length is due to the alternation of the instruments: the second theme (meas. 25-36) appears in the primo part, then repeated an octave lower by the secondo.

Ex. 1-5.   Carr, "Duett for Two Harpsichords," 1st movement, secondo, meas. 1-9 (the primo enters at meas. 9).

---

26. The contents of this manuscript at the Library of Congress, ML96.C28, are listed in chapter 3, note 4. The edition of the duet in Charles A. Sprenkle, "The Life and Works of Benjamin Carr (1768-1831)," 2 vols. (D.M.A. dissertation, Peabody Conservatory, 1970), 2:1-29, is not completely reliable.

It is almost as if this duet were a keyboard arrangement of a work for string orchestra, especially in the second movement, labeled "Minore: Andante affetuoso e expressive," in which the primo part consists only of a high violinistic melody (the primo score reduces to a single staff after thirteen measures), accompanied by the secondo. The last movement is a lively 7-part "Rondeau," with four digressions. Not only is this duet an outstanding work in classical style, it seems to be the only early American keyboard duet for two instruments.[27]

Carr's last keyboard work in sonata-allegro form is "Une Petite Ouverture," published about 1826 as no. 9 of his series *Le Clavecin* and reprinted as no. 1 of the new series *Twelve Airs*, op. 17, in 1829 (see chapter 2 for bibliographical details). Whether originally intended for orchestra or piano, this work represents a homespun counterpart of Rossini's *Il barbiere di Siviglia* overture (which Carr had arranged for piano and published as *Le Clavecin*, no. 4). "Une Petite Ouverture" has a quiet beginning, with an accompaniment of alternating octaves in quarter notes. Then there is a gradual crescendo and rise in pitch, the accompaniment quickening to 8ths and 16ths. After a contrasting second theme, and a short development of only ten measures, Carr provides a complete recapitulation, plus a coda with its own crescendo. This is a curious work, perhaps entertaining for a piano student, but not representing the best American piano music of the 1820s, nor even that of Carr. Whereas relatively undemanding music for the parlor pianist was--and still is--very useful, of course, sometimes it is not necessarily interesting for the listener. Looking at such a work from a perspective of over a century and a half later, especially realizing from his other compositions that he had greater compositional imagination and ability, one cannot help but regret that a keyboard "overture" by this important musical figure of early America did not fulfil a higher expectation.

----

27. Carr also wrote two other multi-movement duets, published about 1804: *Two duetts for the piano forte, composed by B: Carr, in which are introduced some favorite airs*, op. 3 (Wolfe 1596A). Duetto I, in D major, consists of a simple Allegro moderato movement in rounded binary form, then a 5-part rondo based on a "French air." Duetto II, in F major, has as a first movement an ABA arrangement of an "Italian air"; the second a 5-part rondo on an "Irish air." None is long enough to be considered a sonata, or even sonatina. The same is true for two duet collections of Joseph Willson (Wolfe 1997 and 9979). *A Collection of duetts for two performers on one piano forte, selected by J. Willson* [1814-15] comprises seven duets, each fitting on a pair of facing pages, and all in C major; only the second duet is broken into two small movements. *A Collection of airs for three or two performer's* [sic] *on the piano forte, selected and arranged by J. Willson* [1807-10] consists of three pieces, which collectively might be considered a sonatina. The first, a 7-part Andantino rondo in F major, is followed by a Graziano movement in C major, a 5-part rondo. The last is an Allegretto vivace, a 6-part rondo (without a final return to "A"). The third performer doubles the main melody an octave higher.

Stefano Cristiani

The Italian Stefano Cristiani (b. 1768?), who was active in Philadelphia and Washington about 1818-23,[28] published "A Sonata, for two performers on one piano forte" (ca. 1819; Wolfe 2215) that clearly displays his roots in Italian opera. The closing theme in both exposition and recapitulation of the first movement is accompanied by repeated-note chords in the manner of an opera aria. The model seems specifically to be Rossini in the second and last movement, a rondo, which includes a "cresc poco a poco" extended over no fewer than twenty measures, beginning pianissimo and ending fortissimo. This duet is entertaining to play, but still does not match in charm the one by Carr.

Rayner Taylor

One of the most important composers in the early United States, Rayner Taylor (1747-1825), had received his musical training as a member of the Chapel Royal. While still a teenager, in 1765, he became organist in Chelmsford as well as musical director of Sadler's Wells. He came to the United States in 1792, settling the following year in Philadelphia. Six divertimentos in his *Divertimenti, or, Familiar Lessons for the Piano Forte* (Philadelphia, [1797]),[29] are likewise in the sonata tradition.[30] The first movements of nos. 1, 2 (EAKM no. 6), and 5 are in sonata-allegro form, each with two themes, develop-

---

28. He also gave three concerts in Lexington, Kentucky, in late 1822 and early 1823. See Joy Carden, *Music in Lexington before 1840* (Lexington: Lexington-Fayette County Historic Commission, 1980), 50-51.

29. The only surviving copy thus far is at the Conservatory of Music, University of Missouri, Kansas City. As I pointed out in the *Sonneck Society Newsletter* 7, no. 3 (fall 1981): 6, the spelling "Rayner" is derived from this edition, from the list of subscribers and preface to Benjamin Carr's *Masses, Vespers, Litanies* [1805], and from John R. Parker, *A Musical Biography* (Boston, 1825; reprint, Detroit: Information Coordinators, 1975), p. 179. See also Victor Fell Yellin, "Rayner Taylor," *American Music* 1, no. 3 (fall 1983): 49 and 57.

30. There is also a multi-movement work by Taylor in a manuscript at the Library of Congress, M1.A1T, paginated 123-28. The collective title is almost entirely cut off by the binder, too much to restore, but "Divertimento," which would be appropriate according to usage at the time, does not fit the bottom of the letters that remain. The fast movement is an ABACADA rondo; the second, a 3-part "Aria Grazioso: Dolce a [*sic*] Piano"; the third, March & Quickstep. All movements are in D major. On the last page of the manuscript, in a different hand, is an unrelated dance also ascribed to Taylor, entitled "New Jersey."

ments, and recapitulations.[31] All final movements are rondos, except
that of the first which is a three-part minuet. The usual two-
movement form is expanded in no. 6 by the insertion of a three-part
slow Scotch air. Like the Carr divertimentos, these are modest in
size--the first four occupy only two pages of the original publication;
the last two, three pages. Even though the subtitle implies that only
the Ground which precedes the divertimentos was intended for students (". . . To which is Prefixed, a Ground for the Improvement of
Young Practitioners"), undoubtedly the whole collection's intent was
instructional. It seems to have been planned to progress in difficulty;
the last divertimentos are more difficult to play than are the first.[32]
Whereas two-part texture and Alberti-bass accompaniment
predominate, the following repeated-note figuration in no. 4 provides
some challenge for the performer (Ex. 1-6).

Ex. 1-6.   Taylor, Divertimento 4 in F, 1st movement, meas. 15-18.

---

31. The first movement of no. 3 is in 3-part form; that of no. 4
is binary, each half ending with the same material; that of no. 6 is
continuous but with a reference to the initial music at the end.

32. The movements are: "A Ground," in two parts--9 state-
ments of the 8-measure theme in the first part, 8 statements in the
second. Divertimento I in C--Moderato; Minuetto. Divertimento II in
G--Andante Allegro; Rondo-Con Vivace. Divertimento III in D--
Vivace con moderato (middle section in D minor); Giga Rondo-
Allegretto moderato. Divertimento IV in F--Allegretto; Rondo-
Moderato. Divertimento V in A--Larghetto e Cantabile; Rondo-
Allegretto. Divertimento VI in C--Pomposo; Scotch Air-Slow; Rondo-
Con Vivace il moderato.

Mr. Newman

Three sonatas for the pianoforte or harpsichord by the mysterious "Mr. Newman" were published by James Hewitt in 1807-10, then reprinted from the same plates by E. W. Jackson in Boston in 1821-26.[33] Regrettably this set, labeled op. 1, was not followed by others. The sonata-allegro movements, while not large, omit no essential features of the form.[34] The first two sonatas have the movement plan fast-slow-fast. Sonata 3 in D, however, is unique (EAKM no. 13). The 3-part Andante movement that opens the sonata ends on a dominant chord which leads to the Allegro spiritoso in sonata-allegro form (but without the expected repeats). The third movement consists of a repetition of the first fifteen measures of the first movement. It also ends on a dominant chord, and is succeeded by a rollicking 3-part Allegro. Whoever Mr. Newman was, he must have spent much time studying the piano style of Haydn, for he successfully captured his model's good-humored spirit.

Peter K. Moran

The daughter of the Irish-born Peter K. Moran (d. 1831) was only five years old when she performed her father's "Petit Sonata, in which is introduced O dolce concento and St. Patrick's Day; with flute accompaniment (ad Libitum.) as performed at the New York Concerts by Miss Moran, with distinguished approbation."[35] Published in 1820, this work is a sonata only in that it is a multi-movement work; it is certainly not in the tradition of even the simple sonatas by Americans written ten or more years earlier. The first movement is essentially an arrangement, with two variations, of Mozart's "O dolce concento" from *Die Zauberflöte*, and the second movement a setting, in three-part form, of the popular Irish tune. The flute part adds to the charm of the work, but is not essential.

-----

33. Wolfe 6492-6492A. The first is in McClenny-Hinson, 13-17, but one serious editorial omission is the alto *b c' b* following the rhythm of the soprano in the first measure of the Andante. As explained in the Preface, the abbreviation "McClenny-Hinson" refers to Anne McClenny and Maurice Hinson, eds., *A Collection of Early American Keyboard Music* (Cincinnati: Willis, 1971).

34. Sonata 1, all three movements; Sonata 2, 1st movement; Sonata 3, 2nd (of four) movements.

35. Wolfe 6121. Another piece by her father performed by the five-year-old Miss Moran was "A Duett for two performers on one piano forte, in which are introduced the Tyrolese Air & Copenhagen Waltz, as performed by Mr. & *Miss Moran with great applause at the New York Concerts, composed & arranged by P. K. Moran. *Miss Moran was only five years of age when she performed the Primo part of this Duett" [1820], Wolfe 6096.

Alexander Reinagle

The most ambitious American piano sonatas, in length and style, are those by Alexander Reinagle (1756-1809),[36] who came to the United States from his native England in 1786. Their relative difficulty in performance--more difficult than the usual teaching pieces-- probably accounts for the fact that they were not published during his lifetime. The four sonatas in manuscript at the Library of Congress are now available in modern edition (1978) by Robert Hopkins.[37] It is

---

36. The conventional wisdom is that Reinagle was born in 1756, the year he was baptized. Victor Yellin, however, found evidence that both Reinagle and his teacher Rayner Taylor were born in 1747. See his article "Rayner Taylor" (cited above, note 29), p. 50. Lillian Moore, *The Duport Mystery*, Dance Perspectives, 7 (1960): 77, note 38, speculates that since he was described as in his 62nd year (i.e., 61 years old) when he died in 1809, his birth instead must have occurred in 1748. Anne McClenny Krauss, in "Alexander Reinagle, His Family Background and Early Professional Career," *American Music* 4, no. 4 (winter 1986): 425-56, note 6, maintains that the correct year of birth was 1756.

37. The sonatas were first described in Ernst C. Krohn, "Alexander Reinagle as Sonatist," *Musical Quarterly* 18, no. 1 (January 1932): 140-49. Frederick Freedman's edition of the sonatas, announced for publication by Da Capo Press in 1966 and listed as published in the bibliography of Gilbert Chase's *America's Music*, 2nd ed. (New York: McGraw-Hill, 1966), never appeared. Alexander Reinagle, *The Philadelphia Sonatas*, ed. Robert Hopkins, Recent Researches in American Music, 5 (Madison: A-R Editions, 1978) originated in Hopkins's "An Edition of Four Sonatas and Two Sets of Variations for Piano by Alexander Reinagle" (D.M.A. dissertation, Eastman School of Music, 1959). (For a page of corrections to the printed edition, write the Institute of Studies in American Music, Brooklyn College, CUNY, Brooklyn, NY 11210.) Sonata 1 in D is in McClenny-Hinson, 23-37, and is recorded by Anne McClenny for the Music in America series of the Society for the Preservation for the American Musical Heritage (MIA 126), and by Eugene List on *Early Sonatas for the Pianoforte* (Musical Heritage, MHS 733). The second sonata in E major is edited but unfortunately abridged in John Tasker Howard's *A Program of Early American Piano Pieces* (New York: J. Fischer & Bro., 1931), 1-18. Its last two movements are in Marrocco-Gleason's *Music in America*, 191-203, but the last movement is missing a complete digression and return (the "CA" of ABACADA). It was recorded by Jeanne Behrend (Allegro ALG 3024, 1951) and by Arthur Loesser in the Music in America series (MIA 101, 1958). Sonata 3 is recorded by Alan Mandel in *An Anthology of American Piano Music (1780-1970)* (Desto DC 6445/47, 1975). The three numbered sonatas are recorded on a Broadwood grand piano of ca. 1827 in the Metropolitan Museum of New York by Jack Winerock (Musical Heritage, MHS 3359, 1976). All four sonatas are recorded by Sylvia Glickman (Orion ORS 82437, 1982), and she is preparing an edition,

thought that one of them, the unnumbered sonata in F major, is a work for violin and piano that lacks the violin part. Therefore, only the three numbered sonatas survive intact.

Sonata 1 in D major creates a unique problem, because after the two fast movements are two sets of variations. The first, in A major, is an adaptation of the slow movement from Haydn's Symphony 53 ("L'Impériale") in D.[38] Reinagle also used these variations, titled "Haydn's Favorite Andante," in *Twelve Favorite Pieces Arranged for the Piano Forte or Harpsichord by A. Reinagle* (Philadelphia: author, [ca. 1789]).[39] The other, in D major, is a more elaborate set of variations by Reinagle on the Scotch tune "Maggy Lauder" than the set that appears in his collection *A Selection of the Most Favorite Scots Tunes with Variations for the Piano Forte or Harpsichord* (London: author, [ca. 1782]), although the theme and four variations are similar.[40]

———

Four Sonatas, Andante, Theme and Variations, and Adagio for Piano (New York: Da Capo, forthcoming).

38. First identified by M. D. Herter Norton in "Haydn in America (before 1820)," *Musical Quarterly* 18, no. 2 (April 1932): 313.

39. The printed version is a third version, not as highly ornamented as the one in the manuscript. Variation 1 is as Haydn's, but variation 2 is of a complexity intermediate between Haydn's and that in the manuscript. The print has no variation 3, but gives Haydn's variation 4 almost exactly, as in the manuscript. Both the print and Haydn have the 5th variation, whereas the manuscript does not.

40. The "Maggy Lauder" variations in the Library of Congress manuscript furnishes a good example of what a composer may have performed, yet did not publish. The D-major version printed in Philadelphia consists of the 8-measure tune, followed by seven unnumbered variations. Variations 1-5 appear in the manuscript in mostly similar versions. (Variation 3 is different in most respects; the first two measures of variation 4 is different, the rest similar. The reverse holds for variation 5 in which the first two measures are similar and the rest different.) In the manuscript, variations 1-5 (nos. 2-5, numbered 1-4) are followed by more elaborate variants to be played instead of the publication's repeat marks. The variant to variation 5, however, is less elaborate, and is followed by a variation in D minor, again followed by a less elaborate variant (inexplicably, the variant is numbered 5). (The variant is also written twice, the first incomplete, on the original underlying page, but a new page-fragment with the variant to variation 5, and the pair in minor, was pasted over.) On the bottom of this same page is another variation beginning in F major, ending in D minor (numbered 6), followed on the next page by its simplified variant. For the last two of these manuscript variations, the D-major key signature is coupled with a rather quick triplet 16th-note rhythm. Repeat marks and the numbers 7-8 indicate that the last two variations are to be repeated; the last is not a variant. These last four variations are completely different than the print's variations 6-7.

Reinagle first played a piano sonata in public in New York on July 20, 1786.[41] When he settled in Philadelphia that fall, he became more active as a performer. A fascinating entry, "Sonata, Piano Forte . . . Haydn and Reinagle," appears on the program of the first of the 1786-87 City Concerts, 19 October 1786. Succeeding concerts in the series list "Sonata Piano Forte--Reinagle" for November 1, "Sonata Piano Forte and Violin--Reinagle" for November 16, and "Sonata Piano Forte--Reinagle" for November 30. Of the twelve concerts in the series, which continued until March 1787, there is but one more "Sonata Piano Forte--Reinagle," for February 23.[42]

One is tempted to speculate, in comparing these sonatas with the contents of Reinagle's manuscript, that the first, by "Haydn and Reinagle," was Sonata 1 in D major, played with the A-major variations by Haydn. The concerts on November 1 and 30 would account for the other two sonatas, nos. 2 in E and 3 in C. Could the sonata played on November 16 be the unnumbered one in F major, missing the violin part?[43] The last performance of February 23, some three months later, may have been a repeat of one of the numbered sonatas.

Reinagle's chief influences in style were the Bach brothers of London and Hamburg. *Six Sonatas for the Piano Forte or Harpsichord, with an Accompaniment for a Violin*, published by the composer in London in 1783, was heavily indebted to the Italianate style of John Christian Bach, a resident of London. No fewer than three of them use the Italian preference for the two-movement sonata. However, Reinagle subsequently visited Carl Philipp Emanuel Bach in Hamburg, and tried to have some of C. P. E.'s music published in London. The four American sonatas, supposedly composed in 1786 after his arrival in the United States, often display the more impassioned and serious style of the Hamburg Bach.

Both movements of Sonata 1 in D major are organized in sonata-allegro form, but not in miniature as encountered in the other American sonatas. The second key area of both movements contains at least four different thematic entities before the closing material.[44] The second movement is in an exuberant 6/8, and one surprise is that the second theme of the second key area is in duple 2/4--which also returns in the development. These themes are longer than those of his American contemporaries, and there are more of them. In both move-

---

41. Sonneck, *Concert-Life*, 225.

42. Sonneck, *Concert-Life*, 81-83.

43. Since I first wrote the above, Hopkins's edition was published, where in the preface, p. xi, he ventures the same opinion.

44. In the first movement, the themes in the second key area (labeled here themes 2a, 2b, 2c, 2d) are at meas. 21, 31, 41, 49; the closing section at meas. 59. In the second movement, the transition from the first to second key areas begins in meas. 17; the second key themes begin in meas. 27, 53, 61, 81; the closing area at meas. 105.

ments, the development sections involve as many as five (rather than one or two) keys. Reinagle apparently felt that the return to the first theme at the beginning of the development was sufficient, for the recapitulations in both movements do not include them. The recapitulation in the first movement is interrupted by free material and a fermata before the remaining material resumes[45]--foreshadowing a similar place in the first movement of Beethoven's Fifth Symphony. With the influences by the Bach brothers, already cited, there seems to be an additional influence of Domenico Scarlatti in such places as one of the themes in the first movement, in which a measure of music is stated, repeated, then repeated again with an extra measure to accommodate the tonic cadence (see Ex. 1-7).

Ex. 1-7.   Reinagle, Sonata 1 in D, 1st movement, theme 2c, meas. 41-44.

In the recapitulation of the second movement (Adagio) of Sonata 3 in C major, the first theme is likewise omitted.[46] In the first movement, there are as many as eight easily identifiable thematic elements in the exposition,[47] and three new ones in the development (meas. 93, 106, 114). In the recapitulation, instead of restating the expected theme after the transition, Reinagle presents another one, albeit with the same general texture, in the foreign key of D minor (see Ex. 1-8).

---

45. Meas. 104-08. I analyze the recapitulation as beginning at meas. 101. In the second movement, the recapitulation begins at meas. 183.

46. The principal themes begin in meas. 1, 12, 22; the development starts with theme 1 at meas. 26, the recapitulation with theme 2 at meas. 45.

47. Meas. 1, 9 (transition), 23 (beginning of the new key), 31, 37, 42, 57, 67.

This is succeeded by a short cadence, marked Adagio, before the transition material resumes. The remaining material appears in regular order.

Ex. 1-8.   Reinagle, Sonata 3 in C, 1st movement, recapitulation, meas. 157-59.

Another brilliant effect, also recalling Scarlatti, is the accacciatura-like figuration of the transition (Ex. 1-9).

Ex. 1-9.   Reinagle, Sonata 3 in C, 1st movement, meas. 9-10.

Similar is an effect used for one of the themes in the last movement (Ex. 1-10).

Ex. 1-10.   Reinagle, Sonata 3 in C, 3rd movement, meas. 98-105.

The last movement is a rondo with four different thematic elements in the digressions (meas. 17, 41, 76, 204). Although its primary theme has the sunniness of J. C. Bach or Mozart, there is the occasional fire of C. P. E. Bach (see Ex. 1-11).

Ex. 1-11. Reinagle, Sonata 3 in C, 3rd movement, meas. 230-41.

In many ways, Sonata 2 in E major is the most impressive. Each movement is rich with well-constructed and expressive themes, and the overall formal construction is logical, yet not commonplace or obvious. The opening first-theme section contains a theme, repeated and followed by two others, all of 8-measure lengths. The second theme (meas. 36-48) is succeeded by a new group including an alternating hand pattern and interrupting cadenza, both suggesting the style of C. P. E. Bach (see Ex. 1-12).

Ex. 1-12.   Reinagle, Sonata 2 in E, 1st movement, meas. 61-64.

In the development, during the presentation of a variant of the first theme, an inconsequential 3-note motive in the middle voice apparently furnishes the impetus for new material (see Ex. 1-13).

Ex. 1-13.   Reinagle, Sonata 2 in E, 1st movement:

a. Meas. 82-85.

b. Meas. 92-95.

A new melody, related to the opening flourish of the first theme, is
presented no fewer than three times (meas. 114, 120, 135), and the
rhythm is broken by fermatas or adagios four times. The recapitulation, with minor changes, is regular.

The clearest influence of C. P. E. Bach is demonstrated in the
slow movement. The material succeeding the opening cadenza measure
seems particularly close to the fantasy style of Reinagle's model and
friend by the exploitation of frequent alternations of piano and forte,[48]
as does the highly embellished and expressive melody which follows.
Whereas this movement is a fantasy in effect, its formal construction is
related to sonata-allegro design.[49]

The main theme of the Allegro movement is undoubtedly
derived from the initial theme of the first movement, in both the 5-
note descending scale in 16th notes and in the accompanying 8th-note
descending scale (see Ex. 1-14).

---

48. Compare, for example, Bach's Fantasia in *Historical Anthology of Music*, ed. Archibald T. Davison and Willi Apel, vol. 2, no.
296, taken from Bach's *Musikalisches Vielerley* (1770).

49. Themes 1a and 1b are at meas. 2 and 9 in E minor; the second theme section beginning at meas. 17 is in G major. Themes 1a
and 1b return in G major after the double bar in meas. 36 and 39, but
are varied as in a development. The beginning of the 2nd theme area
does not return as such, but the last fourteen measures of the "exposition" return, in E minor, at the end of the second half.

Ex. 1-14.   Reinagle, Sonata 2 in E:

a. 1st movement, meas. 1-3.

b. 3rd movement, meas. 1-5.

Other material related to the first movement is figuration in the second part of the B section similar to that in the first movement (Ex. 1-15), and chains of syncopations (Ex. 1-16).

Ex. 1-15.   Reinagle, Sonata 2 in E, 3rd movement, meas. 62-63.

Ex. 1-16. Reinagle, Sonata 2 in E:

a. 1st movement, meas. 100.

b. 3rd movement, meas. 158-61.

The third digression (C), with its length (124 measures), changes of key (e, G, C, b), and initial theme displaying some characteristics of the A theme, is developmental in style. A mark of Reinagle's command of his craft is evident in the different ways he uses fragments of the main theme in leading back to the restatements of this theme. Two of these transitions involve a "built-in" ritard; the last one involves the same kind of ritard and a cadenza.[50]

The three solo piano sonatas of Reinagle are clearly the best composed in the early years of the United States. They were probably played in concerts only by the composer. Had they been published at that time, sales would have been minimal inasmuch as there were few pianists with sufficient skills. Perhaps there were other sonatas of comparable quality, never published and since lost, by his onetime teacher Rayner Taylor or his friend James Hewitt. We can only be grateful that Reinagle's manuscript survives, and that, in view of recent editions and recordings, we can still enjoy his sonatas.

Anthony Philip Heinrich

The one sonata from a later period, Anthony Philip Heinrich's *La Buona Mattina: Sonata for the Piano Forte*, is unique in form and conception. It was included in the composer's ground-breaking collec-

---

50. Meas. 85-92, 233-40. The principal sections of the ABACADA form begin at meas. 1, 17, 93, 117, 241, 257, 349.

tion *The Dawning of Music in Kentucky, or the Pleasures of Harmony in the Solitudes of Nature*, op. 1 (Philadelphia, 1820), available in modern reprint,[51] and is outside the tradition of the simple sonatas by Carr, Hewitt, or even of the more ambitious ones by Reinagle. Heinrich's sonata consists of a core of three movements. The first is prefaced by an "Alla maniera guista" [*sic*] introduction of twenty-six measures, over half including a voice part, text in Italian, which translates as follows: "Accept the respects of a poor son of Orpheus, exiled in the obscure forests and caves, and alone inspired by the harmonies of Nature."[52] To compound the problem for the performer, the last movement ends with four measures containing more Italian text, translated: "Dear friends, I always wish you the happiest days, farewell."[53]

The ending can stand alone without the text being sung, but not so with the preliminary movement where the added voice part, often in the same range as the right hand of the piano, cannot simultaneously be played by the pianist. Did Heinrich intend the pianist to sing the beginning text, or only think it? Quite probably to sing it, since the piano part is otherwise incomplete.

The previous piece in *Dawning*, "A Serenade adapted for the piano forte and dedicated to the Virtuosos of the United States," also begins and ends with a voice part. Clearly the text was intended only to be thought or spoken. It could hardly be sung by a single individual, considering the range--C to g'', or even g''' if one takes the top of the chord at the end. This work is obviously paired with the sonata, since it immediately precedes, and the text at the end is "Bona Notte, Buonissima Notta." What is more, the sonata is "Especially dedicated to the *Virtuosos* of the United States, not as a *Non plus ultra* or *Noli me tangere* but as a 'firstling' in its kind from the *Back woods* and as a small Morning's Entertainment or '*Buona Mattina*' in addition to the *Serenade* or '*Buona Notte*,' already presented to them by their most humble--A. P. Heinrich, of Kentucky."[54]

The main first movement of *La Buona Mattina*, Allegro di molto, bears only superficial resemblance to the usual sonata-allegro form. Slightly more than halfway through is the sign to repeat the first and second half, and both halves begin with the same thematic material. Absent is a second key area, such as the dominant, and any return of themes from the first half to form a recapitulation in the second half. Indeed, the "development" includes material with almost no relation to

------

51. The sonata, on pp. 25-39 of *Dawning*, is also reprinted in facsimile in John Gillespie, comp., *Nineteenth-Century American Piano Music* (New York: Dover, 1978), 145-57.

52. "Accetate gli Ossequi d'un povero Figlio d'Orfeo esiliato nelle Selve ed Antri oscuri e solamente inspirato dagli Concenti della Natura."

53. "Cari Amicivi auguro sempre felicissimi giorni, Addio!"

54. Italics represent the original all-capital letters.

the exposition. With few exceptions, Heinrich adheres to the main key of D major throughout.

The movement cannot be explained easily with the usual terminology of musical form. It is freely constructed; Beethoven would have named it a fantasy, as he did for his "Moonlight" Sonata. The beginning repeated-note motive with dotted rhythm is succeeded by passagework of no particular thematic content that seems to function as transition. A second theme arrives after a long trill,[55] but it is still in the tonic key (see Ex. 1-17).

Ex. 1-17.   Heinrich, *La Buona Mattina*, 1st movement, meas. 40-44.

The characteristic upbeat of three 8th notes is maintained for the next principal theme,[56] which begins in B minor (see Ex. 1-18).

Ex. 1-18.   Heinrich, *La Buona Mattina*, 1st movement, meas. 66-69.

---

55. Using the pagination in *Dawning*, the theme begins on p. 30, 3rd system, meas. 2. For those using Gillespie's edition, this is on p. 148.

56. p. 31, beginning of 3rd system.

The same D-major key, however, is re-established after only eight measures, and remains until after the beginning of the second half.

The three 8th-note rhythm also permeates a fourth theme in E-flat major, the new key achieved by a striking modulation soon after the beginning of the second half.[57] After further passagework utilizing the same rhythm, the theme is given again, but in the ubiquitous key of D major. The relation between the themes is clearly intended (Ex. 1-19; compare with Exx. 1-17 and 1-18).

Ex. 1-19.   Heinrich, *La Buona Mattina*, 1st movement, meas. 94-97.

The rhythmic motive is also prominent in some of the connecting passagework.[58] Except for the structure of these 8-measure themes, and one brief recall of earlier scalework in the second half, the remainder of the movement is indeed more characteristic of the fantasy than of the usual sonata-allegro design.

Melodic sequence is sometimes a feature of Heinrich's music. One scale passage coming after the second theme is presented in sequence five times, beginning on the pitches *d" e" f"*-sharp *g" a"*, but when the scale returns in the second half there are no similar repeti-

---

57. p. 32, beginning of 3rd system.

58. See, for example, near the end of the first half, p. 31, system 5; after the fourth theme, p. 32, last system; and in the final sections of the movement, p. 33, last system, and p. 34, 5th system.

tions.[59] Another sequence of scales, this time divided between the hands, is heard near the beginning of the movement (Ex. 1-20).

Ex. 1-20. Heinrich, *La Buona Mattina*, 1st movement, meas. 18-22.

In the introductory movement, scales are harmonized by parallel chords in a most unusual manner (Ex. 1-21).[60]

Ex. 1-21. Heinrich, *La Buona Mattina*, introductory movement, meas. 12-15.

59. Compare the beginnings of the 5th system on pp. 30 and 33. There is another correspondence in the alternating intervals which immediately precede.

60. Other sequences: p. 29, bottom two systems; the diminished-seventh arpeggios on p. 31, systems 1-2; right-hand figurations on the last two systems of the same page; p. 32, last system, through the third measure of p. 33.

The 28-measure Andante piu tosto adagio, only two measures longer than the opening introduction, has the same function. A passage with horn fifths recalls a brief spot in the first movement.[61] The key is D minor, until the modulation to the B-flat major of the next movement.

The Finale alla Polacca represents Heinrich's affinity for the popular dance music of his time; it is organized into 8-measure sections,[62] each ending with a tonic B-flat major cadence. The horn fifths of the previous two movements make a brief appearance,[63] although unity among movements may not have been intentional. Several unconventional cadential patterns, such as the following, might be considered examples of clumsy composition if one wishes to criticize Heinrich, or of rugged individualism if one prefers praise (Ex. 1-22).

---

61. System 4 on pp. 29 and 35.

62. Except for one 7-measure section beginning at the end of the 6th system on p. 37.

63. p. 37, system 5.

Ex. 1-22.   Heinrich, *La Buona Mattina*, 3rd movement, meas. 37-40.

Another cadence is deceptively simple, yet it makes one wonder why it hadn't been discovered before (Ex. 1-23).

Ex. 1-23.   Heinrich, *La Buona Mattina*, 3rd movement, meas. 86-87.

No thematic recurrences take place until the last two sections which, with the coda, are based on the same melodic thought.

Heinrich's only sonata is like that of no other composer, most strikingly by the presence of a voice part at the beginning and end, and certainly by the final movement's key of B-flat major, unrelated to the D major and minor of the preceding movements. Heinrich knew the music of Beethoven, whose innovative spirit may have been the guide for the unconventional "Tyro Minstrel of Kentucky."[64]

Heinrich's *La Buona Mattina* sonata represents an early stage of musical independence from Europe in art-music, an independence which later came to its most prominent fruition in Ives's Concord Sonata. Still, the modest and derivative efforts by Hewitt, Carr,

---

64. The self-description is taken from the title-page of "A Serenade," the preceding piece in *Dawning*.

Taylor, and Moller may yet be useful to piano students, and certainly those by Reinagle and Heinrich are worth repeated revivals for the concert hall.

2

Rondos, Brown to Meineke

> That which is liked by everyone, sung by amateurs,
> played by harpsichordists, demanded by listeners, in
> short, the jewel of the present musical epoch, is
> called Rondo.
> --Abt Georg Joseph Vogler, *Betrachtungen der*
> *Mannheimer Tonschule* (Mannheim, 1779)[1]

The apex of the popularity of the rondo in Europe occurred in
the period 1773 to 1786. In the following year, 1787, the first collection of rondos was published in the United States: *Three Rondos for*
the Piano Forte or Harpsichord. Indeed, this was the first original
publication of secular art-music by an American (albeit foreign-born)
composer, William Brown.[2] It was dedicated to no less a figure than
Francis Hopkinson, signer of the Declaration of Independence, first
Secretary of the Navy--and amateur composer. Brown's rondos
predate by one year Hopkinson's own *Seven Songs for the Harpsichord*
or Forte Piano, dedicated to George Washington,[3] the first publication
of secular art-music by a native-born composer.

---

1. As quoted in Malcolm Cole, "The Vogue of the Instrumental
Rondo in the Late Eighteenth Century," *Journal of the American*
Musicological Society 22, no. 3 (fall 1969): 432.

2. *A Selection of the most favorite Scots tunes with variations for*
the piano forte or harpsichord, composed by A. Reinagle (Philadelphia:
for the author by John Aitken, [1787]), advertised as "just published"
on 28 August 1787, may have been the first (Sonneck-Upton, 375).
However, this was largely a reprint of an edition originally published
in London, ca. 1782. See also Robert Hopkins's preface to his edition
of Reinagle's *Philadelphia Sonatas*, viii and xvi.

3. Reprint, Philadelphia: Musical Americana, 1954; 2nd reprinting, New York: Broude Bros, 1959.

Curiously, all of Brown's three rondos are in G major. They are already exceptional in that they all have three digressions (ABACADA, returns indicated by da capo directions), in contrast to most subsequent ones which have only two (ABACA). Yet the representation of the form with letters does not do justice to more subtle relationships which sometimes occur. For example, in the first rondo[4] the "C" section is thematically derived from the "A" section. Similarly, the "D" section of the second rondo includes material derived from sections "A" and "B." The third rondo in G (EAKM no. 1)[5] has no such inner relationship, but its "C" theme is similar to the main theme of the first rondo. In all three of Brown's rondos, the "C" sections are in the parallel minor mode and follow an inner three-part form. Alberti bass accompaniment predominates, yet is often relieved by other textures. The "D" sections are the longest--taking up most of the second page in the two pages allotted to each piece in the original print--and all three rondos end with a section in the dominant key which logically leads back to the tonic of the main theme. In the case of the second rondo, an element from the main theme, with a quicker accompaniment and in the dominant key, is used for the transition from the "D" section to the da capo (Ex. 2-1).

Ex. 2-1.   William Brown, Rondo II in G, end of "D" section, beginning of "A" section.

----

4. Abridged and altered in Carl Engel, comp., *Music from the Days of George Washington* (Washington, 1931; reprint, New York: AMS Press, 1970), 36-39; complete in McClenny-Hinson, 9-12. A facsimile of the Boston Public Library copy of all three rondos is in Wolverton, 461-71. The third rondo appears in facsimile in Carl Engel's article "Introducing Mr. Braun," *Musical Quarterly* 30, no. 1 (January 1944): 63-83.

5. Also in Maurice Hinson and Anne McClenny Krauss, with David Carr Glover, eds., *Music of the Capital City: A Collection of Keyboard Pieces and Songs Performed in Philadelphia during the Early Days of the Young Republic* (Miami, Fla.: Belwin Mills, 1987), 36-41.

The earliest surviving rondo by an American, however, is by James Bremner (d. 1780), perhaps written shortly after he arrived in Philadelphia from England in 1763. His Lesson in B-flat major was copied out about that time by the same Francis Hopkinson, his music student.[6] The piece was never published at that time. It is basically a single binary movement. Two distinct musical ideas are presented in as many keys during the first half. The first of these opens the second half, and then a third ideas intervenes before the final return--in letters, |: A B :|: A C A :|. Indeed, the last "A" in this representation includes a variant of the "B" theme, so the germ of the sonata-allegro form can be seen. Whereas regular phrases of four and eight measures predominate, "A" is untypically five measures in length.

There are two categories of keyboard rondos in early America: those based on existing tunes, and those based on original themes. In contrast with sonatas, rondos of both categories never lost favor; one reason must have been the ease for the listener in recognizing the recurring main theme. Those based entirely on original material will be discussed first.

Independent Rondos

John Christopher Moller

Although John Aitken was the first publisher to engrave music in the United States (see note 2 above) the first American publishers exclusively of music were John Christopher Moller and Henri Capron. The third number of the short-lived series *Moller & Capron's Monthly Numbers* (1793) was Moller's own Rondo in F major (EAKM no. 8).[7] This work, like those of Brown, is a seven-part rondo, of which the fourth part ("C") is also in the parallel minor mode and also has an

---

6. *Francis Hopkinson's Lessons: A Facsimile Edition of Hopkinson's Personal Keyboard Book: An Anthology of Keyboard Compositions & Arrangements Copied in Hopkinson's Own Hand*, notes by David P. McKay (Washington: C. T. Wagner, 1979), 114-15.

7. The EAKM edition gives the date as ca. 1800, but the same work was originally published in 1793; see Sonneck-Upton, 266 and 360.

inner three-part form.[8] The other common element is the traditional
Alberti accompaniment in many passages. But in contrast with
Brown's rondos, Moller's have written-out returns of the main theme,
each preceded by a short cadenza in free rhythm. These cadenzas
probably represent a part of Moller's own keyboard skills, and were
probably a challenge to amateur and student pianists of the time.

Rayner Taylor, August Peticolas

After Brown's, the next independently-composed rondo was
Rayner Taylor's Rondo in G major (McClenny-Hinson, 3-5), published
as early as 1794.[9] Its theme seems to have been inspired by the last
movement, also a rondo, of Mozart's familiar Sonata in C major, K.
545. Both Taylor and Mozart use the relative minor key in the second
digression of the five-part ABACA form, and all returns to the rondo
theme are written out. A notable feature of Taylor's rondo is the use
of cadenza flourishes, in small notes, before these returns (even briefly
in the inner three-part structure of the initial rondo theme) and the
imitation between the hands of the main theme. Taylor's piece
exhibits some traits indigenous to the keyboard, such as the alternating
octaves in one of the thematic returns (Ex. 2-2). In the midst of the
second digression, the hands quickly alternate on the same pitches (Ex.
2-3), but the busy motion is soon relieved by simple two-part horn
fifths (Ex. 2-4).

Ex. 2-2.   Rayner Taylor, Rondo in G, meas. 40-42.

Taylor wrote a modest Rondo Allegretto, also in G major, a part
of the "March & Rondo" printed on a single page in Carr's *Musical
Journal for the Piano Forte* (1803-04, no. 108, p. 14), available in
modern reprint. Although it has two digressions (ABACA), each part
is only eight measures long. The third digression has a change of
tempo (Maestoso), key (dominant), and two breaks in the Alberti bass
to feature more horn fifths in the right hand (meas. 25-37, 97-105,

----

8. For those interested in matters of performance practice, compare meas. 57, 61, and 65, with 16th-note appoggiaturas, whereas at
meas. 81, 85, and 89 the same notes are written as small-note ornaments.

9. Sonneck-Upton, 360; a reprint of 1808-11 is cited as Wolfe
9282.

137-47), the last two identical. These transitions end with cadential flourishes, increasing in difficulty for the performer.

Ex. 2-3.   Taylor, Rondo in G, meas. 56-58.

Ex. 2-4.   Taylor, Rondo in G, meas. 64-68.

"Rondo" by Master August Peticolas, published about 1803 (Wolfe 6964), is extremely simple in thematic material and formal procedure. He was probably the son of the French immigrant painter and music teacher Philippe Abraham Peticolas (1760-1841), both of whom moved to Richmond from Philadelphia in 1804.[10] Even though there are seven parts (ABACADA), all of them except the third digression and coda are unimaginatively eight measures long. Peticolas must have had the financial resources from his father to have published an obviously juvenile piece.

Benjamin Carr

Benjamin Carr wrote four rondos not based on existing tunes. The first is "Rondo from the Overture to the Opera of the Archers or Mountaineers of Switzerland." The opera dates from 1796, but the rondo was not printed until about 1813, as no. 7 of Carr's series *Musical Miscellany in Occasional Numbers*, also available in modern reprint.[11] A shortened ABA version of this rondo--still marked "Rondo"--was printed as Sonata no. 5 in Linley's *New Assistant* (1796--the same year as the opera). The Linley version is somewhat simplified, due to its instructional function, as well as shortened. For

---

10. Wolfe, p. 681; see also Moore, 32.

11. Some minor changes are made in the edition of John Tasker Howard, *A Program of Early American Piano Pieces*, 28-32.

example, the initial rondo theme as printed in Linley's book is a standard sixteen measures long (a musical period comprising two eight-measure phrases), whereas a six-measure extension follows the second phrase in Carr's own publication. Linley's version interestingly avoids the chromaticism of the first cadence (meas. 7), and the sharpened second scale-degree used in several cadences in the "B" section (Ex. 2-5).[12] The "Archers" rondo then continues with a second digression, the "C" of the ABACA design, in the tonic minor, which contains another return of the rondo theme, in F major, as the "b" of the inner "a b a." This factor makes the whole rondo similar in design, but not quite as long (106 vs. 117 measures) as the G-major rondo (ca. 1794) by Rayner Taylor.

Ex. 2-5a.   Benjamin Carr, Rondo . . . Archers, meas. 24-25.

Ex. 2-5b.   Carr, Sonata V from Linley's *New Assistant*, meas. 19-20.

The "Archers" rondo was originally composed for orchestra, and, according to the complete title, "arranged for the Piano Forte." In spite of the late date in which it was first published, the conservative Alberti bass accompaniment, with almost no relief, overbalances any qualities which the opera audiences may have heard.

Carr's two rondos in his *Musical Journal for the Piano Forte* are not transcriptions. The E-flat major Rondo[13] is unique in its slow introduction, with several augmented-sixth chords. This time the Alberti bass does not permeate the main theme section (of 28 measures--long enough for three different musical ideas), but

---

12. "Sonata V" is printed on only one page in the original publication, achieved by using a da capo marking instead of reprinting the initial rondo theme.

13. Vol. 3 [1801-02], no. 60, pp. 13-14; Wolfe 1642.

threatens to do so at the beginning of the "B" section. The pattern, however, is picked up by the right hand, while forte and piano octaves or chords alternate treble and bass registers in the left hand, crossing the right. The "C" section, following the pattern of most rondos discussed thus far, has a change to G minor, with a touch of its relative major, E flat, in the middle.

His "Rondo Performed at the Philadelphia Harmonick Society,"[14] also in E-flat major, is written for instruments with a compass higher than usual. Under the title is printed: "NB: If the Piano has additional keys play those Passages marked 8va: an Octave higher," and indeed the highest note is c''''.[15] The "C" section, in the relative minor key, is based on a theme first heard near the end of the "A" section. Frequent use of bold octaves in both hands and the exploitation of register contrasts make this rondo a successful work.

Breaking the chronology of this discussion, a later independent rondo was published as *Carr's Musical Miscellany* no. 36, about 1816: "The Waltz Rondo, composed for the use of these numbers" (Wolfe 9584; reprint, pp. 139-40). Carr was apparently careful to attribute works to himself only when he wrote them.[16] If he actually wrote "The Waltz Rondo," he may not have wished to claim authorship because of its commonplace themes and too many exact repetitions. The meter of the main theme and first digression is 2/4; the reason for the title is the second digression, labeled "Waltz," in 3/8.

Musical Miscellany no. 48 is "La Bagatelle, composed for the use of these numbers." Perhaps published in 1818, it is likewise undistinguished, although the form varies in details from the usual rondos by Carr intended for the student. In the first digression, the dominant key is not reached until the last part, along with material based on the main theme. The "C" section, in the relative minor, has an inner three-part form--the first and last parts derived from the main theme and the middle part form the beginning of the "B" section. "Calmuck Rondo, composed for these numbers" was published about 1818-19 as *Musical Miscellany* no. 50.[17] Although the style is similarly simple, the form is not usual: ABACADCA coda.

---

14. Vol. 5 [1803-04], no. 116, pp. 21-22; Wolfe 1644.

15. See the photo of the square piano of ca. 1820 by Goulding, D'Almaine, Potter in Rosamond E. M. Harding's *The Piano-Forte* (Cambridge, 1933; reprint, New York: Da Capo, 1973), 81. "Additional keys" extend the range an octave, to c''''. I own an almost-identical instrument by Goulding & D'Almaine, made slightly later (1823 or so), in which the additional keys include a few more notes, to f''''.

16. According to Meyer, "Benjamin Carr's *Musical Miscellany*," 256.

17. Unlocated according to Wolfe 1584, but a copy is at the University of Pennsylvania, reproduced in the reprint.

Carr's Musical Miscellany in Occasional Numbers was succeeded in 1825 by *Lyricks* for the voice and *Le Clavecin* for the piano. Nos. 9-20 of *Le Clavecin* were reissued in 1829-30 as nos. 1-12 of *Twelve Airs*, op. 17, "fingered and otherwise particularly adapted for the improvement of piano forte pupils."[18] Of the four rondos, only one is not based on an existing tune: "La Serenade, composed by B. Carr." Although perhaps useful as a teaching piece, the constant repeated 8th-note chords in the left hand quickly tire the listener.

James Hewitt

After Rayner Taylor's rondo of ca. 1794, there is a gap in the publication of independent rondos until about 1811, the publication date of James Hewitt's D-major "Trip to Nahant" (EAKM no. 15). The main rondo theme is similar to the final rondo movement of Haydn's Sonata in D major, Hob. 19 (Ex. 2-6). Both have in their first eight measures the same harmony, form, character, and almost the same notes. In Haydn's movement, the returns are varied (A B A' C A" A), and Hewitt's formal plan (see below) also includes varied returns.

---

18. Twelve Airs: arranged with variations, or as rondos. Fingered, and otherwise particularly adapted for the improvement of piano forte pupils. By Benjamin Carr. These pieces are placed in promiscuous order, without any regard to progression of study. Philadelphia: B. Carr, 7 Powell Street. Sold also by R. H. Hobson, 147 Chesnut Street, opposite the United States Bank, [1829-30]. Price, singly, 25 cents; collectively, $1 50. Op. XVII. Library of Congress copy. The contents of nos. 1-5 (Wolfe 1877) are: 1) Grand artillery march (Carr; Wolfe 1601); Il cigno (waltz, Carr; Wolfe 1587); 3) The jolly waterman (Dibdin, arr. as a rondo by Carr; Wolfe 2439); 4) Overture to Il barbiere di Siviglia (arr. from Rossini; Wolfe 7637); 5) Overture to La Dame blanche (arr. from Boieldieu; Wolfe 926). Nos. 6-7 are thus far not known. The remaining, with the page numbers of nos. 9-20 (originally printed in parentheses) are: 8) Fantasia for the piano forte on the air Gramachree, by Benjamin Carr; 9) Une Petite Ouverture, composed by Benjamin Carr (pp. 3-5); 10) The Campbells are coming, arranged as a rondo by B. Carr (pp. 6-7); 11) Duett for two performers, by Dale with additions (pp. 8-9); 12) Little Bo Peep, arranged as a rondo by B. Carr (pp. 10-11); 13) La Serenade, composed by B. Carr (pp. 12-13); 14) The Carolinian waltz, composed by B. Carr (pp. 14-15); 15) The Sultan Saladin, as a rondo by B. Carr (pp. 16-17); 16) The Spanish Hymn, with variations by Carr (pp. 18-19); 17) Thema con variazione, composed by B. Carr (pp. 20-21); 18) Di tanti palpiti [from Rossini's *Tancredi*], arranged by B. Carr, as a duett for two performers (pp. 22-23); 19) Drink to me only with thine eyes, with variations by B. Carr (pp. 24-25); 20) The Genoa Ground, with variations by B. Carr (pp. 26-28).

Ex. 2-6.   Franz Joseph Haydn, Sonata in D major, Hob. 19, movement 3, meas. 1-4.

Hewitt's rondo, with the one issued in the 1790s by Taylor, ranks as the finest by Americans issued in the late 18th and early 19th centuries. "Trip to Nahant" (named for a resort town north of Boston), first of all, is marked by the lack of the continuous Alberti bass accompaniments which plague, for example, Carr's "Archers" rondo. The main theme is first given with short-chord accompaniment, and only on its immediate repetition does he use the Alberti accompaniment. Of the first 50 measures (ABA of the overall scheme), only fifteen have this accompaniment. Another measure of quality are a number of sudden (and humorous) rests preceding theme statements.[19]

The formal scheme ABACABA, although generally accurate, does not represent several subtle relationships. The "C" section commences with a new melody in the tonic key, stated twice, but after one of the unexpected rests comes another melody, which (after another sudden measure rest) is restated. The transition to the return of the main rondo theme uses the same material that had similarly been used at the end of the "B" section--but in a varied manner. The octave displacements which characterize Carr's "Rondo Performed at the Philadelphia Harmonick Society" are also prominent in "Trip to Nahant," especially in the final returns of the rondo theme. The final delight is the syncopated treatment of the last return.

19. Meas. 36, 68, 89, 116, plus a fermata in meas. 136.

Victor Pelissier, James F. Hance, Charles F. Hupfeld

By contrast, Victor Pelissier's Rondo in D major, printed in his series *Pelissier's Columbian Melodies* (1812),[20] is more sophisticated in style, in the class of Rayner Taylor's Rondo in G major of 1794. Pelissier's two digressions provide most of the length of the piece.[21] There are as many as six identifiable themes in the first digression,[22] the fifth of them with an augmented second interval between the 6th and 7th scale degrees and an awkward augmented-sixth cadence (Ex. 2-7). The second digression, in D minor, has an inner three-part form which has been frequently encountered, and scale passages which are somewhat challenging to the amateur pianist (Ex. 2-8). This digression ends with a cadenza. The main factor detracting from the quality of the piece is the rather commonplace rondo theme, complete with Alberti bass and the usual period structure.

Ex. 2-7.   Victor Pelissier, Rondo in D major, meas. 52-57.

---

20. The series is dated 1811-12 in Wolfe 6923, but probably it was issued January-December 1812. Available in modern edition in *Pelissier's Columbian Melodies*, ed. Karl Kroeger, Recent Researches in American Music, 13-14 (Madison: A-R Editions, 1984), 169-77.

21. First digression, 69 measures long; second, 50. The main theme is only 16 measures long, its two returns 16 and 24 measures long; the whole work totals 175 measures.

22. Measures 17, 25, 33, 39, 45, 57, with a seventh theme functioning as a transition beginning at meas. 73.

Ex. 2-8.   Pelissier, Rondo in D major, meas. 105-08.

This one rondo, due to its style, was undoubtedly composed for piano rather than an instrumental ensemble. Another such piece from *Columbian Melodies* is his five-part Rondo in F major.[23] Generally, the characteristics and formal organization are Mozartean, as had been the earlier rondos by Rayner Taylor. Indeed, the main theme, like that of Taylor's Rondo in G, is very much like the last movement of Mozart's Sonata in C, K. 545--the first two measures in the right hand of Pelissier's rondo are identical to Mozart's. There are no extraordinary challenges for the performer, but it is a fine work, in classical style.

Pelissier (ca. 1745-ca. 1820), probably of a French background, came to Philadelphia from what is now Haiti in 1792, and became known as a French horn soloist as well as a musical arranger and composer primarily for the theater. Among other piano music in *Columbian Melodies*, several dances, originally functioning as accompaniments to dancing on the stage, were intended for instrumental groups. Nonetheless, some are extensive enough to be in rondo form, and were published in arrangements for piano.[24] His rondos in D and F, however, are best.

The reappearance of the independently-composed rondo at the end of the decade brought also an emancipation from the Alberti bass. James F. Hance's "Le Songe Celeste! a Rondo" (1818-21; Wolfe 3329) is based on an attractive melody (Ex. 2-9). The chord beginning the

---

23. Kroeger ed., 159-63.

24. See Allegro in F, Kroeger ed., pp. 8-11; "Dance as Performed at the New York Theatre in Obi, or Three Fingered Jack," p. 59; "Negro Dance in Obi, or Three Fingered Jack," p. 63; "Dances as Performed at the Philad[elphi]a New Theatre under the Direction of Mr. Francis in The Peasant Boy," pp. 64-67--the section entitled "Tambourine: Allegro"; "Allemande Danced at the Philadelphia New Theatre by Mr. Francis & Mrs. Green," p. 153.

third measure would not have been used by previous American composers. Hance, however, who usually displays better judgement, detracts from the quality of the piece by restating this four-measure theme--albeit with varying settings--no fewer than eight times without relief.

Ex. 2-9.   James F. Hance, "Le Songe Celeste!" meas. 1-4.

The theme of the first digression, and its accompaniment, is more closely related to Beethoven and Schubert than to Haydn or Mozart (Ex. 2-10).

Ex. 2-10.   Hance, "Le Songe Celeste!" meas. 33-40.

After the return of "A," the "C" section provides some tonal contrast in a modulation to the relative minor. The section includes a new musical idea, succeeded by another that appears to be new as well except that it turns out to be a well-disguised version of the main rondo theme (Ex. 2-11). The overall form is A B A C A' B A. Figuration on a diminished-seventh chord in the second half of the last "B" and several modest cadenzas are Hance's only other concessions to contemporary trends of piano style seen in some of his other works.

Ex. 2-11.   Hance, "Le Songe Celeste!" meas. 135-39.

Hance's "The Cossack Rondo" (1827), in comparison, is retrogressive in style.[25] A few exceptions aside, the accompaniment lies within the reach of the left hand. Tonally, there are no keys outside the tonic C major and its relative minor, and each section of the ABACA form is boxed with the length of sixteen measures.

Charles F. Hupfeld (1787-1864) was born in Germany and came to Philadelphia as a youngster, in 1799. With Benjamin Carr and others, he was a founder of the Musical Fund Society and led an active career as violinist, violist, teacher, composer, and publisher. Hupfeld's only rondo is "A Divertimento" (1821-22), dedicated to his wife, one copy of which he inscribed to A. P. Heinrich.[26] Not very impressive as piano music, it consists of a march and trio, each of a regular eight measures in length, succeeded by variant returns of the march in a five-part rondo pattern (A B A' C A" coda).

F. Holden, Frederick A. Getze, William Staunton, Jr.

The unidentified F. Holden is responsible for "Mina, a favorite rondo" (1820-25; Wolfe 3888)--his only published composition--which

25. The Cossack Rondo for the piano forte by I. F. Hance. Price 25 Cents. New York, engraved, printed, & sold by E. Riley, 29, Chatham Street. [2] pp. Bottom of p. [1]: Entered according to Act of Congress, the eighteenth day of June 1827, by Edward Riley of the State of New York. Bottom r.h. corner of p. [2]: Cossack Rondo.2. New York Public Library copy.

26. Wolfe 860; unlocated. A Divertimento for the piano forte, composed & dedicated to his wife by Charles F. Hupfeld. Pr: 50. Copyright. Philadelphia, published by G. E. Blake at his piano forte and music store, No. 13 south Fifth street, [1821-22]. Title-page + pp. 2-5. At top of title-page: (No. 51, Blake's Musical Miscellany). Manuscript note at upper l.h. corner: for Mr A. P. Heinrich with Mr Hupfeld's compliments. Bodleian Library copy, box 14.

is undistinguished in style and unchallenging to the pianist. The only unusual feature is a return of the rondo theme in F major instead of the tonic B-flat major. Of noticeably higher quality is Frederick A. Getze's "Saxon Rondo" (1821?; EAKM no. 23), another so-called rondo in spite of the three-part form. Getze was active in Philadelphia about 1819-42. The left-hand accompaniment has rests on the first and fourth beats of the 6/8 meter for much of the piece, a trait also occasionally used in the right hand as well. Another prominent device is the repetition of short fragments on successive higher tonal levels--the sequence[27]--and, toward the end of the second part, the augmented ("French") sixth chord. These features were rarely used in the United States before the 1820s.

The English-born William Staunton, Jr. (1803-89) wrote some music published in Boston in 1826-29 before becoming a Episcopal clergyman.[28] One of them is "Euterpe, a Rondino,"[29] which is of little interest except for the rondo return in D minor, in place of the tonic F major, just before the final return. The old-fashioned Alberti bass is used in the "B" section.

Charles Thibault

The French-born Charles Thibault (d. 1853?) represents a significant change from the classical styles of Mozart and Haydn and their American imitators. Thibault gave concerts in New York from 1818 until well into the 1830s, and published music until about 1850. He was one of the best composers living in the United States at the time, and his compositions reveal his fine training at the Paris Conservatory, from which he claimed to have received a Grand Premium.

------

27. See meas. 13-14, 46-48.

28. He maintained his interest in music, however. Among his publications at the Library of Congress are *The Church Chant-Book* (New York: Stanford & Swords, 1850), *Fugue for the Organ* (New York: Wm. A. Pond, 1864), *The Book of Common Praise: A Collection of Music Adapted to the Book of Common Prayer* (New York: F. J. Huntington & Co., 1866); and in the *National Union Catalog* are listed many church writings, and *Voluntaries for the Organ* (New York: W. Hall, [ca. 1856]). Staunton had come at the age of 15 to Pittsburgh with his father, moved to Boston by 1826, and became organist at St. Luke's Episcopal Church, Rochester, New York, in May 1827. He also opened a music business where he sold pianos and built pipe organs. He became married in 1831, and was ordained deacon in 1833. I am indebted to James W. Kimball, SUNY-Geneseo, for sending a copy of his article "Rochester's Musical Pioneers," *Rochester Sunday Democrat and Chronicle*, Upstate Magazine section, 2 September 1984, 6-13.

29. Euterpe, a Rondino, composed for the piano forte, by W^m. Staunton Jr. Copy right secured. Boston, published by James L. Hewitt & Co., at their Music Saloon N°. 36 Market S^t. [1826-29]. [2] pp. New York Public Library copy.

"Le Printems, a Rondo," op. 6, of 1823,[30] apparently is his first work published in the United States. It is the first rondo to have an introduction, and this introduction is the only one to incorporate what is essentially an added section, "Rustic Dance." The rhythm (8th-8th-quarter), repeated in the bass on an open fifth, imitates the tambourine. The dance is preceded by a short free section, the content of which subsequently returns to serve as a transition to the main theme.

The rondo form, rather than the standard ABACA or related pattern common earlier in the century, is treated with much more freedom. The structure is best represented by a chart:

meas.	form	key	description
1-8		G	Adagio sostenuto [introduction], meter C
9-55			Rustic Dance, Allegretto, 2/4
56-63			Adagio; transition
64-87	A	D	Allegro non troppo, 3/4
88-103	B	D	
104-23	A	G	
124-39	B	G-D	
140-58	C	D	grazioso
159-70	D	D	spiritoso, triplets
171-84	B'	D	
185-92	A	G	
193-203	A'	g-Bb	
204-21	D	Bb-a-Bb	
222-38	B	Eb	
239-57	C	G	
258-71	D	G	
272-87	A	D	
288-98	coda	D	

Such a summary, however, does not reveal that much of the music is almost developmental in nature--especially in the flat keys toward the end--rather than a clear-cut alternation of themes. Thibault's facile writing includes many decorative scale and arpeggio passages, and in these he often exploits the high range of the piano, as high as *c''''*.

Thibault's second independently-composed rondo (not based on an existing tune) is "L'Adieu," op. 11 (EAKM no. 27), published in

---

30. Le Printems, a rondo, with an introduction for the piano forte, composed & dedicated to Miss Ann Heyward, by Charles Thibault. Op: 6. Copy right secured. Price 1 dollar. New York, published by Dubois & Stodart at the Piano Forte & Music Store No. 126 Broad Way, [1823]. Title-page + pp. 2-11. American Antiquarian Society copy. Wolfe 9336 (unlocated).

the following year, 1824.[31] The introduction, marked "Prelude," is in a style uncannily reminiscent of the first movement of Beethoven's "Moonlight" Sonata. Already in the ninth measure Thibault has modulated from the tonic G major to the distant key of E-flat major--a bold modulation for American composers of this time. The interest in virtuosity which had been growing since the second decade of the century, is seen in the numerous cadenzas, of varying lengths, such as the one at the end of the prelude, and in the continuous scales and other passagework, especially in the digressions. The rondo theme is in three-part form, and a short cadenza scale is an essential part of the II-6/5 chord held in the sixth measure of the eight-measure phrase; each time the cadenza returns it is more elaborate.

The structure of "L'Adieu" is even more complex than that of "Le Printems," for he has manipulated smaller musical units in a manner that supersedes the overall ABACA form, as indicated here (measures not represented are further transitions or extensions):

meas.	large divisions	small divisions	correspondences
1-17	Prelude		
18-	A		
18-25		a	
25-28		b	
29-36		c	
41-48		a	
49-53		codetta/transition	
52-53		b	
54-	B		
54-55		d	
56-57		b	
58-59		e	
60-61		b	
62-64		e	
65-67		c	
74-81	(A')		
81-88		f	after "b"
89-94		e'	
105-16		c	as meas. 29-40
117-27	A	a	as meas. 41-51
128-31		b	as meas. 52-53
132-	C		
136-43		d	after meas. 54-55
151-58	(A")		
159-64	C, cont'd		as meas. 132-35
165-70			as meas. 97-102
173-76		c	from meas. 29-30
183-205	(A')		as meas. 74-96

---

31. It was also reprinted in London's *The Harmonicon* in 1828 (see Wolfe 9330).

216-23 A--elaborated
224-35 coda

There are variant returns of the rondo theme within the "B" and "C" sections (at meas. 74, 151, 183), in addition to the main returns separating the two digressions (at meas. 117 and 216). Tonally, the main key is G major. The related key of D major is used for the first digression and C major for the second, yet there are a number of tonal excursions within these principal keys. This piece represents a marked growth in quality and style for music by an American-resident composer.[32]

Only one impromptu originated in the United States before 1830; because it has rondo characteristics it is being discussed here. The work was written to mark the return to the United States--after a 40-year absence--of the only surviving general in the Revolutionary War: "La Fayette's Return, or The Hero's Welcome, an impromptu for the piano forte," op. 12 (1824; Wolfe 9334), by Thibault. Lafayette had arrived in New York City on 16 August 1824, and would visit every one of the twenty-four states before returning to his native France in September 1825.

Thibault's impromptu comprises four sections. The introductory Allegro maestoso is succeeded by the Allegro spiritoso, rondo-like in its sprightly mood and compound rhythm, and pianistic with its scale passages and hand-crossing. A drum-imitation (16th-note octaves) leads directly to "Hail La Fayette: Marcia maestoso," also with the drum in its midst. The compound rhythm of the second section returns to complete the work, with the drum in the final chords. "La Fayette's Return," dedicated to the "Ladies of New York," is integrated in form and delightful in effect. Amidst the marches and dances by other Americans, and even Oliver Shaw's programmatic "Welcome the Nation's Guest" (see chapter 5), Thibault's musical homage to his fellow-Frenchman is the best piano work associated with Lafayette's visit.[33] As pure piano music, however, "Le Printems"

---

32. This trend is also seen in a much later rondo published in London: Tarentelle, (La Diavoletta.) pour piano. par Chs. Thibault. Ent. Sta. Hall. Price 2/6. London: Leader & Cock, 63, New Bond Street, corner of Brook Street, [1851]. Title-page + pp. 1-7. At top of p. 1: La Diavoletta. Tarentelle. par Ch: Thibault. At bottom of pp. 1-6: L & C 1057. At bottom of p. 7: 1057. London Printed by Leader & Cock, 63, New Bond St. Also reprinted, with imprint on title-page altered to: London, published by A. W. Hammond, Music Seller & Publisher, 9, New Bond Street, Opposite the Clarenden Hotel, [1854]. British Library copies, h.723.v.(9-10). Not only is the 6/8 piece difficult to play, especially at the tempo "Vivo," but it also utilizes the greater range of the mid-century keyboard--to *a''''*.

33. For an account of Lafayette's tour and the associated music, see my article "American Musical Tributes of 1824-25 to Lafayette: A Report and Inventory," *Fontes Artis Musicae* 26, no. 1 (1979): 17-35.

and "L'Adieu" are better. (Five of his rondos based on operatic themes are discussed below.)

La Chasse

In the 1790s first appeared in the United States the type of rondo called "La Chasse." The European craze in the late 18th century for this style, based on horn calls in the hunt, was also shared by the musical public in America. European chasses, sometimes actually incorporating standard horn signals (*sonneries*), were represented in such works as the operas *Tom Jones* (1765) by François André Danican-Philidor and *Diane et Endimion* (1784) by Niccolò Piccini. Some chasse symphonies are François-Joseph Gossec's *Simfonia da Caccia* (1774), works entitled *Simphonie de Chasse* by Karl Stamitz (1775) and Francesco Antonio Rosetti (1782), and Franz Anton Hoffmeister's Symphony "La Chasse," op. 14 (1791). Haydn included some chasse music with quotations of various *sonneries* in his oratorio *The Seasons*, and in his Symphony 31 and Symphony 73 ("La Chasse"). Some chasses for keyboard are Leopold Kozeluch's "La Caccia"[34] (1781), Muzio Clementi's sonata "La Chasse," op. 16 (1787), and works titled "La Chasse" by Adalbert Gyrowetz (1797) and Jan Ladislav Dussek (1796).[35]

As early as 1787, William Brown (whose *Three Rondos*, discussed above, were published the same year) played in Philadelphia Stamitz's "New Overture, La Chasse" and Carlo Antonio Campioni's sonata "La Chasse." Even though none of the chasse works by Haydn was published in the United States during his lifetime, Thomas Jefferson's music collection included keyboard arrangements of Symphony No. 73, and this symphony was performed in New York in 1793 and 1794.[36] An arrangement, as a divertimento, of Haydn's "La Chasse" (taken from the first movement of Symphony 67) was printed in *Carr's Musi-*

---

34. Perhaps the same as: Kozeluch's La Chasse, for the harpsichord or piano forte. Op. V. Pr. [in ink:] 7s/6d. London, printed for J. Bland, at his Music Warehouse, 45 Holborn, where may be had all the above Authors Works & the greatest Variety of Music, English & Foreign. Title-page + pp. 36-46. Top of p. 36: (No 1) La Chasse. Bottom of pp. 36-46: Kozeluch's La Chasse Op 5. Lilly Library, Indiana University copy.

35. These works are discussed in part 2, chapter 4, of Alexander Ringer's "The Chasse: Historical and Analytical Bibliography of a Musical Genre" (Ph.D. dissertation, Columbia University, 1955).

36. Irving Lowens, *Haydn in America*, Bibliographies in American Music, 5 (Detroit: Information Coordinators, 1979), 58 and 61, and item nos. J-4 and J-8.

cal Miscellany series about 1813.[37] The first American publications of
chasses were Campioni's "La Chasse," as arranged by Alexander
Reinagle in his *Twelve Favorite Pieces arranged for the piano forte or
harpsichord* of 1789 (the same work performed in public two years
earlier by William Brown), and James Hewitt's arrangement of
Rosetti's "La Chasse," appearing in *Six Songs for the Harpsichord or
Piano Forte* (1794; Sonneck-Upton, 439, 47-48).

Reinagle's own "La Chasse,"[38] like Campioni's, is in 6/8 meter
and in a five-part rondo form, but one digression--the second--is in
the relative (not parallel) minor. It is influenced by the Campioni and
other chasse pieces in the exploitation of hunting calls and horn fifths
(Ex. 2-12).

Ex. 2-12a. Carlo Antonio Campioni, "La Chasse," meas. 55-58.

Ex. 2-12b. Alexander Reinagle, "La Chasse," meas. 25-32.

37. Wolfe 3492; reprint, pp. 51-54. The source is Haydn's
Symphony 67, 1st movement, and not Symphony 73 as indicated in the
reprint.

38. La Chasse, a new lesson for the piano forte composed in an
easy familiar stile [*sic*] by A. Reinagle [1794]; Sonneck-Upton, 59;
edited by Edward Gold in *The Bicentennial Collection of American
Keyboard Music* (Dayton: McAfee, 1975), 4-6.

John Christopher Moller's "La Chasse," published about 1802-03,[39] is closely patterned after the chasse by Franz Koczwara (composer of the notorious *Battle of Prague*)--the chasse that was thought for some time to be by Reinagle (see Wolfe 5117). Both Moller's and Koczwara's are in D major. Both have two digressions, the first of which is labeled "Minore" in the parallel minor key, including a mid-section in F major. Moller furnishes a cadenza before the da capo that is not found in Koczwara's. Both chasses use the subdominant for the second digression.[40] Only Moller's has a coda. Much of the musical material of the two compositions is remarkably alike, especially in the last few measures of these examples (Ex. 2-13).

Ex. 2-13a. Frantisek Koczwara, "La Chasse," meas. 1-16.

---

39. Wolfe 5887. It may have been composed at least a decade earlier, however. A manuscript book signed "Catherine Akerly's Music Book, Bethle[hem, Pa.], Dec. 19th, 1792," owned by Irving Lowens, begins with "Favorite La Chasse by J. C. Moller." James J. Fuld and Mary Wallace Davidson, *18th-Century American Secular Music Manuscripts: An Inventory*, MLA Index & Bibliography Series, 20 (Philadelphia: Music Library Association, 1980), item 76.

40. Erroneously labeled "Minore" in the Weldon publication of Koczwara's (Wolfe 5117).

Ex. 2-13b. J. C. Moller, "La Chasse," meas. 1-16.

Although these few pieces are the last American chasses for keyboard,[41] "American Rondo" (1820?; Wolfe 1) by the German-American composer Frederick L. Abel (1794-1820), resident of Savannah, Georgia (and a later teacher of Lowell Mason), is stylistically related to the chasse (Ex. 2-14).

Ex. 2-14. Frederick L. Abel, "American Rondo," meas. 1-6.

---

41. One vocal counterpart was composed by a committee: "Rondeau Chasse, selected from the Ode to Cheerfulness, composed by B: Carr & G: Schetky and performed by the Young Ladies of Mrs. Mallon's Academy on Thursday Decr. the 23^d. 1802," *Musical Journal for the Piano Forte* [1802-03], no. 4, pp. 60-62 (Wolfe 1641). It exhibits the horn fifths and 6/8 meter characteristic of the genre, and begins with the text "Tis then with hound & sprightly horn we'll cheerly rouse the slumb'ring morn."

Except for momentary touches of D minor, the tonic key
predominates, yet the rondo scheme is not unusual. The main rondo
theme is in two parts; the second melody, reassigned to the left hand,
returns in the midst of the digression to suggest an overall A B A' C A
form.

Oliver Shaw's "Trip to Pawtucket," which dates from around
1830,[42] likewise includes several passages which imitate the horn (Ex.
2-15). Here he intends the posthorn instead of the hunting horn, confirmed by the engraving on the original sheet music of a coach with
four horses.

Ex. 2-15.   Oliver Shaw, "Trip to Pawtucket," meas. 9-12, 25-28.

42. Trip to Pawtucket, price 12½ cts., composed by O. Shaw.
Published and sold by the Author No. 70 Westminster St. Providence.
1 leaf. Brown University copy. Recorded in E. Power Biggs, *The
Organ in America* (Columbia MS 6161). Also printed in *O. Shaw's
Instructions for the Piano Forte* (Providence: author, 1831), 26.

Rondos Based on Pre-Existing Melodies

Benjamin Carr

Benjamin Carr was the most prolific American arranger and composer of his time, and apparently the first (and almost the last) composer of rondos based on popular melodies.[43] His first such rondos, both based on "Yankee Doodle," however, are part of larger works. At the end of his medley *The Federal Overture* (1794), "Yankee Doodle" serves as the main section, and another melody, "Viva Tutti," as the digression (see chapter 4). Similarly, the popular American tune is used at the end of the "Naval Medley" in *The Siege of Tripoli* (1804-05; EAKM no. 11), and this "Yankee Doodle as a rondo" was also later published separately (Wolfe 1678--undated). Although the setting of the tune in its first eight measures is almost the same as in *The Federal Overture*, the next phrase is not, and there is even a variant of the basic melody. At the end of the main section, a codetta consists of fanciful 16th-note scales and repeated cadences at different octave transpositions. The first digression is at the subdominant level of D major, followed by a fantasy on the rising three-note motive of the beginning of the theme. After the da capo to the "A" section, the third digression ("Minore") initially develops the same motive in a modulation from A minor to the submediant F major and development of other motives. The transition to the last da capo consists of cadenza-like passages culminating in a rising 2½-octave chromatic scale. This ABACA rondo treatment in *The Siege of Tripoli* is more successful than the "Yankee Doodle" in *The Federal Overture*, and deserves modern performance. (He may also have written a set of variations on "Yankee Doodle"--see chapter 3.)

Carr's important collection *Applicazione addolcita: Twelve Airs & a Ground with Variations or Arranged as Rondos*, op. 6, published by Carr and Schetky in Philadelphia in 1809 (Wolfe 1576), contains seven rondos intermixed with five variations. He makes clear on the title page that the collection is instructional: "The certainty that there cannot be too great a number of Pieces proper for Pupils, is the inducement for the present addition to those already published . . .," but not exclusively, for he adds: "To Amateurs, who occasionally wish for some short Pieces of the above kind, this Work is also respectfully submitted."

Carr's rondos in the collection all have two digressions, resulting in the form ABACA. There is also a certain unanimity in the key

---

43. Alexander Reinagle composed a rondo-arrangement, presumably before he came to the United States in 1786: Muirland Willie, a favorite Scotch air made into a rondo by Alex[r]. Reinagle. Edin[r]., printed & sold by Gow & Shepherd Music Sellers No. 16 Princes Street. Pr. 1/6. pp. 2-5. Copy at the British Library, g.352.k.(11), which dates it ca. 1805. This work somehow escaped the notice of Robert Hopkins, who otherwise lists all of Reinagle's compositions in his edition *The Philadelphia Sonatas*, xvi-xxiii.

scheme. Those in the minor mode--"Spanish Fandango" and "Shelty the Piper"--use the relative major key in the "B" sections, and the tonic made major for "C." The others, in major keys, use the dominant key for "B," and minor--either relative minor or parallel minor--for "C." All returns are accomplished with the "D.C." marking, making it possible for most of these rondos to fit on two pages. Sometimes there are tonal excursions within these main keys, such as in the second digression of "Nobody coming to marry me." The main key is D major; the "C" section begins in D minor and modulates to F major, G major, and A minor. In the same digression of "Tid re I," the initial key of the section, A minor, is soon left in a tonal sequence through the keys of F major, E minor, D, C, G, and E major, the last functioning as the dominant to the rondo return in A major. A passage in which a single note is repeated for several measures in the "A" section is also found in the middle of "C."

These rondos are suitable for students and make few demands on keyboard technique. The first digression of "Shelty the Piper" is based on the first measure of the rondo theme followed by an arpeggio. This pattern is repeated three times, and is capped with a 3-octave scale. The first digressions of "Nobody coming to marry me" and "The Rose," and the second of "Spanish Fandango," include hand crossing. The collection's last rondo, "Fishers Hornpipe," does not tax the pianist with more than a few scales. Carr was able to use the material of the main theme in the whole work; the digressions contrast only in key and treatment. The predominant texture in the rondos is the melody in the right hand and Alberti-bass accompaniment in the left.

Carr provided variety in the tunes he chose. "Spanish Fandango" is a sprightly melody in 6/8. "Shelty the Piper" is a Scotch tune, also in 6/8, in which the tonic E-minor harmony often alternates with the chord on the lowered seventh scale degree, D major. The full title is "Shelty the Piper as a rondo, in which is introduced 'Polwart on the Green'," and the second melody is introduced as the "C" section, with a change of tempo from Allegro to Slow, and to common (C) meter.[44] For his rondo based on John Bray's song "The Rose" (Wolfe 1336), Carr likewise introduces another Bray melody, "Soft as yon silver ray" (Wolfe 1342-47), in the midst of the "C" section--preceded and followed in the section by scales and other figurations. "Nobody coming to marry me" is a song by the English composer Thomas Simpson Cooke (Wolfe 2076), but more information about the Vestris

---

44. "Polwart on the Green" is included on p. 54 of two (obviously related) collections of Scotch tunes: John Aitken's *The Scots, Musical,* [sic] *Museum* [1797], and Carr's own publication *The Caladonian Muse* [1798], Wolfe 10170 and 10183. I have not determined if "Shelty's Song" on pp. 83-84 of both collections is the same as "Shelty the Piper." The title is apparently taken from William Dunlap's farce *Shelty's Travels*--this information is from Sprenkle, 1:213.

of "Vestris's Gavot" has not yet been found.[45] "Tid re I" is an anonymous Irish song with alternate title "The Marriage of Miss Kitty O'Donavan to Mr. Paddy O'Rafferty" (Wolfe 9380-84).

In 1812, Carr inaugurated his series *Musical Miscellany in Occasional Numbers* with his own rondo-arrangement of "Tell me soldier," a duet from the comic opera *The Foundling of the Forest* by Michael Kelly, first performed in the United States in Philadelphia in the season 1809-10. The difference of Carr's intended audience between his rondos of *Applicazione addolcita* and "Tell me soldier" are striking. The borrowed melody is presented in a simple manner, at first with simple Alberti bass accompaniment, then with block chords in the left hand. Yet between these two statements Carr already adds a cadenza of scales and tremolos, calling for an extended keyboard range to c''''. The next section (meas. 26-67) consists of four-measure phrases, repeated, and using two harmonic schemes:

meas.	*harmonic skeleton*
26-29, 30-33	I I V I
34-37	V I V I
38-41, 42-45	I I V I
46-49	V I V I
50-53, 54-57	V I V I
58-61, 62-65	V I V I

The only four-measure segment not immediately repeated (meas. 34-37) is given later (meas. 46-49) with different figurations in the right hand. There is no memorable contrasting melody in this section; Carr instead introduces one keyboard idea after another, without much sense of natural progression. There are two measures of final cadence, a fermata, and this is presumably the Fine. The "Tell me soldier" melody, or even its harmony, is not present.

The 2½ pages following (meas. 68-150) are, at least in part, borrowed from another work, as indicated in the explanation "from Bihler."[46] In all likelihood, Carr used a portion of a sonata movement, from the transition section after the first theme onwards. The modulation from C major to G major is accomplished in the first section ending with the fermata (meas. 84), and the material that follows (at least until meas. 109) has the character of a second theme and closing theme. The rest of the section is developmental, although it is all centered on G major. In the return to C major, there is a "Cadenza brilliante" on the dominant-seventh, yet the chord progression afterwards is certainly unconventional, if not awkward (Ex. 2-16). In sum-

---

45. Wolfe 9469-72. Presumably Vestris was European, since Latour wrote piano variations on the dance-tune.

46. Otherwise unidentified; two late 18th-century composers with this name were Gregorius Bihler of Donawert, Germany, and Franz Bihler of Augsburg. Neither is represented in the *British Union-Catalogue*.

mation, this so-called rondo has elements of pasticcio; the only rondo aspect is the overall three-part design--except that the borrowed theme is not even heard at the end, and the overall form is heard as ABCAB.

Ex. 2-16. Carr, "Tell me soldier," meas. 146-50, 1-4 (originally printed with small notes until the "Adagio ad libitum").

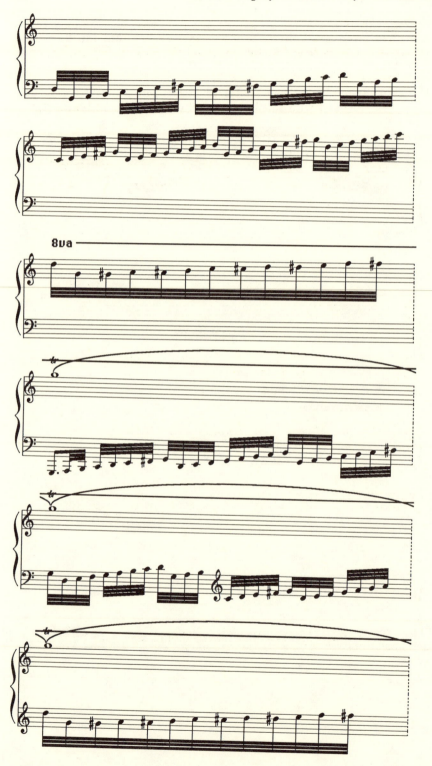

Adagio ad libitum

Da Capo

non troppo Allegro

Carr's rondo-arrangement of the Irish tune "Paddy Carey," no.
35 of his *Musical Miscellany* series, published about 1816, is much
more unified. The "A" section contains a simple setting of the
melody, with Alberti bass accompaniment. But in comparison with the
binary form of the tune as published a few years later,[47] Carr has
changed and expanded on the original tune in several places and even
added some virtuoso writing (Ex. 2-17).

Ex. 2-17a. "Paddy Carey," Riley publication, meas. 9-10.

Ex. 2-17b. Carr, "Paddy Carey," meas. 22-25.

Ex. 2-17c. Carr, "Paddy Carey," meas. 32-37.

---

47. Paddy Carey, a cotillion (New York: E. Riley, [1818-20]);
Wolfe 6720. There are two different publications with the same
imprint, in C major and D major; I used the C-major one for
reference.

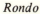

The codetta to the section features a horn-call (Ex. 2-18). The sixteen-measure tune is thereby expanded to a 72-measure "A" section. The horn-call reappears in the "B" section, as does material from the second phrase of the original tune (Ex. 2-19). The right hand, as seen in this example, subsequently crosses over the left hand several times, to sound in the bass. After the da capo, the "C" section begins in A minor with the horn-call, yet includes a variant of the main theme in A major. The digressions end with well-written transitions, both marked "slower and slower," which effectively lead to the rondo theme. The final return is written out and abridged, and is capped with a coda.

Ex. 2-18.   Carr, "Paddy Carey," meas. 62-65.

Ex. 2-19a.   "Paddy Carey," Riley publication, meas. 5-8.

Ex. 2-19b. Carr, "Paddy Carey," meas. 96-100.

"Italian Air, arranged as a rondo for these numbers," *Musical Miscellany* no. 40 (1817?), has some of the same characteristics as other rondos specifically attributed to Carr. Most of the piece is accompanied by the Alberti bass, and provides little challenge to the pianist. Perhaps the simplicity of this work, along with "The Waltz Rondo," "La Bagatelle," and "Calmuck Rondo," discussed earlier, prompted Carr not to use his own name on the publication. The "B" section is in the dominant key, and is initiated with unaccompanied octaves, as in "The Plow Boy."

One arrangement by Carr was not described as a rondo even though it is rondo-like: "A Divertisment [*sic*] on the favorite air of The Plow Boy," *Musical Miscellany* no. 49 (1818?), based on an air from William Shield's comic opera *The Farmer*, first heard at Covent Garden, London, in 1787. The theme was also used for a set of variations as the second movement of James Hewitt's Sonata in C major, op. 5, no. 2, and in Hewitt's C-major "Mount" sonata, and was arranged for another American publication from a rondo movement in a piano concerto by Dussek (Wolfe 8124-27). Perhaps this piece by Carr is best described as a fantasy-rondo, since not only does the main theme recur throughout (ABACA), but also serves as the basis for the development-like digressions. In fact, the theme is given intact within each of the two digressions, but in keys other than the tonic of F major.[48] In the first digression, the theme appears in sequence. At the beginning of the second digression, Shield's melody receives a forceful treatment in octaves in D minor, and again in C minor in the midst of the same section. For what is essentially a false return, albeit in the tonic key,[49] Carr provides a new treatment, the melody in the left hand answered by quick scales in the right (Ex. 2-20).

Ex. 2-20.   Carr, "Plow Boy," meas. 123-24.

At or near the end of each "A" statement, the main theme, unaccompanied and appearing in a high range ($c'''-c''''$), comes from the original air. This represents the plow boy playing a whistle. For several other passages, Carr used the extended range of the piano, to c'''', but also provided alternates for "piano ordinaire" with a limit of f'''.

Examples of pianistic pyrotechniques are embedded in Carr's "Plow Boy" arrangement. A measure of alternating octaves in the initial "A" section is apparently the impetus for this treatment in the first digression (Ex. 2-21).

Ex. 2-21.   Carr, "Plow Boy," meas. 48-49.

---

48. Meas. 55-58 in G major, meas. 101-05 in B-flat major.

49. The final "A" is on the last page, meas. 134.

Alternating octaves and fast scales toward the end of the same digression are likewise challenging for the pianist (Ex. 2-22). In the second digression, broken chords in both hands exploit the full resonance of the instrument (Ex. 2-23).

Ex. 2-22.   Carr, "Plow Boy," meas. 81-83.

Ex. 2-23.   Carr, "Plow Boy," meas. 98-99.

Such pianistic writing, by contrast, is not found in Carr's rondo treatment of "Di tanti palpiti, or Hail to the Happy Day," published about 1823 as *Carr's Musical Miscellany* no. 75. The reason must be that it was also written "also with an Accompaniment for the flute or violin." However, the score reads "N.B: This Piece may be played without the Accomp^t." and indeed the piano part is viable played alone. Nevertheless, the potential presence of the other instrument may account for the lack of pianistic virtuosity characteristic of many other solo piano works by Carr. "Di tanti palpiti" originated as a cavatina from Rossini's 1813 opera *Tancredi*, and in various American imprints appeared as a song, issued with variations by Jean Tatton Latour, William Martin, and Ferdinand Ries, arranged as a rondo by J. C. Nightingale and Carr, and was included in Meineke's medley *Divertimento*.[50] Most of Carr's rondo has an Alberti bass accompaniment and, with the exception of several scales in 32nd notes, is restrained in character. Both digressions, "B" in the dominant of C major and "C" in D minor and B-flat major (relative minor and subdominant to the tonic F major), are based on material of the main theme.

Carr's rondo on "When the hollow drum," the next-to-last (no. 85) of *Musical Miscellany* (ca. 1825), is likewise a disappointment. The original song from Samuel Arnold's *The Mountaineers* was performed as early as 1796 and published within a year or so afterwards (Sonneck-Upton, 466). Carr's arrangement follows the same pattern seen in many of his other rondos. The first digression centers on the dominant key of C major; the second, in the relative minor (D), begins with the main tune in octaves. The problem may have been Arnold's original tune, which is excessively repetitious. The fault is also true of the arrangement by Carr, who adds only a few 16th-note major scales. The rondo was obviously aimed at pianists with only modest abilities. Carr is more exciting when he demands more of the pianist and treats the given melody in more adventuresome ways, as in "Tell me soldier" and "The Plow Boy."

Carr's next published rondo is "The Jolly Young Waterman, a favourite air by Dibdin, arranged as a rondo for the piano forte," no. 3 of his new series *Le Clavecin*, published in 1825 (Wolfe 2439). Carr's arrangement uses some of the same characteristics of others by him--the five-part ABACA form, and beginning the "C" section in the relative minor mode with the two hands in octaves. Instead of newly-composed material for "B," however, there is "Another Air by Dibdin" (Ex. 2-24). What is more, this melody returns after a midsection with chromatically altered appoggiaturas which are not typical of Carr's style (Ex. 2-25). Also unlike his other rondo-arrangements is the altered return of the rondo theme (Ex. 2-26). Carr's plan, however, was to prevent over-familiarity with the rondo theme, since it is used extensively in the manner of a development for the "C" section. Even the final return of the "A" theme is disguised and altered

---

50. Wolfe 7606-15 and 5769. Meineke's *Divertimento* is available as EAKM no. 30.

(Ex. 2-27). In spite of the routine nature of the borrowed theme, Carr's treatment displays touches of imagination.

Ex. 2-24.   Carr, "Jolly Young Waterman," meas. 28–31.

Ex. 2-25.   Carr, "Jolly Young Waterman," meas. 50–53.

Ex. 2-26.   Carr, "Jolly Young Waterman":

a. Meas. 1–4.

b. Meas. 63-66.

Ex. 2-27.   Carr, "Jolly Young Waterman," meas. 129-37.

Such imagination, however, is not continued with his rondo-arrangements in nos. 10, 12, and 15 of *Le Clavecin*: "The Campbells are coming," "Little Bo Peep," and "The Sultan Saladin." All are printed on only two pages of score, a restriction that also applies to their elementary styles, useful only to the young piano student. An element of exoticism is included in "The Sultan Saladin," along with an untypical arrangement of form and key:

theme	key
A	a
B	A
A'	a
B	G-e
A	a
B	A

The last two statements of "B" end with material from the end of "A," a downward octave leap, which return satisfies the rondo-aspect of the arrangement.

Carr, as has been made clear, was the major contributor to the rondo form in the early 19th century--he published as many rondo arrangements of popular tunes as did all the other American composers of the time combined. Admittedly his music survives because he and his father and brother were major music publishers, and most of his rondos--especially those in *Applicazione addolcita*--were intended for the student and not the concert stage. Yet his output is impressive.

Jacob Eckhard, Jr.

The only rondo treatment of "Yankee Doodle" other than the two of Carr is that of Jacob Eckhard, Jr., published in Charleston, where he was resident, in the period 1819-25.[51] The publication, however, eschews the term "rondo"; instead, the tune is only "arranged for the piano forte." The genre is a cross between rondo, variations, and fantasia. After a slow introduction, "Yankee Doodle" alternates with contrasting material, but the returns are varied, as suggested in the following scheme: A B A' C A" D A"'. Section "C" is a short variant of the main tune in D minor, shortly returning to the principal key of F major. Section "D" is a short, free, almost developmental section. Eckhard's treatment is still not as imaginative as that of Carr in his *Siege of Tripoli.*

---

51. Yankee Doodle, arranged for the piano forte by Jacob Eckhard Jr. Copy right secured. Pr. 38. Charleston, published by J. Siegling at his Musical Warehouse 69 Broad Street. pp. [1]-4. Plate no. at bottom of pp. 2-4: 152. Charleston Museum copy. According to Wolfe, p. 1144, the dates for Siegling at this address are 1819-25 or 1828.

James Hewitt

One of the first rondos on a popular tune was James Hewitt's "The Hag in a corner, a favorite Irish air composed & arranged as a rondo," published by the composer about 1810 (Wolfe 3717). But the piece turns out not to be a rondo at all. The whole work is a series of varied eight-measure statements, mainly on the tonic D-major chord but with a cadence on the dominant in the fourth measure. (The one exception is that the initial four-measure phrases begin on G-major chords.) The lively 6/8 piece is obviously related to the Irish jig, and is best put in the category of the dance.

Peter K. Moran

The almost-constant use of the Alberti bass in Peter K. Moran's "Sir J. Stevenson's celebrated air Come buy my cherries, arranged as a rondo" (1819; Wolfe 8651) is not typical of the virtuosity and stylistic freedom in his variations published about the same time,[52] but the arrangement may have been published in Ireland much earlier.[53] The "B" section remains in the tonic of E-flat major, modulating to the dominant only toward the end of the section. "A" returns in the dominant key. In common with Carr's rondos, Moran uses the minor mode for "C," but here G minor, relative of the dominant.

Moran's rondo "The Carrier Pigeon" (1825; Wolfe 6090) is based on his own song issued some three years earlier. (William R. Coppock also used the melody for a set of variations.) The first digression contains two different thematic sections, and, like his "Come buy my cherries" rondo, retains the tonic key. Only for the second digression is there a modulation to the subdominant key of B-flat major. Yet Moran returns to the F-major tonic by means of a sequential device (Ex. 2-28). Again, Moran relies heavily on the traditional Alberti bass and related accompaniments; only occasionally does the accompaniment encompass notes beyond the hand to require the use of the pedal. The two returns of the main theme are varied--the first in its accompaniment, the second by means of 16th-note decoration of the melody. Related traditional accompanimental patterns also mar his rondo on "Mi pizzica mi stimola" (ca. 1830), an aria from Auber's opera

---

52. See, for example, EAKM nos. 20-21.

53. "A celebrated air of Sir John Stevenson, arranged as a rondo for harp and piano" (Dublin: B. Cooke, [ca. 1796]); information kindly supplied by Eve R. Meyer. Another rondo by Moran may have been published on either side of the ocean--there is no imprint: Rondo, by P. K. Moran. pp. 3-7. Bottom of pp. 3-7: The Cottagers. Brown University copy. Neither Eve Meyer nor I have yet identified the tune. The two returns of the theme are varied; the first return is in the dominant key as well.

Masaniello.[54] 16th-note motion persists without relief, and the two digressions display little imagination.

Ex. 2-28.   Peter K. Moran, "Carrier Pigeon," meas. 90-96.

Julius Metz

A popular song "The Hunter's Horn, a new sporting cavatina" by the Welsh tenor Thomas Philipps, who made several tours in the United States in 1818-23, was probably published just after his first New York appearance in 1818, then issued by the same publisher as a piano rondo by Julius Metz (Wolfe 7002, 7005). One feature of the song, ". . . to have heard echo wake to the hunter's horn," set as a dialog between the voice and piano imitating an "echo Bugle," is retained in the rondo toward the end of nearly every section, whether main theme or digression. Metz's arrangement is also out of the ordinary in that the central return of the theme is in the dominant key of G major--and in the left hand--perhaps the only such instance in any rondo of the period. For the second and last digression, he modulates to E-flat major. The "Hunter's Horn" rondo is a successful work, within the capabilities of a talented amateur pianist. Unfortunately he wrote no more rondos.

---

54. Mi pizzica mi stimola, thema from Masaniello, arranged as a rondo for the piano forte and dedicated to Miss McKeon, by P. K. Moran. Published by John Cole, Baltimore, & to be had of Thompson & Hemans Washington, [ca. 1830-32]. Title-page + pp. 3-7. Plate no. at the bottom of pp. 3-7: 530. Library of Congress copy.

Frederick Fest, T. V. Wiesenthals

Another touring musician from abroad was the impetus for another rondo arrangement. Frederick Fest, an unidentified composer of the 1820s from the Philadelphia area, set "The Hymn of Riego" (1824-25; Wolfe 4385), the melody by the Spanish guitar virtuoso A. F. Huerta y Katurla, who was concertizing in the United States at the time. The only unusual feature is that the second return of the rondo theme is in D minor and F major, rather than the tonic D major. The tonic returns in the succeeding coda.

"Laurette, a much admired Italian dance, arranged as a progressive rondo" (1819; Wolfe 9905) by the naval surgeon and amateur (but comparatively prolific) composer Thomas Van Dyke Wiesenthal (1790-1833), his only rondo, is not really a rondo at all, unless the commonly-accepted definitions are stretched to include a pattern of ABCDC. After a brief introduction, three eight-measure themes are given with 8th-note accompaniment, then repeated with a 16th-note Alberti bass. Following a brief four-measure respite, the third section is given again, almost without change. Because each eight-measure theme consists of two repeated four-measure phrases, the effect is of too much repetition.

Thomas Tomlins, William R. Coppock

The traditional ABACA form is followed for "The Bath Waltz, popular air, arranged as a rondo" (1820; Wolfe 9394) by the unidentified Thomas Tomlins. The texture is likewise very simple. But the two digressions have tempo changes: "A Little Quicker" (including a midsection marked "Chearful") and "Slow and with Taste."

William R. Coppock's "Paddy O'Carrol, a rondo in which is introduced a favorite Welch air" (1821-24; Wolfe 2092) is surprisingly the only rondo based on this popular tune, although Moran furnished a set of variations. Coppock (1805-63) was in Brooklyn about 1821-29, and in Buffalo from 1832. The harmonic backbone of the first eight measures of "Paddy O'Carrol" (all tonic except a dominant chord in the 4th measure) is the same that Hewitt used for "The Hag in the Corner" (see above). Coppock's piano style is also straightforward, and relies on the Alberti bass. One passage in the first digression is a rare example of sequences (Ex. 2-29).

Ex. 2-29. William R. Coppock, "Paddy O'Carrol," meas. 41-55.

The second digression must be the one in which the unidentified and unlabeled Welsh air appears, if the redundant 6/8 marking is any clue.

J. George Schetky, William Martin

J. George Schetky (1776-1831), Reinagle's nephew, was active in Philadelphia musical circles from 1787, when he immigrated from Scotland. He was a partner with Benjamin Carr in publishing for about ten years. Schetky was mainly a cellist.[55] There are a few publications of his piano music, however, including "Earl Moira's welcome to Scotland, or the Countess of Loudon's strathspey, arranged as a

---

55. According to Sonneck-Upton, 523, Schetky played cello at a Philadelphia concert as early as 1787--when he would have been only eleven.

rondo" (1823).[56] The melody had been published as early as 1813, and again by Blake at about the same time he published Schetky's rondo-arrangement.[57] The usual five-part scheme is used, "B" concentrating on the dominant key and "C" the relative minor, and the only passage of interest is this Mozartean sequence within "C" (Ex. 2-30).

Ex. 2-30. J. George Schetky, "Earl Moira's Welcome to Scotland," meas. 46-48.

"Le Retour de Kips Hill, arranged as a rondo" (1822-27; Wolfe 5596) by William Martin has some of the keyboard display which is more typical of the 1820s than some of the previously-discussed rondos. The melody does not yet appear in other sources such as a song; one can only surmise from the wording of this title page that it is not original. The rondo theme is heard, with its own midsection, in a flowing 6/8 rhythm, and the "B" section continues without a change of key or of style. Up-to-date accompaniments and figurations are

---

56. Wolfe 7847. In the Library of Congress copy, "No. 58 Blake's Musical Miscellany" (according to Wolfe) instead reads "No. 38." The *Musical Journal for the Piano Forte*, no. 10 (1800), pp. 18-19, has "Lord Alexander Gordons Reel, arranged as a rondo for the piano forte by I. G. C. Schetky," but presumably this is the Philadelphia composer's father Johann Georg Christoff Schetky (1740-1824), who married Alexander Reinagle's sister and remained in Edinburgh. The Library of Congress owns a holograph "A Favourite Menuet or Rondo for the Harpsichord or piano forte by I: G: C: Schetky," probably also the same composer. The holograph was originally in the collection of his daughter (and J. George Schetky's sister) Caroline Schetky Richardson (1790-1852). The music is not the same as "A Favorite Minuet composed by G. C. Schetky" in Reinagle's *Twelve Favorite Pieces* [1789].

57. Wolfe 2645; *Blake's Evening Companion*, vol. 2, book 9 (1823-24), p. 82 (listed in Wolfe, p. 85).

refreshing as in the setting for the "B" theme (Ex. 2-31). The closest to the Alberti bass is this pattern within the midsection of "B" (Ex. 2-32). In the "C" section, elements of B-flat minor and major are intermixed, although the figuration is overused (Ex. 2-33).[58]

Ex. 2-31.   William Martin, "Le Retour de Kips Hill," meas. 54-55.

Ex. 2-32.   Martin, "Le Retour de Kips Hill," meas. 73-74.

Ex. 2-33.   Martin, "Le Retour de Kips Hill," meas. 142-45.

----

58. Wolfe 5596A, a copy of which is also at the New York Public Library, is an altered reprint by Geib & Walker, with "Second Edition" added at the top of the title page. This later version is abridged: pp. 1-3 of the first edition are replaced by re-engraved plates numbered pp. 2-3, in which meas. 46-53 (the final "a" of the inner "a b a" form of the first section) and 73-97 (within "B") are omitted. Pages 4-6 of both editions are then the same.

Charles Thibault

Keyboard display is also a trait of Charles Thibault's music. As indicated earlier, he wrote several rondo-arrangements of operatic arias. In his rondo-arrangement of Gluck's "Che faro senza Euridice," op. 14 (1826),[59] the range is expanded upward to f'''' on a six-octave piano, with a direction to play these passages an octave lower on the "ordinary Piano." This work is not a rondo in the sense that there are digressions to entirely new and contrasting themes; instead, it represents aspects of both rondo and variation. Each of the three returns to the main theme is varied, and the first and third digressions consist of small fantasies based on the same theme. Only the second digression has non-related passagework--which likewise appears both in the last return and in the coda. This work has an interesting structure, as well as providing opportunity for the exploitation of the piano.

Thibault incorporated melodies of Rossini for "Le Gout du jour," op. 15 (1826)[60]--the "taste of the day" being an obvious reference to the introduction of European grand operas to the New York stage in the mid-1820s. This "scherzo" is a conglomerate of rondo and medley, and is a precursor of the mid-century operatic fantasy by Liszt and others. "Le Gout du jour" must have been a delight for those who had favorite Rossini arias in their heads, since Thibault easily moves from one opera to the next. The introduction is based on *Semiramide*, as is the main (rondo?) theme to follow. It returns only briefly, however, before the alternation between material from that opera and *Barbiere*, and eventually *Cenerentola*. There is a definite return of the main theme toward the end, before the final measures based on *Barbiere* and *Cenerentola* material. Is it cleverness by Thibault to glue all this together successfully, or is it that he simply discovered the similarity of much of Rossini's music?

---

59. "Che faro senza Euridice," composed by Gluck, arranged as a rondo for the piano forte by Charles Thibault. Op. XIV. Pr: 100. New York, published by Dubois & Stodart 126 Broadway. Entered according to Act of Congress the fourteenth day of February 1826, by Dubois and Stodart New York. Title-page + pp. 2-9. Library of Congress copy, missing pp. 5-6; a complete copy was kindly supplied by Dr. John Gillespie from the original at the Newberry Library. It is also included on his cassette *19th-Century American Piano Music: A Sampler* (University of California, Santa Barbara, [1986]).

60. Le Gout du jour, three themes from Rossini's operas, arranged as a scherzo for the piano forte, by C. Thibault. Op. XV. Pr. 75. New York, published by Dubois & Stodart 126, Broadway. Entered according to Act of Congress the twenty fifth day of April 1826 by Dubois and Stodart New York. Title-page + pp. 2-9. New York Public Library copy.

For the introduction to "Le Passe-tems des Dilettanti, polacca from the opera of Tancredi," op. 16 (1827),[61] Thibault quotes fragments from four operas of Rossini: *Tancredi*, *Barbiere*, *Otello*, and *La Gazza ladra*. Again, the form is not standard, and in some aspects seems more allied with sonata-allegro than rondo. After the main tune, in the tonic of D major, he modulates to the dominant and a new theme, marked "grazioso" (meas. 73). The next principal event is the return of the main theme in the tonic (meas. 123), after which the second theme recurs but remains in the tonic (meas. 142-82 is equivalent to 69-110). The work is completed with another rondo return and a coda. The only missing sonata-allegro element is a development section.

The next two rondos by Thibault are based on themes from Boieldieu's opera *La Dame blanche*, although neither represents his best work. The horn music of "la chasse" permeates the "Chorus of Highlanders," op. 18 (1827),[62] and there is little relief from the 6/8 meter and G major key. Scale passagework of the introduction form the most important aspect of the middle section.

"Les Charmes de New York," op. 19 (1828),[63] his last published rondo of the period,[64] likewise is disappointing. The introduction

---

61. Le Passe-tems des dilettanti, polacca from the opera of Tancredi, arranged as a rondo for the piano forte, and dedicated to Miss. A. Heward by C. Thibault. Op. XVI. Pr. 100. New York, published by Dubois & Stodart, No. 149 Broadway, [1827]. Title-page + pp. 2-10. Plate no. at bottom of title-page: 10. New York Public Library copy.

62. La Dame blanche, rondo from the celebrated Chorus of Highlanders, composed by Boieldieu, arranged for the piano forte and dedicated to Miss Louisa Durand, by C. Thibault. Op. XVIII. Pr. 50. New York, published by Dubois & Stodart No. 149 Broadway. Entered according to Act of Congress the twentieth day of November 1827 by Dubois & Stodart New York. Title-page + pp. 2-6. Newberry Library copy.

63. Les Charmes de New York, from Boildieu's [*sic*] opera La Dame Blanche, arranged as a rondo for the piano forte and dedicated to Miss Julia Anna D'Wolf, by C. Thibault. Op. XIX. Pr. 75. New York, published by Dubois & Stodart, No. 167 Broadway. Entered according to Act of Congress the twentyth [*sic*] day of August 1828, by Dubois & Stodart New York. Title-page + pp. 2-8. Library of Congress copy.

64. Pazdirek's *Universal-Handbuch der Musikliteratur aller Zeiten und Völker*, 30:120, includes these by "Ch. Thibault": The last rose of summer, fantaisie facile, op. 28; La Diavoletta, tarentelle, op. 29 [I found London imprints in the British Library, dated by the library 1851 and 1854]; La Galicienne, rondo-polka, op. 30; La Locomotion, polka, op. 31; L'Etoile du matin, valse sentimentale et descriptive, op. 32. But, unfortunately, nothing between opus 19 and 28 has yet turned up.

dwells too long on the dominant G, and thereafter the main key of C major persists for as long as 40 measures before relief. No memorable contrasting themes appear; when the main theme is not present in its original guise, or in a variant, there is little more than facile passagework. The final statement of the theme is without variety (meas. 117-24 is almost identical to meas. 29-36), and the succeeding material also receives a verbatim repeat (meas. 128-37, 138-47). The high standards set by Thibault in his earlier rondos based on original themes are not maintained for those on operatic ones, with the exceptions of "Che faro senza Euridice" and "Le Gout du jour."

Christopher Meineke

"The Basket Cotillion or the Castilian Maid" (1824; Wolfe 5758), arranged as a rondo by the German-born Christopher Meineke, is based on a Spanish seguadilla "Castilian Maid" to which Thomas Moore wrote the poetry beginning "Oh! remember the time in LaMancha's shades" (Wolfe 1709-13). Meineke is able to combine a playful use of pianistic figures and scales in both digressions with actual references to the main melody, as in these examples (Ex. 2-34). He is not even constrained to bring back the middle rondo theme in the tonic G major, but here uses the dominant; the tonic G major, in fact, does not return until the end of the second digression.

Ex. 2-34. Christopher Meineke, "Basket Cotillion":

a. Meas. 1-4.

b. Meas. 21-22.

c. Meas. 61-64.

"The Lavender Girl, or Morgiana in Ireland," as a song, was first published in the 1820s (Wolfe 5316-22); Meineke's rondo arrangement was issued about 1824 (Wolfe 5785). The middle return is also in the dominant key. The beginnings of both digressions are disguised by the almost constant Alberti accompaniment, and the lack of contrast in rhythm or figuration, until the coda, detracts from this particular arrangement. The same is true of his "The Rustic Reel" arrangement of the same time (Wolfe 5805).

Meineke's most successful rondos are based on tunes still known today. "Polly put the kettle on," issued in 1828,[65] has several features not found in other American rondos. Within the second digression, Meineke actually changes key signature from C major to E-flat major, followed immediately with a brief moment of melodic imitation and a return of the main theme of the dominant (Ex. 2-35). There is no other return of the rondo theme until the last few measures of the work, within a coda. This work is not especially challenging to the amateur pianist, except for one outburst of 32nd notes within the Allegretto context (Ex. 2-36).

---

65. Polly put the Kettle on, arranged as a rondo for the piano forte by C. Meineke. Philad[a]. published and sold by Geo. Willis 171 Chesnut St. pp. [1]-3. Above title: Entered according to Act of Congress the twenty seventh day of October 1828 by Geo. Willig of the State of Pennsylvania. At bottom of pp. 2-3: Polly put the kettle on. New York Public Library copy.

Ex. 2-35.   Meineke, "Polly put the kettle on," meas. 82-93.

Ex. 2-36.   Meineke, "Polly put the kettle on," meas. 33-35.

The best rondo by Meineke, and one of the best of any by an American before 1830, is "The Drunken Sailor," not only included in his medley *Divertimento for the piano forte in which are introduced the favorite airs of Pipe de Tabac, Di Tanti Palpiti, and The Drunken Sailor or Columbus*, published about 1825 (EAKM no. 33), but also issued as a separate rondo about the same time. The overall form is only that of a three-part rondo with coda, yet the middle section is lengthy (meas. 185-272) and consists of a free fantasy based on the main theme--especially its initial rhythm. In this digression the tonic G major is quickly abandoned for the remote keys of B minor, C-sharp minor, A major and minor. A large proportion of the section is in F major, which modulates through F minor, E-flat major, B-flat major, G minor, and then back to G major with an augmented-sixth chord. Such tonal diversions are found in no other American rondos until then. The coda is especially fine, beginning with its general buildup, its hand-crossing, its unexpected rests, its humorous ending. The high quality of Thibault's "L'Adieu" and Meineke's "Drunken Sailor" represents another milestone matching William Brown's inaugural publication of 1787.

3

A Variety of Variations

From the beginning of the nineteenth century until
about 1830, the craze for the *Thème varié* type knew
no bounds. . . . All composers gave themselves over
to the wholesale manufacture of *Thème variés*; some
of them . . . dedicated their entire life to this kind
of production . . . the victory in this contest went
definitely to Abbé Gelinek, who supplied his publishers with manuscript books containing six *Thème
variés* each . . ., and there are eight hundred known
manuscript books by this Gelinek! The second prize
must be awarded to Czerny, who wrote no fewer
than a thousand works, about half of which are
Thème variés!   --Vincent d'Indy,
Cours de composition musicale (1909)[1]

American composers participated in the same craze. Even
though none approached Gelinek or Czerny in output, several were no
worse in quality, and often were better. The theme and variations was
the most important artistic form for early American keyboard music,
probably because of the familiarity of the tunes often used, some still
known today:

Adeste fideles - variations by J. Righton and Rayner
Taylor
Au clair de la lune - James F. Hance and Christopher
Meineke
Home Sweet Home - William R. Coppock
Mark my Alford ("Twinkle twinkle little star") - James
Hewitt

---

1. Quoted by Robert U. Nelson, *The Technique of Variation*
(Berkeley: University of California Press, 1949), 18-19.

> Malbrook ("For he's a jolly good fellow") - Marthesie
> Demilliere and Meineke
> Marseilles Hymn - George Geib
> Yankee Doodle - Hewitt

James Bremner

James Bremner wrote not only the earliest surviving American keyboard rondo, but also the earliest keyboard set of variations. His "Lady Coventry's Minuet with Variations" is included in the manuscript keyboard book copied by his music pupil Francis Hopkinson[2] probably shortly after Bremner had come to Philadelphia from England in 1763. The set is quite modest in scope and easy for the player. Its only salient features are the change from G major to G minor for the first variation, and that the duple 8th notes of the 3/4 meter become triplets in the second and last variation.

Alexander Reinagle

In common with keyboard music in Europe, American variations are generally of the ornamental or decorative type, in which the theme is presented intact in one voice against different accompanimental patterns, or is broken up into figuration. In what is the first publication of keyboard music in the United States, Alexander Reinagle's *A Selection of the Most Favorite Scots Tunes with Variations for the Piano Forte or Harpsichord* (Philadelphia, 1787)[3] this occurs, for example, in "Laddie lie near me." In variation 1, the melody is broken into 8th notes, in 8th-note triplets in variation 2, and into 16th notes in variation 4. In variations 3 and 5, the melody appears intact in the right hand, accompanied by broken triads in the left. In "Lee Rigg," however, Reinagle slightly changes the harmony in the second half of variations 2-4. The technical demands on the performer are not great. At most, in the third variation of "Steer her up and had her gawn," there are crossed hands, and variation 4 would have called for some hours of practice for the student or amateur pianist (Ex. 3-1).

---

2. *Francis Hopkinson's Lessons*, 112-13.

3. Sonneck-Upton, 375. Of the ten pieces, the first eight are reprinted from the nineteen pieces (including a rondo, with flute, as well as an arrangement of the overture to Dibdin's *The Deserter*) in *A Collection of the Most Favourite Scots Tunes with Variations for the Harpsichord* (London, ca. 1782). See Robert Hopkins's preface to Reinagle's *The Philadelphia Sonatas*, xvi-xvii. Six of the ten sets of variations on Scots tunes in the American publication are edited by Maurice Hinson and Anne McClenny Krauss as *Six Scots Tunes* (Chapel Hill: Hinshaw, 1975), which is the basis for this discussion. A facsimile of the title-page and p. 2 of music is in Richard J. Wolfe, *Early American Music Engraving and Printing* (Urbana: University of Illinois Press, 1980), illustration 18.

Ex. 3-1.   Alexander Reinagle, "Steer her up and had her gawn," var.
4, meas. 9-13.

"Yankee Doodle"

It would seem that "Yankee Doodle" should have been a favorite
theme for variations by American composers, but this is not the case.
The first set was published in 1796 by Joseph Carr in Baltimore and
his son Benjamin Carr in Philadelphia, and may well have been written
by Benjamin Carr even though no attribution is made.[4] The main
argument in favor of Carr is that the first eight measures are almost
identical in treatment to the initial statements of the tune in his rondo
arrangement of "Yankee Doodle" in his *Federal Overture* (1794) and
Siege of Tripoli (1804-05; EAKM no. 11). This otherwise anonymous
set of variations, like other productions of the 1790s, represents European classical procedures in America. The unaltered theme is
accompanied by an Alberti bass in variation 1, broken into 16th-note

---

4. Sonneck-Upton, 480; copy at the New York Public Library.

patterns in variation 2, and given in alternating-octave 32nds (preceded by a rest) in variation 3. The same Alberti accompaniment continues in variation 4, where the right hand crosses for individual notes in the bass, and in the following variation in which the left hand crosses to the treble. Some relief comes with a change to triple meter in variation 6, and the standard minor mode in variation 7. The final variation has the only tempo designation--Presto--and it is capped with a modest coda. If Carr wrote this piece, he may have chosen to leave his name off because of its lack of imagination, or because it was merely a teaching piece. Nevertheless, it remains the first "Yankee Doodle" set of variations in the United States.

An anonymous set of four variations on "Yankee Doodle" (McClenny-Hinson, 1-2), first printed in Philadelphia about 1822-23, had greater success, and was reprinted by many publishers well past the middle of the century.[5] In all but the last variation, only the harmonic scheme is retained--not the melody--in favor of 16th-note patterns in one hand or the other. For the third variation, the first half is in the relative minor key and is based only on the first four notes of the melody; the melody notes are decorated in the last half.

James Hewitt

The setting of "Yankee Doodle" by James Hewitt, first published in 1807-10 (EAKM no. 12), is more extensive: there are nine variations. In all of them the tune is either presented intact or thinly disguised in figuration-work. Variation 8 may be the first by an American with the characterization of a march, a type of variation that becomes more common on both sides of the Atlantic as the 19th

---

5. Wolfe 10078-79. Many copies of this set of variations are in collections of sheet music, with imprints dating into the later 19th century, such as: 1) Philadelphia: George Willig 171 Chesnut St. [1819-53] (Wolfe 10078 variant); 2) Baltimore: G. Willig, plate 654 [1822-29]; 3) Baltimore: John Cole; 4) Boston: C. Bradlee [after 1827]; 5) Boston: Oliver Ditson, 115 Washington St., plate 1194 [1844-57]; 6) New York: Dubois & Stodart, 167 Broadway [1828-34]; 7) New York: Millets Music Saloon, 329 Broadway [1839-60]. Ralph T. Dudgeon found at West Point a manuscript-arrangement for treble instrument, presumably for keyed bugle, by the West Point Band director and keyed bugle virtuoso Richard Willis, entitled "Yankee Doodle with variations By R Willis," dated 1825--the same as the anonymous published set, minus variation 4 (which is quite pianistic). He also found another publication of the variations for piano, identical to the editions listed above, with the imprint: The popular national air of, Yankee Doodle composed with variations for the piano forte by Willis. Philad[a]., Osbourn's Music Saloon, 30 S. 4th St. 2 pp. Plate no. at bottom of pp. [1-2]: 169. Free Library of Philadelphia copy. Willis died in 1830, however, and this publication dates from 1835-42. Whether Willis wrote these variations, or simply arranged them for keyed bugle and then Osbourn attempted to capitalize on his name, is unclear. I presume the set is not by Willis.

century unfolds. Another notable variation is the fourth, in the parallel minor mode, with an impressive Mozartean florid line in the right hand. Hewitt's is the only set on "Yankee Doodle" that is definitely attributed to an American. Another published in this country is by the German Graf Henckel von Donnersmarck (1818-21; Wolfe 2542).

"Mark my Alford" originated as the French melody "Ah vous dirai-je maman," on which Mozart wrote a set of variations, K. 265, and the tune is best known today with the words beginning "Twinkle twinkle little star." The text "Mark my Alford" was written by a Mrs. Melmoth to the familiar melody for the Old American Company's production of Samuel Arnold's ballad opera *The Children of the Wood*, and published in 1795.[6] Hewitt's variations were issued in 1808,[7] and display the fine qualities of this important early American composer. None of the variations is in minor, but the fifth one, Adagio (Ex. 3-2), recalls the treatment to the minor variation in Hewitt's "Yankee Doodle."

Ex. 3-2.   James Hewitt, "Mark my Alford," var. 5, meas. 1-3.

Variation 8 begins with a 16th-note decoration of the tune in the right hand, but in the middle section the melody is more prominent in the left (Ex. 3-3). In most of the other variations, the theme is unaltered, or slightly altered; the varied treatment comes from the left-hand accompanimental patterns. Only in the tenth, and last, variation does Hewitt change to triple meter in a simple, yet sprightly, manner (Ex. 3-4). Even though the set suffers somewhat because Hewitt does not vary the return of the "a" for the "a b a" theme (all returns are indi-

---

6. Sonneck-Upton, 105, 399; Wolfe 1616. Another still different anonymous set of variations on "Yankee Doodle" was published in Albany by John C. Goldberg in 1813-16 (Wolfe 5583), perhaps composed by Goldberg himself, but the title does not so indicate.

7. Wagner ed., no. 28; McClenny-Hinson, 18-22. The edition by McClenny-Hinson is not without some misprints. The work is reprinted in facsimile in Gillespie, *Nineteenth-Century American Piano Music*, 169-73, from Wolfe 3741 (1812-15).

cated with "D.C."), it is nevertheless charming and well worth performing.

Ex. 3-3.   Hewitt, "Mark my Alford," var. 8, meas. 5-9.

Ex. 3-4.   Hewitt, "Mark my Alford," var. 10, meas. 1-10.

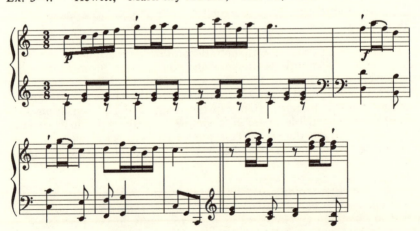

The only other set of variations by Hewitt published in the United States is "Thema with 30 Variations," which appeared in 1803-06 (EAKM no. 10). Hewitt's "Thema" is actually a ground bass, the same that is entitled "The Scots Ground," with six variations, in Robert Bremner's *The Harpsichord or Spinnet Miscellany* (London, ca.

1765).[8] Other American works based on a ground are Benjamin Carr's "The Saxon Ground," with twelve variations, printed as the first piece in his *Applicazione addolcita* (1809), and his "Genoa Ground" in his series *Le Clavecin* (1825). Hewitt's "Thema with 30 Variations" is in the tradition of the ground bass type of variation, as exemplified in two sets by Handel: Chaconne with 21 variations and Chaconne with 62 variations--the first comprising Suite 2, the second the greater portion of Suite 9--both from *Suites de Pieces pour le clavecin*, vol. 2 (ca. 1733).[9] (Both of these are based on the same ground, and the first four measures of Hewitt's treble melody are identical to the first four measures of Handel's bass.)

Hewitt wrote variations on two themes in "Thema with 30 Variations": the ground bass, and the melody which, to the sixth measure, is the descending major scale. Obviously a well-trained musician was at work here. The ground is presented intact in alternation with the soprano melody for the first six variations: the bass in variations 1, 3, 5, the soprano in variations 2, 4, 6. Only once, in variation 7, does the melody appear in the bass. Otherwise, in variations 8, 17, 22, 26, and 30, the melody is unaltered in the soprano. The melody is again heard on the top, in a decorated or altered version, in variations 10, 11, 14, 15, 20, and 21. The ground returns unaltered in variations 9, 12, 14, 21, 25, and 28, and decorated in variation 16. For the remaining variations, only the harmonic structure remains, in favor of keyboard patterns such as the arpeggios of variations 19 and 23, and the crossed hand of variation 27. There is only one so-called double variation--nos. 25-26--in which 16th-note figurations are first written for the right hand, then the left. 16th-note patterns alternate every measure in variation 20. Of particular interest are the cumulative 16th-note rhythm in variation 18 (shared by both hands), similarly with 8th-note rhythm in variation 24, and in the attempt at imitation within the restriction of the form in variation 29.

This one work suggests the fine workmanship of which Hewitt was capable. One can only regret that other, more ambitious, of his works were not printed; they may have been beyond the capabilities of potential purchasers--musical amateurs and students.

Rayner Taylor

Although Rayner Taylor's sixteen variations on "Fye! nay prithee John, a favorite old catch" is related to Hewitt's "Thema with 30 variations" in harmonic pattern and variation technique, it is a London

---

8. Facsimile of the copy at Colonial Williamsburg, with preface by J. S. Darling (Williamsburg, Va.: Colonial Williamsburg, 1972), 10. In addition, the melody of "The Welsh Ground," and the harmony, begins the same way. Robert Bremner may be the father of James Bremner (d. 1780), organist at Christ Church, Philadelphia, in about 1767-74, and music teacher of Francis Hopkinson.

9. *Hallische Händel-Ausgabe*, series 4, vol. 5 (1970).

work, published about 1775.[10]   After his emigration to the United
States in 1792, only two sets of variations appeared, of which one is on
"Adeste fideles" (see chapter 6).   Benjamin Carr's *Musical Journal for
the Piano Forte* (no. 44 [1801], pp. 37-40) includes "Twelve variations
on Ching Chit Quaw, an imitation of a Chinese air performed with
great applause in the entertainment of the Mandarin--the air and
variations composed by R. Taylor."   Indeed, "Ching chit quaw" was a
successful comic trio in the pantomime *The Mandarin*, produced at
Sadler's Wells (of which he was music director) in 1789.[11]   Variations
1-4 display a gradual quickening of rhythmic motion, after which a
variety of treatment is applied to the tune, including a minuet, a giga,
and a siciliana.   In variation 9 the hands quickly alternate playing the
same notes in the treble register, a technique otherwise rare at the
time.   Taylor obviously was a fine musician and composer, and this set
of variations is at least moderately successful, even though he did not
provide any tonal relief by a change of key, or even mode.

Joannetta Catherine Elizabeth van Hagen

   The Van (or Von) Hagen name represents an important musical
family in early American music.   Peter Albrecht van Hagen (1755-
1803), who came to the United States in 1774 from Rotterdam, was the
son of a violinist of the same name who had been a pupil of
Geminiani.   His son Peter Albertus van Hagen (1779/81-1837) was also
a musician.   Peter Albrecht's wife was Joannetta Catherine Elizabeth
van Hagen[12] (1750-1809/10), and except for a march and quickstep by
her son, the only keyboard piece published in the United States by any
member of the family is "The Country Maid or L'Amour est un enfant
trompeur, with variations for the pianoforte or harpsichord by Mrs.
Van Hagen," probably dating from the first decade of the 19th

---

   10.   Fye! nay prithee Iohn, a favorite old catch, with variations
for the harpsicord [*sic*] or piano forte, composed by R. Taylor organist
at Chelmsford.   Price 1s/.   London, printed by Longman, Lukey &
Broderip No. 26 Cheapsd. [ca. 1775].   pp. 1-8.   British Library copy,
g.211.b.(41).   The 3-voice catch, with its words, consists of the
"theme" before the variations commence.   In comparison with Hewitt's
"Thema with 30 variations," the harmonic pattern is barred into four
rather than eight measures, and initially consists of a descending scale
line *d'* to *d* in the bass.   There are actually three melodies involved:
one for each of the original voice parts of the catch.   Another London
publication, with the same date and imprint, is: Martini's favorite
minuet, with variations for the harpsicord or piano forte . . .; British
Library copy, g.271.b.(42), and the Library of Congress also owns a
copy.

   11.   Yellin, "Rayner Taylor," 58.

   12.   Her name is given as Elizabeth Joanetta Catherine von
Hagen in *The New Grove Dictionary of American Music*, and that of
her son Peter Albrecht von Hagen, Jr.

century.[13] This set of variations is impressive, not only for its technical demands--which exceed other American music of the time--but
also for its freshness of style. No one formula persists throughout each
variation. Although the theme itself is simple (Ex. 3-5), the beginning
of the first variation already introduces syncopation and, in its fourth
measure, a note from the opposite mode (Ex. 3-6).

Ex. 3-5.   Joannetta van Hagen, "The Country Maid," theme, meas.
            1-4.

Ex. 3-6.   Van Hagen, "The Country Maid," var. 1, meas. 1-4.

For the comparable place in the second variation, new figuration
briefly appears (Ex. 3-7). Variation 3, with triplets throughout,
includes one passage with chromatic scales in tenths (Ex. 3-8), which
is presented differently in the next variation--followed by a variant
(Ex. 3-9). Variations 5-6, in triple meter, are more consistent in
treatment, and the 32nd-note motion of the sixth variation provides a
showy conclusion. If this work is any indication of Mrs. Van Hagen's
keyboard skills, she must have been a formidable performer on the
concert stage.

---

13. Wolfe 3287. Biographical information on the Van Hagens
can be found in Sonneck-Upton, 508, and Wolfe, pp. 332-33.

Ex. 3-7.   Van Hagen, "The Country Maid," var. 2, meas. 13-15.

Ex. 3-8.   Van Hagen, "The Country Maid," var. 3, meas. 11-12.

Ex. 3-9.   Van Hagen, "The Country Maid," var. 4, meas. 11-14.

Mme. Le Pelletier

Not much information is known about another woman musician, undoubtedly from France, who published her own *Journal of Musick* in Baltimore in 1810-11 (Wolfe 4696). There is speculation that she was one of the French royalists associated with Mrs. Jerome Bonaparte, with connections to St. Mary's Catholic Boys' College and Seminary-- and even that she was a spouse of Victor Pelissier. But by 1813 she had apparently returned to Paris.[14]

Whatever Mme. Le Pelletier's background, her series was elegantly produced. Her only known piano work, "Fantaisie sur un air russe," which appeared in her series as nos. 16-17 (1810; Wolfe 5345), was "composèe pour le forte piano et dèdièe à Madame Dashkoff nèe Baronne de Preuzar" (accents thus). It is an ambitious work, apparently created for pianists with stamina. The most unusual aspect is that the main theme of the rather long (61-measure) introduction reappears after the variations as a short coda. This theme is not the same as the "air russe," given seven variations. One of her favorite devices is giving the right hand the melody, played in the bass, with a left-hand accompaniment in mid-register. The texture is used in the introduction and in the second variation. The other variations are not lacking in pianistic demands, as in variation 3 (Ex. 3-10), or the scales of 32nds and 64ths in variation 7. But each treatment, especially

---

14. Lubov Keefer, *Baltimore's Music: The Haven of the American Composer* (Baltimore: J. H. Furst, 1961), 37-38, 55-56.

broken-chord tremolos in both hands in the sixth variation, often
becomes tiresome, repetitive, and even bombastic. Mme. Le Pelletier's
one contribution to the repertory of the time does not quite succeed.[15]

Ex. 3-10.   Mme. Le Pelletier, "Fantaisie sur un air russe," var. 3,
            meas. 1-2.

Joseph Willson

Although he wrote a number of songs, the English-born Joseph
Willson (fl. ca. 1800-25) left only one surviving work for solo
keyboard: "Henry's Cottage Maid, a favorite air by Pleyel, with variations for the piano forte or harpsichord, composed by Jos[h]. Willson,
organist of Trinity Church, New York," published in 1804-09 (Wolfe
7096). This is a late date to mention a harpsichord on a title-page,
and in fact the set was previously published in London in the period
1792-96 before Willson came to the United States.[16] The theme, from
a Pleyel symphony, is subjected to various figurations, in 16th notes
for variations 1-2, triplet 16ths for variation 3, and rather difficult
32nds in the last variation, no. 4. Although his main activity seems to
have been as organist and singer, Willson must also have been a fine
pianist (Ex. 3-11). Later in the same variation is a cadenza of a

---

15. A more favorable evaluation, along with a facsimile of the
elegantly engraved title-page of Part II of the series, appears in Elise
K. Kirk, *Music at the White House: A History of the American Spirit*
(Urbana: University of Illinois Press, 1986), 37-39. Dolley Madison
was an owner of the *Journal of Musick*.

16. Rita Benton, *Ignace Pleyel: A Thematic Catalogue of His
Compositions* (New York: Pendragon, 1977), no. 1660 (same as RISM
P-4853). The symphonic origin is cited on p. 50.

chromatic scale from *e'* to *e'''*. Willson should have written fewer songs
and more piano music.

Ex. 3-11.   Joseph Willson, "Henry's Cottage Maid," var. 4, meas. 5-8.

A companion set, on an untitled melody by James Sanderson,
published in London about 1796[17] but not in the United States, is
likewise imaginative, especially in the variety of textures in variation
4. Variation 5 is marked "If the Instrument has Additional Keys, the

17. A favorite air, composed by Mr. Sanderson with variations
by Jos[h] Willson author of the variations to Henry's Cottage Maid.
Entered at Stationers Hall. Price 1s. London, printed & sold by W.
Cope at his Music & Instrument Warehouse No. 22 Mount Street near
the Asylum Westminster Road, [ca. 1796]. pp. [1]-5. Bodleian Library
copy, Mus Instr I.233(9).

whole of the following Variation to be played an Octave higher." The highest "additional key" is *c""*.[18]

Benjamin Carr

The enterprising and productive Benjamin Carr composed relatively few keyboard variations. Most of them are contained in his pedagogical collection *Applicazione addolcita: Twelve Airs & a Ground with Variations, or arranged as Rondos*, op. 6 (1809; Wolfe 1576). Five of the airs are sets of variations. The ground is "The Saxon Ground," with no fewer than twelve variations. The set suffers because the harmonic language of the original ground, until near the end, is restricted to tonic and dominant chords. Nevertheless, Carr provides the piano student with a variety of keyboard patterns: broken chords in various rhythms for both hands, 16th-note scales for the left hand (variation 8), then the right (variation 9), then for both in octaves (variation 10). The piece is not particularly enticing for listeners, however, especially if the player observes the da capo to the original ground after each variation.

"The Maid of Lodi" variations in *Applicazione* are of less value for the piano student, but must have been more palatable for the listener mainly because of the popular tune (EAKM no. 14).[19] The melody is buried in the broken triads of the right hand in the first variation, and in the second variation the phrases of the theme in the left hand are answered by scales in the right. The parallel minor and a slower tempo appear for variation 3; the fourth, marked Allegro, brings this modest set to a conclusion.

The variations on Thomas Moore's melody "Will you come to the bower" are also extant in a manuscript copied by Carr himself.[20] The main difference is that the printed version includes fingering; the music of both are otherwise identical. The ornamentation in the first variation is not typical (Ex. 3-12).

---

18. Thus far I have been unsuccessful in obtaining a complete copy of variations on "The Castilian Maid, a Spanish air" (1823-26; Wolfe 9973), by Charles Willson, also of New York, who may have been a son of Joseph Willson. A copy at the New York Public Library is missing pp. 3-4, with variations 3-6. Variations 1-2 and 7-8 have the usual application of arpeggios and scales.

19. On the tune, "The music and words collected by Mr. Shield when in Italy"--Wolfe 8087, printed in Carr's *Musical Journal for the Piano Forte*, vol. 5 [1803-04], no. 101. The original text was "La mia crudel tiranna." The tune was also used in Meineke's *Pot pourri* (1808-09; Wolfe 5803).

20. Clements Library, University of Michigan, which reports that the manuscript came from the Binney family, friends of Carr.

Ex. 3-12. Benjamin Carr, "Will you come to the bower," var. 1, meas. 1-4.

The remaining variations, with such techniques as scale passages, arpeggios, and alternating octaves in the right hand, are not demanding for either listener or performer. The six variations on "Owen" are similar in treatment. The original tune is in the minor mode, and Carr provides a new twist by using the parallel major for the fifth variation.

"Giles Scroggins Ghost," on a song by William Reeve, is also in minor; the third variation again switches to the parallel major, with the characterization "scherzando." The fourth variation, back in minor, features a recurring turn throughout (Ex. 3-13).

Ex. 3-13. Carr, "Giles Scroggins Ghost," var. 4, meas. 1-2.

The last variation, the sixth, is also in major; the duple meter is changed to 6/8, and the tempo marked Presto. The unusual aspect of this variation is that it is almost completely written in parallel octaves or sixths, coming to a rousing end (Ex. 3-14).

Ex. 3-14.   Carr, "Giles Scroggins Ghost," var. 6, meas. 13-19.

    "Savoyard Air" is one of the least successful sets of variations in
the collection.[21] For variation 1 the melody is broken up into repeated
notes, for variation 2 into broken chords, and an Alberti bass
accompaniment is the predominant treatment for variation 4. The only
relief is in variation 3, which introduces a new theme, "supplied by
another Savoyard Air," where 6/8 substitutes for 2/4, and G minor for
the original C minor.
    Later, Carr published separate sets of variations on well-known
tunes of the day. "Away with Melancholy with variations for the
piano forte composed for the use of these numbers" (Wolfe 6200) is
presumably by Carr; it was published about 1818 as a part of his series
Carr's Musical Miscellany in Occasional Numbers, available in modern
reprint. The tune, by Mozart, was also known as "O dolce concento"
from the opera *La virtuose in Puntiglio* (see Wolfe 6278-83), but
originated as "Das klinget so herrlich" from *Die Zauberflöte*.
(Christopher Meineke also wrote variations on the same melody, in his
Pot pourri.) Carr employs the first three notes of the theme, but
thereafter only the harmony--which is rather simple, with only the
three primary chords. Right-hand scales are found in the third variation (Ex. 3-15), followed by similar left-hand scales in the fourth.
For the fifth variation, Carr transforms the melody into a waltz and,
for variation 6, into a march. The set is capped with a coda.

---

    21. Wolfe 1648, pp. 35-37 of *Applicazione*. The last page is
missing in the only known copy, at the Library of Congress, but survives in the reissue (not cited in Wolfe) owned by Columbia University, in which the following imprint is added after the title:
Baltimore, printed and sold at Carrs Music Store No. 36 Baltimore St.
With Variations by B. Carr. "Fishers Hornpipe," pp. 38-39 of *Applicazione*, survives in the same manner (see chapter 2).

Ex. 3-15.   Carr, "Away with melancholy," var. 3, meas. 1-2.

Another in *Carr's Musical Miscellany*, no. 73, "composed expressly for these numbers," is a set of variations on "Come rest in this bosom," which appeared about 1822. The melody was quite popular in the 1820s; it originated as "Fleuve du tage" by Jean-Joseph-Benoît Pollet. The English poetry is by Thomas Moore, and piano variations published in the United States were by the European Kiallmark, and by Americans Christopher Meineke and Peter K. Moran (Wolfe 7162-82, including another set, for the harp, by Eugene Guilbert). The variations supposedly by Carr are likewise in the tradition of the others in *Applicazione addolcita*. 32nd-note scales in the second (of three) variations, and in the short coda provide the only difficulty for the pianist. Considering the modest nature of this set, one can understand why Carr may not have been anxious to label them with his own name.

The origin of the tune "Musette de Nina" is Nicholas Dalayrac's opera *Nina* (1786). Carr's variations, published about 1819 (Wolfe 1625), are not particularly noteworthy, except for some pyrotechnics in the last one (Ex. 3-16).

Ex. 3-16.   Carr, "Musette de Nina," var. 4, meas. 1-2.

Four numbers of Carr's series *Le Clavecin* (1825, partly reissued in 1829-30 as *Twelve Airs*, op. 17--see chapter 2) are sets of variations. Their modest demands are intended for piano students and all are carefully fingered, as with his earlier collection *Applicazione addolcita*. No. 16, "The Spanish Hymn," is now known by its text "Saviour, when in dust to thee," both tune and text presented at the seventh concert of the Musical Fund Society in Philadelphia on 29

December 1824. This arrangement was published by Carr in 1826.[22]
There is room on the two pages for only theme and three variations.
Several short cadenzas are inserted into them, and otherwise the
greatest demand on the performer are one-octave 32nd-note scales in
the last variation. This arrangement, intended for the pianoforte,
might also be tried as accompaniment on the organ for congregational
singing in church.

"Thema con variazione," no. 17, is even more modest, and is the
least interesting of the variation sets in the series. The short eight-
measure theme allows space for five variations, plus coda, on the two
pages; the only departure from the constraints of the theme is in variation 4 with its descending chromatic thirds in the left hand. No. 19,
"Drink to me only with thine eyes," has its share of traditional arpeggios and accompanimental figures. Carr himself explains the feature
of one variation: "N.B. The 3rd Variation contains examples of the
continued Shake; first, as beginning with the under [principal] note,
then with the upper one; and lastly, as played by the left hand." This
set concludes with a short "Coda a la Bolero," with the rhythm two
32nds, 16th, two 8ths.

"The Genoa Ground," no. 20, is in the tradition of Hewitt's
"Thema with variations" (1803-06) and Carr's own "Saxon Ground" in
his *Applicazione addolcita*. As in Carr's earlier ground, this one has
twelve variations, based on not as much a ground or ostinato as on the
general harmonic scheme I IV V I--one chord for each measure, given
twice to fill the eight measures. Some of the variations are paired:
right-hand 8ths in variation 1, left-hand 8ths in variation 2; with
similar treatments in variations 3-4, 5-6, 7-8. Variation 10 is in
minor; the final one, in full chords, is entitled "Air Religieuse."

The Carr variations discussed thus far, however, pale when compared with his fantasia on the Irish melody "Gramachree," originally
written in 1806, but finally published as no. 8 of *Le Clavecin* in
1825.[23] The publication was dedicated to William P. Dewees, to whom

---

22. See "Spanish Chant," arr. Carr, *The Hymnal 1940*, no. 332,
and *The Hymnal 1940 Companion*, 3rd ed. (New York: Church Pension
Fund, 1958).

23. Fantasia, for the piano forte, on the air "Gramachree,"
respectfully inscribed to his friend, William P. Dewees, M.D. by Benjamin Carr. Philadelphia: published by R. H. Hobson, 147 Chesnut
Street, opposite the United States Bank. Price $1. Title-page + pp. 4-
12. On top of title-page: No. VIII of Le Clavecin: a Collection of
Sonatas, Rondos, Marches, Waltzes, Airs with Variations, &c.
Arranged or Composed for the Piano Forte by B. Carr and others. To
be completed in 36 Numbers.--Entered, according to act of congress,
the 26th day of August 1825, by B. Carr of the State of Pennsylvania.
On the title-page of the copy in the Driscoll collection, Newberry
Library, above the title, is written in Carr's hand "Respectfully present
to Mrs. Richardson by the Author." Not in Wolfe, but see no. 1877.
Modern reprint in Gillespie, 48-56. Carr has added these directions
not indicated in the Gillespie edition: p. 55 (p. 11 of the original edition), beginning of 3rd system, "a tempo"; 4th system, measure 1, last

Joseph C. Taws (discussed below) also dedicated his fantasia with variations on "They're a' noddin'." Dewees was the founding president of the Musical Fund Society, and he certainly elicited the best of two composer-members of the Society. (Perhaps Dewees subsidized the publication of these two works, which otherwise would have been too pianistically difficult to attract many buyers.)

Carr's "Gramachree" fantasy is actually a set of variations, yet with a freedom not usually seen in the genre. Although the theme is in F major, the introduction begins in F minor. In an unusual display of key modulation, Carr leaves a C major chord (dominant of F minor) to D-flat major, which serves enharmonically as dominant of four measures in F-sharp major to D-flat minor (eight flats!), and back again to F minor (Ex. 3-17).

Ex. 3-17. Carr, "Gramachree," introduction, meas. 18-23.

3 notes, "Con Spirito"; p. 56 (original, p. 12), beginning, "Andantino Affetuoso." Carr has also added the last 16th-rest, also added in Gillespie's facsimile on p. 49 (original, p. 5), system 5, measure 1. The engraver should have added a bass clef before the last three notes of p. 52 (original, p. 8).

The work was composed much earlier, however. The original version in the composer's hand is at the New York Public Library (Lincoln Center), with the title-page reading "Fantasia with Gramachree, composed by B. Carr, for F. Lucas Jr., Febr. 19th 1806" (*National Union Catalog*, no. 96/390). The musical content and a number of performance directions are not identical in many details, too numerous to describe in detail here. The main differences in the manuscript are that the variations are not numbered, variation 2 of the publication is missing, there is the direction "son harmoniques" for variation 3 through the second system of p. 22 in Gillespie's edition (original, p. 11), and the final six measures are condensed to two measures.

Carr's fantasy-treatment even applies to his presentation of the eight-measure theme ("aria"), which he extends by another seven measures, culminating in a chromatic ascent by the left hand with offbeats in the right (Ex. 3-18).

Ex. 3-18.   Carr, "Gramachree," aria, meas. 11-15.

None of the four variations includes Carr's usual formulas directed to the student or amateur; all are full of virtuoso effects and cadenza elaborations. In the first variation, one can recognize the harmony and melodic content of the theme through the first six measures. Thereafter, the last two measures of the theme are expanded through harmonic and melodic elaboration to six measures. Likewise, variation 2 spreads to thirteen measures; variation 3 to fourteen. Within variation 2 appears a three-octave chromatic scale in thirds (Ex. 3-19).

Ex. 3-19.   Carr, "Gramachree," var. 2, meas. 10-11 (scales printed with small notes in the original print).

The theme is withheld in variation 3--the minor variation--until its seventh measure, and then only half of it. The first part of the variation consists of 64th-note tremolos, including one two-measure buildup, from *piano* to *forte*, on a single D-flat major chord. Only in the last variation is the theme presented intact, quietly, with an elaborated repeat of the last four measures.

Carr's "Gramachree" is his crowning glory, and shows a remarkable growth in style from the classical simplicity of his early works to all the freedom in modulation, harmonic invention, tempo, and virtuosity associated with Romantic piano music. The only earlier work of similar difficulty is his *Siege of Tripoli* of 1804-05 (EAKM no. 11). In many ways, "Gramachree" is more forward-looking than other works published in the 1820s by the younger composers Moran, Meineke, and Thibault.

Philibert Ratel, J. C. Sanders, J. George Schetky, Charles Cathrall

Considering some of the pianistic demands, it is surprising that the variations by Philibert Ratel on James Hook's melody "I have lov'd thee" are his only contribution to the genre.[24] Ratel (dates unknown), probably a French immigrant, was living in Philadelphia about 1814-17; his variations were published in 1816-17. There are an extraordinary ten variations (most of them with cadenzas) and a coda. In these few measures, the accompaniment and general treatment demonstrate Ratel's fondness for varying the rhythm, accompaniment, and general treatment within a few measures (Ex. 3-20). Here, the original melody is embellished in the first two measures, is represented only by arpeggios in the second two, is given plainly in the fifth measure, and then is represented by new figuration. Hook's melody has the form a a' b' a'. Whereas Ratel sometimes provides almost the same treatment for the second section, at other times new ideas are introduced, as in variation 8 (Ex. 3-21).

Ex. 3-20.   Philibert Ratel, "I have lov'd thee," var. 4, meas. 9-16.

24. Wolfe 4073; the citation of Wolfe 658 (Bishop) is an incorrect duplicate.

Ex. 3-21.   Ratel, "I have lov'd thee," var. 8, entire.

Basically, however, these variations suffer from the repeats derived from the original tune, and from a number of places in which Ratel shows his lack of mastery over basic musical materials. In the coda, for example, a diminished-seventh chord becomes an augmented-sixth chord by means of the change from *a″* to *a″*-flat, but in the wrong position. In the succeeding progression, the G-sharp is wrongly doubled, and produces parallel octaves (Ex. 3-22). Nevertheless, such awkwardness is refreshing when compared with other works of the period that are correct, yet common.

Ex. 3-22.   Ratel, "I have lov'd thee," coda, meas. 19-27.

Almost as unusual, albeit more conventional in style, are the variations on "A Favorite German Air," the only published work by an unidentified J. C. Sander. Sander may have been a Philadelphian, since the work was published in that city in the period 1815-19 (Wolfe 7749). He wrote even more variations than Ratel; there are eleven, followed by an unnumbered waltz treatment which turns into an extensive coda. Although the theme is quite simple, and consists of only tonic and dominant chords, Sander altered the harmonic scheme and doubled the length of the first half from four to eight measures in variations 3, 7, and 10. The general musical language is that of the late 18th century. The waltz-coda (2½ pages long in the original publication) is almost a development section, with modulations from the original C major to G and A major. The cadenza, which follows a C-major 6/4 chord, is worth quoting (Ex. 3-23). Such pianistic flair is occasionally produced only by fellow Philadelphians such as Carr.

Ex. 3-23.   J. C. Sander, "A Favorite German Air," waltz-coda, meas. 115-19 (all notes small in the original, until the Finale).

J. George Schetky's only set of variations is on "Young Roscius's Strathspey," probably issued in 1823 (Wolfe 7851). The six variations are well-written, but contain little individuality. A section of variation 5, however, shows a device not seen elsewhere: broken octaves alternating between the hands, joining for the cadence (Ex. 3-24).

Ex. 3-24.   J. George Schetky, "Young Roscius's Strathspey," var. 5, meas. 9-12.

Another Philadelphian, amateur composer Charles E. Cathrall, wrote four variations on what is apparently an original "Air," which appeared in 1825 (Wolfe 1719). His approach is logical but not uncommon: one variation with 16ths, one with triplet 16ths, the third in minor, the last with 32nds.

John C. Goldberg, Marthesie Demilliere, J. Righton

Other variations by amateurs, or by professionals with modest standards, were published or engraved in New York City by Edward Riley in the 1810s. John C. Goldberg was a music teacher and publisher in New York City and Albany. He wrote only one set, "A German Waltz," engraved by Riley and published by himself in Albany about 1813-16 (Wolfe 3147). The three variations are utterly lacking in imagination. Another is "Malbrook with four variations, composed by Miss Marthesie Demilliere," published about 1812-18 by Mr. Demilliere at 33 Chatham Street (Wolfe 2383). Obviously Miss Demilliere must have been delighted that her father published one of her "accomplishments." Undoubtedly Riley engraved it only for his fee, for there are more engraving mistakes than usual (probably due to mistakes in the original manuscript?), and even more serious musical errors. Riley also engraved and published "Adestes [*sic*] Fideles, a Portugueze [*sic*] Hymn, arranged with variations for the piano forte by J. Righton" in 1815 (Wolfe 7481). The unidentified Righton, known only for this one piece, at least had the ability to add an extension-coda after the third variation. The only other variations on "Adeste fideles" by an American are those of Rayner Taylor for organ, although the set by Arthur Clifton's sister Sophia Giustina Corri Dussek (Jan Ladislav Dussek's wife) for harp or pianoforte was published in the United States in the 1820s (Wolfe 2639).

Jacob Eckhard, Jr.

Jacob Eckhard (b. 1757) came to America with the Hessians in 1776 and eventually settled in Charleston, S.C. as church organist, first at St. John's Lutheran Church, then from 1809 until his death at St. Michael's Episcopal Church. His son, Jacob Eckhard, Jr., was the organist at St. John's from 1811 to his death; both died in 1833.[25] Jacob Sr. apparently wrote no keyboard music, but there are five published sets of variations by his son. "Will you come to the bower," published in Charleston about 1813-19 and in Philadelphia about 1813-14 (Wolfe 6057-58), uses the melody by Thomas Moore that was also the basis for variations by Carr and James F. Hance. The theme appears as the top notes of right-hand figuration--16th-notes in variation 1 and triplet 16ths in variation 3--whereas it is intact in the left hand with 16th-note scales in variation 2 and triplet 16th arpeggio patterns in variation 4, played by the other hand. The rhythm quick-

---

25. The father wrote a manuscript book with church music, now published in facsimile as *Jacob Eckhard's Choirmaster's Book of 1809* (Columbia: University of South Carolina Press, 1971); the introduction by George W. Williams provides the biographical information used here.

ens to 32nds in variation 6 for a written-out tremolo which becomes a cliché later in the century (Ex. 3-25).

Ex. 3-25. Jacob Eckhard, Jr., "Will you come to the bower," var. 6, meas. 3-4.

The climax occurs in variation 8 with "brillante" 32nd-note scales in the right hand. The coda, Adagio, comes complete with a cadential 6/4 chord and arpeggio-cadenza, and follows a quiet recapitulation of the theme's second half.

Many of the same techniques are also found in three sets by the younger Eckhard published in Charleston in the next decade: "Washington's March" (1823, apparently an original march), "Masonic Air" (1824?),[26] and "Happy tawny Moor" (1828-31),[27] the last based on a dancing song in Samuel Arnold's opera *The Mountaineers*. All three have Andante variations in the minor mode, the best being from the march (Ex. 3-26).

Ex. 3-26. Eckhard, "Washington's March," var. 5, meas. 5-8.

26. Wolfe 2653, 2650. The decoration in the title, and the words "with variations for the piano forte, by Jacob Eckhard Jun[r]" are identical in these two publications.

27. Happy tawny Moor, arranged with variations for the piano forte by Jacob Eckhard Jun[r]. Copy right. Pr. 50 cents. Charleston, published by J. Siegling at his Musical Warehouse 109 Meeting Street, [1828-31]. pp. [1-5]. Plate no. at bottom of pp. [1-5]: 309. University of South Carolina copy.

In addition, both sets conclude with "brilliant" variations and codas recalling the original theme. The one point of interest in his variations on "The Troubadour" (1823?)[28] is the temporary change of mode from F major to F minor in the second half of the original theme. None of the variations is imaginative, and the rolled *ff* chords in the last one, variation 6, are particularly tiresome. Jacob Jr. must have been American-born. Although he comes from a musical family, his writing, although competent, does not rise above the commonplace.

Eugene Guilbert

Another resident of Charleston, a professional harpist who had come from France in the early 1800s, was Eugene Guilbert (d. 1830s). His only set of variations is on his own song "Arbre charmant," issued in 1824-27,[29] which uses traditional techniques such as Alberti basses and arpeggio patterns. The last variation, no. 8, is in the style of a waltz, and includes a coda. The most striking aspect of the set is the original song; the outer eight-measure phrases in G major are separated by a four-measure segment in G minor. The publication was dedicated to his daughter Margaret. Its companion, dedicated to his other daughter Clementina, is "Tho' love is warm awhile," issued in the same time-period (Wolfe 1223). The original song was from John

---

28. The Troubadour, with variations for the piano forte by Mr. J. Eckhard Jr. Copy right secd. Charleston, published by J. Siegling at his Musical Warehouse 69 Broad Street, [1823?]. pp. [1]-5. Plate no. at bottom of pp. [1]-5: 128. Reproduced in John Joseph Hindman, "Concert Life in Ante Bellum Charleston" (Ph.D. dissertation, University of North Carolina, Chapel Hill, 1971), 235-39, from a copy owned by Josephine L. Hughes.

29. Wolfe 3235. My discussion has to omit variations 3-6, since the American Antiquarian Society copy, the only one available to me, is missing pp. 3-4.

Braham's opera *The Devil's Bridge*, introduced to the London stage in 1812. Several features of Guilbert's variations are unusual, the first being the sudden introduction of E-flat minor and B-flat minor harmonies into the principal key of E-flat major in variation 1. Unique among all early American variations, however, is the fifth, which borrows elements from program music. This is the penultimate variation, in C minor, entitled "Love's funeral march." Within the maestoso setting, *ppp*, comes a sudden *forte* diminished-seventh chord, labeled "scream." The *ff* midsection represents "general desolation." All is well, however, with the succeeding last variation: "Pas Redouble Fantasie: Consolation Friendship and Esteem remains."

Charles Gilfert

Charles Gilfert (1787-1829), possibly an immigrant from Prague, worked in both Charleston and New York City. His variations on "Nina," published about 1813 (Wolfe 3053), is even more demanding for the pianist than Carr's "Musette de Nina" variations on the same tune. Gilfert's second variation is based on the rising arpeggio, like Carr's first. Almost all other variations keep the left hand alternating between the bass and middle registers (Ex. 3-27). They all have cadenzas at the end of the middle sections, before the return to the first part, lasting from three notes (in variation 1) to many more (Ex. 3-28). The fourth variation, in addition, calls for seven measures of constant trills in the right hand. Gilfert's "Nina" variations represents the beginning of more technically demanding piano music published in the second decade of the century.

Ex. 3-27.   Charles Gilfert, "Nina," var. 5, meas. 1-2.

Ex. 3-28.   Gilfert, "Nina," var. 4, meas. 16.

Gilfert's first set of variations published in America, however, is "Haydn's Andante, with six variations" (1804-07),[30] based on the second movement from Haydn's Symphony 53 ("L'Impériale"). This is the same movement, originally theme and variations, arranged by Reinagle in his manuscript (see chapter 1). Gilfert provides decorations or accompaniments of various types in variations 1-3. In the fourth variation, in minor, the treatment is unlike anything of Hewitt's neo-Mozartean style; the unadorned notes of the melody alternate with outbursts of 64th notes (Ex. 3-29).

Ex. 3-29.   Gilfert, "Haydn's Andante," var. 4, meas. 1-8.

---

30. Wolfe 3481, which erroneously cites the slow movement of Symphony 94 ("Surprise").

The theme is played in the treble register by the crossed-over left hand in variation 5. For the last variation, the theme in the left hand is answered by fast arpeggios in the right, in a manner equivalent to Carr's "Maid of Lodi" second variation (EAKM no. 14). For a musician under twenty years of age, Gilfert is skilled indeed.

  Gilfert also wrote variations on "The Maid of Lodi," published in Charleston about 1813-16 (Wolfe 3046). There are minor variations in both Gilfert's and Carr's sets; the more difficult of the two is by Gilfert (Ex. 3-30). One cadenza is even more interesting (Ex. 3-31), but does not match the one in his six variations on Samuel Arnold's melody "Freshly now the breeze is blowing" (Ex. 3-32), of about 1817 (Wolfe 245). The latter set of variations, nevertheless, suffers from the uninteresting harmonic implications of the original tune, which has only tonic and dominant chords.

Ex. 3-30. Gilfert, "The Maid of Lodi," var. 2, meas. 5-8.

Ex. 3-31. Gilfert, "The Maid of Lodi," var. 3, meas. 10.

Ex. 3-32. Gilfert, "Freshly now the breeze is blowing," var. 6, meas. 16.

Probably Gilfert's best variations are those with the intriguing title "Ah! What is the bosom's commotion" (1813; EAKM no. 17), a tune from the English composer Charles Kelly's *The Forty Thieves*. The interest may not be due to Gilfert's treatment, which is not unusual compared with his other variations, but because the original melody is a good one. The alternating right-hand octaves in the fifth variation are a typical challenge of Gilfert's style, but it may be due to the nature of the theme and its frequent pauses that most of the variations do not continue a technique or texture long without a change. The change to triple meter in the last variation, the Adagio cadenza in its middle, and the last two measures (marked "expres"), provide variety that is not often found at the time in American piano music.

Peter K. Moran

An important contributor to American piano music of the late teens and 1820s was Peter K. Moran, who came to New York City from Dublin in 1817. He composed music published in Ireland, and contributed a significant number of songs and piano pieces issued in New York in the 1820s. At least one set of variations was published in Dublin, presumably before he left: "P. K. Moran's Celebrated Variations to the Swiss Waltz."[31] It appeared in no fewer than eleven editions in the United States in about 1817-25 (Wolfe 6127-34). The catchy tune (Ex. 3-33) lends itself to a variety of keyboard patterns, including one which involves the crossing of hands (Ex. 3-34). There is also a modest eight-measure coda.

Ex. 3-33.   Peter K. Moran, "Swiss Waltz," theme, meas. 1-4.

Ex. 3-34.   Moran, "Swiss Waltz," var. 3, meas. 1-4.

The identical harmonic pattern for the theme is also used in his "Stantz Waltz" variations, also for harp or piano (Wolfe 6122-26),

---

31. P. K. Moran's celebrated variations to the Swiss Waltz, for the harp or piano forte, dedicated to Miss B. Reynell. Ent[d]. at St. Hall. Price 2s/0d. Dublin, published by W. Power, 4, Westmorland St. and J. Power, 34 Strand, London. Title-page + pp. 3-7. Brown University and Bodleian Library copies.

which apparently was no less popular. Indeed, both can be played together; one edition of the "Stantz Waltz" variations (Wolfe 6126) includes "N. B.: The variations may be played with the 'Swiss waltz' as a duett for harp & piano forte."

Another set based on an European tune is "Moran's Favorite Variations to the Suabian Air" (EAKM no. 20), for the harp or piano, which uses the melody now known as "Ach du lieber Augustin." The variation techniques are similar to those in "Swiss Waltz" and "Stantz Waltz." Variation 3, however, marked "sotto voce," includes some chromatic writing, and the sixth, "Polacca," features the rhythm short-long-short, characteristic of polacca variations by other composers at the time. The coda, based on a continuation of the Polacca accompanimental pattern, is more lengthy--long enough for several Adagio measures and a finale marked "Allegro et Scherzando."

An identical harmonic scheme and meter is also used for "A Venetian Air, arranged with variations for the harp or piano forte" (1819; Wolfe 6135), but they cannot be played together. The second variation is the one marked "soto [sic] voce"; the following variation is in the minor mode. There are several directions for the harp; perhaps Moran had this instrument uppermost in his mind rather than the piano when composing this set. The virtuoso variation is the fifth (Ex. 3-35).

Ex. 3-35.   Moran, "A Venetian Air," var. 5, meas. 1-4.

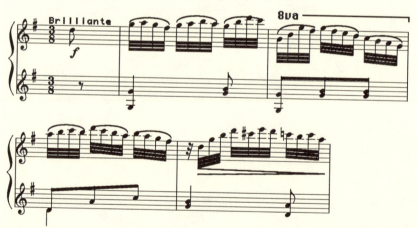

Moran's variations on "Le Retour des Savoyards" (1819; Wolfe 6118) also include directions for the harp: "harmonique" and "natural." The theme does not have the identical harmonic pattern of the two preceding sets, but nevertheless is restricted to the tonic and dominant chords. The polacca rhythm is again found in the fourth variation, and a "Marcia" with dotted rhythms for the fifth. Moran again provided a scherzando coda.

A popular song in America from about 1818 into the 1820s was "The Knight Errant" by Queen Hortense of Holland, as translated from the French by Sir Walter Scott. Other variations on the melody published in the United States were written by Joseph C. Taws and Jan Ladislav Dussek. Moran's is "inscribed to his friend Mr. Julius Metz" in the edition published in 1821 (Wolfe 4349). The variations reveal a number of innovations for Moran. In comparison with the published song, the theme is lavishly decorated with written-out turns and changes of register. Variation 1, marked "Brillante," consists of impressive scales, arpeggios, and other passagework in the right hand; the same treatment for the left hand comes in variation 3. At the end of this variation, Moran breaks the form of the original twenty-measure melody and provides a free section, marked "Digressione" in the score. It is a sixteen-measure extension almost entirely based on the dominant chord. The fourth variation has a similar extension, marked "Scherzando." Although the last variation, no. 5, is not successful (it consists entirely of broken chords), Moran tacks on a decisive coda ending with a low octave trill.

Moran also contributed a set of variations to Pollet's "Fleuve du tage" (also known as "Come rest in this bosom"), which appeared about 1822 (Wolfe 7170). It likewise was written for both harp and piano, and Moran published it himself. It is not one of his best works. His five variations on the Scotch tune "The Bonny Boat" (1826)[32] is better. In variation 2, for example, the theme in the left hand is answered by "brillante" scales and arpeggios exploiting the high register of the instrument, as high as c''''. The "Scotch snap" permeates the following variation. The last one, "Marcia," ends quietly.

Moran wrote several variation sets betraying his Irish heritage as well. One, on "Paddy O'Carrol" (1818; Wolfe 6115), is not outstanding. Neither is "Whistle & I will come to thee my lad,"[33] in spite of a generous amount of hand-crossing in the second variation (Ex. 3-36).

---

32. The Bonny boat, Scotch air, with variations for the piano forte by P. K. Moran. Pr. 50. New York, published by Dubois & Stodart 126 Broadway. pp. 1-5. At bottom of p. 1: Entered according to Act of Congress the thirty first day of May 1826 by Dubois and Stodart New York. Library of Congress copy.

33. Whistle & I will come to thee my lad, a favorite Irish air with variations for the piano forte by P. K. Moran. Price 38 cents. New York, engraved printed & sold by E. Riley, 29 Chatham Street. pp. [1]-4. Bottom of p. [1]: Entered according to Act of Congress, the thirteenth day of July 1827, by Edward Riley of the State of New York. Bottom right-hand corner of pp. 2-4: Whistle & I will come. 4. Brown University copy.

Ex. 3-36.   Moran, "Whistle & I will come to thee my lad," var. 2, meas. 9-16.

On the other hand, "Robin Adair, a favorite Irish melody," for harp and piano (1819; Wolfe 6119) has a sizeable introduction (one page in the original edition). The crossing of hands in variation 2 calls for a pianist with advanced training (Ex. 3-37). The fifth variation, in the relative minor, has the familiar polacca rhythm, although it is not so labeled (Ex. 3-38). This variation, instead of the two-part form of the original theme, returns after a short cadenza to the first part, and then a lengthy (22-measure) transition leads through several related keys back to the dominant of the original key. The last variation, labelled "Valse & Fine" and "Sherzo" (*sic*), also breaks the form of the original theme and goes on to a coda. It is one of Moran's best sets of variations.[34]

---

34. Another set of variations, published in mid-century, has come to light: Kinlock of Kinlock, arranged for the piano forte with variations by P. K. Moran. Boston: published by C. Bradlee 184 Washington Street, [1845-47]. pp. [1]-3. Newberry Library copy. The Music Library, University of Kansas, has another copy with "184" in the street address deleted. The four variations do not reach the standards of Moran's other sets. For example, the first variation simply presents the melody accompanied by the left-hand Alberti bass, and the third variation is little different than the version presented as the original theme. One unusual formula, however, is found for variation 2: the melody in the left hand is repeated a 16th-note later in the right--but the attempt is not very successful. Perhaps Moran lacked enthusiasm for the original tune, which was Scotch and not Irish.

Ex. 3-37. Moran, "Robin Adair," var. 2, meas. 1-4.

Ex. 3-38. Moran, "Robin Adair," var. 5, meas. 1-4.

One of Moran's set of variations is a piano duet. It was published in 1825-26 under the title "Ah beauteous maid if thou'lt be mine,"[35] then re-engraved by another publisher in 1829 with the new title "Fal lal la."[36] As often is the case, the primo part is for the better player, especially in the cadenza within the fourth (and last) variation. Especially effective is imitation in variation 3, in G minor instead of major: a figure is passed from the top down throughout each of the four hands.

The finest set composed by Moran, however, is "A Fantasia for the pianoforte in which is introduced Whitaker's celebrated song Thine am I my faithful fair, with variations" (EAKM no. 21). The term fantasia is doubtless used because of its scope (48 measures) and, for an American, harmonic venturesomeness. The beginning maestoso section in G major is soon left (by means of a Neapolitan sixth) to a dolce section in B-flat major with a simple left-hand accompaniment and a flowing melody based on a short motive. The return to the tonic level is not to G major but to G minor, which effectively prepares the listener for the G-major theme by the English composer John Whitaker.[37] Moran manages to keep the melody notes intact in most of the variations, while surrounding them with differing arpeggio patterns. The treatment in variation 3, where the harmonized melody in the middle is echoed by both hands in the high register, is not found in other piano music by Americans of this period. In variation 4, the melody is retained on the same G-major level with only small adjustments, yet harmonized in E minor. Moran's compositional skill is most revealed in variation 5, which is given a lengthy extension from the tonic of G major to the submediant E-flat major, then E-flat minor, C-flat major enharmonically becoming B major, and then proceeding through A minor to F major, B-flat major, and finally back to G. Duple meter is changed to 6/8 for the last variation, in which there are only traces of the original melody and harmony. This variation is capped with a coda which builds from a "scherzo" beginning to

---

35. Ah beauteous maid if thou'lt be mine, with variations composed and arranged for two performers on the piano-forte, by P. K. Moran. Copyright secured. New York, published and sold by C. & E. W. Jackson, No. 325 Broadway. Also No. 44 Market Street Boston, [1825-26]. Title-page + pp. 2-9. Indiana University copy.

36. Fal lal la, favorite air arranged as a duet for two performers on the piano-forte by P. K. Moran. Pr. 75. New York, published by Dubois & Stodart, No 167 Broadway, [1829]. Title-page + pp. 2-9. New York Public Library copy.

37. The song was issued by five American publishers beginning about 1818, and appeared in at least three musical journals; see Wolfe 9870-77.

a rousing conclusion. This set belongs in the top rank of early American variations.[38]

This fantasy treatment by Moran, and the fantasia on "Gramachree" by Carr, are examples of a trend toward compositional freedom in American piano music of the 1820s. Thomas Hastings was aware of it in 1822, the date of his *Dissertation on Musical Taste*, in which he wrote not about fantasias but "extravagances":

> The object of variations (technically so called) seems, in general, to be little understood. The term itself implies, that they should be made up of ideas that are immediately derived from the ballad or movement, which is made to precede them as their theme. It is evident, that the derivations should be more or less obvious, in proportion to our acquaintance with musick, if they are to produce their required effect. This effect, we apprehend, is

---

38. In the Harding collection, Bodleian Library, filed in a box labeled "Minstrels 1820-42, pre-Minstrel," is a satirical (and today, offensive) set of variations by Moran: Coal Black Rose, tema veried like de big Autors of Nrope [= Europe] and Mernka [America], compose for piany-fort wid companyment for de flute and spectfully dedikated to Missa Rosa Ebony by Sambo Nikaboka Mus.D. member of Conservotie of Haytee! Direkter of Musik to de Teater Afrika!! and Pianist to de King Cristoffe!!!! P. K. Moran. Pr. 50 cts. New-York, published by Firth & Hall, 1 Franklin Square. Entered according to the Act of Congress in the year 1835 by Firth & Hall, in the Clerk's office of the District Court of the Southern District of N.Y. Title-page + pp. 2-7. For pianoforte and "Toottle." Captions and labels: p. 2, theme "La Dame Noir" [a play on "La Dame blanche"], "Imitation of Massa Julus Ets" [Julius Metz]; p. 3, "Imbitation of Massa Playwell" [Pleyel], "Imbitation of Massa Logire" [John Bernard Logier]; p. 4, "Now Tootle tootle! Imbitate Massa Druhee. ha! ha!" [?], "Missa Rosa coss Hand," "Coss de oder hand," "Imbitation of Massa Stybelt" [Steibelt]; p. 5, "From La Dame Blanche," "Imbitation of Massa Tiboo" [Charles Thibault]; p. 6, "Valce: Imbitation of Massa Pee Kee" [P. K. Moran, a parody of his own popular "Swiss Waltz" variations]. The theme is of the 1827 song by George Washington Dixon "Coal Black Rose," of which I have a photocopy (from the Newberry Library) published in Boston by John Ashton, 197 Washington Street, [1824-33]; for the citation of another edition published in New York [1830-31] by P. Maverick, see Harry Dichter and Elliott Shapiro, *Handbook of Early American Sheet Music, 1768-1889* (New York: Dover, 1977), 51. On the song and Dixon, see Charles Hamm *Yesterdays: Popular Song in America* (New York: Norton, 1979), 117-18. The "tema" in Moran's "Coal Black Rose" is not exactly the same as Dixon's; it has elements which are reminiscent of the tune "Spanish Hymn," first given in public in 1824 by Benjamin Carr and published by him in 1826 (see above, note 22)--the year before Dixon first publicly performed "Coal Black Rose."

little thought of by the majority of composers and executants; and most auditors are left to view these ingenious compositions as mere playful extravagances. From their liability of this abuse, variations are not in such request as they formerly were; though the study of them is still useful, in acquiring a knowledge of the derivation of ideas.[39]

William Martin

Another New York pianist and teacher, William Martin (fl. ca. 1822-50), was not nearly as good a composer in spite of his claim, made in 1822 when he first advertised for pupils, that he had been a student of Clementi in London. For his variations on the Scotch tune "O Nanny wilt thou gang with me,"[40] the inherent problem may be the theme itself, which is 28 measures long and contains several inner repetitions. However, Martin chose a device for each of the five variations, and each device persists without relief. The second variation is a march; the third, "Polacca." "O! dear what can the matter be," probably published in 1824 (Wolfe 5595), is better. The familiar tune is not long or repetitious, and Martin's treatment is not as dogmatic. A literal statement of the tune is even abandoned in variation 2 in favor of some momentary imitation (Ex. 3-39). The meter changes from triple to duple in variations 5-6, the latter featuring some hand-crossing (Ex. 3-40).

Ex. 3-39.   William Martin, "O dear what can the matter be," var. 2, meas. 1-2.

---

39. Thomas Hastings, *Dissertation on Musical Taste: or, General Principles of Taste Applied to the Art of Music* (Albany: Websters and Skinners, 1822; reprint, with introduction by James E. Dooley, New York: Da Capo, 1974), 151.

40. An edition different from Wolfe 1701: O Nanny wilt thou gang with me, arranged with variations for the piano forte or harp, by William Martin. Pr [ ] Cts. New York, engraved, printed & sold by E. Riley, 29, Chatham Street, [1819-31]. Title-page + pp. [2]-11. At top of p. [2]: O Nanny wilt thou gang with me. With variations by William Martin. At bottom of pp. 3-11: O Nanny. 11. New York Public Library copy.

Ex. 3-40.   Martin, "O dear what can the matter be," var. 6, meas. 1-
5.

Martin's "Hurrah for the bonnets of blue" (1828)[41] sinks to the
level of the "O Nanny" variations, in spite of the change from 6/8 to
C in the second variation ("Tempo di Marcia") and the succeeding
Allegro variation. What is especially disappointing is the missed
chance for effective writing in variation 4, "Andante con Espressione"
(Ex. 3-41).

41.   Hurrah for the Bonnets of Blue, with variations for the
piano forte by Wm. Martin. Pr. 50 Cts. New York, engrav'd, printed
and sold, by E. Riley, No. 29 Chatham St. Title-page + pp. 2-7. At
bottom of title-page: Entered according to Act of Congress, the eighth
day of April 1828 by Edward Riley of the State of New York. At
bottom of p. 2: Hurray for the Bonnets of Blue, Var: 7. New York
Public Library and Free Library of Philadelphia copies.

Ex. 3-41.   Martin, "Hurrah for the bonnets of blue," var. 4, meas. 1–
4.

In the fifth (and last) variation, the ubiquitous Alberti accompaniment is quite anachronistic. Much of the piece would be just as suitable for harpsichord if it weren't for the notes up to *c″″*.

Probably Martin's best variations are on the Rossini cavatina "Di tanti palpiti" from *Tancredi*, published about 1822.[42] There is no introduction, but the theme itself is presented with some small alterations and a short cadenza. Whereas the figuration in the variations usually incorporates the outline of the theme, sometimes Martin thinks of possibilities which almost become new melodies (Ex. 3-42).

---

42. Wolfe 7608; there is another copy at the Music Library, University of Kansas.

Ex. 3-42.   Martin, "Di tanti palpiti":

   a. Var. 4, meas. 1-4.

   b. Var. 6, meas. 1-4.

Again, Martin typically provides little contrast once a technique is established. One exception is in the first variation, where the sonority at the beginning is almost impressionistic, and a different device begins the second half (Ex. 3-43).

Ex. 3-43.   Martin, "Di tanti palpiti," var. 1:

   a. Meas. 1-4.

b. Meas. 9–10.

In the seven variations, contrasts of meter, tempo, and rhythm help keep the interest for the pianist and listener.

Martin must have been one of the best pianists of New York City, considering the virtuoso demands in these four sets of variations. Still, the lack of free introductions, interludes, cadenzas, or codas is disappointing, especially when one considers the unique creativity found in piano works by his teacher Clementi.

Adam & George Geib, C. H. Levering, William Blondell

Only one set of variations by another English-born composer, Adam Geib (1780–1849) is known. He came to New York in 1797 with his father John and brother George, and had a career mainly as organ and piano builder and music publisher. His five variations on "The Blue Bell of Scotland," dating from 1807-10 (Wolfe 4680), have no relief of tempo or from the constant 16th-note rhythm, and the main technical demand is some hand-crossing in the last variation. In variation 2, however, is a rare example of *Stimmtausch*: the two hands exchange some of the material of the first half for the second half.

There are two sets of variations, however, by Adam's brother George Geib (1782-1842?), who was more active as a performer and teacher. Brought to New York City when only 15 years of age, he enjoyed a long career as pianist, organist, and "professor of music." Yet the variations are not particularly outstanding. "Glen of Glencoe" (1829)[43] includes only two scale-cadenzas and no introduction or coda. The last variation, no. 4, in spite of the "Marcia" designation, retains the 6/8 meter. The second variation has the alternating-hand device occasionally seen in this period (Ex. 3-44).

Ex. 3-44.   George Geib, "Glen of Glencoe," var. 2, meas. 1-4.

43. Glen of Glencoe, Scotch air with variations, composed and dedicated to Miss Perplanck, by George Geib. New York, Bourne, Depository of Arts, 359 Broadway. pp. [1]-3. Bottom of p. [1]: Entered according to act of Congress, on the 13th day of February, 1829, by G.M. Bourne, of the State of New York. Library of Congress copy.

Geib's "Marseilles Hymn"[44] includes only two variations (perhaps due to the length and relative complexity of the theme), followed by two short works, "Vive le Charté, Quick Step" and "The Tri Coloured Waltz." The performer is then directed to "Finish with the March, Page 1." As a result, these variations include an element of the medley.[45]

Even one surviving piece by an unidentified composer, probably American, is more enterprising. C. H. Levering's four "Bounding Billows" variations, published in 1825-26 (Wolfe 5365), have the advantage of a simple theme (with as many as four restatements of a four-measure phrase). The first and last variations require hand-crossing, the fourth variation being the most demanding (Ex. 3-45).[46]

Ex. 3-45.   C. H. Levering, "Bounding Billows," var. 4, meas. 1-4.

---

44. Marseilles Hymn, the celebrated French national air, with variations by George Geib, Professor of Music. Bourne, Depository of Arts, 359 Broadway, New York, [1827-32]. pp. [1]-4. Plate no. at bottom of pp. [1]-4: 22. At end of music, p. 4: Engr[d]. by T. Birch. Brown University copy.

45. Another set of variations, published after the cutoff date of this study: The Minstrel returned from the war, arranged with variations for the pianoforte, by George Geib. Entered according to the Act of Congress, in the year 1832, by E. C. St. Martin, in the Clerk's office of the District Court of the Southern District of New York. Philad[a]. Geo. Willig 171 Chesnut St. pp. [1]-4. Bottom of pp. 2-4: Minstrel return'd. Var: Bodleian Library copy, box 301. There is also a rondo of the same year: Retour de gloire, rondo, pour le piano forte, par George Geib, Professor of Music. New York, Bourne, Depository of Arts 359 Broadway. pp. 1-4. Bottom of p. 1: Entered according to the Act of Congress, in the year 1832, by G. Melksham Bourne, in the Clerk's Office of the District Court of the Southern District of New York. Plate no. at bottom of pp. 1-4: 322. Lilly Library, Indiana University, copy. Neither piece redeems Geib as a composer.

46. According to the *National Union Catalog*, music by Charles H. Levering was published in Detroit in 1851 and 1864.

New York pianist, organist, and "professor of music" William Blondell (fl. ca. 1823-34), is likewise represented by only one set, "A Favorite French Air," issued by two publishers in the late 1820s.[47] The melody was known at the time as "Rousseau's Dream" (from the composer, Jean-Jacques Rousseau), and is now familiarly known with the text beginning "Go tell Aunt Rody." The first variation, while burdened with an Alberti accompaniment, nevertheless contains subtle changes in the treatment of the melody. Variations 2-4 are ordinary. Variation 5, however, features some of the pianistic "tricks" which become more common at mid-century (Ex. 3-46).

Ex. 3-46. William Blondell, "A favorite French air," var. 5, meas. 3-6.

47. A favorite French air, with variations for the piano forte, composed by William Blondell. New York, published by J. L. Hewitt, 137 Broadway. Sold at the Music Saloon, 36 Cornhill, Boston, [1829-35?]. pp. [1]-7. Free Library of Philadelphia copy. Another edition (with a number of engraving errors): A favourite French air, with variations for the piano fort [*sic*] composed by W. Blondell. N. York, lith: and published by E. S. Mesier, 28, Wall-st., [1827-30]. pp. [1-7]. New York Public Library copy.

After a brief extension, the theme is recapitulated with a new accompaniment.

William R. Coppock

Judging from four sets of variations, William R. Coppock was a more able composer. There are only four variations on "C'est tout pour elle" (1829),[48] but in spite of Alberti accompaniment in the theme and variation 4, each variation has some variety. Coppock even provides occasional changes of harmony; for example, the harmony for the first four measures in the theme is I/V/V/I; in variation 1 it is changed to I-V/I/V/V.

From the same year of 1829 comes his variations on "Oh, no, we never mention her," or, according to the title at the head of the music, "Variations sur un theme du suisse."[49] The one interesting feature is variation 4, the last one, composed in the manner of "La Chasse," as are a number of rondos in the century (see chapter 2). The fast 6/8 continues into the finale.

Rarely are American variations based on American-composed tunes. Such is the case, however, with Coppock's variations on Peter

---

48. C'est tout pour elle, French air, with variations for the piano or harp, inscribed to Miss Eliza Oliver by W.R. Coppock. Pr. 25 cents. Philadelphia, published and sold by G.E. Blake No. 13 south Fifth street. pp. [1]-3. Bottom of p. [1]: 12 Gem. Entered according to act of Congress the 4th day of March 1829 by G.E. Blake of the state of Pennsylvania. At bottom of pp. 2-3: C'est tout pour elle. Brown University copy.

49. Oh, no, we never mention her, with variations for the piano forte or harp, composed and dedicated to Miss Lurana Denison, by W. R. Coppock. New York, Bourne, Depository of Arts, 359 Broadway. Entered according to Act of Congress, on the 25th day of March 1829, by G. M. Bourne of the State of New York. Title-page + pp. 3-6. At bottom of p. 6: Engr^d by T. Birch. At top of music, p. 3: Variations sur un theme de suisse, par Coppock. New York Public Library copy.

K. Moran's song "Carrier Pigeon" (1827-31),[50] on which Moran himself wrote a rondo. Unfortunately, Coppock's variations do not rise above the commonplace. In most of the five variations, the right hand is assigned scales and figurations in 16th notes, usually in the same keyboard tessitura above the staff. For variation 4, however, the motion is in 32nd notes throughout, with a full 4-octave range in the right hand from *c* to *c''''*.

Coppock's variations on the familiar "Home sweet home," the original tune of which was "composed and partly founded on a Sicilian air by Henry R. Bishop,"[51] are somewhat more imaginative. The introduction faintly anticipates the initial motive of the theme; the slow coda recapitulates the first two phrases. In a manner reminiscent of William Martin, however, Coppock finds his pattern for a variation, which then persists for the whole variation without change. Perhaps the one with most interest for a pianist is the third variation, the first half of which features some hand-crossing (Ex. 3-47).

Ex. 3-47.   William R. Coppock, "Home sweet home," var. 3, meas. 1-
            4.

---

50. The much admired air Carrier Pigeon, with variations for the piano forte, composed & inscribed to Miss Angelina Van Nostrand, by W. R. Coppock. New York, printed & sold for the Author by Firth & Hall, No. 358 Pearl St., where may be had his other publications, also at the Author's Music Room Brooklyn. Title-page + pp. [3]-6. At top of music, p. [3]: The Carrier Pigeon. Thema Mr. Moran. Variations by W. R. Coppock. Newberry Library copy.

51. Quoting from various editions of the song, published in 1823-25 (see Wolfe 637-44). Publication information on Coppock's variations: Home! sweet home!, a popular Sicilian air, introduction & variations for the piano forte or harp, composed & most respectfully dedicated to Miss Julia Waterbury (of Williamsburgh) by W. R. Coppock. Copy right Sec. Pr. 75 Cts. New York, pub[d] & sold by Firth & Hall at their Piano Forte & Music Store, 358 Pearl St. [1827-31]. Title-page + pp. 3-9. At top of music, p. 4: Home sweet home by Mr. Coppock. At bottom of pp. 3 and 5-9: Coppock's Home. Var. At end of music, p. 9: Engr[d] by T Birch. New York Public Library copy. It was re-issued by the same publisher [1831-43], with street address changed to 1 Franklin Sq. and the addition of the plate no. 3010 to the bottom of pp. 3-9; University of North Carolina, Chapel Hill, copy.

In these three sets, Coppock represents attempts by a piano teacher to supply pieces for the amateur and advanced student that combine a familiar tune with piano techniques learned in the studio.

Henri-Noel Gilles, Gabriel Grenier

The French-born and Conservatory-trained Henri-Noel Gilles (1778-1834), resident of Baltimore from about 1818, is represented only by "The favourite Spanish dance, with variations for the piano forte," copyright in 1825 (Wolfe 3108). It is hardly the usual theme and variations, however. After an introduction is the dance itself, on one page, and then an unmarked variant on another page. The dance returns on the last page, with a coda-like ending. Perhaps the explanation for this strange piece is that it is an arrangement from the original variations for guitar accompanied by piano.

Only one piano work by Gabriel Grenier (dates unknown) has thus far come to light. His variations on "Giles Scroggin's ghost," a tune of William Reeve, were dedicated to and published by another French immigrant, Raymond Meetz. Variations on the same tune had earlier been written by Benjamin Carr in his *Applicazione addolcita*. Grenier must have been well trained in France, according to the ambitious nature of this one work, published in 1822 (Wolfe 7341). The introduction is unusually long, nearly five pages in the original publication. Based on the initial motive of the upcoming theme, it moves from A minor to a section in C minor before returning to A minor, the key of the theme. In the first variation, the theme in the left hand is pitted against triplets in the right, resulting in the cross-rhythm 2 versus 3, not common at the time. In another switch from the norm, variation 6 is in the parallel major; A minor returns in an operatic variation 7. The coda, nearly 2½ pages long, includes the surprise of another tune that begins almost the same way: "Yankee Doodle." Thus, Grenier's "Giles Scroggin's ghost" variations are definitely American, not imported from abroad.

Julius Metz

Three variation sets of the early 1820s by Julius Metz (fl. 1819-57) display an even more imaginative approach. Metz was apparently a relative of Raymond Meetz, the friend and publisher of Grenier. Metz immigrated, probably from France, about 1819 and made his first public appearance as a singer, continuing to give performances as both singer and pianist well into the 1830s. He was the pianist for the New York Philharmonic during its second season in 1842, and so must have been one of the best pianists of the city.

In Metz's "Clermont Waltz" variations (1820; Wolfe 5844), the persistent right-hand busywork and left-hand Alberti patterns common in works by Darley, Martin, and Coppock are kept to a minimum. Textures and registers of the piano are often relieved, as in the second variation (Ex. 3-48).

Ex. 3-48.   Julius Metz, "Clermont Waltz," var. 2, meas. 1-4.

Even in the following variation, the first half of which contains right-hand passagework, the left hand is given a chance in the second half (Ex. 3-49).

Ex. 3-49.   Metz, "Clermont Waltz," var. 3, meas. 9-16.

The beginning of variation 5 consists of parallel tenths in both hands, but Metz finds a different approach for the second half. The coda is initiated with free material, and contains a further variation with 32nd notes, which provides a rousing conclusion.

The melody of "The Vesper Hymn, a Russian air" first appeared in 1818 with music composed or arranged by John Stevenson, and words by Thomas Moore, and was first printed in the United States the following year. Sometimes the tune is ascribed to Dimitri Bortnianski, probably erroneously. The melody, originally issued as a glee, is still used in churches today.[52] Metz's variations were published in 1822 (Wolfe 5850). The simple and straightforward nature of the tune lends itself well for variations, but Metz's is the only set of the period. There are only five variations, yet each one is imaginative. For variation 1, the notes of the theme in the soprano are played alternately by right and left hands. Two-note fragments in variation 2 alternate between the hands as well; this treatment is used throughout, but Metz subtly reverses the hand that leads (Ex. 3-50).

Ex. 3-50.   Metz, "Vesper Hymn," var. 2:

a. Meas. 1-2.

b. Meas. 5-6.

---

52. For example, *Hymnal 1940*, no. 178.

"Brilliante" right-hand scales accompany the melody in the left hand in variation 3. Variation 4 is in minor; the theme is syncopated (Ex. 3-51).

Ex. 3-51.   Metz, "Vesper Hymn," var. 4, meas. 1-4.

Variation 5 is a waltz (in 3/8, erroneously marked 6/8), and indeed is more than double the usual length because of an extension in D minor which actually forms another variation. Although Metz provides no introduction, there is a short coda. Metz's "Vesper Hymn" variations are well worth playing.

Another melody arranged by Stevenson, with poetry by Moore, is "A Temple to Friendship, a Spanish air," to which Metz wrote five variations published in 1823-26.[53] The pianistic device of variation 4 is old, but Metz's placement of the melody in the left hand on the beat, then in the right hand after the beat, is indicative of his imagination (Ex. 3-52).

---

53. A Temple to Friendship, a Spanish air, with variations for the piano forte, composed & dedicated to Miss Helen McEvers, by Julius Metz. Copy right secured. New York, pub [*sic*] by Dubois & Stodart No. 126 Broad Way, [1823-26]. pp. [1]-3. Not in Wolfe; copy at the Music Library, University of Kansas. Compare the same publisher's 1823 edition of the song, Wolfe 8978.

Ex. 3-52.   Metz, "A Temple of Friendship," var. 4, meas. 1-4.

In variation 5, the theme is first distributed to the top voice, then tenor, then the last five notes on the top again (Ex. 3-53).

Ex. 3-53.   Metz, "A Temple of Friendship," var. 5, meas. 1-8.

Metz's best variations are entitled "Spanish Waltz," published in 1818-21 (Wolfe 5849).   The left hand, significantly, has an important role, probably most of all in the third variation where it echoes the right-hand part in canon--a rarity in American piano music of the time.   The harmonic shift from F major to D-flat near the end warrants quoting the entire variation (Ex. 3-54).   Another outstanding representative is variation 4, which resembles a Bach invention (Ex. 3-55).   Metz adds to the five variations an extensive coda which starts in the relative key of B-flat major and contains this well-conceived cadence (Ex. 3-56).   The quality of Metz's variations, especially "Vesper Hymn" and "Spanish Waltz," puts him among the best American piano-composers of the 1820s.

Ex. 3-54.   Metz, "Spanish Waltz," var. 3, entire.

Ex. 3-55.   Metz, "Spanish Waltz," var. 4, meas. 1-8.

Ex. 3-56.   Metz, "Spanish Waltz," coda, meas. 12-16.

James F. Hance, Charles F. Hupfeld

Almost as high in quality is "2nd Grand Fantasie: introduction and brilliant variations to the Russian Dance" (1823-26; EAKM no. 25) by the New York composer and pianist James F. Hance (fl. ca. 1818-33). The introduction, based on the first three notes of the upcoming theme, has a modulation from C major to A-flat major by means of an augmented-sixth chord (still not common in American composition, despite the use by Moran cited above). The right hand then plays a Rossini-style melody alternating between the treble and bass. A cadenza flourish leads to the theme. The techniques in the variations hold no surprises in comparison with others of the 1820s. In some the theme is recognizable--in others, only the harmony and fragments of the theme. The third and fifth variations display the left hand crossing to the treble range--a technique often used by Hance in his other sets of variations and by other American composers of the time. The march style in variation 9 is also common. The unharmonized octaves in variation 7, however, are hardly ever found. The Finale includes a long modulatory sequence through the keys C, D-flat, E-flat, F, G, a, C, which is not typical. The scope and pianism of the Finale does not match that of Moran's "Thine am I my faithful fair," but the propulsion to the end is impressive.

Both Hance and the German-born Charles F. Hupfeld wrote variations on the tune usually called "Hungarian Air," although Hupfeld's is entitled only "A Favorite Waltz" (EAKM no. 19). The theme in the two sets differs in a few unimportant details. Both change to minor for the seventh variation in preparation for the brilliance of the next. In his set, published in 1818-20 (Wolfe 3323), Hance syncopates the melody in his fifth variation and writes for the left hand to cross above the right in two others. Special features of Hupfeld's, published in 1818-20, are some chromaticism from time to time, the theme in the bass for the minor variation, and a polonaise (not "polacca" this time) for variation 9. He breaks the form for the Allegro coda, but still presents the complete theme in its midst.

Hance's other variations are more modest in interest, and were probably of more practical use to the amateur pianist. All, for example, have short codas. "Au clair de la lune" (1824; Wolfe 3318) has one "Marcia" variation; "Will you come to the bower" (1827?)[54] includes metronome markings. The third variation features both hands playing parallel thirds. Still, it is a better set than Carr's on the same tune, issued almost twenty years earlier (described above). "The Marion, impromptu with variations for the piano forte" (1827)[55] is well-written, but suffers from the original theme which uses only tonic and dominant chords.

Christopher Meineke

Another composer who wrote variations on "Au clair de la lune," and on many other melodies as well, was Christopher Meineke (1782-1850). He was born Karl Meineke in Germany (his father had the same name), came to the United States at the age of eighteen, in 1800, and spent his career in Baltimore. In 1817-19 he returned to Europe and supposedly visited Beethoven who praised Meineke's concerto. An early set of variations is "Walze with variations for the harp or piano forte," published in the period 1808-13 (Wolfe 5815). There is little hint of Meineke's later styles. The accompaniments are simple (Ex. 3-57), and the pianist has little challenge.

Ex. 3-57.   Christopher Meineke, "Walze," var. 2, meas. 1-8.

54. Will you come to the bower, favourite air with variations for the piano forte, composed and dedicated to Miss M. Armstrong by J. F. Hance. Op. 15. Pr. 75. New York, published by Dubois & Stodart, 149 Broad Way, [1827?]. Second edition revised by the Author. Title-page+ pp. [1]-7. At head of music, p. [1]: Will you come to the Bower. Brown University copy. See Wolfe 6060, an earlier edition.

55. The Marion, impromptu with variations for the piano forte, composed and dedicated to Miss Sarah Langdon, by J. F. Hance. Pr. 75. New York, published by Dubois & Stodart No. 149 Broadway. Title-page + pp. 3-9. At bottom of title-page: Entered according to Act of Congress the eleventh day of July 1827, by Dubois & Stodart New York. Brown University copy.

The last variation, the sevent, is marked "Tempo di Marcia"--in 3/4 meter!--and is followed by a short coda.

Meineke's "Variations to Hope told a flatt'ring tale, or Nel cor piu non mi sento," issued about the same time (Wolfe 6744), is a noticeably better work. There is an accompaniment for a flute or violin, but the piano part is sufficient alone. The tune, from Paisiello's *La Molinara*, was a favorite since its first American publication as a song in the period 1804-07; others who wrote variations published in the United States are Ignace Pleyel, Joseph Gelinek, and the French harpist Xavier Desargus (Wolfe 6745-48). The one-page introduction opens with a figure based on the upcoming theme, but rising in pitch, not descending. The most immediate effect is from pianistic virtuosity and (for the time) harmonic daring in the use of diminished-seventh chords, as in the last three measures (Ex. 3-58).

Ex. 3-58.   Meineke, "Hope told a flatt'ring tale," introduction, meas. 11-12.

Technical difficulty is also present in the third variation, including not only rapid parallel thirds but also double octaves (Ex. 3-59).

Ex. 3-59.   Meineke, "Hope told a flatt'ring tale," var. 3, meas. 1-8.

Variation 4 furnishes contrast with its high range (to c''''), as does the minor mode of variation 5. The seventh variation is a veritable technical exercise (Ex. 3-60).

Ex. 3-60.   Meineke, "Hope told a flatt'ring tale," var. 7, meas. 1-2.

"Adagio expressive" is the marking for variation 8, where Meineke writes in a florid manner--not unlike Hewitt's reminder of Mozart in "Yankee Doodle"--until the alternating sixths in the sixth measure. This style is rare for Meineke (Ex. 3-61).

Ex. 3-61.   Meineke, "Hope told a flatt'ring tale," var. 8, meas. 1-8.

The 6/8 meter changes to 2/4 for variation 9. The two-page coda includes hand-crossing, a cadenza, an excursion to the key of the flatted sixth, and a dying ("perdendosi") ending.

Meineke's trip to Vienna must have been valuable to his career, because when he returned in 1819 he assumed the post of organist and choirmaster at St. Paul's Episcopal Church, Baltimore, and became a prolific composer of piano music. The variations published in the 1820s are almost all based on European melodies. From France are the following:

> Au clair de la lune (1827)
> Fleuve du tage/Come rest in this bosom (1822-23)
> Madam de Neuville's favourite waltz (1824)
> Malbrouk, a celebrated French air (1829)
> Le Petit Tambour, a favourite French air (1828)
> Pipe de tabac (1825)

"Come rest in this bosom" (Wolfe 7175), also provided with variations by Carr and Moran, relies on broken-chord patterns for many of its variations. One exception is the third (Ex. 3-62); others are the fifth ("Marcia") and sixth ("Allegro di Waltz").

Ex. 3-62.   Meineke, "Come rest in this bosom," var. 3, meas. 1-4.

The tune "Madame de Neuville's Favourite Waltz," presumably French, was popular in the 1820s (Wolfe 5491-96). Meineke's treatment (Wolfe 5790) is of high quality, but is burdened because the theme is a complete waltz in rounded binary form, with trio, and this form (which involves the performance of 40 measures) is retained for all variations. Variation 4, slower in tempo, has an attractive interplay between the hands, and additional contrast of dynamics (Ex. 3-63).

Ex. 3-63.   Meineke, "Madam de Neuville's Favourite Waltz," var. 4, meas. 1-6.

Variation 7 includes arpeggiated right-hand chords, then the broken chords of the left hand are continued in the right (Ex. 3-64). The eighth variation is a polacca. The ninth is a Finale (Allegro animato) in duple meter, with tonal digressions to F major, A minor, suddenly moving to B-flat major dominant, then to G-major dominant broken chords and cadenza. The last few measures include a short Andante respite and an Allegro ending.

Ex. 3-64.   Meineke, "Madam de Neuville's Favourite Waltz," var. 7,
            meas. 1-5.

Meineke's "Malbrouk"[56] is particularly fine. The treatment in
variation 3 is unique (Ex. 3-65), as is the horn-fifths ending (Ex. 3-
66).

Ex. 3-65.   Meineke, "Malbrouk," var. 3, meas. 1-4.

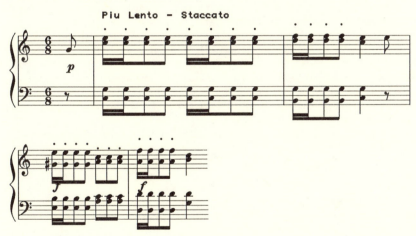

---

56. Malbrouk, a celebrated French air with variations for the
piano forte, composed for and dedicated to Miss E. A. Frickl, by C.
Meineke. Price 38 cents. Baltimore, published by John Cole, [1829].
pp. [1]-4. Bottom of p. [1]: Propriété de l'Editeur, [plate no.] 386.
Brown University copy.

Ex. 3-66.   Meineke, "Malbrouk," coda, meas. 18-21.

His "Le Petit Tambour" variations[57] are less successful.   After
the three variations is a section entitled "Foresters sound the cheerful
horn," based on the harmonic scheme of the first part of the theme.

His set of four variations on Pierre Gaveaux's "Pipe de tabac" is
a part of his medley *Divertimento* (EAKM no. 33), both copyrighted at
the same time, and both using the same plates.[58]   Although it lacks an
introduction and coda, typical of Meineke's independent variations,
this set is worth performing without the other sections of the medley.
Triplet accompaniment is already introduced in the theme section, and
dotted rhythm in variation 1.   In variation 2, the theme, horn fifths in
the left hand, is answered by written-out mordents in the right, and
the hands exchange material in midsection.   Quickly alternating octaves
weaken the quality of variation 3, but the changing textures of the last
variation, the left hand alternating bass and treble ranges, and 32nd-
note motion in the right hand throughout, redeem the set.

Probably the best of Meineke's variations on French melodies is
"Au clair de la lune" (EAKM no. 35), dedicated to Maelzel, whom he
probably met during his trip to Vienna.   The arresting octaves of
variation 2 are followed by two variations in lighter mood and an
effective variation in minor.   The last variation, the sixth, involves
interplay between the top and bottom registers, and, at the end, more
horn fifths answered by *forte* chords.

Supposedly from further east came the tune for "The favorite
Russian air of Ne'er can the rose, with variations for the piano forte"

---

57. Le Petit Tambour, a favourite French air with variations for
the piano forte, dedicated to Miss Anne Elizabeth Adeline Bayly by C.
Meineke. Pr. 38. Baltimore, published by John Cole. Title-page +
pp. 2-4. Bottom of title-page: Copy right secured according to Act of
Congress Jany. 10th. 1828 by John Cole of the State of Maryland.
Plate no. at bottom of pp. 2-4: 302. Top of p. 2: Le Petit tambour.
Variations by C. Meineke. New York Public Library copy.

58. Pipe de tabac, with variations for the piano forte by C.
Meineke. Baltimore, published and sold by Geo. Willig Jr. pp. [3]-5.
At bottom of p. [3]: Entered according to act of Congress the 25[h] day
of April 1825 by George Willig of the State of Maryland. At bottom
of p. 4: Divertimento M. At bottom of p. 5: PIPE DE T. Not in
Wolfe. Duke University copy.

(1824?).[59] These are not among Meineke's best variations, but the syncopation in the sixth variation is well done (Ex. 3-67).

Ex. 3-67.   Meineke, "Ne'er can the rose," var. 6, meas. 1-8.

"The Favorite Swiss Air" theme is as yet unidentified; the sections of the set that have been found[60] are not outstanding (Ex. 3-68).

Ex. 3-68.   Meineke, "Swiss Air," theme, meas. 1-8.

---

59.   Wolfe 5799, which is probably the same as the unlocated Wolfe 735.   The melody, arranged by Bishop, described as "from the comic opera of The Marriage of Figaro," may be different.

60.   The favorite Swiss air, with variations for the piano forte, composed and dedicated to Miss Ann Eliza Fischer by C. Meineke. Baltimore, published and sold by Geo. Willig Jr.   Price 1.D., [n.d.]. Title-page + pp. [2]-11.   At top of p. [2]: The favorite Swiss air.   Pp. 5-8 are missing in the Brown University copy, after variation 3; the Finale is on pp. 9-11.

Several melodies used by Meineke have unknown genealogies. One is "The Much Admired Waltz of Count de Gallenburg."[61] Variation 2 is conspicuous with its brilliant thirds (Ex. 3-69).

Ex. 3-69.   Meineke, "Waltz of Count de Gallenburg," var. 2, meas. 1-5.

The following variation, however, reveals a bad cliché of broken octaves common later in the century (Ex. 3-70).

Ex. 3-70.   Meineke, "Waltz of Count de Gallenburg," var. 3, meas. 5-8.

---

61.   The much admired Waltz of Count de Gallenburg, with variations for the piano forte by C. Meineke. Baltimore, published by John Cole & to be had of Thompson & Homans Washington, [183-?]. Entered according to Act of Congress by John Cole of the State of Maryland, U.S.A. Title-page + pp. 3-7. Plate no. at bottom of pp. 3-7: 527. Brown University copy.

"Look out upon the stars my love" (1824?; Wolfe 5789) is not Meineke's best, but the third variation is catchy (Ex. 3-71).

Ex. 3-71.   Meineke, "Look out upon the stars my love," var. 3, meas. 1-4.

The sixth of the eight variations is another march, and a short Finale concludes the work.

Five sets based on operatic arias are included in Meineke's output. He used two sections of Mozart's "Non più andrai" for the theme of one, published in 1828,[62] and immediately gives it a scherzando treatment for variation 1 (Ex. 3-72). Techniques common with Meineke are found: the right hand alternating between the bass and treble in variation 2, arpeggio chords in variation 3, and an arpeggiated 16th-note chordal accompaniment for the intact theme in variation 4. The fifth and last variation is in 6/8 and marked Vivace.

---

62. Non piu andrai, a favourite air from Mozarts opera The Mariage [*sic*] of Figaro, with variations for the piano forte composed by C. Meineke. Philadelphia, published by John G. Klemm. Pr. 50 Cs. Title-page + pp. 3-7. Plate no. 366. Bottom of title-page: Entered according to Act of Congress the fifteenth day of April 1828 by John G Klemm of the State of Pennsylvania. New York Public Library copy.

Ex. 3-72.   Meineke, "Non piu andrai," var. 1, meas. 1-8.

Meineke's development as a composer can be seen in two sets of variations on a single theme, Mozart's "Away with melancholy" (sometimes titled "O dolce concento"; originally "Das klinget so herrlich" from *Die Zauberflöte*). The first set was included as the last section of his medley *Pot Pourri* (1807-09; see chapter 4). Only the first half (eight measures) of the melody is used. Alberti bass accompaniment permeates all four variations except the second, although the change to triple meter in variation 4 helps. Not only does his new set of 1827[63]

63. Away with melancholy, with variations for the piano-forte, by C. Meineke. Baltimore, published by John Cole, [1827]. pp. [1]-4. Plate no. at bottom of pp. [1]-4: 245. At head of title: Property of the publisher. Indiana University copy. It was also published later by Benteen: Away with melancholy, with variations by C. Meineke. Baltimore, published by F. D. Benteen, [1839-51]. pp. [1]-4. Plate no. at bottom of pp. [1]-4: 132. Library of Congress copy.

use the complete sixteen-measure tune, but there is more variety of texture, rhythm, and keyboard technique. The left hand crosses the right in variations 1 and 5. The right hand answers with a counter-subject in variation 3, to the theme in the left hand. Variation 6 is "Finale: Alla Polacca." This is one of Meineke's successful variation sets, not as much for his inventiveness as much as for his playful treatments of a catchy tune. Certainly it is idiomatic for the pianoforte, with no traces of harpsichord style as in the earlier set.

His variations on the Hunter's Chorus from Weber's *Der Freis-chütz*, published in 1826,[64] was in competition with those by Darley (discussed below), copyrighted less than a month earlier. Meineke's set suffers from the predominance of the three basic chords (I, IV, V) in the original theme. Nevertheless, momentary imitation between the hands enlivens variation 1, brilliant parallel thirds does the same in variation 3, and tonal relief comes with the minor variation 8. Varia-tion 9, a polacca, is capped with a coda based on the last theme of *Der Freischütz*'s overture, balancing this set's introduction.

"Araby's Daughter" from Kiallmark's opera *Lallarookh* is more ambitious.[65] (The theme was later appropriated for the song "The Old Oaken Bucket.") A 24-measure introduction with several tempo changes ends with a cadenza (Ex. 3-73).

Ex. 3-73.   Meineke, "Araby's Daughter," introduction, meas. 29 (after the first chord, all notes printed small in the original).

64. The Hunter's chorus from Der Freyschütz, varied for the piano forte, and dedicated to his pupil Miss Susan Schroeder, by C. Meineke. Baltimore, published by John Cole. Price 1.25. Copy right secured, according to Act of Congress Feb. 14th 1826 by John Cole, of the State of Md. Title-page + pp. 2-14. Plate no. at bottom of pp. 2-14: 194. Wolfe 9692 (unlocated). New York Public Library copy.

65. Araby's Daughter from Lallarookh, with variations for the piano forte, composed and dedicated to Miss Fanny Rundle by C. Meineke. Philadelphia, published by John G. Klemm. Entered according to Act of Congress the twenty first day of July 1826 by John G. Klemm of the State of Pennsylvania. Title-page + pp. 2-10. Plate no. at bottom of pp. 2-10: 276. Brown University copy.

The "Brilliante" variation is the fourth (Ex. 3-74), and similar pyrotechniques are present in the ninth (Ex. 3-75). The coda includes an excursion into the submediant key of A-flat major, but it ends slowly and softly.

Ex. 3-74. Meineke, "Araby's Daughter," var. 4, meas. 1-2.

Ex. 3-75. Meineke, "Araby's Daughter," var. 9, meas. 1-4.

In spite of Meineke's German background, however, Great Britain furnished most of the tunes for his variations. Most of these are Scotch. One is by the Irish poet and musician Thomas Moore, probably with its origin in an Irish folktune. Meineke's setting of "My heart and lute" (1827)[66] begins with a cadenza, and all variations have a cadenza before the da capo as well, except variation 7. This variation, in the relative minor key, is a unique example of a siciliano, which in its midst has a rare example of imitation (Ex. 3-76).

Ex. 3-76.   Meineke, "My heart and lute," var. 7, meas. 13-18.

Meineke provides a coda in which the tempo gradually becomes slower: presto, andante, slentando sempre, dolce, calando, morendo.

"The Welsh air Nos Galen (or New Years Night)" is the same tune now known with the words "Deck the hall with boughs of holly."[67] The fourth variation, marked "resoluto," has the same effect of 16th-note scales in the left hand (Ex. 3-77) as does variation 2 of Meineke's "Au clair de la lune" variations. The basic harmonic pattern of the tune is transformed into an effective Andante cantabile, but which is spoiled, perhaps, by the chromaticism in the fourth measure of variation 6 (Ex. 3-78).

---

66. My Heart and Lute, a favourite air, with variations for the piano forte, composed and dedicated to Miss Ann Williams by C. Meineke. Baltimore, published by John Cole. Copy right secured according to Act of Congress Aug 7, 1827 by John Cole, of the State of Maryland. Title-page + pp. 2-11. At top of p. 2: Introduction. Plate no. at bottom of pp. 2-11: 289. Free Library of Philadelphia copy.

67. The Welsh air Nos Galen (or New Years Night), with variations for the piano forte, composed for and dedicated to Miss De Wees of Philadelphia by C. Meineke. Price 75 cents. (Copyright secured.) Philadelphia, published by Geo. Willig, [182-?]. Title-page + pp. 3-9. Bottom of pp. 3-9: Nos Galen. Free Library of Philadelphia copy.

Ex. 3-77.   Meineke, "Nos Galen," var. 4, meas. 1-4.

Ex. 3-78.   Meineke, "Nos Galen," var. 6, meas. 1-4.

The Polacca, variation 8, does not have the usual long note on the second half of the first beat (Ex. 3-79).

Ex. 3-79.   Meineke, "Nos Galen," var. 8, meas. 1-2.

This set of variations is capped with a coda that has in its midst a return of part of the theme, in chords--something not done elsewhere by Meineke.

Five sets of variations are based on Scotch tunes, equalled only by the number of those with French melodies. "Brignal Banks" (1827)[68] has a cadenza in the middle of all six variations, except the sixth which also functions as the finale. The cadenza of variation 2 is the longest (Ex. 3-80). The fifth variation is a march.

Another march is contained in "Kinloch of Kinloch" (1825).[69] Its seventh variation is an Andante pastorale, similar in treatment to the siciliano in "My heart and lute." The eighth variation is just plain fun (Ex. 3-81).

68. Brignal Banks, a favorite Scotch air with variations for the piano forte, composed and dedicated to Miss Mary Todhunter by C. Meineke. Pr 75 C. Baltimore, published and sold by Geo. Willig. Title-page + pp. 2-9. At top of title-page: Entered according to act of Congress the 26th day of March 1827 by G Willig of the State of Maryland. Top of p. 2: Brignal Banks. Bottom of pp. 3-8: Brignal banks. New York Public Library copy. Another copy at the Free Library of Philadelphia has "Jr" inserted after "Geo. Willig."

69. Wolfe 5783. According to Temperley, *The London Pianoforte School*, 7:xxvi, this tune is from the song "Enchantress, farewell" by George Kinloch of Kinloch, first published in 1798, and harmonized by Beethoven in George Thomson's *Original Scottish Airs*, vol. 5 (1818).

Ex. 3-80.   Meineke, "Brignal Banks," var. 2, meas. 16-17 (originally in small notes between the fermata and "a tempo").

Ex. 3-81.   Meineke, "Kinloch of Kinloch," var. 8, meas. 1-2.

The "Pollacca [*sic*] con Finale" uses the usual polacca rhythmic pattern this time. The whole set is preceded by an introduction with several tempo changes, and dips from the tonic F major into D-flat major and the parallel tonic minor, F minor.[70]

Meineke's "Sandy and Jenny" variations, also issued in 1825 (Wolfe 7809), on a melody by James Sanderson published in the United States as early as 1803-04 (Wolfe 7797), includes a shorter introduction but a sizeable cadenza before the theme (Ex. 3-82).

Ex. 3-82. Meineke, "Sandy and Jenny," introduction, meas. 10 (notes are small after the first chord).

---

70. Another set of variations on a Scotch tune, published after my cutoff date of 1830: Dumbarton's bonny dell, Scotch ballad with variations for the piano forte, composed for & dedicated to Mrs. Robert A. Taylor by C. Meineke. Baltimore, published by F. D. Benteen 137 Baltimore St., [1840-42]. Pr. 37½ net. Title-page + pp. 2-7. Plate no. at bottom of pp. 2-7: 352. Lower right-hand corner of p. 7: Gravé par L. M. Webb. University of North Carolina, Chapel Hill copy. It begins with his usual one-page introduction. Of the seven variations, the second is a march, the third slows to Andantino, in the fourth ("Brillante") the theme appears in alternating octaves, variation 5 is in minor, and after a short cadenza the waltz tempo of variation 6 continues into the coda.

The beginning of the ninth variation, marked "maestoso," is actually march-like (Ex. 3-83), but it merges into a final Andante statement of the theme and a quiet ending. Techniques of other Meineke sets are used, but none are unusual.

Ex. 3-83.   Meineke, "Sandy and Jenny," var. 9, meas. 1-8.

Another Scotch tune, "They're a' noddin" (1824?; Wolfe 5812), likewise ends quietly in its tenth variation. Variation 5, for the first half, alternates scale passages between the hands; the theme is in the right hand of the first measure (Ex. 3-84). Variation 7, in G minor, is marked "Andante con expressione." A waltz is used for variation 8, and polacca for the ninth (Ex. 3-85). A coda, normally found only at the end of a whole set of variations, is attached to this penultimate one.

Ex. 3-84. Meineke, "They're a' noddin," var. 5, meas. 1-4.

Ex. 3-85. Meineke, "They're a' noddin," var. 9, meas. 9-12.

In another unique situation, Meineke wrote variations on a pair of tunes, "The Musical Recreation containing the celebrated airs of Robin Adair and Let us haste to Kelvin Grove" (1829).[71] "Robin Adair" has an introduction, three variations, and a transition and cadenza leading to "Let us haste"--this last a melody first published in the United States in an arrangement by Robert Archibald Smith (Wolfe 8381). The third variation is of interest (Ex. 3-86), but variation 6 is full of pianistic showmanship (Ex. 3-87).

Ex. 3-86.   Meineke, "Musical Recreation: Let us haste to Kelvin Grove," var. 3, meas. 1-3.

Ex. 3-87.   Meineke, "Musical Recreation: Let us haste to Kelvin Grove," var. 6, meas. 1-2.

---

71. The Musical Recreation containing the celebrated airs of Robin Adair and Let us haste to Kelvin grove, with variations for the piano forte, composed and respectfully dedicated to his pupil Miss Frances Donnell by C. Meineke. Pr. $1.25. Baltimore, published and sold by Geo. Willig Jr. Entered according to act of Congress the 18th day of May 1829 by George Willig Jr. of the State of Maryland. Title-page + pp. 3-13. Bottom of pp. 3-7: Robin Adair. Bottom of pp. 8-13: Let us haste to. New York Public Library copy.

The Finale also serves as variation 7, and is over eight times as long as the eight-measure theme; it includes a portion in the submediant key of E-flat major.

The only variations by Meineke on an American tune are "Variations on Gilferts favorite air I left thee where I found thee love" (1828).[72] The original melody, by Charles Gilfert, was issued in 1823 (Wolfe 3042). Variation 5 furnishes one example where Meineke has written an implied 3/4 rhythm in one hand, against the 6/8 of the other--a rare case of rhythmic ambiguity (Ex. 3-88).

Ex. 3-88.   Meineke, "I left thee where I found thee love," var. 5, meas. 1-2.

_____

72. Variations of [*sic*] Gilferts favorite air I left thee where I found thee love, composed for the piano forte and dedicated to his pupil Miss Caroline Turnbull by C. Meineke. Price $1.25. Philadelphia, published by John G. Klemm. Entered according to Act of Congress the twentieth day of March 1828 by John G. Klemm of Pensylvania [*sic*]. Title-page + pp. 2-13. Plate no. at the bottom of pp. 2-13: 356. Free Library of Philadelphia copy.

The seventh variation is a siciliano, strikingly reminiscent of Mozart[73] (Ex. 3-89).

Ex. 3-89.   Meineke, "I left thee where I found thee love," var. 7, meas. 1-2.

The last variation, the ninth, is marked "Rondo di marcia" which, like "Let us haste to Kelvin Grove," has a digression into the submediant of E-flat.

Meineke was the most important composer of variations at the time, if one considers only the quantity. He wrote enough for a statistical analysis of some of the compositional and pianistic techniques and performance directions in the twenty-three sets:

> 12 sets of variations with introduction (or transition before the next variation)
> 7 of these introductions (or transitions) with a cadenza at the end
> 6 variations in the parallel minor mode
> 2 variations in the relative minor mode
> 30 variations which include inner cadenzas
> 15 sets of variations with a finale or coda, or extension of the final variation
> 5 finales or codas with an excursion to the flat submediant key
> 8 finales or codas, or last variations, with a change to triple from duple meter
> 4 sets of variations with a faster ending
> 6 sets with soft and slow ending
> 17 variations featuring the crossing of hands
> 9 variations featuring repeated alternating octaves in the right hand
> 5 variations with the right-hand melody in alternating octaves
> 8 variations with extended arpeggios through the two hands
> 5 variations with extensive use of parallel thirds in the right hand
> 2 variations with extended right-hand trills
> 2 siciliano variations

---

73. Quartet in D minor, K. 421, last movement.

6 march variations
6 polacca variations
2 waltz variations
6 variations with the direction "scherzando"
12 "dolce"
3 "delicatezza"
2 "cantabile"
3 "resoluto"

These variations are not all consistently high in quality; some individual sets by Hance, Metz, Thibault, and Clifton are better. Meineke sometimes tends to rely on well-established formulas. Nevertheless, his variations include many moments of spark and are well-worth investigating and performing.[74] American piano music of the 1820s would have been much the poorer without him.

Arthur Clifton

Arthur Clifton (1784-1832) was a member of a distinguished musical family. His original name was Philip Antony Corri; his father was the song and opera composer Domenico Corri (1746-1825), who moved from his native Italy to Edinburgh in 1781 and to London in 1790. Philip Antony, after composing a number of published songs and piano pieces, and after having been one of the principal founders of London's Philharmonic Society in 1813, left London to escape marital difficulties. He settled in Baltimore by 1817, renamed himself Arthur Clifton, and remarried.[75] Clifton's finest set of variations is

---

74. A fine set of variations from a later time: Thou reighn'st in this bosom, favorite German air with variations for the piano forte, composed and dedicated to Miss Eliza Ann Fischer, by C. Meineke. Pr. 1.25. Published by F. D. Benteen, Baltimore [1839-51]. Title-page + pp. 2-13. In small letters below name of publisher on title-page: W. H. Duffy. Plate no. at bottom of pp. 2-13: 1216. At lower right of p. 13: A. F. Winnemore, Eng^r. Bodleian Library copy, box 301. The tune is the familiar "Du, du liegst mir im Herzen." This is an ambitious work, apparent from the one-page introduction based on motives from the upcoming theme, then a half-page cadenza. Particularly effective is variation 6, in which the tonic B-flat major is changed to B-flat minor, and then there is a modulation to D-flat major. A 4-measure transition leads to the Finale which, after the standard 12-measure variation, becomes a lengthy 85-measure (nearly 4-page) fantasy, mainly related to the theme.

75. Clifton did, however, revisit London in 1821, appearing with his former name as a singer on a Philharmonic Society concert of June 11. See Myles Birket Foster, *History of the Philharmonic Society of London, 1813-1912* (London: John Lane, 1912), 53; my thanks to John Gillespie for pointing out this source, after I had written the article on Clifton for *The New Grove Dictionary of American Music*. Information on Corri's involvement in the founding of the Philharmonic Society, and as singer in its concerts, is found in Foster, 5

"An Original Air with variations," published in Baltimore in 1820
(EAKM no. 22). Perhaps its success is due to the quality of the
original melody (Clifton was primarily devoted to vocal music; his
main interest was in singing and composing songs, and he wrote a
singing method), yet the treatment in the five variations is likewise
masterful. Rather than relying on various stock figurations to vary the
tune, Clifton gives each variation an individual musical characterization. Variation 1 is in the low range, certain notes of the original air
appearing in the 16th-note rhythm shared by both hands. In variation
2, three strong chords are answered by 32nd-note fragments. As if to
balance the low tessitura of the first variation, the third remains high
on the keyboard. Scales and other figurations by the right hand, in
16th-note sextuplets, lift variation 4 to be the high point of the whole
set, in dynamics and virtuosity.

Almost as fine is his "Blue eye'd Mary" variations, perhaps published in 1821 (Wolfe 1912). The original melody was a song, perhaps
by an otherwise-unidentified Robert Tuke, which was also arranged
with variations by an amateur and by the Italian-American Stefano
Cristiani (see below).[76] Whereas the theme is buried in right-hand
figurations and scales of 16th notes in Clifton's first variation, it
appears intact--in three different tessituras--in variations 2-4, with a
variety of rhythmic accompaniments (Ex. 3-90). Untypically for
Clifton, the fifth variation is chordal, almost hymn-like, marked "con
espress." The last variation and coda are based on three-note broken
chords, the theme represented as the high note. Although the workmanship is imaginative, clearly Clifton is restrained by the simple
theme. More variety in harmonic content or key would have helped.

---

and 8-9. Boston's *Euterpeiad*, 22 September 1822, reprinted a London
newspaper's June 17 advertisement from a solicitor, with a £100
reward, for information on Corri's whereabouts. In part, "It has been
reported that the above named P. A. Corri after his arrival at New-
York, proceeded to Philadelphia, thence to Baltimore, and there
married a quaker lady; it has also been asserted that he is returned to
England. The said P. A. Corri has a sharp Italian visage, sallow com-
plexion, black curly hair, black eyes, and is bald on the crown of his
head. He is forty years of age, 5 feet 8 inches high, and has a soft
voice and gentlemanly manners."

76. Wolfe 9418 (Tuke), 893-905 (anonymous song), 1581 (Carr
edition), 90 (variations by an amateur), 2194 (Cristiani variations).

Ex. 3-90.   Arthur Clifton, "Blue eye'd Mary":

a. Var. 2, meas. 1-4.

b. Var. 3, meas. 1-2.

c. Var. 4, meas. 1-2.

Two other sets of variations on popular tunes do not show Clifton at his best. "The Bonny Boat, with easy variations for the pianoforte"[77] is written on the Scotch melody more commonly known with the title "O swiftly glides the bonny boat."[78] The variations are written with the usual formulas--including one with the *passé* Alberti bass--which betray its intended use by students. But the last variation, no. 5, reveals a sprightly character (Ex. 3-91).

Ex. 3-91.   Clifton, "Bonny boat," var. 5, meas. 1-4.

"The Mignonette Waltz" variations, probably first published in 1823 (Wolfe 1937), is burdened by a poverty of harmonic content implied in the given theme; the tonic and dominant chords are the only ones used throughout the four variations.

Charles F. Fisher, T. L. Holden

Another Baltimore musician, about whom almost nothing is known, was Charles F. Fisher. His most ambitious published work is "The White Rose, a favorite waltz" variations, issued about 1823 (Wolfe 2813). (The harmonic scheme of the waltz is identical to "Ach du lieber Augustin," except for the thirteenth measure--dominant instead of "Augustin's" tonic.) None of the variations, however, rise above the commonplace. Like many others, one is in a "Tempo di Marcia"; the sixth and last, marked "Brillante," contains banal 16th-note arpeggios. A unique marking is "Bassoon" in variation 1, where

---

77. The Bonnie Boat, with easy variations for the piano forte, composed by A. Clifton. Baltimore, published by J. Cole [after 1826]. pp. [1]-3. At bottom of p. [1]: Propriété de l'Editeur. Plate no. 354 at bottom of pp. [1]-3: 354. Brown University copy.

78. A Beethoven arrangement, no. 19 of his *Schottische Lieder*, op. 108, was published in Baltimore in 1822; see Wolfe 491.

the right hand crosses to the bass for several measures; yet there is no other clue that the piece is a transcription from ensemble music.

Absolutely nothing is known about T. L. Holden (not to be confused with the also-unidentified F. Holden, whose "Mina" rondo is described in chapter 2), who contributed a modest set of variations on the catchy "Copenhagen Waltz" (1811-17; EAKM no. 16). The tune, also appearing in Hewitt's *Pot pourri*, was used for American-published variations by the English musicians Charles Kelly, Jean Tatton Latour, and Samuel Webbe, Jr., and in a set for harp by Benjamin Carr.[79] Although there is none of the demanding passagework equivalent to Carr's harp variations, Holden's leads to the final "fortissimo et vivace" variation, which would have taken some work for an amateur to master.

William Staunton, Victor Pelissier

The clergyman William Staunton (1803-89), some of whose music was published in Boston in the late 1820s, also wrote variations on "O swiftly glides the bonny boat."[80] Staunton was not afraid to reharmonize, as in variation 2, the first part of which has syncopation between the two hands (Ex. 3-92).

Ex. 3-92.   William Staunton, "O swiftly glides the bonny boat," var. 2, meas. 1-2.

_____

79. Wolfe 4725 (Kelly), 5250-54 (Latour), 9655-58 (Webbe), 1590 (Carr--also included in the *Carr's Musical Miscellany* reprint).

80. O swiftly glides the bonny boat, a favorite Scotch air, arranged with variations for the piano forte by William Staunton Jr. Boston, published by James L. Hewitt & Co. at their music store No. 36 Market St., [1826-29]. Copy right secured. Price 50 Cts. Title-page + pp. [3]-7. Clements Library, University of Michigan copy. Added imprint on Brown University copy: New York, published by J. L. Hewitt & Co. No. 129 Broadway. Seller's stamp at bottom of title-page: Sold by Hewitt & Co. 83 Washington St. Boston.

Variation 3, marked "Brilliante," is characterized by continuous 32nd-note scales and arpeggios in the right hand which would certainly be beyond the abilities of the modest amateur. In a refreshing break from the usual pattern, the fourth variation is followed by an extensive *maestoso* section based on the second half of the theme that leads from the tonic D major to the keys of B minor, C major, E minor, and B-flat major, and to G-sharp diminished-seventh chords which lead to a long cadenza on the dominant of D major. Impressive as the cadenza might have been on the concert stage then, its content might evoke laughter today (Ex. 3-93).

Ex. 3-93.   Staunton, "O swiftly glides the bonny boat," var. 4, meas. 22 (notes are small in the original after the trill).

The last (unnumbered) variation, a Marcia, is spoiled by repeated bombastic D-major chords. Strangely, the work ends softly.

Marches are rarely used as the basis for variations, but Staunton furnished one, "Pittsburgh Quick Step."[81] The five variations are not

81. Pittsburgh Quick Step, with variations for the piano forte, composed & dedicated to Miss Lydia Collins, of Pittsburgh, by Wm. Staunton, Jr. Copy right secured. Boston, published by James L. Hewitt & Co. at their Music Saloon No. 36 Market St. and No. 129 Broadway, New York, [1826-29]. pp. [1]-3. Photostat at New York

marked with high quality in spite of the brilliance of variation 2 ("scherzando") or the evocation of horn fifths ("alla corni") in variation 3.

Another such march is the only offering in this category by Victor Pelissier--"March as Performed by the Philadelphia Military Bands and also at the Olympic Theatre on the 4th of July 1812, with variations for the piano forte," included in *Pelissier's Columbian Melodies* (1812).[82] Pelissier was a professional French horn player, which may explain why this set of three variations are not very impressive. The techniques were done with more imagination by pianist-composers of the time.

Stefano Cristiani

The other set of variations on "Blue eye'd Mary" was first issued in 1819 (Wolfe 2194A), two years before Clifton's, by Stefano Cristiani. Surprisingly, considering that Cristiani had come to Philadelphia and Washington about 1818 with a solid background as an opera composer in Italy, his variations fall short in quality in comparison to Clifton's. One wonders if Cristiani was a good pianist; his writing is clumsy and does not fall easily into the hand. Some of the successful procedures for writing variations are there; the theme shifted to the left hand in variation 3, and the mode made minor in variation 5-- the one before the final variation. But Cristiani's lack of talent and judgement are clearly shown at the beginning of both halves in variation 4, where the added left-hand passagework forms consecutive octaves with the theme in the right hand. It is not surprising that this is the only set of variations by Cristiani published in the United States, and that he disappeared from the musical scene after 1825.[83]

William Henry Westray Darley

William Henry Westray Darley (d. 1858?), an English-born Philadelphia musician (and son-in-law of the English-born American painter Thomas Sully), likewise wrote variations on "O swiftly glides

---

Public Library. Lydia Collins was the sister of Stephen Collins, for whom Stephen Collins Foster was named. The first page of this music is printed in Evelyn Foster Morneweck, *Chronicles of Stephen Foster's Family*, 2 vols. (University of Pittsburgh Press, 1944), vol. 1, opposite p. 51.

82. *Pelissier's Columbian Melodies*, ed. Karl Kroeger, Recent Researches in American Music, 13-14 (Madison: A-R Editions, 1984), 165-69.

83. Cristiani, "late composer of music for all the theatres of the Spanish court" and a "very accomplished performer on the Piano Forte," taught and performed in concerts in Lexington, Kentucky, in 1822-24, however. See Carden, *Music in Lexington*, 50-51, 74.

the bonny boat" (1829),[84] as did Clifton and Staunton. Darley utilizes many pianistic devices, but rarely shows creative imagination in his sets of variations published in the 1820s. For example, variation 1 is based on legato parallel thirds in 16th notes, variation 3 ("brillante") on broken-chord figuration in 32nd notes. A unique direction is "In rowing time" for variation 5 (Ex. 3-94).

Ex. 3-94. W. H. W. Darley, "O swiftly glides the bonny boat," var. 5, meas. 1-4.

The sixth and last variation is a "Marcia," a character variation also used in his 1824 "Hurrah hurrah" variations.[85] The "brilliant" writing in "Hurrah hurrah" applies to the 32nd-note scales of variation 2, and the same in variation 4 for the left hand (Ex. 3-95).

---

84. The favorite Scottish melody O swiftly glides the bonny boat, arranged with variations for the piano forte by W. H. W. Darley. Price 75 cents. Baltimore, published and sold by Geo. Willig Jr. Entered according to act of Congress, the 3rd day of August 1829 by George Willig Jr. of Mar^d. Title-page + pp. 3-9. At top of p. 3: O swiftly glides the bonny Boat. On bottom of p. 4: O swiftly glides the. On bottom of pp. 5-9: O swiftly glides. New York Public Library copy.

85. Wolfe 2275. *Carr's Musical Miscellany in Occasional Numbers*, nos. 79-80, printed together, includes Darley's variations and the original song, "Now fleecy snows descend around, a favorite ballad adapted to the popular Swedish air of Hurrah! Hurrah!"

Ex. 3-95.   Darley, "Hurrah hurrah," var. 4, meas. 1-4.

Only occasionally does Darley relax for a slower variation in the minor mode, as in the sixth variation.

Darley's variations on the Scotch tune "They're a' noddin," published in 1824 (Wolfe 2277), are probably his best, due to several departures from his usual formulas. The set includes a minor variation (no. 7, "espres."), and a newer device in which the melody is given with right-hand offbeats[86] (Ex. 3-96). The rhythm of the "polonaise" characterizes variation 6--a technique also found in the fifth variation ("Pollacca") of Darley's "Romaika" variations[87] (Ex. 3-97). Another character variation in "Romaika" is the fourth, "a la Valse." Darley's

---

86. Yet this device was also used in "Martini's favorite Minuet with variations for the harpsichord or piano forte composed by R[ayner] Taylor organist at Chelmsford" (London: Longman, Lukey & Broderip, [ca. 1775]), variation 6. Library of Congress copy.

87. The Romaika from Moore's Evenings in Greece, arranged with variations for the piano forte by W. H. W. Darley. Pr. 50 C. Baltimore, published and sold by Geo. Willig Jr., [ca. 1830?]. pp. [1]-5. At bottom of pp. 2-5: Romaika Var. The Brown University copy also has a seller's stamp: Sold by H. Goodwin, Hartford.

four variations on the Scotch tune "Kinloch of Kinloch" (1829)[88] include one (no. 3) with the same offbeat device as in his "They're a' noddin" set.

Ex. 3-96.   Darley, "They're a' noddin," var. 5, meas. 1-2.

Ex. 3-97.   Darley, "Romaika," var. 5, meas. 1-2.

As distinct from some popular melodies used for variations, "Love's Ritornella" has the advantage of several secondary dominant chords, as well as a fermata at the end of the "b" phrase in the a b a structure. Darley includes small cadenzas at these fermatas in all seven of his variations, published in 1830.[89] Variation 3 consists of the

88. Kinloch of Kinloch, favorite Scotch air, arranged with variations for the piano forte by W. H. W. Darley. Baltimore, published and sold by Geo. Willig Jr., [1829]. pp. [1]-3. Bottom of p. [1]: Entered according to act of Congress the 25h [*sic*] day of February 1829 by George Willig Jr of the state of Maryland. Clements Library, University of Michigan copy.

89. Love's ritornella, the much admired air, arranged with variations for the piano forte by W. H. Darley. Philad[a], published & sold by J. Edgar 68 S. Fourth St. Pr. 50. pp. [1]-6. Bottom of p. [1]: Entered according to act of Congress the 26th day of May 1830 by J. Edgar of the State of Penns[a]. New York Public Library copy.

unaccompanied tune in the left hand, answered by a rapid ascending
scale in the right, the same technique in variation 3 of Benjamin Carr's
"Maid of Lodi" (EAKM no. 14). (One wonders if Darley might have
studied with Carr in Philadelphia.) Darley gives variation 4 the same
waltz treatment he had in "Romaika," but certainly rare for the time
is variation 4: "A la Bolero" and its rhythm 8th-two 16ths-four 8ths
(compare with the ending of Carr's "Drink to me only with thine
eyes," described above).

Since Darley arranged the music for the production of Carl
Maria von Weber's *Der Freischütz* given in Philadelphia in 1825, it is
not surprising that he also composed variations on one number from
this opera, the Hunter's Chorus.[90] The theme is the longest Darley
used--58 measures--and all of the six variations, until the last one,
incorporate the same length. The last one again uses the "Polonaise"
rhythm. Certain repetitions of figurations in the fifth variation are
tiresome. Better is the third, "Resoluto," which uses the same
approach as the third variation in "They're a' noddin" (Ex. 3-98).

Ex. 3-98.   Darley, "Hunter's Chorus," var. 3, meas. 1-4.

In all his variations Darley relies on rapid scales and figurations,
which indicate that he must have been an accomplished pianist. If he
had more imagination to modulate to other keys, to provide free intro-

---

90. The Hunters Chorus, from Von Weber's opera of the Freys-
chutz, with variations for the piano forte, as performed at the
Anniversary Concert of the St. Cecelia Society of Philad[a]. composed by
W. H. W. Darley. Price 75 cents. Philadelphia, published & sold by
G. Willig 171 Chesnut St. Entered according to act of Congress the
seventeenth day of January 1826 by Geo. Willig of the State of
Pennsylvania. Title-page + pp. 2-9. Engraving of two hunters with
rifles and a dead bird on the title-page. New York Public Library
copy.

ductions or codas, and to search for fresh keyboard patterns, his stature as a composer may have been higher.

George Pfeiffer, Theodore F. Molt

The first two piano pieces with a Canadian association were both published in the United States. George Pfeiffer was a music teacher in Philadelphia, where his "Canadian Dance" variations were published in 1817.[91] The theme is very simple, with only tonic and dominant harmonies, and the seven variations have little merit, except perhaps for the offbeat accompaniment in variation 1, two lowered sixth scale degrees in variation 2, and the division of the melody between the hands in variation 3. Theodore F. Molt's "Post Horn Waltz" variations, published in Philadelphia perhaps before 1823 when he moved to Quebec City, is on a theme with the same harmonic restriction.[92] There are more demands on the player, however, including several two and three-octave arpeggios and a "brillante" seventh variation in which the two hands cross to complete four-octave arpeggios. Quebec City was the home of one of Canada's first piano builders, Frederick Hunt, who was active beginning in 1816, and where Molt became organist of Notre-Dame Basilica and married the daughter of Frederic-Henri Glackemeyer (1751-1836)--that city's pioneer music teacher and importer of pianos and sheet music.[93]

Oliver Shaw

Oliver Shaw (1779-1848), one of the few American-born musicians in this survey, made music his profession after becoming blind. (He was an early music teacher of Lowell Mason.) From 1807 until his death, he was located in Providence, Rhode Island. Shaw wrote only five sets of piano variations, all modest. One, "Westminster Waltz," appeared in *O. Shaw's Instructions for the Piano Forte* (1831). The three variations are carefully fingered and exploit various 8th-note patterns for the benefit of the student who was reaching the end of

---

91. Wolfe 6966. Facsimile in Elaine Keillor, ed., *The Canadian Musical Heritage* 1: *Piano Music I* (Ottawa: Canadian Musical Heritage Society, 1983), 1-5. She speculates that perhaps Pfeiffer had visited Canada, and that "the tune for Pfeiffer's variations has a rhythm typical of many French-Canadian folk-dances" (p. v).

92. Not in Wolfe; facsimile (with corrections) in Keillor, 6-11. Wolfe, p. 575, speculates that Molt (who was apparently also the author of an 1835 piano tutor) was of German background--he wrote a song "Know'st thou the land" also with the German text "Kennst du das Land."

93. Keillor, v, vii.

this published course of instruction. "The Sisters," a duet (1827),[94] has the primo player give the melody in octaves for variation 2, and the same for the secondo part in the following one. A march-like style in variation 4 finishes this pleasant but modest contribution.

The other three sets are also on waltzes, probably intended for those with slightly more ability. "Aerial Waltz" (ca. 1824; Wolfe 7915) advances to the use of 16th and 32nd notes. The only distinguishing feature of "New Bedford Waltz" (1832)[95] is that the waltz itself is in three sixteen-measure segments. The three variations contain traditional 8th-note arpeggios and scales in the right hand. The same characteristics are also present in the three variations written on "Nassau Waltz," published sometime between 1823 and 1848.[96]

Charles Thibault

An important pianist-composer with fine European credentials was Charles Thibault (d. 1853?), who claimed that he had received the Grand Premium of the Royal Conservatory of France. He gave concerts in New York City from 1818 until well into the 1830s, and published music until about 1850. Like one set of variations for harp published earlier in Paris,[97] his first American set, on "Robin Adair"

---

94. The Sisters, an air with variations for two performers on one piano-forte, composed & dedicated to Misses L. M. & H. N. Fearing by Oliver Shaw. Pr. 50. New York, published by Dubois & Stodart, No. 169 Broadway, [1827]. Title-page + pp. 2-7. New York Public Library copy.

95. New Bedford Waltz, composed and respectfully inscribed to Miss Mary Read, by Oliver Shaw. Providence: published by the Author 70 Westminster Street. pp. [1]-4. At bottom of p. [1]: Entered according to Act of Congress in the year 1832, by Oliver Shaw in the Clerk's office of the District Court of Rhode Island. Brown University copy.

96. Nassau Waltz, with variations for the piano forte composed & dedicated to his friend Miss Harriot Adeline Brown by Oliver Shaw. Providence: published by the Author, No. 70 Westminster St. pp. [1]-3. Brown University copy.

97. Fantaisie pour la harpe avec variationa [*sic*] sur la romance favorite de Joconde, composée et dédiée à M^r. Nicolo de Malte, par Charles Thibault. Prix 6 fr. à Paris, Chez Ch^{les} Bochsa Pere, auteur editeur et M^d de Musique Rue Vivienna No. 26, prez celle Faydeau, [1812-15]. Title-page + pp. 2-15. At head of music, p. 2: Fantaisie pour la harpe, sur la romance favorite de Joconde. Bibliothèque Nationale copy. Although for harp, it also works well on pianoforte. The fantasy functions as a long (3-page) introduction on the upcoming theme, long enough for one return of initial material and an excursion from the main key of D major to F major and other keys. The five variations are technically demanding for the performer, and are capped by an impressive cadenza and return to the initial material of the fan-

(1819),[98] commences with an elaborate introduction based on the upcoming theme. At times almost developmental, the music moves from the main key of G major to C minor, G minor, and D minor, and to a section in G major which, in sonata-allegro context, would have been a second theme. There is even a short section in E-flat major before the return to the principal key, cadenza, then simple statement of the theme.

Not only does the introduction of "Robin Adair" instill new quality into American piano music, but so do the variations. Each of the first two variations has its own characteristic treatment--the first, 16th triplets; the second, written-out mordents in 32nds. Both hands quickly move from one register to another, and frequently cross (Ex. 3-99).

Ex. 3-99.   Charles Thibault, "Robin Adair," var. 2, meas. 1-2.

Short cadenzas precede the final measures of both these variations. By contrast, such rhythmic activity ceases in variation 3, Andante, in

---

tasy. My thanks to Dr. Martha D. Minor for obtaining a copy in Paris.

98. Robin Adair with introduction, variations & finale, for the piano forte, composed and dedicated to Miss Fanny Laight by Charles Thibault. Copy right secured. All copies signed by the author. New York, published by the author. To be sold at Meetz's Music Repository Broad-Way. Valotte's Music Store William St. Riley's Music Store Chatham St. and at the author's Provost Street. Price $1.50 cts. [1819]. Title-page + pp. [2]-12. At bottom of p. [2]: Engrav'd and printed by E. Riley 29 Chatham Street New York. Manuscript inscription at the top of title-page: To Mr H. K. Sowell this book is presented with sincere esteem by the author Ch^s Thibault. Wolfe 9337 (unlocated). American Antiquarian Society copy (courtesy of Arthur Schrader)--the first of a bound volume of ten works by Thibault.

which there are several striking modulations: C major, F major then F minor, to A-flat major. The A-flat enharmonically becomes G-sharp, the third of E major--of which the leading-tone D-sharp serves as the new tonic of E-flat major. Its subdominant A-flat chord then functions as a lowered submediant in the return to C major. Such command of chromatic and enharmonic modulation is unusual in the United States before 1830.

The main feature of the fourth variation is a sustained trill, not difficult to perform except that the trill also appears in the middle of three voices at the beginning of the second half. Pianistic difficulties increase in the following "Minore agitato" variation 5, in A minor, with a more extensive cadenza toward the end. The trend continues with variations 6-7, this last ("Brillante") having virtuoso 32nd-note passagework for the right hand. The finale, with meter changed to 6/8, begins as the last variation, then continues freely into an exciting coda, still based on "Robin Adair." In this, Thibault's first American set of variations, a new standard of pianistic and compositional musicianship was established.

Thibault retreated somewhat from such brilliant pianism in his next publication, variations on an unidentified "Russian air" (1820).[99] Its introduction, again based on the principal theme, is shorter (27 measures, versus the 62 measures of "Robin Adair"). Passagework of 16th triplets ("Commodo") in variation 1 is succeeded by 32nds ("Brillante") in variation 2. The next, based on the dotted march rhythm, is coupled with a constant change of register not used by other composers for this type of variation (Ex. 3-100).

Ex. 3-100. Thibault, "Russian air," var. 3, meas. 1-4.

99. Russian air with an introduction and variations, for the piano forte, composed and dedicated to Miss Cornelia Juhel, by Charles Thibault. Price 1 dollar. Copy right secured. New York, published by W. Dubois at his Piano Forte and Music Store No. 126 Broadway, [1820]. Title-page + pp. 2-9. Wolfe 9338 (unlocated). Duke University copy.

Variation 4 is permeated with a figure of four 32nd notes, the last three of which are repeated (changing the thumb and first fingers). Relief from passagework is provided in the siciliana of variation 5, but a bariolage figuration of 32nds in the right hand of variation 6 is demanding enough for an alternate to be provided "for those who have small hands." The principal motive of the final variation ("Fieramente") is a five-note ascending or descending scale in 32nds, similar to one variation in Arthur Clifton's "Original Air" published the same year (see above).

Unfortunately, "Le Souvenir," op. 7 (1823; Wolfe 9339), for piano or harp, does not represent his best writing, perhaps due to the repetitions of phrases within the a a b a theme, or due to the limitations of the harp. The last variation (unnumbered, but the sixth), a march with the direction "fieramente," is more representative of Thibault's flair (Ex. 3-101).

Ex. 3-101. Thibault, "Le Souvenir," var. 6, meas. 1-8.

Thibault better shows his fine skills as composer in "L'Esperance, a fantasia with variations on a French theme," op. 8, published in 1824-25 (Wolfe 9331). It was one of the several Thibault piano works also published, in abridged form, by *The Harmonicon* (London, 1828).[100] The high quality is already noticeable in the two-page introduction, based on the first measure of the upcoming theme. Of pianistic interest are virtuoso flourishes in the right hand, and a cadenza just before the theme; of harmonic interest is a modulation from the tonic D major to the unrelated F major. When the key returns to D, it is D minor, soon touching B-flat major. A motive, imitated between the soprano and tenor, is used for the return to D major (Ex. 3-102).

Ex. 3-102. Thibault, "L'Esperance," introduction, meas. 31-35.

For the first variation, the melody is elaborated with broken chords; for the second the theme in the left hand is accompanied by a consistent figure in the right (Ex. 3-103).

Ex. 3-103. Thibault, "L'Esperance," var. 2, meas. 1-4.

---

100. The 45-measure introduction is reduced to 4; variations 3, 5, and 6, with transitions, are omitted; and the 41-measure coda is condensed to 18 measures.

The usual pattern of variations is broken after the second when Thibault introduces an extra section ("con fuoco") in B minor. The same material reappears as a transition from the B-flat major of variation 5--in sequence through G minor, A minor, and B minor, to the regular D major of the next variation. The "marcia" variation, no. 4, is pianistic (Ex. 3-104), like his "Greek March of Liberty," nos. 1-2. The coda is a continuation of variation 6, combining some of its characteristics with a touch of variation 2.

Ex. 3-104. Thibault, "L'Esperance," var. 5, meas. 1-8.

The variations on Kalkbrenner's air "La Bretonne," op. 9 (1824; EAKM no. 31) is Thibault's finest, and probably ranks as one of the best of the period. The introduction, rather than being aimless flourish, is based on a melody, given once and then again in a new guise. The rhythm of the theme is previewed in a brief transition. The theme, also with a a b a form, is nevertheless more interesting than that of "Le Souvenir." Thibault already provides an unusual aspect at the end of the first variation: a short section in the relative minor. Variation 2 features repeated unisons or octaves in the right hand, slightly changed to include a trill figure upon its return at the end. The third variation, a pastorale, is among his best piano writing; it, too, includes an extended section in the relative minor at the end, then a repeat of the initial treatment of the variation. Variation 5 is a waltz; Thibault adds an extension to the "b" part before the return to "a." The variation unobtrusively slips into a coda (meas. 251) which brings the whole set to a conclusion.

Denis-Germain Étienne

Another product of the Paris Conservatory was Dennis-Germain Étienne (1781-1859), who had won first prize in harmony and accompaniment in 1800. He moved to New York City in 1814 or 1815 and had a career as pianist there and in other cities into the 1850s. He was also one of the first players in the New York Philharmonic in 1842, both as pianist and horn player. Unfortunately only two of his compositions have thus far been found: *Battle of New Orleans* (1815; see chapter 5) and "O! Pescator dell' onda, a Venetian barcarolle varied for the piano forte," published in the period 1828-34.[101] It is not near the quality of those by Thibault. This is not to suggest that Étienne's set is not technically demanding; in spite of scale passages in 32nd notes (as high as f''''), his treatment in each variation is consistently applied without relief, and there is almost no harmonic variety. A metronome marking is provided for all variations. The binary theme is uneven in phrase length--3 + 5 measures--the structure of which is kept in almost all of the twelve variations. (The one exception is variation 9, in the parallel minor mode, where the repetition of the initial three measures, in C minor, is shifted to its relative major of E-flat.) The introduction is short. Not until the extensive coda (67 measures), a continuation of variation 12, does Étienne manage to break from the restriction of the theme to venture to other keys, most notably B major. Obviously he must have been a fine professional pianist, but his potential as composer is not realized in this work.

---

101. O! Pescator dell' onda, a Venetian barcarolle varied for the piano forte, and dedicated to Miss Juliette Burgière by D. Etienne. Pr. 75. New York, published by Dubois & Stodart, No. 167 Broadway, [1828-34]. Title-page + pp. 3-11. Library of Congress copy.

Joseph C. Taws

An impressive Philadelphian composer is Joseph C. Taws, who wrote a modest amount of piano music including two sets of variations. It is difficult to separate him from his father, Joseph Charles Taws (also spelled "Tawes" or "Tawse"). The father arrived in the United States from Scotland in 1786, almost the same year as another prominent Philadelphia musician, J. George Schetky, also from Scotland. "Charles" Taws is best known as a maker and dealer of pianos and organs as well as a teacher of piano and theory. Two sons, James B. and Lewis, were also instrument makers.[102] One of Charles' organs was the three-manual instrument built for St. Augustine's Catholic Church about 1800,[103] presumably the one that Benjamin Carr's *Voluntary for the Organ* (EAKM no. 5) inaugurated. Charles Taws also sold sheet music in 1807-14, and published a few pieces in 1813-19.[104] "Joseph C." Taws is undoubtedly his son "Joseph Carr Taws," to whom Benjamin Carr willed "Bach's Fugue."[105] Joseph C. Taws for a time kept a bachelor's house with Schetky and Carr, and all three were founding members of the Musical Fund Society in 1820.[106] Perhaps Taws was taught by his namesake, Carr. Joseph C. Taws was also involved in the publication of a collection written in honor of Lafayette's visit in 1824, including his own "Pennsylvania Lafayette March."[107] Inexplicably, nothing is known of him after 1824.

The first of Joseph C. Taws's variation sets is on Queen Hortense's melody "The Knight Errant," published about 1821 (Wolfe 4347). The set is not of the quality of Peter K. Moran's on the same tune, which appeared at the same time. Most of the five variations treat the theme with broken chords or 16th-note scale patterns; the most enterprising pianistic device is the crossed left hand in a few places. The fourth variation is in the character of a march, labelled

---

102. Robert A. Gerson, *Music in Philadelphia* (Philadelphia: Theodore Presser, 1940; reprint, Westport, Conn.: Greenwood, 1972), 45.

103. Orpha Ochse, *The History of the Organ in the United States* (Bloomington: Indiana University Press, 1975), 80.

104. Wolfe, pp. 1134, 1160, 1168.

105. The will is quoted in Ronnie L. Smith, "The Church Music of Benjamin Carr (1768-1831)" (D.M.A. dissertation, Southwestern Baptist Theological Seminary, 1969), 293-95.

106. Louis C. Madeira, *Annals of Music in Philadelphia and History of the Musical Fund Society* (Philadelphia, 1896; reprint, New York: Da Capo, 1973), 53, 67.

107. Wolfe 4657. See also my article "American Musical Tributes of 1824-25 to Lafayette: A Report and Inventory," *Fontes Artis Musicae* 26, no. 1 (1979): 17-35.

"en Militaire."   In keeping with the purpose of *Carr's Musical Miscellany in Occasional Numbers* (of which this is no. 49), the "Knight Errant" variations must have been intended for the piano student or amateur.

Taws's "Air with variations for the piano forte with an accompaniment for the flute or violin and violoncello" [1820][108] is suitable for piano alone, but probably works better with the other instruments.   The theme is a waltz, coincidentally with the same harmonic structure as "Ach du lieber Augustin."   Taws incorporates a full repertory of devices; "scherzando" with dotted rhythms in the first variation, 32nd-note scales through two octaves or more in the second variation, duple meter in the third, hand-crossing in the fourth, "brillante" arpeggios in the fifth, "cantabile" parallel tenth scales in the sixth, "alla polacca" for the seventh, "con brio" 32nd-note scales for the left hand in the eighth, the relative minor key in the ninth-- followed by a cadenza--and a change to duple meter for the tenth variation.

On the other hand, Taws's "Fantasie in which is introduced the favorite Scotch air of They're a' noddin with variations for the piano forte as performed at M. Aime's concerts" (1824; Wolfe 9212) is definitely a concert piece, written for a professional pianist.   The work has Musical Fund Society connection; it was "composed & most respectfully inscribed to Dr. W. P. Dewees, President of the Musical Fund Society of Philadelphia," and the copy in the Driscoll collection at the Newberry Library has a manuscript inscription to the sister of Taws's fellow-member: "for Miss C[aroline] Schetky with the Authors best respects."

The extensive (29-measure) introduction, of a virtuoso nature, is based on the initial three-note motive of the upcoming theme. Already in the sixth measure the key changes from G major to E major--with E minor used as well.   Broken diminished-seventh chords are more typical of Taws's younger contemporaries Chopin or Liszt than of most American music from the 1820s (Ex. 3-105).

Ex. 3-105.   Joseph C. Taws, "They're a' noddin," introduction, meas. 26-28.

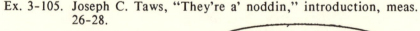

---

108.   Wolfe 9209.   Taws gave a public concert in New York City on 2 July 1824, including this work as well as the "They're a' noddin" variations (see below); Delmer D. Rogers, "Public Music Performers in New York City from 1800 to 1850," *Yearbook for Inter-American Musical Research* 6 (1970): 21-22.

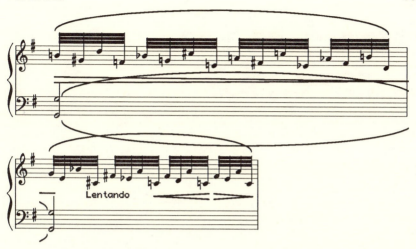

For variation 1, the melody is broken up into 32nd notes; in the second variation the melody is capped with an additional line by the crossed left hand (Ex. 3-106). In the midst of the prevailing rhythm 16th-32nd-32nd in variation 3, Taws suddenly inserts an imitation of the bagpipe (Ex. 3-107).

Ex. 3-106. Taws, "They're a' noddin," var. 2, meas. 1-4.

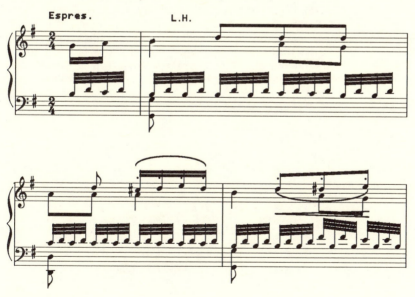

Ex. 3-107. Taws, "They're a' noddin," var. 3, meas. 9-10.

Several touches of adventuresome harmony are found in the next two variations; one in variation 5 foreshadows the style of barbershop quartets (Ex. 3-108). In variation 6, the theme in the alto, if accented by the thumb of the right hand according to the rhythm of the original tune, results in a new texture rarely seen in piano music of its time. The sixteen-measure theme is expanded to twenty measures in the minor variation, the ninth, to accommodate excursions from G minor to A-flat and E-flat major. The character variation is the tenth-- "Polacca"--with the typical 3/4 rhythm: 8th-quarter-8th-8th-8th.

Ex. 3-108. Taws, "They're a' noddin":

  a. Var. 4, meas. 1-2.

b. Var. 5, meas. 8-10.

The "Fantaisie" of the title must refer to the extensive coda, consisting of over five pages of the thirteen pages of music in the original publication. The coda represents almost another set of variations, but without the restrictions in form, melody, and key of variations 1-10. After a brief modulatory transition, the opening portion of the theme receives a treatment in G minor, then A-flat major. An Andante section has the complete theme in the left hand, in E-flat major, accompanied by a florid right hand--sometimes with 64th notes--ending with an uncommon cadence (Ex. 3-109). The following Allegro would likewise have the complete theme, in G major, except that there is no return of the last "a" in the original form a a b a. The next section, in E minor, with triplet 16ths, has only the initial "a a." A short statement in G major leads to this abrupt change of key (Ex. 3-110). The theme is complete in the E-flat major section. For the following Allegro (marked "Brillante"), in G, the first nine measures represent an almost exact return of the treatment in variation 3, as do the succeeding nine measures of variation 1. The characteristic of variation 3 again resumes for two eight-measure segments, the last even more climactic, with an augmented-sixth chord resolving to the opposite mode (Ex. 3-111).

Ex. 3-109. Taws, "They're a' noddin," coda, meas. 44-46.

Ex. 3-110. Taws, "They're a' noddin," coda, meas. 88-93.

Ex. 3-111. Taws, "They're a' noddin," coda, meas. 117-23.

On the basis of this one work, Joseph C. Taws deserves praise as a native-born composer with high qualities similar to the foreign-trained professional immigrants Meineke, Clifton, and Thibault. If Taws was the student of Benjamin Carr, great credit is also due to the teacher.

Frederick A. Wagler, Miss R. Brown, "A Lady," Maria Penniman

Besides those of Meineke, Darley, and Taws, a third set of variations on "They're a' noddin" was composed by the Washington musician Frederick A. Wagler (dates unknown). Its most important aspect is that it was a part of the collection of lithographs of music by Henry Stone published in 1823--apparently the first in this country.[109] Although the set is his most ambitious published piano work, Wagler's seven variations are quite undistinguished.

---

109. For the contents of the collection, see Wolfe 2002; Wagler's variations are cited as Wolfe 9557. The University of Kansas music library has the Stone collection, complete except for pp. 53-64. In Wolfe's listing of contents, the second item, "Coleridge's song of peace," is on pp. 6-7; p. 8 contains a "Waltz." Meves's "Within a mile of Edinburgh" is on pp. 65-68, not 65-72. The items missing in the Library of Congress and New York Public Library copies are: pp. 73-82, "Ei, ei, mein liber Augustin," by I. L. Wellin of Vienna (theme and 15 variations); pp. 83-84, "The harp of love, sung in the character of Frances in The Spy, composed and arranged by R. Willis"; pp. 85-89, "Juvenile improvement, I. C. Calcott" [*sic*]; p. 90, "Three Waltzes," Woelfl. Further on these lithographs: Edward N. Waters, "Music," *Library of Congress Quarterly Journal of Current Acquisitions* 16 (November 1958): 24-26; Edith A. Wright and Josephine A. McDevitt, "Henry Stone, Lithographer," *Antiques* 34 (July 1938): 16-19.

After the early set of variations by Mrs. Van Hagen, none by women composers was published until the late 1820s. An otherwise unidentified Miss R. Brown apparently played variations on a Scotch air in a Boston concert on a harp, and these were published in an arrangement for harp or piano.[110] In the theme section, added small notes in the tenor are supposedly meant for the piano; directions "Ettouffe" in variation 1 and "Harmonic" in variation 3 are for the harp. The set is undoubtedly more successful for the harp; there is little of interest for the pianist. The variations in Miss Isabella Nixon's "Rose of Lucerne"[111] have style-markings "Pastorale," "Scherzando," "Legato" (the fourth variation is unmarked), "Marcia; Brillante." The second half of the "Scherzando" variation features one-octave finger slides.

The only other instance of the slide in variations is near the end of "Oft in a stilly night," coincidentally by a woman composer but identified only as "A Lady."[112] In this case, the slide ranges over two octaves, and serves as a transition from the fifth variation, in C minor, back to the tonic C major of the coda. (The only other American precedent for the slide is the double slide, in sixths, in the battle sec-

---

110. Scotch Air, with variations as performed by Miss R. Brown on the harp at the Boston Concerts, arranged for the harp or piano forte by G. Adams. Boston, published by James L. Hewitt & Co. at their Music Store No. 36 Market Street, [1826-29?]. pp. [1]-3. Another issue, with the same title information but with different plates, has the imprint: Boston: published by C. Bradlee Washington Street, [1827-34]. New York Public Library copies. I have been unable to further identify the melody, but the first 4 measures, taking away the dotted rhythm, are almost identical to "Polly put the kettle on."

111. The Rose of Lucerne, arranged with variations by Miss Isabella Nixon. New York, published by Dubois & Stodart 167 Broadway, [1828-34?]. Pr: 38: pp. [1]-4. Brown University copy. The New York Public Library has the following, probably by a different composer with the same surname: The Victoria Waltz, air, with variations for the piano forte, composed & inscribed to Miss Augusta Browne (of Philadelphia), by Mrs. Nixon, Cincinnati. Pr 50 C. New York, published by Dubois & Bacon, 167 Broadway, [1835-37]. Title-page + pp. 2-5.

112. Oft in a stilly night, with variations for the piano forte, by a Lady. Philadelphia, published and sold by Geo. Willig 171 Chesnut st, [1827]. Price 50 cts. pp. 1-5. At bottom of p. 1: Entered according to the acts of Congress April 23d 1827 by T. Birch of the State of N.Y. Fred J. Betts Clerk of the S.D. of N.Y. At the bottom of pp. 2-5: Oft in a stilly. Var. At bottom of p. 5: Engr^d by T. Birch. Brown University copy. This set of variations is reproduced in Judith Tick, *American Women Composers before 1870*, Studies in Musicology, 57 (Ann Arbor: UMI Research Press, 1983), 67-71. The melody is Scotch, as arranged by John Stevenson (see Wolfe 8921-26).

tion of Carr's *Siege of Tripoli*.) One of the other variations is somewhat challenging: the 1½-octave arpeggio accompaniment and several
32nd-note runs in variation 2. The ubiquitous "Marcia" appears as
variation 3.

One of the most unique sets of variations was written by a 13-
year-old girl: "German Waltz with nine variations for the piano forte,
composed by Miss Maria Penniman, at the age of thirteen years, pupil
of Mr. F. C. Schaffer," published in Boston in 1821 (Wolfe 6940).
What is even more unique is that Miss Penniman was blind. About
four years later she became the pupil of Anthony Philip Heinrich, who
wrote a 24-page duet for her, "The Minstrel's Entertainment with his
blind pupil, or a divertimento for 4 hands on the grand piano forte,
dedicated to Miss Maria Penniman" in *The Sylviad* (1825, no. 5).
Even discounting the help Miss Penniman may have had in composing
her "German Waltz" variations, they are not any worse than other sets
written by well-established "professors of music." The theme itself
consists of two eight-measure halves, yet there is an additional eight-
measure section added to all variations but nos. 2, 3, and 8. Traditional techniques are used, such as adding different accompaniments,
surrounding the theme with extra figuration, or (for variations 5 and
7) assigning the theme to the tenor voice. The last variation is a
march. Miss Penniman must have been extraordinary at the keyboard
if she could accurately perform variation 4 with its treacherous hand-
crossing (Ex. 3-112).

Ex. 3-112. Maria Penniman, "German Waltz," var. 4, meas. 1-5.

Anthony Philip Heinrich

Heinrich himself wrote only one set of piano variations before
1830, on Haydn's familiar "God save the Emperor" melody. The
variations form the first part of a collection of pieces with the general
title "The Minstrel's Petition, or a votive wreath for the piano-forte;
humbly presented to Her Majesty Charlotte Augusta, Empress of

Austria," in *The Dawning of Music in Kentucky* (1820), available in modern reprint.[113] The performer is directed to proceed directly from the variations to the other works in the "votive wreath": five minuets, an Austrian Landler, "The Fair Traveller, of the Post-Ride from Prague to Vienna, a descriptive waltz," and a lengthy "Empress March." However, the "Emperor" variations are quite self-sufficient, especially since the five minuets and the waltz "are more especially intended for the Violin."

The "Emperor" variations are the only American ones on Haydn's melody, and are the most ambitious, even eccentric, ones written before 1830. Haydn's unadorned setting is given as the theme. In a break with tradition, the meter is changed to 3/4 and the mode from G major to G minor for variation 1. In effect, this variation, marked "Mesto, alla Introduzione," is a free treatment, standing in place of a free introduction. Although Heinrich does not stray from the G-minor tonality for long, there is a momentary shift to A-flat before the cadence to the dominant for the end of the first phrase (Ex. 3-113). In general, Heinrich follows the outline of Haydn's melody and harmony, a half-measure of the theme being expanded to a full measure in 3/4.

Ex. 3-113. Anthony Philip Heinrich, "God save the Emperor," var. 1, meas. 6-9.

113. Pp. 216-50; Wolfe 3620. The variations are on pp. 219-26. *Dawning* is reprinted as Earlier American Music, 10 (New York: Da Capo, 1972). The variations are also edited by Neely Bruce in "The Piano Pieces of Anthony Philip Heinrich Contained in *The Dawning of Music in Kentucky* and *The Western Minstrel*" (D.M.A. dissertation, University of Illinois, 1971), 270-86.

However, for the second phrase, the last two measures of the original theme are compressed into a flurry of 16th-note decoration (Ex. 3-114).

Ex. 3-114. Heinrich, "God save the Emperor," var. 1, meas. 12-14.

The main notes of the third phrase are well-hidden in the tenor (meas. 15-17), the c''-sharp d'' accompanied by 32nd notes "con licenza" (Ex. 3-115).

Ex. 3-115. Heinrich, "God save the Emperor," var. 1, meas. 17-19.

The first half of the fourth phrase receives a chordal treatment, separated with further 32nd-note passagework (meas. 20-22); the second half is almost completely buried in Heinrich's imaginative pianism (meas. 23-26), as is the entire fifth and last phrase (meas. 26-31). The remaining of the variation is a coda which is an elaboration on the tonic G; it ends on a thick G-minor chord positioned below the bass staff. The outbursts of 32nd-note activity, the minor mode, and the descent toward the end results in effective somberness. This is Heinrich at his impassioned best.

Haydn's formal and harmonic outline are retained in variation 2, which is the identical length of the theme. The prevailing rhythm, into the second phrase, is 8th-16th-16th. The theme, however, is quickly buried, and one finds its notes only with difficulty (Ex. 3-116).

Ex. 3-116. Heinrich, "God save the Emperor," var. 2, meas. 5-8.

In the last half of the third phrase, the theme's notes begin to appear clearly in the top voice. For the last phrase, the theme is at first on the bottom of the left-hand figuration, then the top (Ex. 3-117).

Ex. 3-117. Heinrich, "God save the Emperor," var. 2, meas. 16-18.

The surprise comes at the end, when the right hand descends to *G'* below the staff and the left hand rises to *g"*--the hands are crossed, five octaves apart!

Variation 3 begins conventionally, the theme intact on top accompanied with 16th-note accompaniment. Beginning with the second phrase, however, the theme is buried in the manner of variation 2. The formal pattern is broken in his treatment of the third phrase; two measures substitute for the original four. (Heinrich previously avoided representing the same phrase in variation 1.) As if to compensate, an extra measure is added to the fourth phrase; the variation is nineteen measures long instead of twenty. In the fourth phrase the theme constitutes a part of the right-hand figuration, migrating to the left (Ex. 3-118). The opposite occurs for the last phrase. The prevailing motives in the variation are parallel thirds or sixths, and repeated 16th notes--this last figure often beginning on the note above.

Ex. 3-118. Heinrich, "God save the Emperor," var. 3, meas. 10-14.

Syncopation is the unifying device for variation 4, either of 8th notes or of 16ths. The theme is included in the left-hand chords for the first two phrases, then migrates from one hand to the other thereafter. In the twentieth measure the marking "alla Cadenza" signals a free section ending on a D dominant chord with a three-measure trill on top and chromatic figuration underneath. This cadence leads directly to the last variation in which the undisguised theme consistently appears in the left hand for the first four phrases, on top for the last. Rapid crossing of the right hand occurs in the first three measures. The main motive for the rest of the variation incorporates four 16th notes, the first of which is tied from the previous beat (Ex. 3-119).

Ex. 3-119. Heinrich, "God save the Emperor," var. 5, meas. 14-16.

The rhythm quickens toward the end, continuing into the seven-measure coda. Except for one subdominant, the coda has only dominant and tonic chords. These are juxtaposed in one bizarre passage. At first, right and left hands agree on these two chords, then they disagree for a measure until the coordination resumes (Ex. 3-120).

Ex. 3-120. Heinrich, "God save the Emperor," var. 5, meas. 21-23.

     If some American composers of the 1820s may be criticized for
repetitiveness, overuse of stock figuration, occasional exhumation of
the anachronistic Alberti accompaniment, and lack of novelty, Heinrich certainly is not guilty. The "Emperor" variations are not in the
mold established in Europe by Czerny and Gelinek; instead, Heinrich's
fondness for disguising the theme is more akin to the serious variations
of Beethoven, Schumann, and Brahms. The "Emperor" variations do
not lack in virtuosity, nor passion, nor imagination. This music was
not intended for the amateur pianist, nor the popular concert hall. It
makes extraordinary demands on both performer and listener, and is
far ahead of its time. Eccentric works of Ives took nearly a half-
century to be accepted by performers and audiences after they were
written. Heinrich's works are now available in modern reprint; perhaps they too will revive after more than a century and a half of
neglect.

4

A Potpourri of Medleys

The public concert of the late 18th and early 19th centuries was not the serious occasion which is often presented today. Music was still considered to be a form of entertainment. Modern-day counterparts are the informal concerts by the Boston Pops and other orchestras, and concerts by the town band on a summer evening. Both types still include arrangements of various popular tunes known as the medley.

Oscar Sonneck's study *Early Concert-Life in America* furnishes testimony from early newspapers that the medley was a prominent part of 18th-century American concerts as well. Examples of medleys on late 18th-century programs are: "Medley, familiar airs on the Piano Forte, Mr. Vogel" (Baltimore, 16 April 1798); "The Concert to conclude with the Federal Overture [by Carr]" (Norfolk, 7 October 1796); "Pot-pourri of Marshall, on the Forte Piano" (Norfolk, 17 April 1797); and "A Medley on the Pianoforte, Mr. Guenin" (Philadelphia, 3 March 1795).[1]

Benjamin Carr

A modest, yet significant, number of publications of medleys further reveals that they were also played by amateurs, at home. The first published American medley was *The Federal Overture, as performed at the Theatres in Phil[a]delphia and New York, selected and compose[d] by B. Carr*, which appeared in 1794.[2] The sections in *The Federal Overture* are:

---

1. Sonneck, *Early Concert-Life*, 57, 60, 61, 142.

2. Facsimile reprint with an excellent essay by Irving Lowens (Philadelphia: Musical Americana, 1957). The essay was reprinted, with corrections, in Lowens's *Music and Musicians in Early America* (New York: Norton, 1964), chapter 5.

	meter	*key*	*tempo*
[introduction, based on "Yankee Doodle"]	¢	E*b*	Spirito
No. 1 Marseilles March	¢	G	[Andante]
No. 2 Ca ira	¢	G	[fast]
[transition]	C	g-E*b*	Larghetto
No. 3 O dear what can the matter be	6/8	E*b*	Slow
No. 4 The Irish washer woman	6/8	G	[fast]
No. 5 Rose Tree [from Shield's *Poor Soldier*]	2/4	G	Andante
No. 6 La Carmagnole	6/8	G	Allegro
[transition]	C	G-c	Larghetto staccato
No. 7 Presidents March [by Phile]	2/4	E*b*	[Maestoso]
No. 8 Yankee Doodle	(2/4)	E*b*	Allegro
No. 9 Viva Tutti	(2/4)	B*b*	[Allegro]

As revealed by Irving Lowens, the political significance of *The Federal Overture* is that it contains several tunes associated with the Federalists--"President's March" and "Yankee Doodle"--and several symbols of anti-Federalism: "Ça ira," "La Carmagnole," and "Marseilles Hymn." The remaining are politically neutral. Carr was attempting to unite in this medley the symbols of the Federalists and the anti-Federalists. The last tune, "Viva tutti," was known with the words "Here's a health to all good lasses," and was discovered by Donald Krummel to come from Pietro Guglielmi's 1772 opera *Il carnovale di Venezia*.[3] *The Federal Overture* is important in the history of American music because it contains the first American printing of "Ça ira" (the expression is attributed to Benjamin Franklin) and "Yankee Doodle."

In a medley, the composer simply selects and arranges the popular tunes. A variety of meters, tempos, and keys (as indicated in these summary content lists) seems to have been important. Usually the introduction and transitions furnish the only opportunities for display of skill. For his introduction, Carr used "Yankee Doodle" in this manner, following the opening flourish (Ex. 4-1). The original performances of *The Federal Overture* were by instrumental ensembles, described as a band or orchestra; the publication is an arrangement for pianoforte. (Indeed, perhaps all of these medleys were originally intended for orchestra.[4])

---

3. Donald W. Krummel, "'Viva Tutti': The Musical Journeys of an Eighteenth-Century Part-Song," *Bulletin of the New York Public Library* 67, no. 1 (January 1963): 57-64.

4. "Whether James Hewitt's potpourris, *New Medley Overture* (1799-1800) and *The New Medley* [sic] *Overture* (1801-02), published for piano, are reductions of orchestral scores is uncertain; probably such piano scores, of which a large number appeared during the Federal era, served as the basis for ad hoc orchestrations depending on the instrumental resources at hand." *The New Grove Dictionary of*

Ex. 4-1.   Benjamin Carr, *The Federal Overture*, meas. 1-6.

In several passages what must have originally been string tremolos (in which a note is played with rapidly alternating bow) is transferred as the keyboard tremolo, in which notes of a chord are rapidly alternated (Ex. 4-2).

Ex. 4-2.   Carr, *The Federal Overture*, meas. 22-24.

The same kind of writing, with the opening flourish, returns in the transition between tunes 2 and 3. The transcription is not particularly demanding on the accomplished pianist, with the possible exception of one measure near the end of the introduction (Ex. 4-3).

American Music, s.v. "Orchestral music."

Ex. 4-3.   Carr, *The Federal Overture*, meas. 49-50.

The ending of *The Federal Overture* is not quite as simple as the above list of tunes might indicate. The "Yankee Doodle" section includes, as cadential material, an imitation of change ringing. The familiar bell-scale is called "rounds," the falling third pattern "Queens" (Ex. 4-4).

Ex. 4-4.   Carr, *The Federal Overture*, meas. 308-16.

The tune "Viva tutti" lasts only 25 measures; the section continues with a return of "Yankee Doodle," in E-flat, then with contrasting material in C minor based on "Yankee Doodle." *The Federal Overture* concludes with a da capo to the "Yankee Doodle" section, including the change ringing. The combination of the familiar tunes and the well-organized formal scheme at the end are factors which must account for the success of this medley in performances for several years after its premiere in 1794.

In a manuscript at the Library of Congress, attributed to Benjamin Carr on the basis of the handwriting and the signature "BCarr" on the first page, is a work entitled *Medley Overture* which is undoub-

tedly by Carr.[5] The work is unusual because of its great length--
longer than any other American medley--and because, with one
exception, it uses concert music for its sources rather than popular
tunes. The score is generous for its designation of instruments, and
might be considered a short orchestral score even though it is entirely
playable on the keyboard. In common with Carr's *Federal Overture* are
the same familiar bell peals in nos. 3 and 18 of the following list of
contents (the item numbers are editorial):

		meter	*key*	*tempo*
1.	[introduction, including indication "Horns & Clarinets"]	C	C	Spirito
2.	[untitled]	(C)	F	Andantino
3.	[untitled, followed by "Tutti with Bells"]	(C)		All°
4.	[untitled, a duet labeled "Hor[n]"]	3/4	B*b*	Mod[erato]
5.	Tutti [in the form A B da capo]	[2/4]	B*b*	"same time"
6.	[transition]	[C]	g	Adagio
7.	[untitled, "Bassoon" l.h., "Hautboy" r.h.]	3/4		Pathetic
8.	[untitled, two bass clefs, "violincello"]	C	d	Slow
9.	[untitled]	[6/8]	F	Allegro
10.	[untitled, "Hautboy" r.h., "Piano Forte" l.h.]	2/4	B*b*	Andantino
11.	["Tutti"? "vio solo"]	[C]	B*b*	Andante
12.	Horns. A set of Hunting Notes. The Call in the Morning.	6/8	C	
13.	Tutti [introduction material]	C	C	All° Con Spirito
14.	[untitled; "Bassoon Solo"]	[C]	F	Moderato

---

5. The manuscript is cataloged as ML96.C28 case. The complete
contents:

		meter	key	tempo
15.	[introduction material]	[C]	F	Allegro Con Spirito
16.	[Haydn, Symphony 53 in D "L'Impériale," 2nd movement, theme and variations 1 and 5; "Piano Forte"]	2/4	A	Andante
17.	Minuet & Trio [3rd movement from the same Haydn symphony, but without the trio]	3/4	D	Allegro
18.	[untitled; "Trumpets" r.h., "Kettle Drums" l.h., interspersed with "Bells" material of no. 3 and "Tutti with Bells"; midsection with "Pizz." and "col arco" directions, followed by "Da Ca[po]"]	[C]	D	Pomposo
19.	[Handel, Organ Concerto in F, op. 4, no. 4, 2nd movement, meas. 1–8, 37–40, 53–56; "solo organo"]	(C)	B♭	Andante
20.	[transition; B♭, ending on E dominant chord]			Larghetto
21.	[untitled]	3/2	C	Affetuoso
22.	[Malbrook; "Clarinetts & Horns"]	[6/8]	C	All°
23.	[untitled, followed by direction "The Next Movement more Stately"]	3/8	C	Slow
24.	Fortis°. with Trumpets & Kettle Drums	3/4	C	more Stately

Pot Pourri Ecossois, in which is introduced several of those Scotch Melodies sung by Mrs. French, Mr. Phillips &c, arranged for these numbers, was published in 1820 as *Carr's Musical Miscellany in Occasional Numbers*, no. 63. Carr, as editor of the series, probably arranged this medley; that there is little original material may have been the reason he left his name off. The short introduction is only seven measures long.

	meter	key	tempo
Introduction, based on "Maggy Lawder"]	C	C	Moderato
Auld Lang Syne	2/4	C	
Moggy [Maggy] Lawder	C	C	
Auld Robin Gray	(C)	F	
The White Cockade	2/4	F	Allegro
Robin Adair	3/4	C	[Andante]
Reel	C	C	Moderato
Oh Nanny [wilt thou gang with me, by Charles Thomas Carter]	(C)	C	Slow

Bruce's Address [= Scots wha hae wi' Wallace bled]	(C)	(C)	Bold
Roy's Wife	(C)	C	Affetuoso
Reel	C	C	[Allegro]

A bit of virtuosity, typical of Carr, appears at the end of the "Robin Adair" section (Ex. 4-5).

Ex. 4-5.   Carr, *Pot Pourri Ecossois*, meas. 85-89.

John Christopher Moller

The term "medley" for a loose collection of popular tunes is already used for an early piece, *Meddley with the most favorite Airs and Variations* (1795-97; EAKM no. 3) by John Christopher Moller. It has several movements; perhaps some of the untitled tunes were well-known at the time, but these remain thus far unidentified. The work begins with a 6/8 Moderato, in C major and binary form, succeeded by a duple-meter Allegro which is constructed like the exposition of a sonata-allegro movement. The Allegro has two contrasting themes, using the tonic and dominant keys. The initial 6/8 section is then literally repeated, and eight measures of the Allegro return--this time in A minor. Four measures in A major lead to the siciliano in A minor which ends with an extensive cadenza. The concluding air and five variations of this piece is on the tune "Je suis Lindor," on which Mozart had also written a set of variations, K. 299a.[6] *Meddley* has aspects of three of the important keyboard forms of the time: sonata, variations, and medley. It is like no other American work of the period.

James Hewitt

James Hewitt wrote more medleys than any other American composer of the time. His first, *The New Federal Overture*, published in 1797 (EAKM no. 5) was undoubtedly given this title to contrast with the popular *Federal Overture* by his friend and music publishing colleague Benjamin Carr. (Hewitt bought Carr's publishing establishment in New York City in 1797, and each sold the music published by the other.) The contents are:

	meter	key	tempo
[introduction]	¢	d	Largo
Yanky [sic] Doodle	2/4	D	Allegretto
French air	3/4	d	Andante
Presidents March [by Phile]	2/4	D	Maestoso
Air in Rosina [by William Shield]	6/8	D	Allegretto
Allemand	2/4	d	Allegro
French air	C	D	Andante
Oui noir mais pas si diable	2/4	G	Allegro
Ca Ira	(2/4)	G	[Allegro]
Pauvre Madelon [by Samuel Arnold]	C	G	Andante
Airiette	6/8	D	Gayment
Washingtons New March	¢	D	Maestoso
[Yankee Doodle]	2/4	D	[Allegretto]

There are two more tunes than in Carr's *Federal Overture*, and Hewitt uses three of the same ones: "Yankee Doodle," "President's March," and "Ça ira." The style of the introduction is not unlike the introduction of a Haydn symphony; the sudden appearance of "Yankee Doodle"--instead of the usual symphonic first theme--after the dominant cadence would be startling to a modern audience. The unbroken string of no fewer than five French melodies, with a sixth

---

6. Other titles on the same melody in the *National Tune Index* (hereafter abbreviated as NTI): "Vous l'ordonnez," "Serenade du Barbier de Seville," "Air in the Spanish Barber," "Romance," "The Spanish Barber," "Tell tale eyes can ne'er dissemb."

near the beginning, shows a definite anti-Federalist (pro-French republic) bias, although these are surrounded by the two President's marches and "Yankee Doodle." "Washington's New March" is unique, and apparently was not published elsewhere (Ex. 4-6).

Ex. 4-6.   James Hewitt, *The New Federal Overture*, meas. 277-80: "Washington's New March."

The federal overtures of Carr and Hewitt are related in more ways than title and tunes. Near the end of Hewitt's *New Federal Overture* is a coda based on "Yankee Doodle," borrowed almost exactly from the introduction to Carr's *Federal Overture* (Ex. 4-7), as well as "rounds" (compare with Ex. 4-4).

Ex. 4-7a.   Hewitt, *The New Federal Overture*, meas. 338-end.

Ex. 4-7b.   Carr, *The Federal Overture*, meas. 15-18.

The title of Hewitt's next medley describes the setting for performances of this type of work: *A New Medley Overture, as performed
at the Theatre with Great Applause, selected and composed by J. Hewitt*
(published by Hewitt in New York, B. Carr in Philadelphia, and J.
Carr in Baltimore in 1799-1800; Sonneck-Upton, 323). Again, the
introduction resembles the opening of a symphony, this time up to the
point where a contrasting second theme is expected. The audience
instead hears "Hail Columbia," now so-titled since Joseph Hopkinson's
text was applied in 1798 to Philip Phile's "President's March." Hewitt
incorporates melodies which represent a wide mixture from theater and
national origins, framed with American patriotism:

	meter	key	tempo
[introduction]	¢	C	All. con spirito
Hail Columbia [by Philip Phile]	2/4	C	[Maestoso]
Way worn traveller [from Samuel Arnold's *The Mountaineers*]	2/4	C	Allᵒ
Within a Mile [of Edinburgh, by James Hook]	C	C	Andante
Black joke [an Irish tune]	6/8	C	Allᵗᵒ
[transition]	C	a	Largo
Scotch Air [also known with the title "A Galic Air," first line beginning "Dear Myra, the captive ribband's"]	C	A	Andante
French Air	2/4	A	Allᵒ.
[unidentified tune]	6/8	A	Allᵗᵒ.
Hey dance [to the fiddle and tabor, Irish tune from *The Lock and Key* by William Shield]	6/8	F	[Allegretto]
Scots Air	3/4	F	Adagio

Governor Jay's March [by Hewitt]	¢	C	[Maestoso]
[Yankee Doodle]	6/8	C	[Allegro]

An almost identical title, not to be confused with the above, is *The New Medly* [sic] *Overture*, "as perform'd at the Theatre with Great Applause, selected and composed by James Hewitt" (1802; Wolfe 3762). (One version is available in the Wagner ed., no. 7.) The introductory material is the most extensive of any published medley, and the beginning (if not borrowed from some other composer) is Hewitt at his best (Ex. 4-8).

Ex. 4-8.   Hewitt, *The New Medly Overture*, meas. 1-7.

The section is followed by a short Allegro maestoso section, in octaves, which in turn is suddenly succeeded by more serious music (Ex. 4-9).

Ex. 4-9.   Hewitt, *The New Medly Overture*, meas. 29-32.

This, of course, is lifted directly from Mozart's Piano Concerto in D minor, K. 466, and Hewitt provides the entire orchestral exposition.[7] As in *A New Medley Overture*, the first quoted tune is "Hail Columbia."

	meter	key	tempo
[introduction]	C-¢	d	Largo-- Allº. maestoso
[Mozart, Piano Concerto, opening]	(¢)	d	[Allegro]
Hail Columbian [sic] ["President's March" by Philip Phile]	2/4	D	[Maestoso]
The Blue Bell of Scotland [attributed to Dorothea Bland Jordan]	C	D	[Andante]
Scotch Reel	¢	D	[Allegro]
Highland Reel	(¢)	D	[Allegro]
When pensive [I thought of my love, from Michael Kelly's *Blue Beard*]	6/8	D	Andante
[Garry Owen]	6/8	G	[Allegro]
Sweet passion of love [by Michael Arne]	3/4	G	[Andante]
[free material, or an unidentified tune]	6/8	G	Allº.
[Garry Owen]	(6/8)	A	[Allegro]
Yankee Doodle	6/8	D	[Allegro]
Pipe de Tabac [by Pierre Gaveaux][8]	2/4	D	Allᵗᵒ.
[coda]	C	D	Allº.

The coda--almost one page long in the original publication--is an impressive piece of original writing by Hewitt, with a strong unison beginning, an effective buildup in the middle, and an exciting ending.

Hewitt's *Pot pouri* [sic], printed in Carr's *Musical Journal for the Piano Forte* in 1800-01 (nos. 38 and 40, pp. 25-32), available in modern reprint, is the first printed medley in the United States with that name. (Hewitt wrote another with the same title, correctly spelled, described below.) It is also the first to include a keyboard

---

7. The quotation from Mozart is not included, nor cited, in the edition by Wagner. He obviously used another imprint, Wolfe 3763. Also, he misidentifies the tune "Garry Owen" as "Irish Washer-woman."

8. "Tobacco was immortalized by James Hewitt's *Pipe de tabac* in the early 1800s" (*New Grove Dictionary of American Music*, s.v. "Advertising, music in").

version of "Malbrook" (now known with the words "For he's a jolly good fellow"). The introduction is, again, the equivalent of the beginning of a symphony--up to the second theme--and prefaced with a thirteen-measure Largo. The setting of Kelly's "When pensive I thought of my love" is similar, but not identical, to the one in *The New Medly Overture*.

	meter	key	tempo
[introduction]	¢-C	d-D	Largo--Allegro molto
Sigh no more Ladies [Shakespeare text; unidentified melody]	¢	A	[Allegretto]
Let the Sultan Saladin	¢	a	[Allegretto]
[Monsieur] Nong Tong Paw	6/8	A	Allegro
When Pensive [I thought of my love, from Michael Kelly's *Blue Beard*]	(6/8)	E	Andante
Malbrouk [*sic*; followed by a 24-meas. transition modulating from A minor to G major]	(6/8)	A	[Allegro]
Blaise et Babet [from the opera by Nicholas Dezede, but not from the Overture]	(6/8)	G	[Allegro]
[untitled]	¢	g	Allegro
["The Harriott"?, followed by 8 measures in G minor, ending on a B♭-major chord]	2/4	G	Allegro
The Wounded Hussar [by Hewitt, followed by an 11-measure transition]	C	E♭	Andante
Malbrook	6/8	C	Allegro
Poor Mary [not the song by Carr]	3/4	A	[Andante]
[untitled]	2/4	A	[Allegro]
March in Pizzaro [by Hewitt]	¢	D	[Maestoso]
[untitled; "Rough and smooth"?--NTI]	6/8	D	[Allegro]

Two of the untitled sections are the most interesting. The one in G minor features momentary imitation between the treble and bass; if the tune is Hewitt's own it does him credit (Ex. 4-10). The Allegro in A major certainly is original since it is quite pianistic (orchestral?) in style, and modulates to several related keys (Ex. 4-11).

Ex. 4-10.   Hewitt, *Pot pouri*, meas. 236-40.

Ex. 4-11.   Hewitt, *Pot pouri*, meas. 371-79.

What is surprising about Hewitt's *Scotch Medley*, which he published in 1804,[9] is that he used none of the 132 tunes in *The Caledonian Muse* (1798; Wolfe 10183), "printed and sold at B. Carr's

---

9. Wolfe 3775. The American Antiquarian Society copy is complete; but that at the Library of Congress, in which the bottom third of the folio for pp. 1-2 is missing, has the names of the 7th and 9th tunes written only in manuscript, not printed. In both copies the redundant 6th measure of p. 2 is crossed out by hand.

Musical Repository, Philadelphia; J. Carr's, Baltimore; and J. Hewitt's, New York"--in turn obviously taken from John Aitken's *The Scots Musical Museum* (Wolfe 10170) of the previous year. Hewitt's contribution as composer is modest; he added only a short eleven-measure introduction and an even shorter coda, and there is little need for modulatory transitions.

	meter	*key*	*tempo*
[introduction]	3/4	F	Larghetto
Nae gentle Dames	6/8	C	Vivace
My love is but a Lassie yet	2/4	C	Vivace
O Misk Misk [NTI: "Oh open the door, Lord Gregory"]	3/4	a	Larghetto
Duncan Gray [came here to woo]	C	A	All^{to}.
My Patie is a lover gay [title: "Corn riggs are bonny"]	C	A	[Allegretto]
She['s] fair & Fause	6/8	a	[Andante]
O my love like the Red Rose	2/4	F	[Allegretto]

Olla Podrida, the Spanish equivalent of the French *pot pourri* (both literally meaning "putrid pot"), is the title of a series of three medleys by Hewitt also published in 1804 (Wolfe 3757-59). Hewitt's contributions to *Olla Podrida No. 1* are modest; there is no introduction and only a short coda.

	meter	*key*	*tempo*
The Island [by Charles Dibdin]	6/8	G	Allegretto
Since Kathlean has prov'd so unkind [= "Since Kathleen has prov'd so untrue," from Shield's *The Poor Soldier* (1782); the correct meter is 9/8!]	6/9	G	[Allegretto]
Beneath a Green Shade [a lovely you, Scotch tune]	3/4	G	Andante
March	C	D	[Maestoso]
Tink a kink [= Tink a tink, from Kelly's *Blue Beard*]	2/4	G	[Andante]
Joe Anderson my Joe [= John Anderson my Jo]	C	g	Andantino
Scotch Reel	6/8	e	[Allegro]
My Nannie O [1st line "While some for pleasure pawn"--Scotch tune]	C	e	Adagio
Laly [i.e., "Lady"] Spencer's Allemande [NTI: "Lady Charles Spencer's Fancy"]	2/4	G	[Allegro]

By contrast, *Olla Podrida No. 2* is more demanding of the pianist, indicating that the entire set of three was originally intended for keyboard and not an arrangement of music first composed for a theater orchestra.

	meter	key	tempo
Allen a Roon [other Irish titles: Eileen Aroon, Ellen a Roon; Scotch: Robin Adair]	3/4	D	Andantino
Duncan Davis [= Duncan Gray]	2/4	G	[Allegretto]
[untitled; perhaps "Master Jackey"]	(2/4)	D	[Allegro]
Les Visitts	(2/4)	D	[Allegro]
[My boy Tammy, Scotch tune]	C	d	Lanto [Lento?]
Rondo des Visitandines	6/8	D	[Allegro]
The way worn traveller [from Samuel Arnold's *The Mountaineers*]	2/4	D	[Allegretto]
March	¢	D	[Maestoso]
Waltz	3/8	D	[Allegro]
[coda]	(3/8)	D	[Allegro]

The virtuosity follows the dominant chord at the end of "Rondo des Visitandines" (Ex. 4-12).

Ex. 4-12.   Hewitt, *Olla Podrida No. 2*, meas. 127.

Olla Podrida No. 3 is the most amazing of all Hewitt's medleys, due to the ambitious nature of its introduction, which is 2½ pages long in the original publication. In most aspects, the introduction is in sonata-allegro form, lasting well into a development. The usual key scheme, however, is backwards, since the prefatory twenty-measure Largo is in the key of C major, the Allegro moderato immediately following in C minor. This first theme section ends on a C-major chord which seems to function as dominant of F major. Yet a modulation, not without some awkwardness, leads to the second key area of A-flat major (Ex. 4-13).

Ex. 4-13.   Hewitt, *Olla Podrida No. 3*, meas. 40-48.

The most elegant theme of the A-flat section is the second (Ex. 4-14). After a strong cadence, the key abruptly changes to the original C minor, then the keys of F and A-flat major. The manipulation of first theme material and these modulations are characteristic of a development. The section ends with C-major chords, and these function as dominant to the F-major key signature and a new theme. After fifteen measures, the first quotation, "Washington's March," is heard--unless the introduction is also derived from some pre-existent symphony or sonata.

Ex. 4-14. Hewitt, *Olla Podrida No. 3*, meas. 58-61.

	meter	key	tempo
Introduction			
[introduction, meas. 1-20]	C	C	Largo
[1st theme and trans., meas. 21-44]	₵	c	Allegro moderato
[2nd theme section, meas. 45-66]		A*b*	
[development, meas. 67-87]		c-F-A*b*-F	
Major [new theme, meas. 68-103]		F	
Washington's March [I]	₵	F	[Maestoso]
Red Cross Knight [by J. W. Callcott]	(C) (C)	B*b*	
The Friar of Orders Grey [by Callcott]		F	Adagio
Polly put the Kettle on	2/4	C	[Allegro]
Oh Lady Fair [by Thomas Moore]	2/4	C	Moderato
Giles Scroggin's Ghost [by Reeve]	2/4	a	[Moderato]
Tid re I [or The Marriage of Miss Kitty O'Donovan to Mr. Paddy O'Rafferty]	6/8	A	[Allegro]
[midsection]	2/4	a	Moderato
[Tid re I]	[6/8]	A	Allegro
[Giles Scroggin's Ghost]	2/4	a	Moderato
Hail Columbia [by Phile]	2/4	C	[Maestoso]
Governor Lewis's Waltz [by Hewitt, and coda]	3/8	C	[Allegro]

Hewitt's last published medley, *Pot Pourri* (1818-20; Wolfe 3768), not to be confused with his earlier--and misspelled--*Pot Pouri* discussed above, is one of his least interesting. The introduction begins with octaves of potential quality, but there is lack of variety in their sequential repetition (Ex. 4-15).

Ex. 4-15.   Hewitt, *Pot pourri*, meas. 1-9.

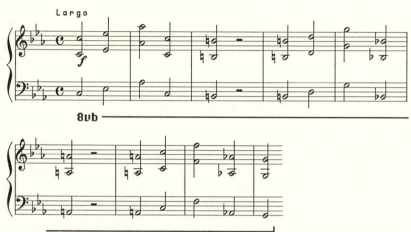

The rest of the section is static, and the harmonies consist mainly of tonic and dominant chords. In the string of tunes, the midsection of "Copenhagen Waltz" is titled "Bohemian Air." It is not labeled this way in other published single editions (see Wolfe 2085-88), but Hewitt adds new material after the "Bohemian Air" section, before the return of the main waltz tune, to create a sizeable segment lasting 2½ pages in the original publication. The one-page coda is based on "Copenhagen Waltz" material.

	meter	key	tempo
[introduction]	C	c	Largo
Mozarts Waltz	3/4	C	
March [Hewitt's "Governor Strong's New March"]	C	C	[Maestoso]
Robin Adair	3/4	F	
Lord Moira's Return to Scotland	C	F	All°
Copenhagen Waltz	3/8	F	
Bohemian Air	3/8	C	
[Copenhagen Waltz]	[3/8]	C	
[coda]	[3/8]	C	

Julius Metz

The last published "pot pourri" appeared a few years later: Julius Metz's *Petit Pot Pourri* (1821-23; EAKM no. 24). It contains some of the elaborate scales and other piano figurations typical of the period. The whole is unified by one meter (3/4) and tempo.

	key
Polonaise	C
Trifler Forbear [a polacca in Henry R. Bishop's *The*	G
Farmer's Wife--Wolfe 829-31]	
Like the gloom of night	C
No more by sorrow	C
[Polonaise, as at the beginning]	C

Metz's competence as a fine composer and pianist is obvious in the subtle change into the extension-transition after the first tune (meas. 23-38), the modulation to E-flat major after the G major of the second melody, and the general exuberance of his style.

Christopher Meineke

Pot Pourri is also the title used by Christopher Meineke for the earliest of his two medleys. It was published in Baltimore in 1807-09 (Wolfe 5803), within the first decade after Meineke had emigrated from Germany to Baltimore. In contrast to many of Hewitt's medleys, this one has no indications of a piano transcription from orchestral music. Like Moller's *Meddley*, discussed earlier, Meineke's has several returns of themes, and two of them are presented with at least one variation.

	meter	key	tempo
[introduction]	2/4	G	Allegro vivace
Away with Melancholy [Mozart's "Das klinget so herrlich" from *Die Zauber-flöte*]	¢	C	
[introduction material, varied]	(¢)	C	Allegro
March	2/4	C	[Maestoso]
Walz	3/8	G	
Walz [Ach du lieber Augustin]	3/8	G	
Italian Air [The Maid of Lodi, "collected by Mr. Shield when in Italy" (see Wolfe 8087), with one variation]	6/8	G	
Away with Melancholy [with four variations]	C	G	
[coda]	(C)	G	

The incorporation of variations for some of the tunes is likewise an important feature of Meineke's medley *Divertimento for the piano forte in which are introduced the favorite airs of Pipe de Tabac, Di Tanti Palpiti, and The Drunken Sailor or Columbus*, published in 1825 (EAKM no. 33). For example, the initial "Marcia" includes in its midst (meas. 21-28) a variant--the main melody broken up into 16th notes. Pierre Gaveaux's "Pipe de tabac" is presented with four variations, the rhythmic motion increasing from 8ths to 32nds. This section was published separately at the same time from the same set of plates (see chapter 2). The following "Waltz" is a thinly-disguised variation of "Pipe de tabac," but in D major instead of G major. "Di tanti palpiti," the melody taken from Rossini's *Tancredi*, receives no variation treatment, but substitutes an extensive excursion from the tonic G major to B-flat major (meas. 148-51), and provides another example of the high quality of compositional craftsmanship Meineke had acquired since his early years in Baltimore. (Probably this was a benefit of Meineke's trip to Vienna in 1817-19--the trip during which he is reported to have met Beethoven.) "The Drunken Sailor," also published separately at about the same time (Wolfe 5770), and discussed in chapter 2, is one of Meineke's most successful works. It shows imagination in breaking the pattern of the usual rondo or set of variations, in the use of modulations to distantly-related keys, and in the clever way the basic melody and rhythm is worked out. Meineke's *Divertimento* must have been a success on the concert stage; it rises far beyond the level of pedagogical and amateur music so common earlier in the century.

Meineke wrote one more medley in the 1820s: *The Rail Road, a characteristic divertimento for the piano forte; in which is introduced a variety of national and popular airs*, copyrighted in 1828.[10] The introduction consists of a musical shout (Ex. 4-16). The national airs are the "Star Spangled Banner" and "Hail Columbia"--each in short seven-measure statements--and "Yankee Doodle" with three variations and transition. The popular airs are "Polly put the kettle on" and a Waltz with trio. The remainder of the medley is "Rondo: Speed the Plough."[11] The form of the "rondo" is ABCDEAFGH-coda, the coda based on "A." The patriotic section is successful because of the composer's individual treatment of the familiar tunes; the arrangement of the remaining popular tunes is more commonplace.

---

10. Publication information: the title continues "composed by C. Meineke. Baltimore, published by John Cole. Price 75 Cents. Copy right secured according to Act of Congress. July 23rd. 1828 by John Cole of the State of Maryland." Title-page + pp. 2-8. Plate no. at bottom of pp. 2-8: 321. New York Public Library copy. The title-page has an engraving, signed "J. Sands Sc.," of a lady, with hat and parasol, and a gentleman with top hat and cane, looking at a departing railroad car ("Ohio" on the back, "Velocipede" on the side). In cartoon balloons, the lady says "Give my Love to all my nine Cousins and tell Aunt Polly that I'll drink tea with her in Cincinati [*sic*] tomorrow evening and bring the new bonnet and the gigot Pattern and the Flounces and All"; the gentleman says "Dont [*sic*] forget to drop my Letter in the Post Office at Wheeling so it may get to N. Orleans the next day."

11. No composer; see Wolfe 8482 and Sonneck-Upton, 406.

Ex. 4-16.   Christopher Meineke, *The Rail Road*, meas. 1-6.

Arthur Clifton

Arthur Clifton's *National Divertimento for the piano forte, in which are introduced Hail Columbia! with a new trio, and Yankee Doodle! with variations*, published about 1821 (Wolfe 1938)--pure musical patriotism--is more concentrated and effective. In the second half of "Yankee Doodle" the traditional lowered seventh scale degree, used since its first appearance in Carr's *Federal Overture*, is raised and the melody modernized (Ex. 4-17).

Ex. 4-17a. Carr, *The Federal Overture*, meas. 291-94.

Ex. 4-17b. Arthur Clifton, *National Divertimento*, meas. 75-78.

Clifton adds a touch of modernity in his chromaticism within variation 2 (Ex. 4-18).

Ex. 4-18. Clifton, *National Divertimento*, meas. 101-14.

Of the five variations, the character variation is the fourth, marked "Capricio," in the relative minor key of A.

Clifton's last medley, published about 1832-33, consists of a traditional patchwork of Scotch and Irish tunes. According to the title-page, *Medley Overture* was "originally composed for a full orchestra and arranged for the piano forte."[12] Clifton's contributions are largely restricted to the introduction and coda. The sections are:

	meter	*key*	*tempo*
Introduction	C	D	Larghetto [*sic*]
Scots wha ha'e [wi' Wallace bled]	C	D	Andante
O 'tis love	6/8	D	Allegretto
Lewis Gordon	2/4	D	Andantino
Paddy O'Rafferty	6/8	D	Allegro
Irish Lilt	6/8	G	[Allegro]
Cruckeen Laun	C	a	Andantino --Piu moderato
There's nae Luck [about the house]	(C)	A	Vivace
Reel of Tullochgorum	(C)	A	Vivace
Money in both Pockets	6/8	D	Poco piu lento
Young may moon	(6/8)	D	Piu moderato
Auld Robin Gray	C	D	Andante cantabile
Bonny Highland Laddie	C	D	Allegro
[coda]	(C)	D	vivace

William R. Coppock, Peter K. Moran

William R. Coppock furnished only one modest piece that has characteristics of the medley, *The Village Wake: petite brilliante divertimento for the piano forte*, published in the period 1827-31.[13]

------

12. Medley Overture; in which the following favourite airs are introduced: Scots wha ha'e wi' Wallace bled; Oh! 'tis love; Lewis Gordon; Paddy O'Rafferty; Irish Lilt; Cruskeen lawn; There's nae luck about the house; Tulloch Goram; Money in both pockets; The young May moon; Auld Robin Gray; and The bonnie highland laddie, originally composed for a full orchestra and arranged for the piano forte, by A. Clifton. Baltimore: published by John Cole & Son (Property of the Publishers). Title-page + pp. 3-11. Plate no. on pp. 3-11: 683. Library of Congress copy.

13. The Village Wake: petite brilliante divertimento for the piano forte by Coppock. New York, pub'd by Firth & Hall at their piano forte & music store 358 Pearl St. [2] pp. Bottom r.h. corner of p. [1]: E. Riley Engraver New York. New York Public Library copy.

The piece is entirely in 6/8 meter, marked "Vivace pastorale," and in C major. After a short three-part beginning, subsequent sections are marked "Bells," "Chime," and then perhaps the only quotation, "Hark the Bonny." A da capo marking indicates a return to the first section.

Peter K. Moran's sole contribution is *Honi soit qui mal y pense: Divertimento for the piano forte* (1830).[14] The principal tune, by George Alexander Lee, is joined by two others: the one marked "Rossini" is from the Tyrolean chorus in act 3 of *William Tell*; the other, "Weber," is the first number in act 1, scene 3, of *Der Freischütz*. "Honi soit" returns, followed by a coda of brilliant scales. This, with the extended transition to the Rossini section, represents the independent piano medley--not an arrangement of a work first heard by an instrumental ensemble. Moran's divertimento is also unified by centering on one key, F major, and by the presence of a single rhythm (three 8ths, 8th rest, quarter) to accompany all three tunes.

James F. Hance

Moran's *Honi soit* was not the only opera-oriented medley of the 1820s; Charles Thibault wrote several, but presented the operatic melodies in integrated pieces he termed "rondo" or "scherzo" (see chapter 2). James F. Hance issued two such pieces, both based on Rossini's *Il barbiere di Siviglia*. "The Opera Waltz" [1827][15] has much repetition and little imagination. Hance is partially redeemed by "Fragments from the opera Il Barbiere di Siviglia, arranged as a divertimento" (1827),[16] which at least has an introduction with two "fragments" and a dominant-seventh cadenza, leading to an arrangement of "Coro, mille gracie mio Signore."

These so-called "divertimentos" mark the fading of the piano medley as such in the United States after the 1820s. (A. P. Heinrich's *A Divertimento, di Ballo, for the piano forte, comprising a grand waltz, and galopade*, published in 1823-26 [Wolfe 3597], is not a medley but a suite of two dances, as indicated by the title.) One of the last is *The Constellation: popular airs founded on the same harmonies, selected,*

14. Honi soit qui mal y pense: divertimento for the piano forte, composed & arranged by P. K. Moran. Pr. 50. New York, published by Dubois & Stodart, No. 167 Broadway. Entered according to Act of Congress the thirteenth day of September 1830 by Dubois & Stodart New York. Title-page + pp. [2]-6. New York Public Library copy.

15. The Opera Waltz (The motives from Il Barbiere), arranged for the piano forte by J. F. Hance. New York, published by Dubois & Stodart, 149 Broadway, [1827]. pp. [1]-3. Library of Congress copy.

16. Fragments from the opera Il Barbiere di Siviglia, arranged as a divertimento for the piano forte, by J. F. Hance. New York, published for the author & sold at the principal music stores. Entered according to law by J. F. Hance March 23 1826, J. Dill clerk. Pr. 75 cts. Title-page + pp. [2]-7. Bottom of p. 7: Engrd by T Birch. Brown University and Washington University copies.

composed & arranged for the piano forte or harp, by J. F. Hance,
copyrighted in 1826.[17] Hance, as seen by the title, gathered several
tunes with the same harmonies, with this suggestion at the bottom of
the last page: "These pieces produce a delightful effect being performed together as a round on several Instruments, or as Duetts on
Harp and Piano." The pieces, all sixteen measures long, in triple
meter, and all based on simple tonic and dominant harmonies, are:

> Introduction (Moderato)
> Hungarian Air [= Hungarian Waltz]
> Tyrolese Air
> Ach du Lieber Augustine
> Vienna Waltz
> Sequel to the Vienna Waltz

Hance had previously written variations on the "Hungarian Air"
(Wolfe 3323). This is pure entertainment music. It isn't often that one
finds a keyboard piece in the form of a round!

---

17. Publication information: pp. [1]-3. At the bottom of p. [1]:
Entered according to law by J. F. Hance January 23[d] 1826 James Dill
clerk N.Y. At the bottom of p. 3: Engr[d] by T. Birch. Above the title
is engraved a lyre with an upward spray of light beams and ten stars.
New York Public Library copy.

5

EUROPEAN AND AMERICAN KEYBOARD BATTLES

In comparison with the mass, motet, sonata, concerto, and symphony, music historians have neglected the genre of battle music, in spite of the fact that battle pieces were written as long ago as the 15th century--the date of Heinrich Isaac's *A la battaglia*. Battle pieces for keyboard were apparently more popular in the first fifty years of the United States than was the hallowed keyboard sonata. As many as sixteen battle pieces by European composers were published in the United States between 1793 and 1828. Practically none of them, even the notorious one by Koczwara, is played or even known today. The composers themselves are unknown. The only battle piece given an occasional performance or recording is Beethoven's *Wellington's Victory*, but it is usually cited as an example of a lapse of taste by an otherwise master-composer. But this type of music can hardly be ignored by historians simply because modern tastes have changed.

European Battle Pieces

European pieces that were published in the United States have a number of features in common--battles usually follow the same general form.[1] Louis Emmanuel Jadin's *La Grande Bataille d'Austerlitz,*

---

1. Raoul Camus kindly shared a copy of a printed folded sheet from the München Staatsbibliothek entitled "Zergliederung eines vom Kapelldirektor I. F. Kloeffler gesetzten Instrumental-Tonstücks, eine Bataille vorstellend. Das Orgester wird in zwen Chöre getheilet" (Analysis of an Instrumental Piece Setting Forth a Battle Set by Ensemble-Director I. F. Kloeffler. The orchestra is divided into two choirs [sections]). The general formula is described in detail, including the overture, the entrance of the armies, the battle effects, the lament for the wounded, and the celebration of victory. The "Nachricht" at the end advertises that Kloeffler (of Bentheim-Steinfurth) will present his battle-piece on 3 January 1787, with two orchestras of 50 players, that had been successfully received in London, Berlin, Copenhagen,

surnommée La Bataille des Trois Empereurs (published 1808)[2] commences with a musical portrayal of "the dawn of day," and Karl Kambra's *The Battle off Trafalgar* (1808; Wolfe 4708) with "the sun rising." Victor Dourlen's *Bataille de Jena* (1807)[3] starts with the calling of the soldiers ("Sommeil des Soldats"). A march and at least one trumpet call is included in almost all of them, and about half include a cannon--the military kind, not the musical--usually depicted with a low chord or note. The second main section is the battle itself, where the composer shows his avant-garde imagination and the player is given an opportunity for virtuoso display. One unfortunate result of battles is that some of the participants inevitably are wounded or killed; therefore the third section, which is almost always present, is slow and usually chromatic, depicting the cries of the wounded or lamentation for the slain. The two exceptions are Dourlen, in whose battle the demise of Prince Ferdinand is substituted (complete with his last words), and Kambra, who portrays the shooting of Lord Nelson.

All battles are followed by shouts of victory or trumpet calls, then some celebration, usually a fast dance or march. The unidentified C. Ogilvy, of Tannadice (Scotland), wrote *The Battle of Waterloo*, which ends with a triumphal chorus--for voices!--stolen from Purcell. The text begins "Britons strike home, revenge your country's wrongs."[4] Another feature commonly found is the use of national songs. Franz Koczwara's *The Battle of Prague* (editions in the United States from 1793 and continuing throughout the 19th century; Sonneck-Upton, 39, and Wolfe 5097-5116) Jonathan Blewitt's *The*

Königsberg, St. Petersburg, and Moscow. What is more, the descriptive summary, in printed form, will be available free to the audience.

2. Wolfe 4594. The piece was first published in Paris in 1806, "dédié à S A. I. Monseigneur le Prince Joseph, grand électeur de l'empire." Georges Favre, *La Musique française de piano avant 1830* (Paris: Didier, 1953), 61, 69.

3. Wolfe 2544. The "Military" Finale was also printed in Carr's *Musical Journal for the Piano Forte*, vol. 5 [1803-04], no. 110, pp. 15-16--Wolfe 2545. Dourlen also wrote a *Bataille de Marengo, sonate militaire pour le piano-forte*, op. II [2], published in 1801--Favre, 118.

4. This piece was printed in the United States from 1818 (Wolfe 6634) until at least 1899, with authorship changing to the original arranger, "G. Anderson, organist"--or with neither name. The final chorus was likewise sometimes dropped, so that the work would end with the "Lamentation for the slain." Strangely, I found no British edition at Cambridge University, the Bodleian Library, and the British Library. Nor is it located (as of 1985) at St. Andrews University, the University of Aberdeen, or the National Library of Scotland, according to Elizabeth Ann Frame of the first of these Scottish institutions.

Battle of Waterloo (1816-18),[5] and John Gildon's *The Victory of Salamanca* (1812-14; Wolfe 3026) use "God save the King." *The Battle of Jena* (1807-09; Wolfe 2888) by Georg Friedrich Fuchs includes "Malborough s'en va t'en guerre" (the tune also known as "Malbrook," and now with the words "For he's a jolly good fellow"). Kambra's *Battle off Trafalgar* appropriately has "Rule Britannica." François Devienne includes the "Marseilles," "La Carmagnole," and "Ça ira" in *The Battle of Gemappe* [Jemappes] (1796; Sonneck-Upton, 37) and Philipp Jacob Riotte's *The Battle of Leipsic* (1818)[6] quotes Haydn's national anthem. *The Bastile* (1793; Sonneck-Upton, 37) by the unidentified composer Elfort ends with the same "Go to bed Tom" that is also quoted in Koczwara's *Battle of Prague*, and then a solo song "Short be ever the possession, short and hateful be the reign of Tyranny's unjust oppression . . ." and chorus beginning incongruously with the text "Isle of Liberty and beauty Ireland still be this thy share."

Almost all of these battle pieces include descriptions of the story in the printed editions. In the American editions, the descriptions are in both French and English in Bernard Viguerie's *The Battle of Maringo/Bataille de Maringo* (1802; still in print in 1870)[7] and in Jadin's battle, only in French for Dourlen, and the rest in English. Joseph Mazzinghi's *Battle of the Nile* (1807; Wolfe 5662) has no text at all, but seems to follow the same general plan of the other pieces in effects and tempos.

These battle pieces are not easy to play. Considering that most keyboard music printed in the late 18th and early 19th centuries in America was intended for amateurs, one may ask why these pieces were printed at all. Perhaps there were some accomplished amateur performers. Many kinds of special keyboard techniques depict drums, guns, bullets, swords, galloping horses, and the confusion of battle. In Koczwara's *Battle of Prague*, the Prussians attack, with the right hand, the left-hand Imperialists (represented by an Alberti bass). Prussian cannons are fired by crossing the right hand over the left for isolated low notes. Rapid descending scales in the treble represent "flying bullets," and sword attacks are rolled chords in the right hand accompanied by "horses galloping" (triplet Alberti bass). Heavy cannonfire is depicted by rapid rising scales in the left hand and general rifle fire in the right. Kambra's *Battle off Trafalgar* and *The Conquest of Belgrade* (1795; Sonneck-Upton, 87) by Schroetter (J. H.

---

5. Wolfe 880. The "Triumphal March" toward the end (p. 11) is the same music as in Blewitt's *Battle of Waterloo*, p. 5, in the midst of the battle, where it is captioned "Genl. Bulow Entering The Field To Aid Prince Blucher."

6. Wolfe 7500. The original title: *Die Schlacht bei Leipzig*.

7. Wolfe 9479-85. Recorded by Neely Bruce in *Piano Music in America*, vol. 1: *19th Century Popular Concert and Parlor Music* (Vox SVBX 5302, 1972). The piece was originally published in Paris in 1800, as op. 8 (Favre, 119-20).

Schroeter?) also feature crossed hands for cannons. Devienne wrote repeated-notes *A* against *b*-flat to represent the marching of advancing infantry. One special effect by Viguerie is the X'd circle, **Ⓧ**, a sign for a tone cluster--stretching the hands on all the keys of the lower three octaves. The fermata was similarly used by Heinrich Simrock in *The Battle of Wagram* (1810),[8] but such an effect is not found again until the "experiments" of Charles Ives. Extended passages of diminished-seventh chords in Elfort, Viguerie, and Kambra depict the fury of battle or the wounding and killing of troops.

Such usage foreshadows by a number of years an important component of the harmonic vocabulary of Liszt and others. In Blewitt's battle, a written-out low trill in octaves gives the sound of "the drums beat to charge," or the "rolling of drums" in Jadin. Blewitt's right-hand tremolos are the musical equivalent of the clashing of swords, and his unique effect is the ascending two-octave thumb-slide found in the section describing the flying enemy. When the enemy is "repuls'd and beaten," right-hand arpeggios gradually descend, diminuendo--a device previously used by Viguerie.

Simrock pictures running fire by rapid repeated notes ascending two octaves. For another of his techniques, the right hand alternates in 8th notes the octaves *A* and *a*, against which "the cannon should be express'd, with the left hand, by pressing the notes indistinctly and holding them during the four bars to give effect." In Gildon's piece, the news of *The Victory of Salamanca* is celebrated in London by rockets, musically shown by ascending two-octave scales in 32nds, and pictorially above the score by ascending broken lines separating into explosive bursts at the top.

Most of the battle sections of these pieces follow no standard musical form, but represent the events portrayed. Fanfares and marches are placed as the story unfolds, and the battle sections are free fantasies using a variety of keys. A few battle sections, however, show traces of sonata-allegro form. The "Battle" section in *The Battle of Jena* by Fuchs has a syncopated first theme in F major and a contrasting second theme in the dominant key of C major. After a busy development (presumably representing the thick of fighting), there are representations of "Cavalry," "the Emperor change[s] his position," "Charges," "Retreat of the Prussians . . . with the Swort [*sic*]" ("Slower Chasse mouvement"), "Groans of the Wounded" (still *à la chasse*), and the quote of "Malbrook" (cited above), comes a complete recapitulation of both themes, in the tonic key.

For another example, the first theme section, in D major, of Devienne's *Battle of Gemappe* describes "Cavalry advancing," and the "attack" section takes the place of a second theme section in the dominant key. After a "development" with key signature of one flat, the recapitulation is only of the "attack" material. The "movement"

---

8. Wolfe 8255. I used Wolfe 8255A (unlocated): The Battle of Wagram, a favorite sonata for the piano forte, by H. Simrock. New York, printed & sold at J. Willson Musical Repository 62 Broadway, [1812]. Title-page + pp. 2-10. Brown University copy.

ends on the dominant, leading to the "complaint and cries of the wounded."

Likewise, the battle section in Kambra's *Battle off Trafalgar* follows the identical key pattern--D major, A major, a "development" with a one-flat signature, then a return to D major and thematic material from the first key area. The section is interrupted when Lord Nelson is shot with a German augmented-sixth chord. The battle resumes in the tonic key without the return of previous themes.

Except for the earliest two, the battles represented by the European pieces represent the conflicts associated with the French Revolution and the Napoleonic wars. The *Battle of Prague*, the first of the genre discussed here, concerns the successful attack in May 1757 by Frederick II, the Great, and his Prussian forces against the men commanded by Charles of Lorraine, brother-in-law of the Holy Roman Empress Maria Theresa. Unexplained in Koczwara's piece is the section of Turkish music, or the quotation of "God save the King"-- except that he wrote it about 1788 for a London public. Schroetter's *The Conquest of Belgrade* is motivated by the taking of the city, occupied by the Turks, by the Austrian army on 8 October 1789. Devienne's *Battle of Gemappe* represents the offensive authorized by the French Revolutionary National Convention on 6 November 1792 against the Austrians at Jemappes, located west of Mons in Belgium-- the first successful battle of the new government.

Mazzinghi's *Battle of the Nile* describes the defeat by Admiral Sir Horatio Nelson of the French ships on 1-2 August 1798, thereby dooming the planned French conquest by Napoleon of the Middle East. The *Battle of Maringo* by Viguerie concerns the contest at Marengo, in northern Italy, in which the army of Napoleon, then first consul, defeated the Austrians on 14 June 1800. After this success, Napoleon returned to Paris to take both military and political charge of France.

Napoleon, since crowned Emperor, suffered a setback by his navy in the *Battle off Trafalgar* (music by Kambra), near Gibraltar, on 21 October 1805, by the British navy under Admiral Nelson, who died as a result but certain of his victory. This ended the naval power of France in favor of the supremacy of the British navy for another hundred years. Napoleon was victorious, however, in December of that same year. A coalition of the Russian Alexander I and the Austrian Francis II were defeated in Moravia in *La Grande Bataille d'Austerlitz, surnommée La Bataille des Trois Empereurs* by the third emperor, Napoleon. One result was the formal abolishment of the Holy Roman Empire the following year. The battle music is by the French composer Jadin.

Further Napoleonic battles are represented by Dourlen's *Bataille de Jena* and Fuchs's *Battle of Jena* in Germany on 10-14 October 1806, in which the French were victorious over the Prussian army of King Frederick William III. However, Napoleon did not win the *Battle of Wagram* against Archduke Charles Louis, brother of the Austrian Emperor Francis I, near Vienna on 5 October 1809. The musical depiction is by Simrock. Several months later, Napoleon signed the Treaty of Schönbrunn ceding 32,000 square miles of Austrian territory.

The British army under Lord Wellington, in combination with Portuguese and rebel Spanish forces, conquered the French army in the *Victory of Salamanca* in northern Spain on 22 July 1812; the musical description is by Gildon. Another defeat for the French was Napoleon's at the *Battle of Leipsic, or the Liberation of Germany* in October 1813 against the Prussian General Gebhard von Blücher and the Swedish Crown Prince Jean Bernadotte, along with the Russians from the east led by General Levin Bennigsen. The composer for this work is Riotte. Napoleon's final defeat, of course, was the *Battle of Waterloo* in Belgium, by the British under the Duke of Wellington and the Prussian army led by the same Prussian General von Blücher, on 16-18 June 1815. The British composers commemorating this important event in battle pieces were Blewitt and Ogilvy.[9]

American Battle Pieces

The same features are also found in battle pieces by American composers during the same period.[10] They use low notes or chords to represent the sound of cannons, and have trumpet calls, shouts or acclamations before or after the fight, and a section of grief for the wounded. The American author Thomas Hastings was well aware of battle pieces, according to his book *Dissertation on Musical Taste* (1822). In the section "Of the Imitative," he wrote:

> If his piece is a battle, for instance, each of its
> movements must have a conspicuous title placed over
> it: and the particular battle the composer had in
> view, and the leading circumstances attending it,
> must be made known to us before we are sure of
> comprehending his meaning, or forming any ade-
> quate conception of his design. The style of a march
> indeed is so well settled, that we can readily imagine
> from it that some section of an army is in motion;
> and the trumpet of victory may also tell of conquest.
> The imitations of the groans of the wounded may be
> so pathetic, and so different from all the rest of the
> piece, that we can easily imagine the field of battle

----

9. There must be a long list of European battle pieces concerning this event. One example, found by Raoul Camus at the Bibliothèque Royale, Brussels: La Grande Bataille de Waterloo, ou de la Belle-Alliance (fait historique), composée pour le piano-forte, et très-humblement dédiée a Son Altesse Roijale Le Prince d'Orange, Prince Héréditaire du Roijaume de Païs-Bas, par son très-obéissant et très dévoué serviteur D. F. Ruppe, Mâitre [*sic*] de Chapelle à l'Université de Leide, oeuvre XXIII. Leide: auteur, n.d. Title-page + pp. 3-19. The final two sections are "Air Anglais National" (God save the King) and "Hurrah des Prussiens pour saivans."

10. Julia Elmira Henning, "Battle Pieces for the Pianoforte Composed and Published in the United States between 1795 and 1820" (D.M.A. document, Boston University, 1968), chapter 3, consists of an analysis of the American battle pieces.

to be covered with the distressed victims of the conflict. But *who* were the vanquished? In *whose camp*
was heard the trumpet of victory? and which army
and what section of it, was in motion? Here we are
left in entire uncertainty. Had each army a style of
musick perceivably different from the other--could
the march, the trumpet of victory, and even the
groans of the wounded, be all given in a style pecu-
liarly national; the composer might then advance one
step farther in his representation: and were each
division of the contending armies furnished with its
peculiar musical dialect, a second step might be
gained. Still it would be necessary for us to understand all these varieties of style, before we could
fully comprehend this musical designer with the aid
of an interpreter.

What is here wanting is supplied in dramatic
musick by the action of the plot and by scenick representations. . . . Under such circumstances, the
musician is sufficiently furnished with interpreters.
We have become so interested in the plot, that if he
now gives us the march, the trumpet of victory, or
the groans of the wounded, we readily imagine their
particular application.[11]

Still, the specific method with which these musicians presented battle
pieces to an audience is not clear. Were there placards? Did an
assistant speak the captions as they came along? Did the performer?
Was the action pantomimed? Answers to these questions have yet to
be answered.

Filippo Trisobio

The first extant battle piece by an American resident is
apparently *The Clock of Lombardy, or the Surrender of Milan to General Buonaparte* (1796-98), composed by Filippo Trisobio and published by him in Philadelphia (Sonneck-Upton, 65-66). The composer,
who had come to the United States from London only two months
after the battle, having previously been in Lisbon, was probably
Italian. He died in Philadelphia in 1798, two years after he arrived.
Strictly speaking, this is not a battle piece, since the surrender took
place without fighting. Napoleon entered Milan in May 1796 after
defeating the Austrians nearby at the Battle of Lodi Bridge. This
"capriccio for the piano forte" therefore has no battle scene; instead,
the main movement is the seventh section below, consisting of four
variations.

    1. Allegro maestoso: Entry of General Buonaparte
       into the Milanese Territory

---

11. Hastings, 113-14.

2. Adagio: General Buonaparte Convokes the Corps
    of Officers of his Army to communicaet [*sic*]
    his orders
3. Largo: The City of Milan intimidated at the
    sight of the army orders the great bell of the
    Senate to be rung--Great confusion and Con-
    sternation
4. Presto: The Senate resolves to dispatch an
    Estasette to General Buonaparte to learn his
    Intentions
5. Presto: General Buonaparte reads the Dispatch
    Signed by the Intendant of the Senate
6. Allegro: The General answer[s] in two words[:]
    money and the Castle
7. The Band plays during the General repast
8. Allegro: The Troops under arms
9. Quick March to take Possession of the Castle
10. Moderato: The Garrison open[s] the Gates of the
    Castle and present their arms to General
    Buonaparte--No. 9 repeated
11. Minuetto: General Buonaparte satisfied with the
    Submission of the Milanese, orders a Grand
    Entertainment in which the Gentry dance
    Minuets
12. Allegro: The Soldiery with the Country Girls in
    the dance peculiar to the Country Allessandrina

One section unique to the battle repertory is the second--an
instrumental "Recitativo ad Libitum." Otherwise, the music has little
to commend it.

James Hewitt

The first piece about an American battle was James Hewitt's
Battle of Trenton (Wagner ed., no. 33);[12] the original edition (1797)
includes a title-page showing a likeness of its dedicatee, General
Washington. This is the famous battle in which Washington and his
troops crossed the Delaware on Christmas night, 1776, and surprised
the Hessians, capturing them with a short fight. An early quotation is
"Washington's March" (Sonneck's Group I, sometimes given in early
editions with the title "Washington's March at the Battle of Trenton").
The "attack" section, with the traditional cannons and bombs
represented by low notes in the bass played by the crossed right hand,
resembles sonata-allegro form in some aspects. The first-theme section
in D major is succeeded by new material in A major, then A minor
and F major. There is no clear beginning of a development section; a

---

12. Abridged in Carl Engel, comp., and W. Oliver Stunk, ed.,
Music from the Days of George Washington, 8-21; this is the edition
used for the recording by E. Power Biggs, *The Organ in America*
(Columbia MS 6161, ca. 1960).

contrasting passage "begging quarter" in D minor substitutes. A quasi-recapitulation occurs with the caption "the fight renewed." The "grief of the Americans for the loss of their comrades killed in the engagement" quotes the Scotch folktune "Roslin Castle," frequently associated with funerals. (Somehow Hewitt got his information wrong: no Americans were killed, two were frozen to death, and only four wounded.) "Yankee Doodle" is given with an imitation of drums and fifes. The final Allegro is a complete ABACADA rondo.

The Battle of Trenton, published by Hewitt, however, never indicates that he actually composed it.[13] It has just been discovered[14] that most of the music was actually adapted from another battle piece, published in Edinburgh about five years earlier: *The Siege & Surrender of Valenciennes* by Natale Corri (the uncle of Philip Antony Corri/Arthur Clifton).[15] Even Hewitt's title-page is a mirror-copy of Corri's, with the addition of Washington's head between the flags and an angel holding a wreath over the head. Hewitt's "Army in Motion" is Corri's "Assembling of the Combined Armies," "Acclamation of Americans" was originally "Acclamation of the Soldiers," and the final section, "General Rejoicing," is taken (without a written-out cadenza flourish at the fermata) from Corri's "Rejoicing." Hewitt's main contribution is the substitution of American tunes for Corri's Austrian ones.

The first three descriptive pieces by Americans were *Overture in 12 Movements, Expressive of a Voyage from England to America*, by Jean Gehot, and Hewitt's *Overture in 9 Movements, Expressive of a Battle*, played at subscription concerts by these composers and others on 22 and 26 September 1792, just after their arrival from England, and Hewitt's *Overture to Conclude with the Representation of a Storm*

---

13. The Battle of Trenton, a sonata for the piano-forte, dedicated to George Washington. New York, printed & sold by James Hewitt at his Musical Repository, No. 131 William Street; B. Carr, Philadelphia & J. Carr, Baltimore. See Sonneck-Upton, 39. A later edition [1812-14] published in Philadelphia by G. E. Blake (Wolfe 3683), however, was "composed for the piano forte by James Hewitt."

14. By Raoul F. Camus, reported at the Sonneck Society meeting in Shakertown and Centre College, Kentucky, 17 April 1988. This is one of the early benefits of his forthcoming *National Tune Index: Early American Wind and Ceremonial Music, 1636-1836* (New York: University Music Editions)

15. The Siege & Surrender of Valenciennes, for the piano forte or harpsichord, with an accomp^t for a violin, composed by Natale Corri, dedicated by permission to the Marquis of Huntly. Edin^r, printed for Corri & Co and to be had at D. Corri, N°. 6 Dean Street Soho London.

at Sea, performed on 1 April 1794. But none of these survives.[16]
Hewitt's later *Military Sonata* (1813-15; Wolfe 3743) proves not to be a
battle piece, but merely an introduction followed by two marches.

Another descriptive piece by Hewitt survives, however: *The 4th
of July, a Grand Military Sonata for the Piano Forte Composed in
Commemoration of that Glorious Day* (1801).[17] Although not a battle
piece as such, it has some of the same effects and general form. The
day breaks with a cannon and a siciliana in 6/8 meter.

> Siciliana: Day break
> The General Beat: Fife and Drum
> Maestoso: Assembling of the People
> Distant March--Horse advancing--Trumpet
> March: The Artillery
> Quick Step: Rifle Men
> Quick March: Infantry
> Allº. con Spirito--Firing small arms
> The Reveillee: Fife [and] Drum
> Shouts of the People
> Maestoso: Hail Columbia
> Finale: Allegro

The equivalent of the battle section is the one marked "Allº. con
Spirito--Firing small arms." Like *The Battle of Trenton* and several
European battle pieces, the section has traces of sonata-allegro form:
theme groups in the tonic C major and dominant G major, the equivalent of a development beginning with "firing small arms," and a
strong return to the tonic key, if not the "exposition" themes.
National tunes quoted in the final pages are "Hail Columbia" and a
rondo reminiscent of "Yankee Doodle."

Oliver Shaw

Another descriptive non-battle piece is *Welcome the Nation's
Guest: A Military Divertimento* (1824; EAKM no. 28) by the Rhode

---

16. Sonneck-Upton, 320-21. (Gehot's first name is given as
"Joseph" in *The New Grove Dictionary of American Music*.) One later
example of a Canadian descriptive piece is "A Storm on the Lake
(Barcarolle): A Souvenir of Toronto" (1884) by William Horatio Clarke;
facsimile in Elaine Keillor, ed., *The Canadian Musical Heritage* 1:
Piano Music I, 236-46.

17. Wolfe 3697; facsimile of the title-page is on the endpaper of
Wolfe, vol. 2. Recorded by Alan Mandel, *An Anthology of American
Piano Music (1780-1970)* (Desto DC 6445/47, 1975). The work was
originally performed on 4 July 1797 in New York City (Sonneck, *Early
Concert-Life*, 212).

Island resident Oliver Shaw.[18] It was composed in honor of Lafayette's visit to Providence in August 1824, and the captions outline the events of that visit. A thick low chord at the end of the first section, obviously borrowed from the battle genre, represents the "signal cannon."

> Introduction: Larg[h]etto
> Quick step: The General approaches the town
> The town's committee advance[s] and receive[s] the General
> Grand March: The General enters the town escorted by the military and citizens
> Andante pastorale: The General alights and is escorted on foot to the State House while the Misses strew his path with flowers
> Maestoso: Reception by the Governor and distinguished citizens
> Finale: The General's departure for Boston, amid the acclamations of the citizens

The indications "trumpets" and "tutti" perhaps suggest that the original may have been performed by a band, but more likely Shaw was simply imitating the band on the piano. The finale, in 3/8, includes passages of horn fifths, a similar technique previously used by J. S. Bach to imitate posthorns in his *Capriccio sopra la lontananza del suo fratello dilettissimo* of 1704.[19]

Benjamin Carr

Benjamin Carr's *The Siege of Tripoli*, op. 4 (1804-05; EAKM no. 11) reveals virtuoso imagination not encountered again in the composer until 1825, when his *Fantasia on Gramachree* was published. The siege represents the bombardment of Tripoli by the American

---

18. The Rhode Island Historical Society, Providence, owns a manuscript version of this piece, on 4 pages numbered 24-27, entitled "Welcome Friend of Washington." Some of the more important differences with the published version: missing are meas. 19-20, 23, 62, 94-105; the caption at meas. 40: "Marshals advance and receive the General at the line"; add "in general" to the end of the caption at meas. 44; the caption at meas. 78: "The General alights and is escorted on foot to the State House while the Misses clad in white strew the path with garlands and flowers"; caption at meas. 106: "General's departure for Boston amid the cheers of our ten thousand citizens." My thanks to Dr. Bruce Degan, of Simpson College, Indianola, Iowa, for supplying a copy.

19. For citations of other American music composed during Lafayette's tour of the United States, see my "American Musical Tributes of 1824-25 to Lafayette: A Report and Inventory," *Fontes Artis Musicae* 28, no. 1 (1979): 17-35.

Commodore Edward Preble in 1804. The bashaw of Tripoli, on the Barbary Coast (present-day Libya) had declared war on the United States three years earlier in an attempt to acquire more tribute money in return for allowing American ships to sail the Mediterranean unmolested by pirates. The scene opens with a morning gun--a low A-major chord which reappears several times during the piece--on a calm morning sea. Marches represent the American Marines and the enemy Moors. Two separate sections are represented: the boarding of the Tripolitan ship on August 3 (meas. 112-45), and the sending of a fire-ship into the harbor on September 4 (meas. 145-81). The siege section bears no resemblance to sonata-allegro form; the principal key is D major until the Americans begin to board the enemy ship, when it changes to F major. The climax is a unique upward double glissando in sixths describing the blowing up of the vessel Intrepid.[20] Confusion and the destruction of a tower are portrayed with diminished-seventh chords, and a descending four-octave scale represents the flight of the barbarians back to port. After the lament, the crew relaxes with a naval medley.[21] The work ends with a rondo on "Yankee Doodle," which Carr later published separately.

Peter Weldon

Peter or Pedro Weldon, of indeterminate origin but probably from a Spanish-speaking country, arrived in New York City from Jamaica[22] about 1797 and likely left for London about 1810. The

---

20. The technique had been used for "The powder magazine is blown up" in Ferdinand Kauer's *La Conquete d'Oczakow: Sonata militaire* (London: Bland, [1789?]; Special Collections, University of Kansas, copy) concerning the battle of 17 December 1788. Even though there is no actual written direction to slide the parallel sixths on the keyboard, the intent is clear. Other European examples: sixths in the cadenza of Mozart's "Lison dormait" variations, K. 264 (1778), octaves near the end of Beethoven's "Waldstein" Sonata, op. 53 (published 1805).

21. The tune beginning at meas. 249 is "Fisher's hornpipe," the identity discovered after the edition in EAKM was published. According to Henning, the first tune (meas. 195-200) is "Welcome welcome brother debtor"; the third (meas. 222-25) is "The sailor's complaint" or "Come listen to my ditty"--information supplied to her by Arthur Schrader.

22. Robert Stevenson found a reference in the 9 September 1788 issue of the Kingston (Jamaica) *Royal Gazette* that on that day Weldon (replacing the previously announced Samuel Patch) played a piano concerto at the house of Mr. Byrn in the Beef Market. In the following issue the paper related that "he played in so agreeable a manner that no occasion was given for lamenting Mr. Patch's absence." My thanks to Prof. Stevenson for sharing this information. See his article "Música secular en Jamaica, 1688-1822," *Revista Musical de Venezuela*, año 4, nos. 9-11 (January-December 1983): 149-50.

scenes and portraits engraved on his two battle pieces published by himself in New York about 1809-12 are particularly elaborate. Both were re-issued in London. *The Battle of Baylen, and Surrender of General Dupont's Army to the Patriotic Spanish Army under the Command of Generals Castanos & Reding*, also with the Spanish title *La Battala de Baylen, y redicion de el General Dupont al exercito espanol patriotico al mando de los General Castanos y Reding*, was first copyrighted in 1809.[23] Parts for violin and bass survive with the London edition. The events described in this "historical and military piece" occurred in Seville and Baylen, southern Spain, in May-July 1808. The conflict between the forces of the Spanish Ferdinand VII and Napoleon's French army in the Peninsular War resulted in the surrender of the army of French General Dupont to a combination of Spanish, Portuguese, and English forces. Weldon's portrayal is accompanied by both English and Spanish captions, of which the English is as follows:

> Introduction, Moderato: The Supreme Junto of Seville deliberating on the situation of their Country--The Royal Colours hoisted and Ferdinand the Seventh declared King of Spain amidst the acclamations of the People
> Grave: Sorrow of the Patriots for the captivity of their Sovereign and the depradations committed in their Country
> Furioso: The Patriots unanimously join the Royal Standard of Ferdinand the Seventh under the Supreme Junto of Seville
> Conciliating: The Junto of Sevilla proclaim peace with England in the name of Ferdinand the Seventh
> Allegro, Resolute: War declared against Buonaparte
> Moderato: General Castanos takes command of the Patriots resolved to expel their enemies
> Ferdinand the Seventh's March, Majestic: The Patriotic Army (under the Command of General Castanos) March from Sevilla against the French Army under General Dupont
> The Attack, Allegro: The Patriotic Peasants advancing with their long Pikes--Troops of General Reding advancing--Peasants advancing--Firm columns of Patriotic Infantry--Shouts of the

---

23. Wolfe 9730. The title-page is shown in Wolfe, *Early Music Engraving and Printing*, illustration 28a. London publication information: London, printed by Goulding, Phipps, D'Almaine & Co. Music Sellers to their R.H. the Prince & Princess of Wales, 124, New Bond Strt. & 7 Westmorland Strt. Dublin. Engraved page + title-page + pp. 3-15; violin part, title-page + pp. 2-7; bass part, pp. 1-4. British Library copy.

> Patriots [for] Ferdinand the Seventh--The French
> Infantry retreating--The French Cavalry
> advancing--The French Cavalry give way--
> Duponts Army defeated retreats to the
> Mountains--The Patriots comfort their wounded--
> Duponts situation become desperate attacks the
> Patriots with all his force--The French Infantry
> give way--The French Army entirely routed--
> Dupont surrenders to the Patriots--Shouts of the
> Patriots for Victory and Ferdinand the Seventh--
> Trumpets of Victory
> Grave: Sorrow of the Wounded--Burial of the Dead
> The Patriots and Peasantry Rejoice at Victory

A rare return occurs among the small descriptive sections: the music of the "Conciliating" returns in a variant version for the "Moderato." The score includes the traditional low thick chords or notes for cannons or guns, and fanfares of trumpets and drums. Otherwise, it suffers from the persistence of D major.

The main exception to the sameness of key is the battle section, in which the sonata-allegro tradition is even more faint than in some of the previous battle pieces. The tonic D major eventually modulates to the dominant key, climaxing in the "Shouts of the Patriots [for] Ferdinand the Seventh." The quasi-development is in B minor. When Dupont attacks, the tonic key and some of the previous material returns, and similar scales resume in a quasi-coda when the French army is completely routed. Almost as many elements of the form are absent as are present.

Weldon's *The Siege of Gerona/El Sitio de Gerona*, published in New York about 1810-12,[24] includes parts for violin and bass in its American edition. This concerns the besieging of Spanish patriots in Gerona, located in northeast Spain, by the French in 1809. The captions are likewise in English and Spanish.

> La Gran Marcha Militar de Gerona: Don Mariano
> Alvarez [footnote: Governor of Gerona] having
> recieved inteligence [*sic*] that the French are
> advancing in great Force against Gerona Review
> the Patriots who are resolved to bury themselves
> in its ruins rather than surrender
> Allegro: The French Army under the Command of
> General Verdier approaching Gerona--French
> Signal Cannon to halt--A Flag of Truce Advances
> before the Walls of Gerona and demands Dn.
> Mariano Alvarez to deliver up the City and
> Forts--The Governor promptorily refuses--First

---

24. Wolfe 10167; my thanks to Carleton Sprague Smith for sending a photocopy of the New York edition. London imprint is the same as for *The Battle of Baylen*; title-page + engraved page + pp. 4-13, no parts for violin or bass. British Library copy.

Garrison Signal Cannon--Second G. Signal
Cannon--French Signal Cannon for attack

Allegro: The French make a furious attack upon the
outworks--Are repulsed and driven back by the
Patriots--The French make a second attack--Are
again driven back by the Patriots--The French
commence a regular siege--Small arms--Shot from
the Castles--The French receive
Reinforcements--The French throwing up
redoubts and preparing to bombard the City and
Forts--Shells falling into the City and Forts--A
White Flag with a dispatch advances before the
walls of Gerona--The Governor answers no Flag
of truce can be admitted--General Verdier with
five thousand five hundred men marches in three
columns to storm the three breaches of Santa
Lucia, Quartel de Alemanes and Puerta de S^{nt}
Cristobal--Are repulsed by the Patriots--The
Patriotic light Troops make a sortie from the
Castles and make great slaughter amongst the
French--The Patriots return to the Castles--The
Patriots having withstood a dreadful siege of
Months against numerous enemy and finding their
Magazines nearly exausted [*sic*] become uneasy--
Anxiety of the Patriots at perceiving through
clouds of dust an army advancing

Marcha del General Blake: The Patriots rejoice at
perceiving them to be a detachment from General
Blake Commanded by General Conde

Allegro: Joy of the Patriots upon joining thier [*sic*]
brave Comrades who had cut thier way through
the French lines escorting 2000 Mules loaded with
supplies

The arrival of the supplies on 4 June 1809 did not end the siege; the
French did not give up until the following December 10.

Weldon's piece holds no musical surprises. The basic key is C
major, kept throughout but again with the exception in the attack section where there are touches of minor mode and modulation to the
dominant of G major as a secondary key area. A brief recapitulation
occurs at the end of the section just before General Blake's march. A
three-octave descending scale represents the first garrison signal cannon, and quick descending scales in 32nd notes describe falling shells.
At the beginning of the third section, the French are driven back with
a series of descending first-inversion triads (Ex. 5-1). All in all,
Weldon's elaborate editions, however, are not matched by the quality
of the music.

Ex. 5-1.   Peter Weldon, *The Siege of Gerona*, 3rd section, meas. 1-9.

Francesco Masi

The four remaining American battle pieces in the first quarter of the 19th century concern the War of 1812 between the United States and Britain. *The Battles of Lake Champlain and Plattsburg*, published in 1815,[25] is the only battle piece by the Italian immigrant Francesco

25. Wolfe 5622; Newberry Library copy.

Masi (d. 1853). He arrived in Boston in 1807, and advertised his services as teacher of a number of woodwind, brass, and string instruments, and on the piano. Masi's musical description is of the engagement that occurred on 11 September 1814. The captions are:

> Maestoso: The approach of the Land, and Naual [*sic*] Forces--The Colours hoisted, and men Called to Quarters
>
> Grave: Confusion of the Inhabitants
>
> Allegro moderato: The Fleet and Army, animated by their Officers
>
> Allegro: The Millitia [*sic*] and Volunteers, join the Regulars
>
> Trumpett: Cheering the Green Mountaineers--The Americans make Disposition for Battle
>
> Grand March: The Enemy Aproach [*sic*] the Fort
>
> Allegro Mol[to]: Attack--The Americans make a Sortie from the Forts--The British retreating [and] Americans pursue--The Drum and Fife Signals for the Americans to form--The British Comander [*sic*], rallies his Troops--Enemy Defeated again
>
> The Trumpetts of Victory
>
> Poco piu adagio: Americans Confort [*sic*] their Wounded--Cannon Signal to Inform the Army, of the Success of the fleet
>
> Allegro: Attack, The Roaring of the Artillery from the fleet--The Enemy Ships Strike their Flag--The Sailors Rejoicing at the Victory
>
> Largo: Cries of the Wounded--Burial of the Dead
>
> Allegro: Victory, Grand National Salute, on account of the Victory
>
> Finale: Yankee Doodle

Masi was not a very good composer; along with the misspelling, his score includes some errors and instances of awkward parallel fifths and octaves. The basic tonality of the battle piece is D major, made minor for the two slow sections; the only other relief is G major in the sixth section, the grand march.

As in Weldon's two pieces, Masi's battle section has a semblance of sonata-allegro form: the secondary dominant key of A major is reached in the sixteenth measure (after the American sortie), and the development is reflected in various keys as the British commander rallies his troops. Some material from the second key area returns in the section representing the roaring of the artillery from the fleet, ending in a cadence similar to that before the earlier development. As in Hewitt's *Battle of Trenton*, the battle section begins as the right hand, in 16th notes, represent the Americans, and the slower British, in quarters and 8ths, are in the left hand (Ex. 5-2).

Ex. 5-2.   Francesco Masi, *The Battles of Lake Champlain and Plattsburg*, 7th section, meas. 1-4.

Philip Laroque

The last battle of the war, at New Orleans on 8 January 1815, ironically took place two weeks after the signing of the peace treaty, but before this news had reached the armies. The Americans were led by Andrew Jackson, and the victory not only restored American military pride but also catapulted Jackson to fame, eventually resulting in his election to the presidency. General Sir Edward Pakenham and two fellow British generals were killed in the action.

The musical results in three pieces describing the battle are noticeably better than in the works by Weldon and Masi. New Orleans resident Philip Laroque wrote the first of them: *Battle of the Memorable 8th of January 1815*,[26] published that same year with a title-page including an engraving of "The Heroe of New Orleans," General Jackson. Texts are in both English and French.

> Andantino: the day begins
> The enemy fires a Congreve rocket as the signal of
>   attack
> Tempo 1°. moins lent: the light increase[s]
> The enemy formed in a very close colum[n] advan-
>   ce[s] toward our left--the enemy presses his
>   March, the firing begins on our left--the fire of
>   the enemy begins--the colum[n] of the enemy
>   begins to breake [*sic*]--the colum[n] falls back--
>   our fire slackens--Shouts of joy
> Yankee doodle

---

26. Wolfe 5227; facsimile of title-page on front endpaper of Wolfe, vol. 3.

All°.: the enemy forms again--a rolling fire on both
sides--Death of General Pakenham--Surprise and
consternation among the enemy
Funeral March
All°.: the fire of our Musketry is heard towards the
wood--Rolling fire--can[n]on
Andante: Generals Gibbs and Keane are wounded
All°.: the enemy sends a column towards our right--
the enemy takes possession of a redoubt--the
enemy drives out of the redoubt--the enemy falling back to their camp
Andantino: Whilst our men are assisting the wounded
of the enemy his soldiers lying into a ditch fire
on them--Fire of the British--Our men continue
to relieve the wounded of the enemy
Fanfare: The signal of Victory
All°.: The enemy sends a flag of truce for a suspen-
sion of arms
Triumphal March
Rondo Finale

Laroque's piece includes a number of special effects. The Con-
greve rocket is portrayed with a 64th-note scale (or glissando?)
upwards, a written-out trill, then an arpeggio downwards and another
trill (Ex. 5-3).

Ex. 5-3.   Philip Laroque, *Battle of the Memorable 8th of January
1815*, 2nd section.

In the fourth section, the marching of the enemy consists of repeated chords. After the "firing on our left" with a left-hand Alberti bass accompaniment, the fire of the enemy begins in the right-hand part with a quickening of the rhythm to 16ths. Further along, "the column falls back" and "our fire slackens" with a gradual lowering of pitch and decrease of motion from 16ths to 8ths to quarters (Ex. 5-4), a device also used later when the enemy falls back to their camp in the tenth section. For the following scene, in which the wounded enemy soldiers are aided by the Americans who are in turn fired upon by the British, Laroque alternates the tempos of Andantino and Allegro. No semblance of sonata-allegro form is used; instead, the music closely follows the action with a variety of keys, unified by the A major of the beginning and end. His is one of the most imaginative American battle pieces. In its performances in New Orleans in 1816, 1817, and 1818, the medium was not piano but orchestra.[27]

Ex. 5-4.   Laroque, *Battle of the Memorable 8th of January 1815*, 4th section, ending.

27. Henry Kmen, *Music in New Orleans: The Formative Years, 1791-1841* (Baton Rouge: Louisiana State University Press, 1966), 224. My thanks to Frederick Crane for pointing this reference out to me.

Peter Ricksecker

The X'd circle ⊠, the sign for playing all notes of the lowest three octaves in Viguerie's *Battle of Maringo*, is also adopted by the composer Peter Ricksecker (who also served as a Moravian missionary) in *The Battle of New Orleans* (1816; Wolfe 7479) to represent cannon, although without a specific explanation of the sign for the performer. It recurs throughout the piece. Captions are again in both English and French.

Grave: The Americans await with calmness the
approach of the Enemy; who are seen advancing
from a distance--Drums beating to Arms--Word
of Command (𝕏)

Allegro: The Americans forming in order of Battle
(𝕏)--The British Drums are heard (𝕏)

British March

The British begin the Attack--They are repulsed by
the American Infantry & Artillery (𝕏)--Sir
Edward Pakenham is mortally wounded--
Tremendous fire--The repeated attacks of the
English being frustrated; they are totally routed
and fly from the Field of battle (𝕏)

Shouts of Victory (𝕏)

Lento con Expressione: Lamentation of the wounded
and dying

Gen: Coffee's March

Gen: Carroll's March

General Jacksons March

Rondo Majore-Minore-Majore--Coda

Ricksecker's piece is straightforward in musical effects, one of the best
being the quickening motion that opens the fourth section (Ex. 5-5).

Ex. 5-5.   Peter Ricksecker, *The Battle of New Orleans*, beginning of
4th section.

He is the only one, on either side of the Atlantic, to describe the
battle, in the passage "tremendous fire," by moving in sequence
through the entire circle of fifths. Otherwise, the work suffers from
the stubborn key of D major and the predominance of marches.

Denis-Germain Étienne

The French-born Denis-Germain Étienne (1781-1859), who settled in New York City about 1814-15, contributed *Battle of New Orleans*, published during the year following the battle (Wolfe 2718).

> Andante: The Night Calm--Dawn of Day
> Lento
> Quick Step: Distant March of the Enemy--Beat to Arms--Charge of Trumpets in the American Camp
> Allegro non troppo: Turning out and mustering of the Americans--Order of Battle under Arms
> Lento: Profound silence--Faster: British advance--Attack the Camp--Death of the British Commander
> Lento e mesto: Lamentation of his Officers and followers
> Allegro: Furious Attack by the Americans--Terrible Carnage--Total defeat of the British--Shouts of Victory
> Tempo di marcia: Hail Columbia
> Allegro: La Victoire est à nous
> Yankee Doodle

The one fault of the work is that no section has a key-signature other than that of C major (or minor, for the six measures of the second section). On the other hand, Étienne's is the only American battle piece to specify an instrument with percussion stops:

> C: Sign of the Drum Pedal for the Canon
> Ө Sign of the Drum Pedal with the little Bells

The first is used primarily in the fifth section, the one in which the battle commences, and the seventh section for the passage of "terrible carnage." The second sign is withheld until the triumphal "Hail Columbia."

One passage is a primitive predecessor of the famous crescendo in Ravel's *Daphnis et Chloë*; here, the "Dawn of Day" rises, with a crescendo, on a broken G-major chord below the treble staff up to f''' (Ex. 5-6).

Ex. 5-6.   Denis-Germaine Étienne, *Battle of New Orleans*, 1st section, ending.

Another gradual rise in pitch and dynamics represents in broken octaves the British advance and attack on the camp in the fifth section. Plenty of broken diminished-seventh chords depict the fury of battle. For the "Furious Attack by the Americans," Étienne summons all the power he could muster--a quotation from Mozart's *Don Giovanni*. To complement the "dawn of day," the "Total defeat of the British" is shown with a gradual descent of pitch, from *c‴*, dying ("perdendosi") to *G* (Ex. 5-7).

Ex. 5-7. Étienne, *Battle of New Orleans*, 7th section, ending.

Several factors must have been responsible for the popularity, on both sides of the Atlantic, of these battle pieces. One was the general interest in military matters and military heroes. Twenty battles are represented in the music described here, and the period involves important revolutions and wars. Another reason must have been the growing appeal of descriptive music, which evoked one's imagination in a manner lacking in abstract sonatas or rondos.[28] The most impor-

28. An obvious example is the storm section of Beethoven's Symphony 6 ("Pastorale"). Another, for piano, is Daniel Steibelt's "Storm Rondo," or "The Storm: A Descriptive Piece of Music," published in the United States in seven editions, 1806-20s (see Wolfe 8581-87), and still in print in 1870.

tant reason, however, was interest in virtuoso performance in the ever-increasing number of public concerts.

This suggests that techniques used to describe battles are not devoid of historical value. Strings of arpeggios, flashy scales, and extended passages of diminished-seventh chords are not typical of Mozart and Haydn in Europe. Yet Koczwara's *Battle of Prague* was written during Mozart's lifetime (both died the same year). Programmatic and descriptive aspects of battle pieces would seem to be additional and important elements of the growing Romanticism in music. Virtuosity is another important feature of the 19th century, and it is certainly clear in battle pieces. Indeed, special effects which first appear in battle pieces furnish the model for new and particularly pianistic techniques and harmonic styles in the late sonatas of Beethoven and in much of the piano music of Liszt in Europe, and in some of the compositions of Heinrich and Gottschalk in the United States.

6

ORGAN MUSIC,
BREMNER TO ZEUNER

The subject of early American organ music is limited, not because there weren't fine organists but because only rarely did they write their organ compositions down. Modern recordings of older American organ music, unfortunately, include much music that may not even have been played on the organ at the time. The pioneering recording by E. Power Biggs, *The Organ in America*,[1] for example, includes only one work written definitely for the organ--Selby's "Fuge or Voluntary" in D. The rest was written for harpsichord or pianoforte.[2] Some anthologies also bend the category of organ music, such as Jon Spong's *Early American Compositions for Organ (of the*

---

1. (Columbia MS 6161, ca. 1960).

2. Admittedly, some of this early music, such as the several marches, Billings's "Chester," and Oliver Shaw's "Trip to Pawtucket," is just as successful on a chamber organ in a secular setting. But others--John Christopher Moller's Sonata [VIII] in D, Hewitt's *Battle of Trenton*, and William Brown's first Rondo in G--specify harpsichord or pianoforte on their original title pages. The greater value of the recording is in the opportunity to hear the historic American organs and the valuable essay on these organs by Barbara Owen.

Similarly, Janice Beck's *Anthology of American Organ Music, Volume I: The Eighteenth Century* (Musical Heritage OR A-262) has only one real organ composition: Selby's Voluntary VIII in A--but this work was composed and published in England before Selby came to the United States. In the notes by Charles B. Beck, one finds the rationale "It is clear, nevertheless, that most keyboard music was intended to be played on any keyboard instrument." In that case, why do not organists play Mozart, Haydn, and Beethoven piano sonatas on the organ? A good argument can be made to play James Bremner's "Trumpet Air" on the organ, but it is certainly far-fetched for the songs of Francis Hopkinson or the choral works of Billings.

18th and 19th Centuries),[3] but in this case the lack of citations of the sources, or even of original titles or media of performance, make it difficult for those seeking genuine organ music from early America. Another such collection is Samuel Walter's *Organ Americana: Compositions by Early American Composers*,[4] which has no genuine organ music from before 1830. Much more faithful is an organ anthology more recently edited by Barbara Owen: *A Century of American Organ Music, 1776-1876*, and sequels with the same title, volumes 2-3.[5] Ms. Owen had written a valuable survey, "American Organ Music and Playing from 1700," as early as 1963,[6] and her tour-de-force is *The Organ in New England*.[7]

There were a number of accomplished organists in 18th-century America, the first being Charles Theodore Pachelbel (1690-1750), the son of the famous Johann Pachelbel of Nuremberg. Unfortunately, Charles left little of his own music; even an often-cited Magnificat in C for two choirs and organ was apparently composed before he came to the New World. None of Pachelbel's organ music survives.

James Bremner

James Bremner (d. 1780), organist at Christ Church, Philadelphia, contributed one piece definitely for organ--his "Trumpet Air" in D major.[8] It is in the tradition of the English trumpet air or voluntary written nearly a century earlier, such as the famous "Purcell's Trumpet

----

3. (Nashville: Abingdon, 1968).

4. (Nashville: Abingdon, 1976), complete with Hammond organ registrations.

5. (Dayton: McAfee, 1975-76; Melville, N.Y.: Belwin-Mills, 1983). Hereafter, these are cited as *Century*, 1, 2, or 3.

6. *Organ Institute Quarterly* 10, no. 3 (autumn 1963): 7-13.

7. (Raleigh: Sunbury, 1979).

8. Owen, *Century*, 1:8-9; Spong, 1-2; Howard, *A Program of Early American Piano Pieces*, 19; or the original source reprinted from the manuscript at the University of Pennsylvania, *Francis Hopkinson's Lessons: A Facsimile Edition of Hopkinson's Personal Keyboard Book*, 119. A few corrections for those using Owen's edition: beginning, the marking is "Largo" instead of "Andante"; meas. 3, last l.h. *a'* is 8th note (rest missing), and there is no slur in the r.h. to meas. 4; meas. 4, "Echo"; meas. 6, "Trump."; meas 8, "diminuendo"; meas. 10, "Swell"; meas. 12, "echo"; meas. 13, r.h., 8th-note *a'* should be 8th-rest, add "Trum." to last two notes; meas. 16, "diminuendo"; meas. 17, "Echo," r.h., 2nd beat is *e' d'* dotted 8th-16th, l.h., 2nd beat 8ths *a a* instead of *A*, last l.h. note is unison *d'*.

Voluntary" by Jeremiah Clarke.[9] The closest genre is the march, with its relatively stately tempo (Andante), and predominance of dotted rhythms. Certainly the "horn fifths" are closely allied to band writing of the 18th century, and are readily found in other march compositions of the time. Organists can certainly advance the cause for American music by substituting Bremner's piece for one of the now-ubiquitous Clarke airs.

William Selby

William Selby (1738-98) immigrated from his native England in 1771, and served as organist at important churches in Boston (including King's Chapel and Trinity Church) and Newport, Rhode Island. The year he arrived, he was soloist in an organ concerto, perhaps one of the first keyboard concertos to be performed in the United States. Selby's Voluntary in A major was published about 1770 before he came, in a collection *Ten Voluntarys for the Organ or Harpsichord*.[10] The form and style is that of a French overture, as developed in the orchestral music of Handel. The initial Andante is characterized by dotted rhythms and short 32nd-note scales leading to the strong beats. (All of the short notes should be performed even shorter than notated.) Toward the end of the section are cadences to the related keys of E major, B major, and finally C-sharp minor. The key of A major returns for the beginning of the "Fuge." This is not a strict contrapuntal work in the tradition of Bach. After the exposition for three voices, the subject returns only three times. Interspersed is free material, including Alberti bass accompaniments for the right hand as well as for the left, scales and other patterns in sequences, and several cadences prepared by pedal points. These pedal points, up to three measures long, would tend to indicate that the primary intended instrument was the organ, except that similar held notes were normally repeated by 18th-century harpsichordists when the sound died. A better indication is the title "Voluntary," the label commonly used for free organ works used in church.

---

9. "Trumpet Voluntary" and probably also the "Trumpet Tune" are by Clarke. See Charles Cudworth and Franklin B. Zimmerman, "The Trumpet Voluntary," *Music: A.G.O./R.C.C.O.* 3, no. 9 (September 1969): 28-30; or Franklin B. Zimmerman, *Henry Purcell, 1659-1695: An Analytical Catalogue of His Music* (London: Macmillan, 1963), nos. S-124-25.

10. (London: C. and S. Thompson). Edited in Owen, *Century*, 2:8-11; Marrocco and Gleason, *Music in America*, no. 72, pp. 186-88; and William Selby, *Two Voluntaries for Organ*, ed. Daniel Pinkham (Boston: E. C. Schirmer, 1972). All of Selby's keyboard works (Voluntary in A major, Fugue or Voluntary, and "A Lesson") are in *Keyboard Music of William Selby*, ed. Linton Powell (Boston: Boston Music Co., 1979).

Selby's second surviving voluntary, "A Fuge or Voluntary" in D major, was printed about 1800.[11] The subject is more prominent in this voluntary because of its length--eight measures, versus three measures for the A-major voluntary. Although there are again only three voices (sometimes later on reduced to two), the exposition has four entrances, alternating tonic and dominant. After a short free section, the subject returns twice more, in tonic. Contrapuntal texture is then abandoned for further episodic material: one section accompanied with the Murky bass figure (alternating octaves), the next with the Alberti pattern in the right hand, and another with the Alberti in the left. The final statement of the fugue subject is given in octaves by both hands.

In the same collection printed about 1800 is included a three-movement work entitled "A Lesson." Although an edition for organ was prepared by E. Power Biggs, and one movement is included in Barbara Owen's anthology, there is no particular reason to suspect that the work was intended for the organ.[12] "Lesson" is instead the British term for the harpsichord suite. Even though it can well be played on a chamber organ--as can much harpsichord music--use on a church organ may not be appropriate, especially the "Jig." The Allegro and final "Jig" are in rounded binary form--the initial key and material returning before the end of the second half. The middle Andante movement is a five-part rondo, the second digression in minor. The general style is that of early Classical music from the third quarter of the 18th century.

Francis Linley

Francis Linley (1771-1800), blind from birth, was chosen organist of St. James Chapel, Pentonville, London, and married a wealthy blind lady. But because "his affairs becoming embarrassed,"[13] he came to the United States in 1796. In that same year was issued his *A New Assistant for the Piano-Forte or Harpsichord*, published by the Carrs in Baltimore, Philadelphia, and New York. It contains some teaching pieces by Linley, and six sonatas attributed to Benjamin Carr. A new edition, without the sonatas, was issued the same year, and again in 1814-15 (Sonneck-Upton, 289-90; Wolfe 5393). Linley returned to his birthplace, Doncaster, in 1799 and died the following year, before the age of thirty.

Three organ voluntaries by Linley are available in modern edition. Two of them are from one of the first organ tutors published in

---

11. Sonneck-Upton, 77, 151. See also John McKay, "William Selby, Musical Emigré in Colonial Boston," *Musical Quarterly* 57, no. 4 (October 1971): 609-27.

12. William Selby, *A Lesson for the Organ*, ed. E. Power Biggs (New York: Associated, 1955). The last movement, "Jig," is in Owen, *Century*, 2:7.

13. *Grove's*, 5th ed.

England, his *A Practical Introduction to the Organ in Five Parts, viz. A Description of the Organ, Preludes, Voluntarys, Fugues, & Full Pieces, and a Selection of all the Psalms in General Use with Interludes*,[14] the 12th (!) edition of which is dated about 1810. The C-major voluntary is a modest work, largely comprising suspensions and sequential patterns. His G-major voluntary comes from *Organ Study* of 1836 by the Philadelphian Thomas Loud (to be discussed below); Loud's source is unknown.

Linley's best work is the A-major voluntary from the London publication, specified for the trumpet stop in the same manner as Bremner's. Linley exploits the contrast between the solo stop on the Great division and the contrasting softer Swell, in both cadential echoes and in dialogues between the manuals. At almost exactly the halfway point, the beginning material returns in the dominant key.[15] The final ten measures call for full organ; the ending cadence, borrowing a trait of Handel, is marked "Adagio."

Christian Latrobe

Although no solo keyboard music by American Moravian musicians has survived, nine short preludes by an English Moravian represent the kind of music heard in many American churches. Christian Ignatius Latrobe (1758-1836) nevertheless had an American

---

14. The title-page continues with: Humbly Inscribed by Permission to Dr. Arnold Organist & Composer to his Majesty, by F. Linley. Op. 6. Twelfth Edition Corrected and Enlarged. London: Wheatstone & Co., 20 Conduit Street Regent Street. This publication, a copy of which is in the British Library, is 120 pages long. The voluntaries are in the third part, "Eight Voluntarys for the Organ, Composed for the Use of Young Practitioners, are expressly calculated to shew the proper Method of Mixing the Stops. These Voluntaries are intended for performance after the Psalms." The voluntaries in C and A are in Owen, *Century*, 1:14-15 and 16-19. In the original publication, the title to the one in C is "Voluntary 2" (not Owen's "Introductory Voluntary"), the tempo is Larghetto (not Adagio), and the only registration is "Flute & Stop Diapason" (not "Diapasons or Dulciana and Flute" plus later stop changes). There are also number of musical discrepancies (Ms. Owen used a copy in the New York Public Library, perhaps another edition), the most important of which is that the original concludes with a cadence to the dominant, then continues with another movement, Allegro, for the flute stop. The "Trumpet Voluntary" in A major in Owen's edition is the 3rd movement of "Voluntary 7" in A minor; the only important addition to the edition is "Tru[mpet]" to the last note of meas. 52 and "Sw[ell]" at the end of meas. 64. The original publication has additional notes *A'* in meas. 54-58 and the last measure, available on the typical late 18th-century English organ and on American organs of the time based on English designs.

15. I wonder if the first *b* in measure 44 (Owen's edition, p. 17, last system, 1st measure) was a mistake by the original printer for *f*.

connection--his brother was Benjamin Latrobe, who was the third architect for the United States Capital building, and designed the Bank of Pennsylvania in Philadelphia, the State Capital of Virginia, and the Catholic Cathedral in Baltimore. Nine preludes by Christian Latrobe were included in an appendix to L. B. Seeley's *Devotional Harmony* (London, 1806), and they are published in an edition by Karl Kroeger.[16] This is the only surviving Moravian organ music from either side of the Atlantic. For their limited frame, they are formally logical, occasionally adventuresome in harmony, and useful for today's organist with limited technical ability.

Music from Carr's *Masses, Vespers, Litanies*

Suffering in comparison is the seventeen-measure Largo in E-flat major by the Scotch immigrant J. George Schetky (1776-1831). Schetky was a collaborator with Benjamin Carr in music publishing during the first decade of the new century. This work is one of seven organ pieces included in Benjamin Carr's *Masses, Vespers, Litanies, Hymns, Psalms, Anthems & Motets, composed, selected, and arranged for the use of the Catholic Churches in the United States of America of 1805*.[17] The section of organ pieces is headed:

> As it is necessary in the performance of Mass or Vespers, occasionally to play some appropriate strain on the Organ as at the beginning of each, previous to Tantum ergo &c likewise on those mornings when Solemn Mass is not sung, the following few

> Select Pieces

> either as Preludes Interludes or Voluntaries may in some instances not be unacceptable.

The works (pp. 32-36) are:

> Jom[m]elli, [untitled]
> Dr Arne, Largh°
> Pleyel, Adagio
> B: Carr, Adagio
> R: Taylor, The Subject from "Adeste Fideles"

---

16. Christian I. Latrobe, *Nine Preludes for Organ*, ed. Karl Kroeger (Charlotte, N.C.: Brodt Music Co., 1978). Latrobe's Three Sonatas for the Pianoforte, op. 3 (London: J. Bland, [1793?]) are included in *The London Pianoforte School*, ed. Temperley, 7:29-50.

17. (Philadelphia: Carr & Schetky, [1805]). The last three pages, renumbered 70-72, were also issued with the last two editions of *Select Harmony*; see Wolfe 7722B-C.

Schetky, Largo
B: Carr, Variations to the Sicilian Hymn

Carr's "Adagio" is short enough to repeat in its entirety here (Ex. 6-1).

Ex. 6-1.   Benjamin Carr, "Adagio" from *Masses, Vespers, Litanies* (1805).

All of the other American pieces are available in modern editions.[18]

Carr's variations on the "Sicilian Hymn" (the tune is now most associated with the title "Sicilian Mariners" and the hymn-text beginning "Savior, like a shepherd lead us") is straightforward in the treatment given in the three variations.[19] 16th-note counterpoint in the left hand accompanies the melody in variation 1; the same motion decorates in the right hand for variation 2, with occasional outbursts of 32nd-note scales. The last variation, marked *f*, is more stately.

"Adeste fideles" by Rayner Taylor[20] is the most adventuresome of all his keyboard variation sets, including those for pianoforte.[21] It omits a simple presentation of the theme, instead beginning with the first variation (Taylor does not mark the variations with numbers). Only the last variation retains the 8 + 12-measure structure. In variation 1, instead of returning to the tonic C major in the ninth measure, Taylor stays in the dominant and compensates by restating (in a new treatment) the last eight measures in the tonic--thereby extending the variation from 18 to 28 measures. Variation 2 is characterized by tonal excursions. In the first part the key is A minor; instead of the expected E-major dominant chord in the eighth measure it is E minor. In the following four measures, A minor returns, suddenly succeeded by C minor for what would normally be the final eight measures. Again in compensation, the last eight measures are provided again, but in E-flat major--ending with a cadence in C minor. Such freedom in key is untypical for the early 19th century, and is probably not

18. Owen, *Century*, 1:22-25 and 30-33, for Taylor's "Adeste fideles" variations and Carr's "Sicilian Hymn" variations; Owen, *Century*, 2:17, for Schetky's "Largo"; Owen, *Century*, 3:9, for Carr's "Adagio." This last piece was also included in an earlier version of this chapter: "American Organ Music before 1830: A Critical and Descriptive Survey," *Diapason*, November 1981, 1, 3, 7. A facsimile of the entire *Masses, Vespers, Litanies* is included in Sprenkle, "The Life and Works of Benjamin Carr (1768-1831)," 2:79-212.

19. In comparison with Owen's edition, the original has repeats for each 8-measure segment throughout; there is a flat on the first *a* and a natural on the following *A* in the 7th measure of variation 1; in variation 2 the two *c'* notes in meas. 4-5 are tied and there is a natural on *b'* in meas. 7; throughout the piece the trills are given as "tr."

20. Taylor is provided with a biography, and a glowing account of his abilities as organist, in John Rowe Parker's *A Musical Biography* (1825), 179-82. Other American organists given biographical surveys are George K. Jackson and Sophia Hewitt Ostinelli, and there are articles on church music, chanting, the organ, and the voluntary.

21. Owen's edition omits the repeats for the first 8 measures of all three variations and the last 12 measures for variation 3; the 8-measure coda is marked "Largo Andante"; and triplet 16ths are indicated with the signature 12/16 (even as the other hand retains 2/4) in variation 3.

encountered again in organ music until Ives's variations on "America" at the end of the century. Taylor's last variation features brilliant 16th-note triplets. A subdued treatment of the theme's last eight measures serves as a short coda.

Carr's *Voluntary*

The most extensive and important organ piece written around the turn of the century is Benjamin Carr's manuscript *Voluntary*, "compos'd for the op'ning of the New organ at St. augustines church Philadelphia, respectfully presented by the Author to his Friend A Reinagle Esq." (complete in EAKM no. 5).[22] This is a large-scale voluntary, in five movements, in the manner of a number of voluntaries by late 18th-century English composers. At this point, it might be enlightening to quote the description of the organ voluntary in John Rowe Parker's *A Musical Biography*, published in Boston in 1825:

> A voluntary is generally understood to signify an unwritten or extemporary piece of music as distinguished from the execution of a copy. This is a species of performance for which the organ is peculiarly adapted, and which is susceptible of more of the impress of genuine feeling than any other description of music. The imagination, unchecked by the fetters which the act of writing necessarily imposes, gives life and vigour and maturity to its creations, even in the very moment of their conception. Emotions of the soul which cannot be embodied in language, become by the medium of melodious sounds, transfused into the breasts of the hearers, communicating a sensation not to be expressed, and imparting a tranquil pleasure but rarely otherwise experienced. . . . But laziness has crept in here as elsewhere, and it is now as customary for a voluntary to be played from a copy, as it is for a sermon to be read from a book. . . . Diapason pieces and andante movements seem best to suit the commencement and middle of the service, and fugues of sober character, wheth[er] *ex tempore* or otherwise, are admirably adapted to the close. There are no organ passages more deservedly popular than those performed on the swell; when judiciously employed they have a wonderfully captivating effect; but they are liable to a very serious objection, viz. that as the organ is at present constituted, they

---

22. The third movement is also in Owen, *Century*, 1:26-29. Charles Wilhite, in "An Early American Organist: Benjamin Carr," *Clavier* 12, no. 2 (February 1973): 24-31, includes an edition of the second and third movements.

necessarily abstract one foot from the service of the
pedals.[23]

The first movement of Carr's voluntary, "Largo ad lib," is a
mixture of different musical ideas, organized merely by the gradual
addition of stops, in this order: stopped diapason, open diapason, principal 4, stopped diapason, flute, violoncello, fifteenth, tierce, twelfth,
and trumpet (full organ). The basic key is C major, but at a tempo
change to Adagio there is an abrupt move from an A-minor chord,
mildly smoothed with a trill on *a'* which then serves as a leading tone
to B-flat major. Following a short Andante in C minor (resembling
the style of a Bach trio sonata--the only such instance in Carr's works)
is an even more striking modulation to B minor. The B then serves as
a leading tone back to C major. The remainder of the movement
includes flourishes of 32nd-note scales, a short dialogue of Choir and
Great, a brief return of material heard earlier, and strings of suspensions over a walking bass in the manner of a Corelli trio sonata.
An Aria for the violoncello stop in E-flat major is in repeated
binary form, and concludes with another unusual passage modulating
to its tritone, A major. The third movement, Allegretto in A major
for the flute stop, is likewise in a repeated binary structure, generously
endowed with 16th-note figuration, often with the Alberti pattern and
often in sequence. The contrasting Andante, for the "Choir organ or
Diapasons," is the weakest movement. One idea is succeeded by
another, and none of them returns. One "German" augmented-sixth
chord doesn't save it.
The fifth movement, a fugue in C major, is a vivid contrast with
the strict Germanic fugue style as represented by Charles Zeuner (to
be discussed below). Carr's is instead in the free-voiced style of the
Italian Baroque, as represented by Handel. Not only is the subject a
long one--including a scale fragment given in sequence no fewer than
five times--but is introduced by both hands in octaves. After the
exposition (three entrances, but only two voices) is a lengthy episode
with sequential passages (up to twelve repetitions), none related to the
fugue subject. Almost at the center of the movement, the subject
returns, the first two measures in octaves for both hands! Carr then
provides another exposition, again with three entrances. The counter-
subjects are new, and the chordal outbursts which accompany the third
entrance (in C minor instead of major) are even bizarre. The next
episode is devoid of counterpoint, especially considering the inclusion
of an Alberti bass. The final measures, with wide-ranging scales and
arpeggios, are exuberant.
This voluntary is unique in early American organ music. In
spite of its idiosyncrasies, it nevertheless deserves inclusion in today's
organ recitals and church services.

---

23 Parker, 223-25.

Thomas Loud, Jr., Benjamin Cross, Charles Hommann

The Organ Study, a book intended for Episcopal services, was published in 1836.[24] The compiler was Thomas Loud, Jr. (d. 1834). It is possible that the 1836 edition is a reissue of an earlier edition, and that all the contents predate 1830. Loud emigrated from England to Philadelphia about 1812; he began making pianos in 1816, and with three brothers established the important piano-making firm of Loud Brothers which was active from 1822 to 1837.[25] Loud's two voluntaries in E-flat major are both slow and chordal, and musically bland. In both, initial material later returns, with specified changes of manual and registration. They are the first in this survey to call for an independent pedal part.

Likewise bland for the church-goer is the Voluntary in C major by Benjamin Cross (1796-1857). Cross, born in Philadelphia, was a student of both Rayner Taylor and Benjamin Carr, graduated from the University of Pennsylvania, and was one of the founders of the Musical Fund Society and its most important member after Carr and Schetky both died in 1831. Carr and Cross must have been close, for Cross was a witness to Carr's will, written in 1830, and one of the beneficiaries was Cross's son--named Benjamin Carr Cross.[26]

The voluntaries in F major and E-flat major attributed to Hommann are probably by Charles Hommann, Jr., who with his father, Charles, Sr., were other founding members of the Musical Fund Society. Hommann was the violin teacher of another son of Benjamin Cross, Michael H. Cross (b. 1833).[27] Hommann's voluntaries are also short, but the chromatic harmonies foreshadow a later Victorian style.

------

24. This is the source in Owen's *Century*, vol. 1, for voluntaries in E-flat and B-flat by Loud (pp. 34, 36), Cross in C (p. 39), and in *Century*, 2:14 for Hommann's Voluntary in F, and presumably also for Hommann's Voluntary in E-flat in *Century*, 3:8.

25. It is difficult to distinguish Thomas Loud, father and son. For further information, see Daniel Spillane, *History of the American Pianoforte* (New York: author, 1890; reprint with introduction by Rita Benton, New York: Da Capo, 1969), 112-18. The article in *The New Grove Dictionary of American Music* has information on Thomas Loud (I) (ca. 1762-1833), who came from England about 1816; and Thomas Loud (II) (no dates given).

26. The will is quoted in Sprenkle, 1:293-95.

27. Gerson, *Music in Philadelphia*, 141. It is difficult to separate the Hommanns. Madeira, *Annals of Music in Philadelphia and History of the Musical Fund Society*, 76, lists for a 1821 Musical Fund Society concert Mr. [J. C.] Hommann, Sr., cello; [J.] C. Hommann, tenor [viola]; J. Hommann, double bass. The *New Grove Dictionary of American Music* article is on Charles Hommann (ca. 1800-d. after 1862), son of German immigrant John C. Hommann, and brother-in-law of Charles F. Hupfeld.

For the most part, the United States remained a musical colony of England for its first fifty years. A beginning of influence from Germany occurred in 1800, when the 18-year-old Christopher Meineke arrived in Baltimore, where, in 1819, he became organist at St. Paul's Church, which he served until his death.[28] Although he wrote much piano music, none for organ has yet been found.

Charles Zeuner

The most important organ composer in American before mid-century was another German immigrant, Charles Zeuner, who was born Heinrich Christopher Zeuner in Eisleben, Saxony, in 1795. Among his teachers was Johann Nepomuk Hummel. Although some sources state that he came to the United States in 1824, the first definite evidence of his presence was a concert in Boston in early 1830, in which he displayed his talents as composer, organist, pianist, and vocalist.[29] Later that year he became organist for the Handel and Haydn Society, due to the influence of Lowell Mason, and to the dismay of James Hewitt's daughter Sophia Hewitt Ostinelli, who had been organist since 1820. Zeuner also became organist of King's Chapel, Boston, for an unspecified time. He eventually also became president of the Society for 1838-39, but was asked to resign because of habitual absences at meetings. Another point of contention was Zeuner's criticism of Mason for borrowing secular music and rearranging it for

----

28. Francis F. Beirne, *St. Paul's Parish Baltimore: A Chronicle of the Mother Church* (Baltimore: St. Paul's Parish, 1967), 79, quotes a newspaper clipping of 1820: "An Oratorio was lately performed at St. Paul's Church. The music was indeed sweet, but the result was much sweeter, for, after deducting all necessary expenses, it placed the handsome sum of $703.67 in the hands of the ladies directors of the Female Charity School, a well managed and highly interesting institution." Beirne, however, indicates that Meineke had just come from Germany (apparently not realizing he had originally come to Baltimore in 1800), and remained as organist until 1855--five years after his death. Nonetheless, "He is recorded as giving numerous piano recitals and having many pupils. His teaching brought him a good income and by wise and careful investing he amassed a sizeable fortune." My thanks to Richard J. Cox, of the Baltimore Historical Society, for bringing this book to my attention.

29. A piano concerto by Zeuner was performed in New York City on 14 July 1929, but he was not mentioned with the five German musicians involved. Delmer D. Rogers, "Public Music Performers in New York City from 1800 to 1850," *Yearbook for Inter-American Musical Research* 6 (1970): 22.

church use. Soon he moved to Philadelphia, where he continued his activity as organist until his death by suicide in 1857.[30]

To Zeuner goes the honor of publishing the first collection of organ music in the United States. In 1830 appeared his *Voluntaries for the Organ*, "composed and dedicated to the Handel and Haydn Society, Boston by Ch. Zeuner."[31] The six pieces would have been useful to the church organist of the day, but are not of sufficient musical interest to revive now. Three, entitled Fantasia, are marked "After Service." They are the longest of the set, 2 or 2½ pages long in the original publication, and are with moderate to fast tempos. All of them have recapitulations of initial material, in what might be considered a miniature sonata-allegro plan. The three voluntaries, with slow tempo markings, are for "Before Service," and are somewhat shorter: the maximum is 1½ pages. Two of them have the same formal structure; the other, less than a page long, is too short for a return.

The Voluntary in G, and also presumably a Cantabile in D,[32] are taken from Zeuner's second organ publication, *Organ Voluntaries*,[33] which dates from 1840 and therefore lies beyond the time-limits of this study. Nevertheless, in style and form they are similar to the voluntaries of the 1830 collection.

Zeuner's best keyboard works are the twenty fantasies and fugues in his hand at the Library of Congress. They are all marked "für die Orgel" except for two pieces (nos. 4 and 6) which are evidently for piano. The biggest problem for the researcher is determining if they were composed in Germany and then brought to the United States, or composed after he came. Thus far, I am inclined to believe they are American. The fifth is "dedicadet [*sic*] to Mr: Bigham" (Brigham?)--a name more likely to be encountered in Boston than in Germany. The tenth piece, in D major, had the original title "Fuga a 2 voce et Introduction" crossed out in favor of "Introduction. After the Service. by C. Zeuner." It calls for manual notes down to *A'*, which is more typical of English-style organs in Boston with a small pedal division and compensating extension on the keyboard below *C*,

---

30. This biographical information comes from William George Bigger, "The Choral Music of Charles Zeuner (1795-1857), German-American Composer, with a Performing Edition of Representative Works" (Ph.D. dissertation, University of Iowa, 1976), chapter 2. Since my own article on Zeuner in *The New Grove Dictionary of American Music* appeared, more detailed information, and a preliminary list of works, is now available in Karl Loveland, "The Life of Charles Zeuner, Enigmatic German-American Composer and Organist (1795-1857)," *Tracker* 30, no. 2 (1986): 19-28.

31. "Boston, published by C. Bradlee, 164 Washington St.," copyright 4 August 1830. Title page + pp. 3-13. Newberry Library copy.

32. Owen, *Century*, 1:40-41; *Century*, 3:13.

33. (Boston: Parker and Ditson).

than German organs. The direction in English "without Pedal" is used
for the beginning of the Introduction, and also for the "Fuga a 2
voce," marked "Full Organ (without Pedal)."

This same D-major fugue, without its introduction, is one of six
fugues in another Library of Congress holograph book with the title
"Fuga IV."[34] It is a lively jig-type which displays some of the contrapuntal intricacies of Bach. The subject is inverted several times,
and, except for two free passages, the episodes are tightly organized on
material from the main subject. In spite of the two voices, the exposition has four entries.

"Fuga III" in D major[35] includes a passage near the middle in
which the opening upward scale of the subject, in the left hand,
alternates with its inversion in the right. Just before a fermata, the
three-measure subject appears in the right hand, but the first two
measures are likewise inverted. Zeuner manages to present the opening scale in the three voices every measure in several places, most
notably in the drive to the final cadence. "Fuga I" in D minor,[36]
from the same source, is another well-crafted work. A 19th-century
counterpart to a three-part invention of Bach, it likewise includes
several instances of imitation in stretto.

-----

34. Owen, *Century*, 2:18-19. The principal differences from the
manuscript of fantasies and fugues are as follows. Add "Allegro
molto" and "sempre forte" to the beginning. The last beat of the following measures has an 8th-rest and 16th-note instead of the 8th-note
and 16th rest: 6, 13-15, 20, 23, 40. The upper-8ve pattern in the left
hand of these measures are instead repeated notes: 7, 16-17, 34-37.
The right-hand of measure 18 is: *a'*-sharp *f'*-sharp *g'*-sharp *a'*-sharp *b'*
g'-natural *f'*-sharp *e'*. The right-hand *c'* of meas. 24 is natural, as is
the left-hand *c'* of meas. 38. The fugue ends with two additional
measures, the first an 8th-note chord *G B d g* / *d' g' b' d"*, and
appropriate rests, the second a full-measure (half note!) *D F-sharp A d*
/ *d' f'-sharp a' d"*, both marked *fz*.

35. Owen, *Century*, 2:15-17. This is taken from the Library of
Congress holograph book that includes "Fuga IV." Some corrections:
add trill also to meas. 17, first *e'*, and meas. 22, first *e*; meas. 19, *a'*-
sharp is natural; meas. 32, add natural to *c"*; meas. 39, add editorial
natural to first *c'*; meas. 45, add sharp to *c"*; meas. 67, add appoggiaturas *f'/d'* (written as quarter notes) before the r.h. *c' e'*; meas. 72,
change *a* to *b*.

36. Owen, *Century*, 3:14-15. Some corrections to the edition:
meas. 4, *g'*-flat should be sharp, and add a sharp to the last *c'*; meas.
8, add editorial flat to the last *b'*?; meas. 10, the sharp on *e'* should be
natural; meas. 14, *b'*-flat should be natural; meas. 18, omit flat on *e'*.

"Fuga a 3 voce" in C major[37] is based on a subject which reminds one of early Bach or Buxtehude. Although the returns of the subject, after the exposition, are often shortened, all of the episodes are based on material from the subject. Over a dominant pedal point near the end, the upper two voices are written in strict canon for several measures.

"Jesus meinen Zuversicht,"[38] from the same holograph book, is one of the few organ chorales by an early 19th-century American, although it may have been written in Germany. The chorale tune, in traditional barform (AAB), is introduced by a full twelve measures of the motivic accompanimental material (characterized by a two-note "sigh" and 16th-note scale fragment) that forms the basis for the remainder of the piece. Foreshadowing the quality and some of the character of the Brahms organ chorales, Zeuner's quiet setting warrants use in either recital or church service.

The organ music of Zeuner is a highlight of this survey. The fantasies and fugues represent proof that the "back to Bach" movement was not a monopoly of the 20th century. They are masterfully crafted and, with the *Voluntary* by Carr, deserve resurrection today in church services and recitals. Later 19th-century organ music by Americans such as Dudley Buck and John Knowles Paine represents a complete assimilation of Germanic styles. Yet quality is already to be found in works from the first thirty years of the century, and we, as Americans, should be proud to present some of this music to our musical public.

---

37. Owen, *Century*, 1:42-45. Thus far I have been unable to find the source for this fugue. I am working on an edition of Zeuner's fantasies and fugues for the series Recent Researches in American Music (Madison: A-R Editions). My student Betty Pursley has just (1987) completed "Charles Zeuner's Concerto No. 1 for Organ and Orchestra: An Edition and Commentary" (D.M.A. dissertation, University of Kansas, 1988); apparently this work, dated 1830, is the first keyboard concerto to be composed in the United States.

38. Owen, *Century*, 3:16-19. In the holograph, this setting is followed by a harmonization with figured bass and melody, perhaps intended to accompany a congregation, in which the phrases are separated by short elaborated interludes. Some additions and corrections to Owen's edition: the 2-note "sigh" has slur markings throughout; add indications for pedal in meas. 12 (beginning with *c*)-16, 19-23, 35-39, 67-end; meas. 5, omit sharp before *a*; meas. 6, l.h. *b* should be *a*; meas. 7, add flat before first *d'*; meas. 11, *b* should be *f*; meas. 19, *D* should be octave *C/c*; meas. 20, add flat before last *d'*; meas. 23, add fermata; meas. 30, add flat before *e'* and tie *d'* to the next meas.; meas. 36, add editorial natural to second *c'*; meas. 37, add sharp to last *D*; meas. 52, first *a* should be *b*-flat; meas. 55, a better alternate to the editorial alto might be 8th-rest and 16ths *a'*-sharp *b' c" b'* tied to *b' c" b' a' g' f'*; meas. 58, *a* should be *f*; meas. 60, add editorial natural to last *g*.

7

Pianoforte Tutors in England and America

The United States, because of its origins as a colonial province of the British Empire, remained musically dependent on its parent for some years after the War of Independence. Even when piano instruction books were written by resident American musicians, they were often heavily dependent on those by English authors. Therefore, this examination, although focused on the United States until about 1830, begins with a survey of selected instruction books published in England. All of them were presumably imported into the United States, and some were reprinted here.

English Instruction Books

Preceptor; New Instructions

Among the earliest piano instruction books published in London were *The Preceptor for the Piano-Forte Organ or Harpsichord* (ca. 1785?) and *New Instructions for Playing the Harpsichord, Piano-Forte or Spinnet* (ca. 1790?).[1] Both are slim volumes (34 and 36 pages), and provide a quite concise introduction to the elements of music, notation, and playing. In eleven pages, *Preceptor* explains:

> Note values, rests, the dot
> "Other Characters": accidentals, bar, repeat, direct, "ligature or tye," pause or stop (fermata), stroke (slanted lines for repeated 8th notes, two for 16ths, etc.)
> "The Time" (meter): common, triple, compound
> "The Graces": shake, turned shake, beat, "apogiatura," turn, forefall, backfall
> Fingering, including five "rules," and examples

---

1. Monuments of Music and Music Literature in Facsimile, series 1, vols. 16 and 15 (New York: Broude Bros., 1967).

> "A Scale shewing the Keys of the Harpsichord": drawing
> of the gamut, with clefs, matched with the keyboard

New Instructions treats the same elements, but the drawing of the gamut is inserted before the section on Time, and separate material on the "stave," ledger lines, and clefs is added at the beginning. Many of the explanations are almost identical. In the section on graces, the obsolete forefall and backfall are omitted, but further material dealing with elementary theory is added:

> "Of Keys"
> "Of Intervals"
> "Of Concords"
> "Of Discords"
> "Of Playing Thorough Bass"
> "To play Harpeggio . . ."
> "There are various Cadences or Closes . . ."

In both books, simple and carefully-fingered pieces are provided for the student in progressive difficulty--fifteen in *Preceptor* and eighteen in *New Instructions*. Four of the pieces are duplicates. A few songs are even included, with texts. Featured in *Preceptor* are two "Lessons" by James Hook, the last with an additional part presumably for flute or violin. Both books end with identical instructions on tuning, and almost-identical dictionaries of foreign terms used in music.

John Christopher Moller

John Christopher Moller (1755-1803), probably born in Germany, spent some time in England, and wrote two instructional books before coming to the United States. His opus 5, published about 1784, is a collection of small sonatas written for students (see chapter 1): *Eight Easy Lessons for the Piano Forte or Harpsicord for Young Practioners* [sic]. Opus 6 is an instruction book, *A Sett of Progressive Lessons for the Harpsichord or Piano Forte*, issued about 1785.[2] The imprint for op. 6 is "for the Author by Longman and Broderip"; it was then reissued about 1795 "for the Author by J. Cooper." The ten lessons, all by Moller, are followed by "Short and easy INSTRUCTIONS for playing the HARPSICHORD or PIANO-FORTE" which indeed prove to be short--they are on only three pages. Nevertheless, all the explanations of the 1785 *Preceptor*, but not including the section on fingering, are there--not exact, but at times quite close.

The tutor was also published about 1801 with the title *A Compleat Book of Instructions, for the Piano Forte, Harpsichord, or Organ, A Set of Progressive Lessons, in Various Keys, with Cadence &*

---

2. The copies at the Library of Congress and British Library are dated 1792 and 1795. However, Ronald D. Stetzel, in "John Christopher Moller (1755-1803) and His Role in Early American Music," 1:357-58, found a notice in the *London Public Advertiser* for 3 January 1785.

Preludes . . . Composed by J. C. Moller, Music Master, to their Majesty's School, Queen Square.[3] The contents are identical, but in the new publication the instructions are at the beginning, the pieces afterwards. In both books, a dictionary of Italian musical terms appears at the end.

James Hook

Obviously, London music publishers were issuing competing piano instruction books in the mid-1780s. *Preceptor* was issued by John Preston, *New Instructions* by Anne Bland, Moller's *Sett* by Longman and Broderip. Preston also published James Hook's *Guida di musica*, op. 37, about 1785, but his *New Guida di musica*, op. 81 (1796) was issued by Bland, now in partnership with E. Weller.[4] Hook's latest tutor, "on a new & improved plan," is not derived from the others. The section on the elements of music and notation is only five pages long. In comparison with the 1785 *Preceptor*, some aspects are condensed, others expanded, still others left out altogether:

> Scale or gamut, with exercises; clefs
> Flats, sharps, accidentals
> Note values, the dot
> Time: common, triple, compound
> Shakes and graces: shake, turn, turn shake, beat, trill, transient shake, "apogiatura"
> Major and minor keys

For the first time in these instruction books, the trill and transient shake are realized beginning on the principal, not upper, note. The remainder of the 33-page book is devoted to the lessons, all by Hook,

---

3. "London, pubd. by J. Cooper, 8, Winchester Court, Monkwell Str. Wood Str. Entd. at Sta. Hall, & sold by J. Fentum, 78, Strand, & by R. Watts, Blackman Str. Borough." Charles Humphries and William C. Smith, *Music Publishing in the British Isles*, 2nd ed. (Oxford: Basil Blackwell, 1970), 115, list Cooper at that address ca. 1801, although the New York Public Library dates its copy as ca. 1803. Oddly enough, not even Stetzel has taken notice of Moller's position as "Music Master, to their Majesty's School, Queen Square." Is this version of the book a reprint from an earlier edition of the 1780s, when Moller could have held such a position? In 1801 he was in New York. *Baker's*, 6th ed., although citing Stetzel's dissertation in the article on Moller, does not mention Moller as even being in London.

4. New Guida di Musica, Being a Compleat Book of Instructions for Beginners on the Piano Forte or Harpsichord on a New & Improved Plan, to which is added Twenty-Four Progressive Lessons in Various Keys with the proper Fingering throughout, composed by Mr. Hook, op. 81.

with two pages at the end with fingered scales in the twenty-four major and minor keys.[5]

Jan Ladislav Dussek

Jan Ladislav Dussek (1760-1812), born in Bohemia and pursuing his career mainly on the continent, fled the French Revolution in 1788 to continue his career in London. He married Sophia Corri and was in business with his father-in-law Domenico Corri until the business failed in 1800 and he returned to the continent. *Dussek's Instructions on the Art of Playing the Piano Forte or Harpsichord* was first published in 1796 by Corri, Dussek & Co., then within a few years was issued in a French translation in Paris, and in Leipzig translated to German. It is the most detailed book thus far, as confirmed by its size (47 pages) and the continuation of the title: "Being a Compleat Treatise of the first Rudiments of Music & containing General & Exemplified Rules & Principles on the Art of Fingering, Making the Compleatist Work ever offered to the Public." On seven large pages, ten "Lessons" present the rudiments:

1	Notes (pitches)
2	Gamut or scale
3	"Accidents"
4	Character and length of the notes
5	Triplet or sextuplets
6	Bar
7	"The Characters of Time" (meter)
8	"Legature" or tie, stroke
9	Graces or ornaments: "apogiatura," shake (plain, beat, short, turned, continued, grace & shake), turn (plain, inverted, sharp, after the note), slur, "The Cadence or Reprise"
10	Of the different "cliffs," with drawing of the keyboard

One innovation is at the end of the ninth lesson: the "cadence" is the fermata sign, which indicates the note should be held, "or to introduce Voluntary Graces, Evolutions agreable [unintentionally from *agrément*?] to his Taste and Fancy."

Dussek's endeavors at being "the compleatist" are directed to the section entitled "Rules for Fingering." Dussek met and may have studied with Carl Philipp Emanuel Bach in Hamburg in 1782. This section is obviously influenced by Bach's *Versuch*, chapter 1, but is not directly borrowed from it. On 23 pages, generously endowed with musical examples, are presented these "rules":

---

5. Hook's book, probably *New Guida di musica*, was first published in the United States in 1812, although the earliest extant copy dates from 1817-18; see Wolfe 4049-4049A.

1 "How to Ascend with the Right Hand in sharp Keys"
2 "How to Descend with the Right Hand, in sharp Keys"
3 "How to ascend with the Right Hand in those Keys where you meet with Flats"
4 "How to descend, with the right hand, in Flat Keys"
5 "How to ascend with the Left Hand"
6 "To descend with the left hand"
7 "How to ascend, and descend with the left hand in the flat Keys"
   Examples of various passages for both hands
   "Of Harpeggio Passages"; "Of Double Notes"; "Octaves"; "Chromatic Passages"
   Rule the Last: [hand position]

Nine pages of fingered scales and arpeggios follow, in thirteen major and minor keys (including both F-sharp and G-flat), arranged in the ascending circle of fifths from C upwards.

Only four pages are devoted to six simple one-movement "Lessons"--one in F major, the others in C. However, Dussek's dictionary of terms is the most extensive thus far encountered--also on four pages. The foregoing comprises the first book of *Dussek's Instructions*; the second, designed to be purchased separately, is "Six progressive Sonatinas wth. accomp^t. ad Libitum" by Ignace Pleyel, op. 32. Shortly afterwards, Dussek also issued six more Pleyel sonatas, op. 32. The whole "package" then consisted of three books, each of which could be purchased separately or together.

Muzio Clementi

Among the earliest instruction books to be devoted specifically to the pianoforte, and certainly the most important to be published in England, is *Clementi's Introduction to the Art of Playing on the Piano Forte: Containing the Elements of Music; Preliminary notions on Fingering with Examples; and Fifty fingered Lessons*, first issued in 1801.[6] The title-page specifically mentions his "Six Progressive SONATINAS" as a supplement--the sonatinas of course have had a long life. The tutor had as many as twelve editions, 1801-30, as well as translations published in France, Belgium, Germany, Italy, and Spain. The first edition published in the United States was the eighth, in 1820-21 (Wolfe 1882). Clementi's explanations vary little from those of his English predecessors:

---

6. London: Clementi, Banger, Hyde, Collard & Davis; facsimile of the 1st edition, 2nd issue (1804), with introduction by Sandra P. Rosenblum (New York: Da Capo, 1974). Rosenblum's extensive introduction is most helpful by describing differences in the various editions and in relating Clementi's book to others tutors of the time.

"Preliminaries": note names, "stave," ledger lines
"Clefs"
"The Scale, or Gamut," with exercises
"Intervals," with examples
"Tenor, Counter-tenor, and Soprano clefs explained"
"Figure, Length, and relative Value of Notes; with their respective Rests"
"Time and its Divisions": simple common, simple triple, compound, triplets, sextuplets
"Sharps, and Flats &c."; order of accidentals in key signatures
"Various other marks": pause, sign of repeat, bars, abbreviations
"Style, Graces, and marks of Expression, &c.": staccato, legato, broken chord, dynamics, arpeggio
"Appoggiaturas, and other Graces in small notes explained": appoggiaturas, turns, shakes, beats
"Major and Minor Modes or Keys; vulgarly called Sharp and Flat Keys"
"Explanation of Various Terms" on tempo and style

An important innovation was the legato, "played in a smooth and close manner; which is done by keeping down the first key, 'till the next is struck; by which means, the strings vibrate sweetly into one another."

Clementi then follows with a complete section on fingering, although not as extensively explained as in Dussek's book. There are two-octave scales for both hands, in the major keys, each followed by its relative minor key arranged in ascending fifths (C a G e D b, etc.), then the chromatic scale. The following section, "Extensions and Contractions &c.," represents the pianistic pyrotechniques for which Clementi was famous. It includes repeated notes, rapid octaves, parallel or alternating thirds and sixths, and repeated figures reaching beyond the confines of the octave. The fifty pieces are in the principal major keys, up to four sharps or flats, similarly followed by the relative minor keys. Whereas the tutors by Moller, Hook, and Dussek have pieces exclusively by the compiler, Clementi's furnishes works "by Composers of the first rank, Ancient and Modern." Some of these are Mozart, Handel, Corelli, Couperin, Storace, Pleyel, Haydn, Rameau, Scarlatti, C. P. E. Bach, J. S. Bach, and Clementi's pupil J. B. Cramer--but none by Clementi himself. However, he furnished his own short preludes to the section of pieces that introduce each new key.[7]

Philip Antony Corri

The most extensive book of this period, however, is by Dussek's brother-in-law Philip Antony Corri. His sister Sophia, as mentioned

---

7. The prelude keys are not quite organized like the scales; they alternate a series of ascending with descending fifths (each followed by its relative minor): C F G B-flat D E-flat A A-flat E.

above, married Dussek. In Baltimore, under his new name Arthur Clifton, he published considerably shorter tutors, *New Piano Forte Preceptor* and *New and Improved Piano Forte Preceptor* (to be discussed below), as well as a voice tutor, *New Vocal Instructer*. Apparently he was equally gifted as teacher and performer of voice and piano; his songs and piano pieces published in England and Baltimore are likewise of high quality.

The extent of the sales and impact of his London instruction book is not known. The title page is worth quoting in full:

> L'Anima Di Musica, An Original Treatise upon Piano Forte Playing, in which musical expression & style are reduced to system, the rudiments of music, the art of fingering, the nature of touch, and of preluding, are illustrated with suitable examples, together, with twenty seven exercises, twenty progressive lessons, and above two hundred progressive preludes, in every key & mode and in different styles, so calculated, that variety may be formed at pleasure, a dictionary is also added, explaining every term used in music, the whole written & composed by P. Antony Corri. 1810. London, printed for the author (and to be had of him, 36, Norman Street) by C. Mitchell, 51 Southampton Row, Russell Square and also, to be had at all the principle [*sic*] music shops.[8]

The book is divided into four parts: Rudiments & Theory, Practise & Fingering, Expression & Style, Preluding. Although a few excerpts from the works of Clementi and Dussek are used in the third part, *L'Anima* reveals no direct, or indirect, borrowing from those two books. Dussek's material on rudiments and theory (not including scales and fingering) fits seven pages; Clementi's was the longest thus far with fourteen. Corri's first part, however, is an unprecedented twenty-two pages. Among his innovations is lesson 5, "of counting and beating the time," which involves beating with the hand and counting aloud, a new explanation of syncopation, plus the following outburst:

> It is a matter of surprize to me that so few scholars, or Amateurs who affect to play well, understand any thing about Time.
>
> How often do we hear a performer rattle thro' a Sonata, perhaps with great execution and force--but who cannot play an Adagio or even a simple ballad or air in good Time. Why?--Because it is so much trouble to count--the acquiring execution and brilliancy of finger is the study of years; whereas the perfect knowledge of Time, is the study of a few hours.

---

8. Title-page + ii + 118 pp. Copy at British Library.

Lesson 7, on the clefs, is very thorough: not only are all the C-clefs included (with the "Tenor, or Voce Umana" clef), but also the "Baritone, or Bass Tenor" (F-clef on the middle line). Within the chapter on the appoggiatura, Corri proposes some new terminology. The "forcing or leaning graces" are auxiliary notes to be played "with emphasis and exactly with the Bass," and includes what others term the slide; the "leading or passing graces" follow the principal note without emphasis, and the "anticipating grace--or anticipation." Within lesson 11, "Of the Scale and Moods [modes]," is a drawing of a harmonic circle, giving the keys and key-signatures in a circular form. Corri also provides a description of the difference between the piano and harpsichord at the end of the first part. The pianoforte

> is capable of more expression than either that Instrument [the harpsichord] or the Organ. . . . Whereas on the Piano Forte, the performers taste is express'd at pleasure by the degree of touch or pressure given to the keys, and, with proper fingering, has the peculiar property of blending the sounds imitative of the Voice and like the pencil in the hands of an Artist, may produce that Light and Shade-Harmony of coloring, and combination of effect, which so delight the Senses.

The "compleatist" tutor on fingering still remains Dussek's, with thirty-two pages, as compared to Clementi's five and Corri's seventeen. Corri, however, raises Clementi's concern with the legato style to a new height. In a section concerning the changing of the finger on a key, he explains:

> In slow movements and passages that have more than single parts, it [finger-changing] is the only way of linking the notes & should be particularly attended to, as without it, the melody would be broken and unconnected, whereas this method blends the notes, and produces, the SOSTENUTO or CANTABILE style which this Instrument is so peculiar for . . ..

Corri completes his second section with an additional thirteen pages of the twenty-seven exercises and the twenty progressive lessons promised on the title page.

The most unusual and useful part of Corri's book is the third part. Expression is defined as "the Soul of Music; It is the Eloquence of Sound, and gains access to the Heart, whereas Music without expression is unmeaning and has no charm." He draws analogies with the delivery of poetry, with painting, and dancing. The means of expression on the piano are "Touch, Emphasis and Modulation of Sound--that is; the crescendo, diminuendo, and degrees of forte and piano--Besides which, expression is produced by the protraction of Time, by the Italians termed, TEMPO RUBATO but more properly should be styled TEMPO PERDUTO." Corri discusses the varieties of style: reel, march, song or pathetic air, and the types exhibiting varieties of style: the overture, concerto, sonata, and divertisement, which "combines brilliancy with feeling, the energetic with the pathetic." It is here that Corri commences with a description of legato, several gradations of staccato, and degrees of touch (dynamics). Of great value are the three pages devoted to "Emphasis," in which Corri describes the various methods of shaping a phrase, by means of articulation and dynamics.

Of equal importance, and likewise rarely seen discussed in print, is the succeeding section, "Of the Appoggiando . . . commonly tho' erroniously [sic] called SLURRING, . . . but if it must be anglicised let it be termed properly, LEANING." However, Corri here describes the practice commonly termed arpeggio, or breaking a chord beginning with the bottom note. The signs are

but the practice is to be applied even when not specified. The appoggiando should not be indiscriminately used on all chords, but only on the longer ones that need emphasis. A number of examples are accompanied by detailed reasoning on applying this practice, derived from the harpsichord style, which has been lost by modern pianists who are reluctant to arpeggiate chords that are not specifically marked.

Part the Fourth, "Of Preluding,"[9] begins with the following:

> Every performance should be introduced by a prelude, not only to prepare the Ear for the key in which such an air is to be played, but to prepare the fingers, and therefore should in general consist of some rapid movement intermixt with chords, Arpeggio's [sic] or other passages.

This quotation likewise represents a tradition which has been lost in the 20th century. Corri does not pretend to impart the art of improvisation, but nevertheless provides a number of examples as models, arranged in progressive order, and in all major and minor keys (arranged in the circle of fifths, e.g. C G D A, etc.). The "first style" has only "perfect" (root in bass and soprano) and seventh chords (on the dominant); the second style admits the sub-dominant chord. This harmonic vocabulary is retained for the third style, but the chords are arpeggiated (broken both upwards and back down). With the fourth style Corri writes "coda's [sic] or finales" in which a more advanced pianistic ability is expected for the flourishes of scales and arpeggio in 16th notes. For the fifth style, "capo's [sic] or introductions, with suitable coda's [sic] forming entire preludes" present the nucleus of what receives the final form in the sixth style, "complete preludes or capriccios." As to the performance of these preludes, "all formality or precision of time must be avoided; it must appear to be the birth of

---

9. Part 4 was later reissued as *P. A. Corri's System of Preluding*, in London by Chappell & Co. (1812?) and by P. T. Latour (1823?). Copies are in the British Library.

the moment, the effusion of fancy, for which reason it may be observed that the measure or time is not always mark'd at preludes."

Whereas short preludes, usually introducing a new key, are often furnished in piano instruction books on both sides of the Atlantic, nowhere else does one find a complete step-by-step method for the student to learn how to improvise on his own. Corri's book is probably the best of its time emanating from England. Clementi's, however, was still the most influential.

Neville Butler Challoner

The English harpist, violinist, and pianist Neville Butler Challoner (1784-d. after 1835)[10] wrote a piano tutor which appeared in the United States with two titles: *New Guida di musica, or Book of Instructions on the Piano Forte* (ca. 1819), and *A New Preceptor for the Piano Forte* (1817?).[11] Challoner endeavors to compromise between one method in which the pupil is made to understand all the principles of music before touching the piano--"The Editor is acquainted with one instance where a young Lady received instructions (in this manner) TWO YEARS! before the Piano Forte was used . . ."--and others (referring to Clementi's book by name) in which the instrument is used at the very beginning to aid in understanding the basic elements of music. Challoner "wishes to recommend a plan of Instruction *between* those above noticed. . . ." He explains the staff, notes, clefs, gamut, time values, and meters. Only then are these principles applied to the piano. Simple exercises are then intermixed with further explanations of chords, accidentals, repeat marks, the fermata, staccato, triplets, and marks of abbreviation. The common keys, in Clementi's order of ascending alternating with descending fifths (but only to A and E-flat major), are each introduced with fingered scales. Ornaments are not completely treated until the end of the book, along with a concise dictionary of dynamics and tempo terms. A few of the pieces are arrangements of popular melodies. The student is then referred to Challoner's edition of twenty-four lessons of extracts from Mozart, Haydn, Beethoven, Steibelt, Kozeluch, and Pleyel, also available from American publishers.[12]

------

10. Wolfe, p. 175, gives his birth date as 1784, and cites his first appearance as violinist the previous year! *New Grove* has a short article.

11. Wolfe 1753-54 and 1756-57. For the second, I used a variant of Wolfe 1756 published in Philadelphia by George Willig, located at Baylor University. The contents of *New Guida* and *New Preceptor* are identical.

12. Wolfe 1758-59, in which these lessons are called "sonatas" or "petite sonatas"--but none is an entire sonata.

John Baptist Cramer

John (Johann) Baptist Cramer (1771-1858), Clementi's pupil, is still known as a composer of technical etudes. Although born in Germany, and spending over a dozen years abroad after the death of his teacher, Cramer's principal residence was London. His *Instructions for the Piano Forte* was first published in London in 1812, the first American edition in 1821 (Wolfe 2159). The third edition, issued in Philadelphia in the period 1821-24, was reprinted by subsequent publishers in later years.[13] Cramer's *Instructions*, 3rd edition, does not display as much indebtedness to the book by his teacher Clementi as one might suspect. The wording of the explanations and definitions is completely different from Clementi's.

The differences are most obvious in the organization of the material. Some of the changes parallel those Clementi made in later editions. For example, Clementi explains the C-clefs in some detail, near the beginning, but relegates this material to the back of the book for the 8th edition (1814-16). So does Cramer. However, Cramer presents the complete gamut and the accidentals later in his book than does Clementi. The most important difference is that Cramer uses the device of providing a good deal of information related to the "lessons" in footnotes, information that Clementi had given in a more abstract manner. These explanations include such matters as ornaments, repeat strokes, fermatas, arpeggiando, and staccato marks. An index for the terms, provided right after the title-page, guides the user to these notational devices. Two new elements, compared with Clementi's 1st edition, are pedal markings, and going from a black to a white key with one finger. Pedal markings were added to Clementi's 5th edition (1811), and finger-gliding to the 8th.

Cramer leaves for the end the C-clefs, intervals, arpeggiated chords, "tremando" (tremolo), a complete explanation of the pedal signs, and three new matters not otherwise found in Clementi's editions: transposition, musical accent, and syncopation. Tempo names are not defined as such until the dictionary, on the last two pages. In his 5th edition, Clementi had introduced pieces in the keys only to two sharps or flats (omitting E-flat, A-flat, A, E of the earlier editions), but restored E-flat and A in the 8th edition. Cramer's 3rd edition presents pieces in the upwards circle of fifths from C to E, then downward from F to A-flat--each immediately followed with its relative minor, as in Clementi. Each key is introduced with a small prelude. Some of the traditional composers are still represented-- Haydn, Mozart, Handel, Steibelt, Viotti, Dussek, Beethoven, and

---

13. Wolfe 2160. Of the later imprints, Brown University has several copies and several editions, including a 5th edition (Boston: John Ashton, [1824-44]). The Harding collection at the Bodleian Library, Oxford, has one, dated in pen 1831, published in New York by S. Ackerman, and another, without date, published in Baltimore by George Willig, Jr. with a large engraving of a lady before a square piano, opposite the title-page.

Clementi himself--but there is also a generous portion of popular tunes, and one contemporary composer, Bochsa.

In general Cramer's is a very complete and logically organized book. There are twenty-one pages of instructions (versus Clementi's nineteen), not including all of the material presented in footnotes with the lessons. Although Cramer's 53 pages are ten less than Clementi's 1st edition, Clementi's fifty pieces are matched by only thirty-seven. Yet included in Cramer's "package" is a supplement: *J. B. Cramer's Sequel to his Celebrated Book of Instructions for the Piano Forte, Consisting of Expressly composed & Newly Arranged Pieces, Each preceded by a Short Prelude Fingered by the Author.*[14]

The most important aspects of both Clementi's and Cramer's books are the emphasis on the practice of scales and various types of pianistic figurations--important for the virtuoso--and the growing concern for a singing, legato style, aided in some cases by silent finger-substitution. Cramer's version of the legato, as a footnote to the fourth lesson, contrasts with the disconnected style prevalent in the previous century: "This style of playing is termed in Italian Legato, it is generally used, unless some particular mark should direct to the contrary." Clementi had been more specific:

> The best general rule, is to keep down the keys of the instrument, the full length of every note [unless the contrary is marked]. . . . The notes marked [with slur,] called legato in Italian, must be played in a smooth and close manner; which is done by keeping down the first key, 'till the next is struck; by which means, the strings vibrate sweetly into one another [addition from 5th ed., 1811: "and imitate the best style of singing"]. N.B. when the composer leaves the legato, and staccato to the performer's taste; the best rule is, to adhere chiefly to the legato; reserving the staccato to give spirit occasionally to certain passages, and to set off the higher beauties of the legato.

John Freckleton Burrowes

One of the later English tutors is a textbook: *The Piano Forte Primer, or New Musical Catechism, Containing the Rudiments of Music: Calculated either for Private Tuition, or Teaching in Classes*, by John Freckleton Burrowes (1787-1852), published by George E. Blake in Philadelphia in 1820 (Wolfe 1403). It had been originally issued in London in 1818, and was subsequently reprinted in New York. The instruction is in the time-honored format of pupil's questions answered

---

14. (Philadelphia: G. E. Blake, n.d.). The copy in the Starr collection, Lilly Library, Indiana University, is only seven pages long, but is immediately followed, in the same binding, by pp. 1-15 of Christopher Meineke's *New Instructions for the Piano Forte* (ca. 1823), Wolfe 5781.

by the master. As stated in the title, musical rudiments are covered in the 56 small-sized pages. No teaching pieces are included.

Ornaments in English Instruction Books

Modern performers who are accustomed to begin Mozart's trills on the principal note, and to place "grace notes" before the beat, will be surprised at the degree of unanimity in favor of the upper-note trill and on-beat appoggiatura in these books, published about 1785-1825. The signs and realizations are summarized here.

Appoggiatura. The general rule is as clear in Cramer as in the other books:

> . . . whatever length is given to the Appoggiatura, is taken from the following large note, with which it is always played Legato: about one half of the Large note is generally given to the small one.

New Instructions further explains: ". . . when put before a dotted Note, then the little Note is most commonly played two thirds of the Time, and the remaining third part only used by the principal Note." These two principles are illustrated with many examples in the tutors. The note values of the written appoggiaturas themselves vary, but generally are one degree smaller. For example, an appoggiatura to a half note would be written as a quarter, and played as a quarter. Corri emphasizes that the appoggiatura is played on the beat, with the bass, and adds in a footnote: "The general fault, is playing the Appoggiatura before the Bass" (which is still true today!). Corri also explains why the following passage is written the first way, and not the second (which is its realization).

"The difference . . . is that the appoggiatura . . . is played with more emphasis--being a leaning note . . . --whereas being written as equal notes . . . should be played with equal touch."

Some variance with these general principles is found with the short appoggiatura, as demonstrated in these examples.

Clementi, Dussek:

Challoner:

Dussek:

Challoner:

Clementi, Challoner:

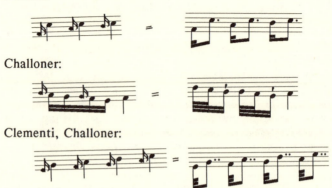

The outmoded forefall and backfall (   ) are explained only in *Preceptor*.

    Turn. Realizations of the usual turn sign vary, but with very little perceptual difference.

    Preceptor, New Instructions, Hook, Dussek:

Clementi, Corri:

Moller:

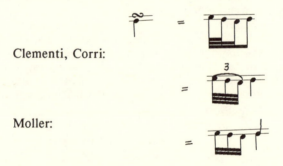

The inverted turn, with the sign ₂ or ∿, is the same except that the first note is the lower. The authors of the books wrestle with the problem of the raised lower note, but Clementi's suggestion is the most succinct: "The LOWEST note of EVERY sort of turn is MOSTLY a semitone." The accidental is sometimes added below or to the left of the sign, but its absence, according to Clementi's statement, does not mean that it should not be used. Corri has three indications for the turn with accidental:

As for a turn on a dotted note, Corri is the most illuminating:

> When the turn is placed after the note--play the note first--and the turn rather late, unless it is a pathetic movement in which case the turn may be played slow--leading to the next note--but without inter- ruption. . . . When the Turn is placed over the dot of a note in common time of 3/4--begin the Turn

just before the dot and end with it making a stop
between the turn and subsequent note. . . . When
the turn is over the dot of a note in Triple Time, . .
. it is played exactly in the place of the dot--that is,
with the Bass note and neither before nor after.

Shake. The signs for the shake (never called the trill) vary considerably in these books: *Preceptor, New Instructions,* Clementi (8th
edition): ⌀ ; Moller: ‖ ; Dussek, Clementi (1st edition): ＼; Hook,
Clementi, Challoner: ∾ ;[15] *New Instructions,* Clementi (8th edition): *tr.*
The number of repercussions for a half-note or quarter-note shake is
from six to eight notes, sometimes with the last one longer. The sign
for the turned shake, in which the repercussions end with a turn, is
universally *tr*; Clementi, however, provides the alternate signs ∿ ⟳ ∿̃.
New Instructions is alone in stating that *tr* "may be played either as a
plain Shake, a turned Shake, or a Turn only, at the Discretion of the
Performer." Corri derives the shake from the turn:

> The Shake *tr* is formed from the Simple Turn--and
> guided by the same rules being merely the two first
> notes of the turn repeated in rapid succession so long
> as the time will admit, concluding with the other two
> notes, which latter notes are denominated the turn of
> the Shake.

Corri further explains:

> Note; the number of notes in the shake are not
> limited, the more the better, as they cannot be too
> swift--the Turn must be played as late as possible so
> to connect it with what follows--and by no means to
> make any interruption except in the case of a dotted
> note. . . .

Furthermore, according to Corri, the two examples would be played
alike:

There are no books which advocate a shake or turned shake beginning
on any note other than the upper auxiliary.
     Other types are the continued shake (Dussek, Clementi, Cramer)
or long shake (Corri), always indicated with *tr*; and the shake with a
prolonged appoggiatura, called "grace & shake" (Dussek). What Corri

---

15. Challoner's *Instructions for Playing the Piano Forte* (Boston:
C. Bradlee, [ca. 1831]), 28, still uses the upper-note trill. Copy in the
New York Public Library.

describes as a shake beginning with an inverted turn () is termed by Clementi a "prepared shake."

As in German treatises of the late 18th century, the modern concept of the trill commencing on the principal note begins to form in the varying realizations of shakes on shorter notes. Since these differences cannot easily be summarized, some examples are here given:

passing shake, Moller:

short shake, Dussek:

short shake beginning by the note itself

    Clementi:

    Clementi:

transient or passing shake, Clementi:

transient shake

    Hook:

    Cramer:

Corri: shakes on short notes, descending, require no turn; but do when ascending:

In spite of the ubiquitous sign *tr*, the only author using the term "trill" is Hook, who has this unusual sign and realization:

Beat. The English equivalent of the mordent is the beat, although the signs and realizations are often closely allied to the turn and the shake. *Preceptor*'s beat is identical to the mordent, or French *pincé*; that of Moller, Hook, and Dussek imply a preceding appoggiatura, like the French *port-de-voix* (lower appoggiatura) combined with the *pincé*. Clementi incorporates all of the signs and practices, and then some.

Preceptor:

Moller:

Hook:

Dussek:

Clementi:

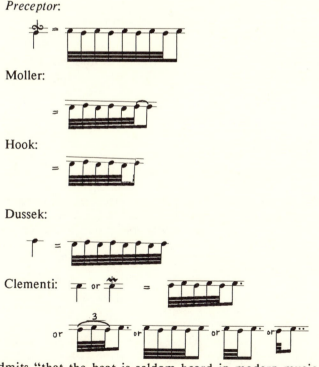

Clementi admits "that the beat is seldom heard in modern music." In the 8th edition, Clementi omits the first sign, and expands his disclaimer: "In modern music . . . we make no use of the long or continued Beat; but the short Beat [the last realization above] has sometimes a good effect, for the sake of emphasis."

To further confuse the issue, Corri makes the beat what others might term a short shake; in German, *Schneller*:

> The BEAT ⱴ is a double appoggiatura, beginning on the principal note--and must be executed with brilliancy and articulation.

Challoner does not mention the beat.

Staccato. No distinction between dashes and dots are made in the instruction books published before 1800. Clementi is the first to explain that dashes indicate the shortest notes, the dots less short, and dots under a slur still shorter yet. Corri calls the dashes "staccato," the dots "disgiunto." Cramer is the most specific:

> These small Dashes (ı ı ı ı) shew that the notes must be played in a distinct and separate manner, giving about one fourth its usual length, and lifting the fingers from the keys, as if a Rest intervened. . . . This style of playing is termed, Staccato, (detached). N.B. When Dots (· · · ·) are made use of, the notes must have half of their usual length.

In another place, Cramer names the dots under a slur "mezzo staccato."

American Instruction Books

John Thomas Schley

The first extant keyboard instructional material in the United States is in a manuscript commonplace book probably copied and used by John Thomas Schley of Frederick, Maryland. Schley was born in Germany in 1712, came to America about 1739, and died in 1790. His book contains a great many works for piano and organ (some composed by Schley himself), undoubtedly compiled for his pupils. At the beginning are eight pages designed for the beginning student (the page numbers are editorial):

1	There are Six sorts of Notes in Music [note-values and rests]
2	The Treble Cliff or G; the Bass Cliff or, F.
3	Gamut: The Treble Scale; the Bass Scale; The Chromatic Scale, or, All the Keys with the Semitones
4	[Signs: sharp, flat, natural, single & double bars, repeat mark]
5	Common Time; Triple Time; Compound
6	Position of the right Hand; Position of the Left Hand

7	[Alternating] Thirds for the right Hand; Thirds for the Left Hand
8	[Alternating] Octaves for the right Hand; Octaves for the Left Hand

In the midst of the book (pp. 287-90) is material on the figured bass, followed by a page on "The art of Fingering the Piana [*sic*] Forte." A crowded page entitled "A Short Dictionary of Musical Terms" is at the end of the book. None of this material seems derived from any published tutor.[16]

Francis Linley

Francis Linley (1771-1800) was in the United States in 1796-99, and was responsible for the earliest keyboard tutors published in the young country. Inexplicably, two editions of the same tutor were published by Joseph Carr in Baltimore during two months of 1796.[17] *A New Assistant for the Piano-Forte or Harpsichord . . . by F. Linley, Organist of Pentonville* (in London) was first advertised for sale August 6. *Linley's Assistant, for the Piano-Forte . . . a new edition* was advertised the following September 30.[18] The two publications are essentially the same in the instructional material, but with new typesetting. *A New Assistant* contains "Twelve Airs or short Lessons progressively arrang'd: To which is added Six Sonatas, one of which is adapted for two Performers." The six sonatas are by the publisher's son and Philadelphia business partner Benjamin Carr. Ten of the airs, somewhat reordered, again appear in *Linley's Assistant* along with others to make a total of twenty-four, plus three songs.

---

16. An inventory of the contents is in Anne Louise Shifflet, "Church Music and Musical Life in Frederick, Maryland, 1745-1845" (M.A. thesis, American University, 1971), and in James J. Fuld and Mary Wallace Davidson, *18th-Century American Secular Music Manuscripts: An Inventory*, MLA Index & Bibliography Series, 20 (Philadelphia: Music Library Association, 1980), no. 18. My thanks to Ms. Davidson for loaning a microfilm of the manuscript.

17. Both are described in Sonneck-Upton, 289-90.

18. The only surviving copy of *Linley's Assistant*, at the Maryland Historical Society, contains many manuscript additions in the instructional portion. The Society suggests these may be in the hand of Eliza E. Ridgely of Baltimore; if true, the book was used at least ten years after it was printed, for Mrs. Ridgely was born in 1802--see Lubov Keefer, *Baltimore's Music: The Haven of the American Composer* (Baltimore: J. H. Furst, 1962), 79. Eliza Ridgely, who subsequently married the son of Maryland's governor, is the subject of a 1818 painting by Thomas Sully, now at the National Gallery in Washington. Roslyn Rensch, *The Harp: Its History, Technique and Repertoire* (London: Duckworth, 1969), 132, and plate 37b.

The "necessary rudiments for Beginners" in both editions are concisely printed on four pages:

> Staff
> "Examples of the Notes on the Lines"
> "Scale of the Notes and Keys": notes matched to a
>   drawing of the keyboard
> "Gamut for the Piano Forte or Harpsichord"
> "Explanation of Musical Characters": clefs, note
>   values, slur, pause, bars, repeats, shake
> "Of Time": note values

The approach, layout, and explanations are different from any English instruction book discussed thus far. On the one hand, the notes are printed on the staves, even with some redundancy, as "1st line E," "2nd Ledger Line C." The same material is presented in another manner on the second page, where a drawing of the keyboard is matched to the notes on the staves; and, in case the student missed it the first two times, on the third page where notes on a complete gamut are labeled. On the other hand, the "Explanation of Musical Characters" is mislabeled; the various musical signs are only named, not explained. Clearly, a student using this book would need a teacher to fill in the gaps.

After the "lessons" are printed a set of "Short Preludes for Beginners" (each only two measures long) in the eight principal keys (up to three flats and four sharps), fingered three-octave scales in the same keys, and a second, more elaborate, set of eight preludes "for those more advanced in Practice." A further two pages is devoted to "Rules for Thoro' Bass," filled out with a table of the intervals. A short dictionary of terms fills the last page. The same typesetting for the dictionary in *A New Assistant* was also used by Joseph Carr for his 1796 anthology of music *The Gentleman's Amusement* (page numbers for both publications appear on the same page).

Linley's Assistant was reprinted in 1814-15. Additional material, including explanations of graces, was added, and new music was substituted for the old.[19]

George Gilfert, Andrew Law

A New and Complete Instructor for the Piano Forte, published by George Gilfert (d. 1814) in New York in 1802-03 (Wolfe 4495), may have been new, but it is not very complete. The rudiments are presented on only two pages, with a one-page dictionary at the end. The thirty-six pieces are mostly popular tunes, and include two which are distinctly American: Phile's "President's March" and "Washington's March" (Sonneck's Group I). The keys do not venture beyond three sharps or flats. Preludes in six keys conclude the playing material.

Even more modest is Andrew Law's eight-page *The Art of Playing the Organ and Piano Forte, or Characters Adapted to Instruments*

---

19. Wolfe 5393. I have been unable to obtain a copy.

(1809; Wolfe 5323). The book is a futile attempt to transfer to the keyboard Law's four shape-note system, expanded by means of adding dots to fill out the seven notes of the scale. The entire book is devoted to explaining the notation system; there is nothing about playing on the keyboard, nor pieces.

James Hewitt

A distinct improvement was made in James Hewitt's *A Complete Instructor for the Piano Forte, with proper mode of Fingering, Illustrated by a variety of examples, consisting of the most Favorite Airs*, first published by Hewitt himself in New York in 1797-99, when he was associated with the Carrs of Baltimore and Philadelphia.[20] Hewitt reissued the book in 1805 with a slightly altered title page and some different "favorite airs."[21] The contents of the instruction section are:

> Staffs, clefs (including four C-clefs and the baritone clef)
> Note values, the dot, rests
> "Gamut for the piano forte with additional keys": $F'-c''''$
> Musical signs: bar, repeat, direct, slur or "legature," hold or pause, accidentals, triplet, slash
> "Of Time": meters
> "Of Shakes and Graces"
> "Of sharps and flats and their positions": key signatures, major & minor "moods"

This organization is different than Linley's books, and from the ones previously published in England. Yet, Hewitt must have known *New Instructions* (ca. 1790), for the wording of the sections on note values and the musical characters, as well as the tuning method and dictionary on the last page, is exactly the same. Likewise, the ornaments are taken directly from Hook's *New Guida di Musica* (1796). The rest of Hewitt's material is apparently original. After five simple untitled "lessons" is an anthology of twenty-eight pieces, many of which are popular tunes, arranged in no particular order of difficulty or key. The American "Yankee Doodle," "Washington's March" (I), and "Hail Columbia" are balanced by one French allemande and two French airs, not to mention "God save the King."

---

20. Wolfe 10237. I have been unable to obtain a copy.

21. Not in Wolfe; copy at the Clements Library, University of Michigan. The title page is altered as follows: . . . most Favorite Airs, by James Hewitt. Price 1 25/100 Dollr. New York, printed and sold at J. Hewitt's Musical Repository No. 59 Maiden Lane, [1805]. Instructions on pp. 2-5, Lessons I-V on pp. 6-7, titled pieces on pp. 7-18, tuning method and dictionary on p. 19.

The most ambitious book for pianists published in early 19th-century America is Hewitt's *Il Introductione di Preludio, Being an easy method to acquire the Art of Playing extempore upon the Piano-Forte, Interspersed with a variety of examples, showing how to modulate from one key to another, and from which a knowledge of the Science of Music may be acquired, Composed & Dedicated to John R. Parker, Esqr*, by James Hewitt, published about 1807.[22] Parker, the dedicatee, was of Boston, later became a music publisher, issued *The Euterpeiad* in 1820-23, and was the author of this country's first biographical musical dictionary, *A Musical Biography* (1825). In Hewitt's preface to *Il Introductione di Preludio*, he suggests the purpose of the book:

> How is it that we can so easily distinguish the Style of a Professor from that of an Amateur? It is because he knows when and where to strengthen the Discords, and to soften the Concords; The Teacher at each new Lesson, is often obliged to repeat the same Instructions, because the Scholar, from want of knowledge in the Theory, cannot comprehend from whence certain Chords derive their origin.

Later in the same preface, Hewitt acknowledges:

> In Justice to Mr. Gretry, I confess to have avail'd myself of the assistance of a work of his, from which I have taken some of the examples that compose the following Treatise; The liberal part of the Profession, I hope will not censure me, for selecting from the works of so great a Master.

Il Introductione is indeed a translation and edition of André Grétry's *Méthode simple pour apprendre à préluder en peu de temps avec toutes les ressources de l'harmonie* (Paris, 1801/02).[23] Grétry's book, which uses the fundamental bass theory of Rameau, instructs the reader on the chords, chord progression, modulation, and fugue. Hewitt, however, had his own contributions. For example, the first four pages, on the diatonic, chromatic, and enharmonic scales as an

---

22. Wolfe 3724. The list of 179 subscribers to *Il Introductione* is also interesting. Headed by New York's Governor D. D. Tompkins and New York City's Mayor DeWitt Clinton, it includes the following musicians or music publishers: J. L. Berkenhead (teacher of Oliver Shaw), G. E. Blake (12 copies), B. Carr (6 copies), P. Erben, G. Graupner (6 copies), S. Holyoke, P. A. Von Hagen, S. Hewitt (Sophia Hewitt, James's daughter), S. H. Jenks, Dr. G. K. Jackson, F. Mallet, W. Pirsson, J. & M. Paff, E. Riley, G. Shetcky [*sic*] (6 copies), J. Wilson (2 copies). The Harvard University copy was owned by Eliza T. Martin, of Newport, one of the subscribers.

23. Facsimile reprint, Monuments of Music and Music Literature in Facsimile, series 2, vol. 102 (New York: Broude Bros., 1968).

introduction to modulation, had not appeared in Grétry. In one example, illustrating chord progression from one key to another in the manner of a prelude, instead of retaining Grétry's "Air du Roi et le Fermier," Hewitt substitutes Gaveaux's "Pipe de tabac," which he had already used in *The New Medly Overture* (1802).[24]

Hewitt's most significant contribution is probably a series of pieces at the end, presumably his own, which are not in Grétry's book. They are three pieces labeled "Preludio" in C major, A minor, and D minor, "Capricio" in B-flat major, "Preludio" in F major, and "Capricio" in G minor. These are obviously written to illustrate how one might improvise. Some suffer from the persistence of pianistic patterns, such as the broken chords in the pieces in minor mode and the syncopation of the F-major prelude. The other ones, however, are worth reviving. Another Hewitt contribution is the one-page essay on the capriccio after the first three preludes.[25]

In spite of the fact that most of Hewitt's book is taken from Grétry, one must admire him for recognizing a need for such a book, for his erudition in acquiring and translating the original French, and for understanding it enough to alter it and provide additional examples for his American readers.

Gottlieb Graupner

Johann Christian Gottlieb Graupner (1767-1836) was born in Hanover but went to London in 1788 where he played in the orchestra that Haydn conducted in 1791. Graupner came to the United States in 1795 and settled in Boston two years later, where he taught, performed on various instruments, and was the city's foremost music publisher until about 1825. *Rudiments of the Art of Playing on the Piano Forte, containing Elements of Music[,] preliminary remarks on Fingering with Examples, thirty fingered Lessons, and a plain Direction for Tuning, Arranged by Gottlieb Graupner* first appeared in 1806, issued in a second edition in 1819, with subsequent printings to at least 1827, all from Graupner's own press (Wolfe 3202-03).

---

24. *Introductione*, 31; *Méthode*, 56-57. *The New Medly Overture* is in Wagner's edition, no. 27.

25. Hewitt's other interjections:

p. 8	last line and example
p. 9	last paragraph, to Gamut, p. 10
p. 12	all until the last two paragraphs
p. 14	example from Rameau; example at bottom
p. 15	right-hand of example in middle of the page; example headed "Another Progression"
p. 18	first paragraph and examples
p. 24	material beginning with 3rd paragraph
pp. 27-28	examples of modulations
p. 32	first example, through p. 33--this substitutes for Grétry, pp. 62-63.

"Arranged by Gottlieb Graupner" is correct, for very little is original. The 21-page "rudiments" portion of the first edition is copied wholesale from Clementi's *Introduction*. The major changes made by Graupner were to substitute new material on the clefs and gamut, and to expand some of the matter concerning note values.[26] Therefore, Graupner's *Rudiments*, without acknowledgement, represents Clementi in the United States before Clementi's own *Introduction* was finally published here in 1820-21. Indeed, the title page of both editions advertises that Graupner's Musical Repository has "Clementi's new patent Piano Forte's [sic] superiour to any others yet known." Whereas a two-page dictionary, headed "A Table of Technical Terms by the Alphabet," provided an opportunity for Graupner to show his depth of musical knowledge, it turns out to be a selection from the dictionary at the end of Dussek's book.

The second edition of Graupner's *Rudiments* includes a new preface with a paragraph worth quoting:

> Of all Instruments as yet known, the Piano Forte
> claims precedence as an accompaniment to the
> human voice; and its use has become so universal,

---

26. Specifically, the differences are (the page numbers on the left are Graupner's):

p. 1 "Table of all the Clefs"
p. 2 "On the Table of Clefs"
p. 3 "Scale of the Notes and Keys," in place of Clementi's "Scale or Gamut"
p. 4 specific notes for the "Exercises" for treble and bass notes
p. 4 omits Clementi's section "Tenor, Counter-Tenor, and Soprano clefs explained"
p. 5 "Figure, Length, and relative Value of Notes" section expanded to add (to the chart based on the semibreve) similar charts based on the minim and crotchet; explanation of the dot condensed
p. 6 Clementi's N.B. (middle of p. 5) omitted
p. 10 Clementi's list of tempo markings (p. 13) shifted to after the section on keys
p. 13 Graupner omits Clementi's (p. 10) second sign for the inverted turn; omits dot after the second realization of the shake; realization for transient or passing shake changed from to .
p. 14 omits the vertical line from the 2nd beat sign; adds at end of line, in small type (as if an afterthought):

The only other such realization is *Preceptor*'s.
p. 15 Clementi's paragraph "Let the pupil" (p. 15) omitted.

that the education of a young lady is hardly thought to be complete without it. But the excellence of the Piano, as an accompaniment to the voice, is not its greatest recommendation. As a Solo Instrument, if we take into view its power of combination, it is perhaps superior to all others; and accordingly we find, that the greatest masters of modern times have successively exercised their talents in eliciting its various powers; which, indeed, are now so far developed, that it is probable no further improvements of much importance will be made.

The new edition has a few changes, including nine new terms (not, this time, from Dussek), two drawings of the hand "ready to strike" and "when it strikes," four new pages of exercises, and (before the directions on tuning on the last page) a short explanation of the damper pedal on "the English Square Piano (which is almost universally used in this Country)" and the English grand piano which also has the una corda pedal. There is a total increase of eleven pages.[27]

The remainder of both editions consists of thirty "lessons," arranged by key in a manner also used by Clementi: C a F d G B-flat E-flat A E. Indeed, five of the pieces are directly taken from the first edition of Clementi's *Introduction*. Lessons 1, 2, 4, and 5 are attributed to Graupner; no. 7 is taken from Linley's *New Assistant*.

---

27. More details on 2nd edition changes:

p. 5   Tables of note values recast; new charts based on the quaver and semiquaver added.

p. 10   New terms: direct, fuga, lentando, largo assai, musico, non, non troppo, largo, obligato, overture, rinforza or R.F. Term dropped: vivo.

p. 14   Add short section, "Exercises for the Double Shake"--trills on thirds.

p. 18   Omit scale of semitones.

pp. 19-24   Add the following exercises: "Gamut for exercising both Hands together, very quick"; "Exercise for ascending by thirds with both Hands together, very quick"; "Exercise for accustoming the two Hands to go together in the space of an Octave" (in the keys C G D A E F--here is retained the "General Remarks" paragraph, referring to the scales on pp. 17-18); "Exercise to accustom the two Hands to go in contrary directions"; "Other Exercise"; "Exercise and Examples where it is necessary to deviate from the established principles of Fingering." (Clementi's "Of Extensions, Contractions &c." resumes here.)

pp. 26-28   Add the following sections: "Exercise for both Hands"; "Of Fingering the Chords."

The other works are popular tunes and excerpts of Handel, Naumann, Pleyel, Hook, Corelli, Bergfeld, Scarlatti, Haydn, and Bach.[28]

In spite of Graupner's grand theft, his (and Clementi's) *Rudiments* represents a significant advance in thoroughness and technique, over a period of more than two decades. Anyone who mastered the contents certainly rose beyond the level of the mere dilettante.

George K. Jackson

Dr. George K. Jackson (1745-1822), another Boston musician, prepared a pianoforte tutor which was not published until after his death. Jackson was one of the best educated musical figures in Boston in the early 19th century. Born in Oxford, he was a fellow-pupil with Rayner Taylor of Dr. James Nares. Jackson received his doctorate at St. Andrews University in 1791, and came to the United States five years later. After spending time in various cities, including New York City (where he was organist and director of music at St. George's Chapel), he moved to Boston in 1812, where he remained (except during the war with England) until his death. He was organist in several prominent Boston churches, including King's Chapel, Trinity Church, and at the newly built St. Paul's Church (where he received a handsome salary).

Jackson was also the publisher of some music, an activity continued by his sons Charles and Edwin W. In 1825, Edwin W. Jackson published his late father's *I-Rudementi-da-Musica or Complete Instructor for the Piano Forte, Including most of the Favourite Airs Songs & Dances, Arranged & Fingered in Progressive Order, also for the Flute & Violin, the whole Composed, Selected & Adapted by Dr. G. K. Jackson.*[29] In only five pages, Jackson presents the rudiments:

> Scale (gamut)
> "Characters": note values
> Signs: accidentals, bar, bind (ligature), pause, repeat
>   sign, slur, staccato, crescendo & diminuendo
>   signs, stroke
> "Cliffs"

---

28. The pieces taken from Clementi are: Air in Atalanta, Handel; Gavotta, Corelli; Larghetto, Pleyel; Minuetto, Scarlatti; Polonoise [from French Suite 6], Bach. Nonetheless, this one work of J. S. Bach is his first published in the United States--Clementi, of course was one of the important champions of J. S. Bach's music in England in the late 18th century. The Linley piece is the third in *New Assistant*. In the 2nd edition of *Rudiments* there is another piece by Graupner and fourteen other substitutions, including Pleyel's "German Hymn with Variations."

29. Copy right secured. Price $1. Boston, published & sold by Edwin W. Jackson No. 44 Market St. Title-page + pp. 2-40. Instructional section on pp. 2-6; music, pp. 7-40. Wolfe 4525 (unlocated). Harvard University copy.

Table of note-values
"The Marks of Time": meters
Ornaments: turn, inverted turn, turned shake,
    "apogiatura"
Fingered scales

The ornaments reflect English practice of the late 18th century. At the beginning of the "lessons" (pieces), the keys of C, G, F, and D are each carefully introduced by the proper hand-position for their execution, in a manner previously used by Cramer. Of the three pieces in each key, the first were composed by Dr. Jackson himself. The twenty-one remaining ones, in the same keys, reflect a repertory of late 18th-century England--the composers are Samuel Arnold, William Shield, and Stephen Storace--plus other popular tunes and dances which by this time are somewhat outdated. Five of the pieces, towards the end, may have been borrowed from Hewitt's 1805 book, although they are sometimes slightly rearranged. Jackson's book is elementary, covering the needs of the beginning pianist. Modest as it may be, this offering is at least freshly written.

Oliver Shaw

Although Oliver Shaw had studied with Graupner in Boston, the London publication *New Instructions* (ca. 1790), not Graupner's tutor, was the source for some of his modest eight-page *A Plain Introduction to the Art of Playing the Piano Forte, to which is added a selection of progressive airs, songs, &c., arranged by Oliver Shaw* (1811; Wolfe 7977). The rudiments are presented in only three pages. Unlike his teacher, however, Shaw borrowed in a less obvious manner.

Characters: "stave," ledger lines, "cliffs" (including
    the C-clef), braces
Note values, rests, the dot
Other signs: bar, repeat, slur, pause, accidentals, tri-
    plet & sextuplets, staccato, stroke
"Apogiaturas"
"Of Time" (meter)
"Scale or Gamut"

The wording of *New Instructions* is here changed somewhat. Before the lessons, Shaw includes a half-page "Dictionary of Musical Terms" which is excerpted, and the definitions sometimes condensed or reworded, from the dictionary at the end of Dussek's book. The first four lessons are apparently original. The fifth is by his previous teacher "I. L. Beaurkenhead" (John L. Berkenhead, also blind, of Newport, Rhode Island), the sixth is Arnold's song "Fresh and strong," and the last, "French air," is a variant of "Mark my Alford." For its succinctness, *Plain Introduction* is well named.

Twenty years later, in 1831, Shaw issued a more complete tutor:

O. Shaw's Instructions for the Piano Forte, Being a
plain introduction to the Art of playing that Instrument, in three parts. Part 1st Containing the Rudi-

ments of Music & Scales in all the Major & Minor
Keys with the proper fingering marked Also a Dictionary of foreign terms used in Music. Part 2nd
Containing 24 Progressive Lessons. Part 3rd Comprising a Selection of easy popular Songs Marches
Waltzes &c progressively arranged, With the fingering marked by the Author.[30]

The first part is an expanded version of the first 3½ pages of his *Plain
Introduction*. The expansion, however, is not Shaw's, but is borrowed
from Cramer. Therefore Shaw's contribution, for the most part, consists of combining what he had earlier used from *New Instructions* with
the update from Cramer. He even substitutes Cramer's dictionary of
musical terms for that borrowed from *New Instructions*.[31]

     Part 2 is completely new and might actually be by Shaw. Fol-
lowing the example set by Cramer, the lessons are arranged by key, up
the circle of fifths to E major, then down the flat side to E-flat--but
with no minor keys. The third part consists of a potpourri of other
music: the songs "Bounding Billows" and "Pleyels Hymn" on one page,
"Home Sweet Home, arranged as a quick step" and "Tivolian Waltz"
on another; with Shaw's own "Rondo," "Westminster Waltz Variations," "Trip to Pawtucket," "Gov Fenner's Slow March," and "Gov
Jones' Slow March" on the last six pages. Shaw had published his own
pieces separately.[32] The 1831 book represents the long life of instruc-

---

     30. Providence, published & sold by the Author, No. 70 West-
minster St. Entered according to Act of Congress in the year 1831 by
Oliver Shaw in the Clerks Office of the District Court of the United
States for the District of Rhode Island. Title-page + pp. 3-28. Brown
University copy.

     31. Specifically:

p. 3	Characters (old)
p. 4	"Time Table"; "Of the Dot" (Cramer)
p. 5	"Of the Sharp, Flat and Natural" (Cramer)
pp. 5-6	Triplets, staccato, stroke (old)
p. 6	Appoggiatura, turn, turned shake (new)
pp. 6-7	Bar, slur, pause
p. 7	"Of Time" (old, but last paragraph from Cramer)
pp. 7-8	"Of Keys and their Modes" (Cramer)
p. 8	"Scale or Gamut" (old; last paragraph new)
pp. 9-10	Scales (Cramer)
pp. 11-12	"A Dictionary of Italian and Other Words Used in Music" (Cramer)
p. 12	"Abbreviations Explained"

     32. The Rondo and "Westminster Waltz" variations, with
another song "The Test of Affection," were issued as: Original
Melodies, consisting of airs, waltzes, songs, &c., intended as progressive pieces, composed & arranged for the piano forte, by Oliver Shaw.
Copy Right secured. Providence, published by the author, No. 70

tional material first published about forty years earlier, plus some more recent material from Cramer--but even this is nearly twenty years out of date.

George E. Blake

George E. Blake (1775-1871), active as a Philadelphia music publisher from about 1803 to about 1840, issued *New Instructions for the Piano Forte, with the proper mode of fingering Illustrated by a variety of examples, Selected from the best Authors, by George E. Blake*, published sometime in the 1810s (Wolfe 856). In a short introduction, he admits that he has "published the following Instructions selected from the works of Clementi, Linly [*sic*], Dussek, Hook and other celebrated composers." Ironically, Blake's borrowings are usually not without change, and large chunks are apparently original. The dictionary, printed before the tutor begins, is from Dussek--the definitions sometimes amplified--as is the section on ornaments. The material of the notes on the staff lines and spaces, the gamut and drawing of the keyboard, and material on note values, are taken from Linley, yet with an additional explanation below the keyboard and a drawing of the hand on the keyboard. The section on the accidentals is only partially adapted from Hook, the material on the slur and stroke from the London *New Instructions* (ca. 1790). Clementi furnished the fingering and order of the scales. The rest is probably Blake's own.[33] Twenty-nine lessons provide no titles or composers'

Westminster St. [1827-30?]. pp. 1-4. New York Public Library copy. Another copy at Brown University, with the same title, includes the pagination 23-26, as in the 1831 *Introduction*, with the Rondo, "Westminster Waltz" variations, plus "Trip to Pawtucket."

33. The contents and sources:

p. 3	"Modern Music . . ." (Dussek)
pp. 3-4	"Music is divided . . ." (Linley)
p. 5	"The Names of the Notes" (Hook); Exercise apparently Blake's "Of Sharps, Flats and Naturals" (adapted in turn from Hook)
pp. 6-7	"Of Notes, their different lengths &c." (chart from Linley)
p. 7	"Of Time"; slur or "legature" (from *New Instructions*), staccato, stroke (*New Instructions*), hold (Dussek)
p. 8	"Of Shakes and Graces"--from Dussek, sometimes recast: tie missing from realizations of plain shake, and from grace and shake; "passing shake" is new, perhaps adapted from Clementi's "transient or passing shake":

names, but four of them are taken directly from Linley.[34] The tuning method is from *New Instructions*, which in turn borrowed it from *Preceptor*.

Francesco Masi

The only Italian immigrant musician to write a pianoforte instruction book was Francesco Masi (d. 1853). In the period 1816-18, before he moved from Boston (where he had arrived in 1807) to Washington, D.C., he published *New Instructions for beginners on the piano forte entirely on a new plan with a few alternative lessons, and a compleate rules,* [sic] *of thorough bass, composed by Francesco Masi*.[35] Although Masi may have adopted material from an Italian tutor, there are few traces of any previously published in English. The same subjects, however, are covered:

> "The Letters made use in Music . . ."
> "Steves [*sic*], and Ledger, Lines"
> "The Scale or Gamut," clefs
> "Of Flats Sharps and Naturals"
> "Of Notes, their different length, and the proportion they bear to one another"
> "An Explanation of the five lines and five spaces"
> "Steve and Ledger Linis" (*sic*)
> "Of Notes and their different lengths" (charts)
> "Of Time"
> "The different degrees of time Explained"
> "The different Cliffs used in Music" (including 4 C-clefs)
> "The Major and Minor Moods with their respective Sharps and Flats in regular Progression"
> "Explanation of the Marke for Embelishment &c." (*sic*): plain shake, turned shake, passive or short shake, continued shake, turn, beat, slur, "apogiatura"
> "Accidents," "Scale of Semitones," exercises

The signs and realizations of the shake, turned shake, "passive or short shake," are the same as Dussek's; the slur and beat are like Moller's. Nowhere else, however, is found Masi's execution of "the Apogiatura in slow time":

---

34. No. 11 (Linley no. 3), 19 ("Mark my Alford" variant, no. 6), 20 ("La belle Catherine," no. 9), 21 ("[French air]," no. 11).

35. Boston, printed and sold by F. Masi No. 71 Newbury Street. Title-page + pp. 2-21. Instructions, pp. 2-7; pieces, pp. 8-21. Not in Wolfe; Newberry Library copy.

Masi's book, as can be surmised from the above, is not very well organized, and abounds with spelling and typographical errors. The worst example is at the bottom right-hand corner of the fifth page, where three short sentences explaining the flat, sharp, and natural are crammed into a bit of space otherwise devoted to "Time." Yet the "Accidents" at the top of the seventh page is the heading of a chromatic scale, not the explanation of the accidentals. The "entirely new plan" of the pieces in the rest of the book is likewise obscure. After a few exercises is a simple ground with two variations, two pages of five lessons each based on a pre-determined position of the hand, another page with three unnumbered lessons (one being the often-borrowed no. 3 of Linley), and three one-page pieces, each labeled "Sonatina." The "complete rules, of thorough bass" reveal no rules at all. Figured bass scales in C major and all the sharp keys, to C-sharp major, are called "Gamut" nos. 1-8. Each is succeeded by a "lesson"--a freely composed figured bass--and another such pair in the relative minor. The flat keys are provided only four "gamuts," to A-flat major/F minor. Next are four unexplained figured basses, each in C major and followed by the same in G, D, and A. Seventeen further "gamuts" for the right hand, all in C, and some kind of exercise for both hands, are likewise unexplained. The three lessons on the last page, while playable on the keyboard, seem more like duets for two treble instruments; why they appear in a piano instruction book is a mystery.

Arthur Clifton

Ten years after P. Antony Corri's *L'Anima di musica* was published in London, his *New Piano Forte Preceptor* appeared in Baltimore under his new name Arthur Clifton.[36] The 1820 book is almost as condensed as the 1810 is complete. Clifton covers almost all of the same material, but sometimes in a different order. It is enlightening to compare the contents:

---

36. New Piano Forte Preceptor, containing the Rudiments of Music and Principles of Fingering, rendered easy for the youngest pupil, also; useful and improving exercises, the major and minor scales and short preludes in every key with directions for the position of the hands, and an explanation of musical terms &c. &c. by Arthur Clifton. Copy right secured. Price $[1]. The sequel to this work is; A sett of Twenty-Six easy lessons (just published). Baltimore, published by the Author and to be had of him, No. 4 South Gay Street. Also just published, his New Vocal Instructor. [Pasted underneath:] Secured according to the Act of Congress the twenty first day of November, 1820, by the Author. Initialed "AC". Instructions, pp. 3-14; exercises, pp. 15-27. Title-page + pp. 3-27. Library of Congress copy.

Corri, *L'Anima*		Clifton, *Preceptor*	
pp. i–ii	"Address," "To the Scholar," table of contents		
p. 1	Part I, "Of the Rudiments and Theory"--Lesson I: "Of the Notes"	p. 3	"The Notes": staff, gamut "Scale of Notes . . ."
pp. 2–3	"The Gamut, or Scale" including basic clefs, and exercise	p. 4	"The Characters of the Notes": time values including dot, triplet
pp. 3–5	Lesson II: "Of the Accidents" plus exercise	p. 5	"The Accidents," "The Order of Sharps & Flats at the Clef"
pp. 5–6	Lesson III: "Of the Characters, and length of the notes, which form Measure and Time" including dot, triplet		
pp. 6–7	Lesson IV: "Of Time and Measure"	pp. 5–6	"Of Time"
pp. 7–9	Lesson V: "Of Counting and Beating the Time"	p. 6	"Exercise for Learning the Position of the Notes,"
pp. 9–10	"Of Syncopated Time"		"Exercise for Learning Sharps and Flats"
pp. 10–11	Lesson VI: "Explanation of the Double Bar--Tie, and other Signs"	pp. 7–8	"Explanation of Signs and Terms"
pp. 11–13	Lesson VII: "Of Clefs"		
pp. 13–15	Lesson VIII: "Of the Graces and Ornaments"--appoggiatura, "forcing or leaning graces," "leading or passing graces," "anticipating grace or anticipation"	pp. 8–11	"Graces and Ornaments"
		pp. 12–13	"Explanation of Italian terms used in music; not before, explained" (*sic*)
pp. 16–17	Lesson IX: "Of the Turns"		
pp. 18–19	Lesson X: "Of the Shake and Beat"		

The twenty-five pages are small in size, versus the earlier book's 118 large pages. Although the explanations are rewritten, occasionally traces of the London publication show, such as the layout of the gamut, the musical example of the "tie," and the (albeit abbreviated) definitions in the dictionary. In *L'Anima*, Corri visualized the semi-breve (whole note) as a "whole Sound," the smaller note values as a "half [sound]," down to the thirty-second sound. Even more appropriate is Clifton's use of equivalent American currency: a dollar, half-dollar, quarter-dollar, down to the "thirty secondth of dollar."

Most of the ornaments are transmitted into the 1820 publication. The "forcing grace" ("two or more graces preceeding the note") and "leading grace" ("which follow the note") survive, as do some of the actual musical realizations of ornaments. The execution of the beat

changes slightly; Corri's ♪ = becomes in Clifton.

The many pages of fingered scales of 1810 are reduced for the 1820 book. Part IV of Corri's book, "Of Preluding," is represented by the final two pages in Clifton's, which contain the simple cadential formulas, in all keys, previously labeled the "second style." There are no pieces in the *New Piano Forte Preceptor*, and no copy of the promised "Sett of Twenty Six easy lessons" has yet been found.

Perhaps Corri's ambitious *L'Anima di musica* would have had a greater success in England had he not left that country. It may be that the competition from such books as those by Clementi, Cramer, and

Challoner were too great. Corri-Clifton's *New Piano Forte Preceptor* is likewise a fine book, even for its size. Unfortunately, Clifton did not republish *L'Anima* in Baltimore as well; perhaps the level of playing in the United States was not high enough for sufficient sales.

Seven years after *New Piano Forte Preceptor*, the Baltimore publisher John Cole issued a new edition, *Clifton's New and Improved Piano Forte Preceptor* of 1827.[37] The rewrite of the section on rudiments is sometimes more dependent on the earlier *L'Anima di musica* than on the 1820 *New Piano Forte Preceptor*. The contents of the numbered "Instructions" are:

1	Drawing of piano keys, gamut
2	Staff
3	"Of the Clefs & Nomenclature of Notes"
4	"Of the Sharps, Flats, and Naturals" (rewritten from *L'Anima* lesson 2)
5	"Of the Characters and Value of Notes" (condensed from *L'Anima*, lesson 3, but with reference to American currency, as in the 1820 book)
6	"Of Time and its Signature"
7	"Of Ornaments and Graces"
8	Double bar, repeat, pause, tie, "abbreviations" ("a repetition of notes")

These are followed by short sections: "General Rules for Fingering," hand and arm position at the keyboard (with drawing taken from *L'Anima*), and a short dictionary. The ornaments are nearly the same as in the 1820 publication, but the explanations are rewritten and the examples are different. The "forcing grace" is there, but not the "leading grace." The beat, also labeled as "a double Appogiatura" (*sic*), is to be "played with emphasis and briliancy" (*sic*); the notated rhythm of its execution is the same as in *L'Anima*. The upper-note shake is still very much alive: "The SHAKE *tr* is a frequent repetition of the two first notes of the common turn."

---

37. Clifton's New and Improved Piano Forte Preceptor, Book the First: Containing the Rudiments of Music, Exercises and Rules for fingering with the Major & Minor Scales, and a correct explanation of every Term and Sign used in Music. Also, Thirty favourite Tunes, Newly and progressively arranged as Easy Lessons. The Second Book will contain Exercises for the improvement of fingering; Preludes in various Styles &c. Baltimore, Published by John Cole. Copy-right secured according to Act of Congress, Oct. 15, 1827 by John Cole of the State of M^d. Title-page + pp. 3-20. Plate no. on pp. 3-20: 294. Instructions, pp. 3-8; exercises, pp. 9-11; "Three Easy Lessons," p. 11; tunes, pp. 12-19; scales, p. 20. Duke University copy.

The thirty short tunes are all newly selected from the popular repertory of the day, and are capped with "Washington's March" (I). Although the three tutors are by the same person, each of them was freshly written.

Christopher Meineke

The first piano tutor by a German immigrant was Christopher Meineke's *A New Instruction for the Piano Forte, Containing the Rudiments of Music Explained in a concise manner, and a Sett of Lessons Calculated to establish the True Method of Fingering and afford an agreeable Study for Pupils* (1823).[38] Meineke had come to the United States in 1800, at the age of eighteen. The book is his own, but the brevity of "The Rudiments of Music" section, only four pages, leaves little room for originality. Meineke quickly covers this material:

---

38. Philadelphia: George Willig; Wolfe 5780. On the last page of this edition is this N.B.: "As the finger'd scales are to be had seperately [*sic*] in every Music store, they were omitted in order to diminish the size of this work." The price on the title-page is $1. Another imprint, price $1.50, Wolfe 5781, instead reads: "N.B. As the finger'd scales are to be had seperately in every Music Store, they were omitted in order to diminish the size of this work; but since this work was published, the scales have been added." Indeed, in the Free Library of Philadelphia copy, the scales are added--but they replace pp. 9-10! This copy is otherwise the same as Wolfe 5780, in contradistinction to the description in Wolfe. It is also curious that for the copy at the Lilly Library, Indiana University, of *J. B. Cramer's Sequel to his Celebrated Book of Instructions* (Philadelphia: G. E. Blake, n.d. [1814-41]), the seven pages of pieces are followed immediately by the two pages of the Meineke scales, then the pages of Meineke's New Instructions, Wolfe 5781, complete except for the missing title page. Blake, of course, was a competitor of Willig in Philadelphia; probably the assemblage was accomplished by a user, not a publisher. The fingering and arrangement of Meineke's scales are taken from Cramer's *Instructions*. This is ironic because of an European publication, presumably by the same Meineke and not his father: Gammes et Preludes dans tous les tons pour le piano-forte, par C. Meineke. Prix 1 fl. A Offenbach s/M, chez Jean André, [1808]. Title-page + pp. 2-15; copy at the Library of Congress. Meineke's (Cramer's) two-octave scales are arranged so that e.g. C major is on the left and C minor on the right; in *Gammes et Preludes*, C major is followed by A minor, etc.

"Of the Notes"
"Of the Clefs"
"The Gamut and Finger Board"
"The Intervals"
"The Scale or Gamut": diatonic and chromatic scales
"Flats and Sharps" and explanations of "Triplets or
    Triols," double bar, pause, "reference" (as in "da
    capo al signo" [*sic*]), points ("staccatto"), slur
"Of Graces": "apogiatura," shake, turn
"Marks of Abbreviation"
"Characters of the Notes": charts based on the semi-
    breve, minim, crotchet, quaver
"Dots after Notes"
"Of Rests"
"Of Time": meters
"Of Fingering" (a short paragraph)
"Musical Terms": a short dictionary

The ornaments, usually a good guide to the source of borrowing, are not like any others. The shake, for example, is as follows:

Obviously the *tr* should have been over a note one step lower. Five simple exercises are followed by twenty-seven short pieces which progress through the sharp keys to E major, then through the flat keys to E-flat major. The last piece, in G major, is "Washington's March." George Willig, the publisher, also sold *New Guida di Musica* by Challoner (discussed above) for those wishing a more complete book.

The only American publication of its time devoted to the physical exercise of the fingers was *Exercises for the Piano Forte, Being a Supplement to Meineke's Instruction*, issued by Blake in 1828.[39] Not pleasant pieces, instead, they are a number of scale fragments and other patterns designed to strengthen the fingers and enhance their independence.

Meineke's tutor was issued in a 3rd edition, "revised & enlarged by the author," in 1840.[40] There are minor changes in wording, and the turn signs are reversed. The scales are included before the pieces,

---

39. Philad* published & sold by Geo Willig 171 Chesnut St. pp. [1]-3. Bottom of p. [1]: Endterd [*sic*] according to Act of Congress the seventeenth day of November 1828 by Geore [*sic*] Willig of the State of Pennsylva. Bottom of p. 2: Exercises by Meineke. Bottom of p. 3: Exercise by Meineke. University of Virginia copy.

40. I have not yet found a 2nd edition. The 1840 edition has the same title-page as the 1823 one, except after Meineke's name is: Revised & enlarged by the author. Third edition. Price $1 nett. Philadelphia, George Willig 171 Chesnut St.; copyright notice of 1840. Library of Congress copy.

but the dictionary is omitted. Some substitutions of more current popular tunes are made in the twenty-eight "lessons"--in spite of the title page, only one more than the earlier edition. What is significant about the 3rd edition is that the 18th-century trill, beginning on the upper auxiliary, and the British terminology of quaver, crotchet, etc., has persisted as late as 1840.

Peter K. Moran

Perhaps not coincidentally, the exact wording of Meineke's title was also used in 1828 for *Moran's New Instruction for the Piano Forte, Containing the Rudiments of Music Explained in a concise manner and a Sett of Lessons Calculated to establish the True Method of Fingering And afford an agreeable Study for Pupils.*[41] Peter K. Moran had been successful in Dublin before he immigrated in 1817 to New York City. According to the introduction, this pianoforte tutor was "undertaken at the request of the publishers, and which has been rendered as simple as possible." One unique feature is that there are no drawings of the staves or keyboard--indeed, there is no music at all in the instructional portion. Instead, the "preceptor" is expected to write the musical notation on a separate "Lecture Table," which can be viewed by a number of pupils at the same time. On only three pages are seven sections, each followed by questions to be asked of the pupils:

1	Stave
2	Notes: pitches on the staves
3	"Time Table": time-values, using British terminology
4	"Of Sharps, Flats and Naturals"
5	"Of Time and its divisions"
6	"Of Scales"
7	"Of the Common Chords, Major and Minor"

Some of the composers represented in the small pieces are Mozart ("Non più andrai"), Rossini ("Di tanti palpiti"), and Steibelt ("Storm Rondo")--but these composers are not named. Moran included three works of his own, and also named his New York colleague the French immigrant Charles Thibault as the arranger of "Russian Air." In a manner reminiscent of Cramer, explanations of various notational signs such as the turn, appoggiatura, staccato, and "pause" (fermata) are in footnotes to pieces in which the sign is first introduced. The shake, *tr*, "begins from the note above, and ends on the principal note, when at the end, it is followed by a Turn"--an implied explanation of that in Cramer's book.

----

41. Price 2 Dollars. New York, published by Dubois & Stodart No. 167 Broadway. Title-page + pp. 2-23. Copyright notice, dated 22 November 1828, on p. 2. Instructions, pp. 3-7; Lessons 1-24, pp. 8-20; Dictionary, p. 21; scales, pp. 23-25. Duke University copy.

Benjamin Carr

The most extensive and detailed piano instruction book of the 1820s was by the then-venerable Benjamin Carr. He published *The Analytical Instructor for the Piano Forte*, op. 15, in 1826, five years before his death.[42] It is in three parts. The first of them contains a painstaking explanation, step by step, of the basic rudiments of music. In the second part, further explanations accompany an anthology of "thirty favorite airs." In the third part, an appendix, the pupil is exposed to further aspects of music, including a table of ornaments and a dictionary of terms.

The Analytical Instructor is a large work--59 pages. In the introduction, Carr provides his rationale:

> In the introduction to this work, it may not be amiss to apologize for its apparent bulk. Elementary books of instructions were formerly made as small as possible; but the object of facilitating the progress of the pupil has caused the gradual admission of much explanatory text into works of this kind, and at the present day European instruction books have become considerably extended. It would be a great mistake to suppose that this extension has added in any degree to the labour of the scholar: on the contrary; it has been the means of diminishing it, and of shortening the time employed in the study of music.

He then continues to explain that the first part is of the simple elements, the second for somewhat more advanced pupils, and the third "for a higher class of pupils, and will be found useful and interesting to those who are tolerably advanced in practical music."

Carr had been a teacher in Philadelphia some thirty years:

> In the long course of his professional occupations, the Editor has occasionnally [*sic*] found it useful to present to his pupils the introductory part of their studies in the form which he has here detailed;

---

42. The Analytical Instructor for the Piano Forte, by B. Carr. Op. 15. Price $3. In Three Parts. [Vignette of a lady playing a square pianoforte by I. C. Darley, engraved by P. E. Hamm.] Either of the parts may be had separately at 1.25 Cts. each part. Philadelphia, published by B. Carr, Proprietor and Author. Part II title-page: Part ["2" in Ms.] of the Analytical Instructor for the piano forte by B. Carr. In three parts. Price separately 1 Doll. 25 Cts. each part. The complete work $3. Philadelphia, printed for B. Carr. Copy-right secured according to law. Title-page + pp. [22]-46. Part III title-page is the same except for Ms. "3." Title-page + pp. 47-59. Copy from the Hunt collection at Columbia University; other copies are in the collections of the Library of Congress, Lester S. Levy, the Pennsylvania Historical Society, and the Free Library of Philadelphia.

> and some fifteen years since he prepared the
> materials of a class-book for his own convenience in
> this kind of instruction. The request of some
> friends, who were desirous of procuring a copy of
> this book, has led to the present publication.

Carr's approach is quite different from those needing a teacher
to explain all aspects of music concentrated on a few pages. The staff
itself takes 1½ pages to explain. To identify notes on the keyboard
Carr includes six drawings, first showing only "D" between two black
keys, finally expanding the musical alphabet to the octave A-G. Five
pages later the pupil is allowed to discover more notes of the staff, and
not until four further pages does he see the full keyboard range. The
only note values in Part I are the "minum," crotchet, and quaver; in
Part II Carr introduces the semiquaver, semibreve, and finally the
demisemiquaver. The keys are likewise gradually presented in Part II,
but only to four sharps or flats. Parts I and II each conclude with a
"Recapitulation of all that has been learnt."
    The more advanced materials in Part III include such matters as
the common chord, the key signatures, modulation, enharmonic spell-
ings of notes and double sharps or flats, and the remaining aspects of
notation (128th notes--"double demisemiquavers"--and 256th notes--
"demisemidemisemiquavers"). The only apparent borrowing in Carr's
book is "A Compendium of the Graces & Embellishments of Music as
exemplified by Dr. Callcott," whose *Grammar of Music* appeared in its
first American edition in Boston in 1810.[43] Although the descending
appoggiatura continues to be on the beat, taking half the value of the
principal note, what is called an "ascending grace" is shorter:

The turn beginning with the upper note is called the "unprepared
turn"; when it begins on the principal note, it is "prepared." The
inverted turn survives unchanged. The shake, however, "may begin
either on the note written or the note above." For the "chain shake"
(on all notes of an upward scale) and "continued shake," as well as the
explanations in Part II, are all realized beginning on the principal
note.[44] The "passing shake or mordente [*sic*]" has two possible

---

43. Wolfe 1469. It was first published in England in 1806. The
National Union Catalog lists further editions published in Boston as
late as 1877.

44. All shakes in Carr's *Lessons and Exercises in Vocal Music*,
op. 8 (Philadelphia, [1811]) begin on the principal note. See his song
"The vi'let nurs'd in woodland wild" from that publication, with his
original and detailed performance directions, in Benjamin Carr,
Selected Secular and Sacred Songs, ed. Eve R. Meyer, Recent Researches in American Music, 15 (Madison: A-R Editions, 1986), 79-86, as
well as the general remarks on Carr's performance practice on pp. xiv-
xv.

realizations:

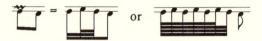

There is also some material "Of Musical Expression," which describes the usual places where notes should be emphasized, depending on the meter, and cases in which other notes should receive more stress: "Accent is governed by rule, Emphasis by the fancy of the Composer." The only other previous writer on this subject was Corri, in 1810. The page on the tuning of the piano even includes the gauge of wire needed to replace strings.

Many of Carr's earlier publications and compositions, such as *Applicazione addolcita* (1809), were intended for the piano student. Another should be mentioned here: *Preludes for the Piano Forte, Selected & Composed by B: Carr: To which are added the Diatonic and Chromatic Scale, with the Fingering marked*, op. 13, first published in 1820 (Wolfe 1638). The fourteen preludes, with up to three flats or four sharps, are intended for the more advanced student; they are more difficult to play than those appearing in, for example, *Applicazione addolcita*. Besides those by Carr, other composers cited are Petrini, W. H. W. Darley, J. C. Taws, and "partly from Cramer." The scales at the end are in the "most usual Keys," major and minor, including those with only four sharps or flats, plus the chromatic scale. James F. Hance, of New York, also published two pages of *Scales by Contrary Motion, with Modulations through the Major Keys in Sharps* in 1825 (Wolfe 3327). The scales are linked with simple modulations to the next key, leading to B major on one page and to D-flat major on the next.

Although music publishers in the United States kept piano students well supplied with new instruction books by native authors, in addition to those imported or reprinted from England, the material is not significant for its originality--until Carr's book of 1826. Ornament signs and realizations originating in English tutors, notably those published in 1801 or before, had an extended life here. 18th-century performance practices were extended through the first quarter of the 19th century in the United States, in spite of more up-to-date "advances" in continental Europe. The impressive quantity of piano instruction books made available during the first fifty-five years of this country's existence attests to the rapid growth of pianism being made in certain segments of American society.

8

THE FIRST AMERICANIST: ANTHONY PHILIP HEINRICH

> The truth is, I fear, that the reason of your composi-
> tions not having the success they deserve, in the
> (perhaps redundant) portion of harmonic science you
> have infused into them, so far beyond the capacity
> or powers of execution of any of our ordinary
> amateurs of music; and if I might venture to give
> advice to a composer of your experience and knowl-
> edge, it would be to counsel you to keep your
> science a little more in the back-ground than you do
> at present, or at least to throw it into the accompani-
> ments, and not let it interfere so much with the
> simplicity of your airs. The perpetual variety of
> your modulations, though they show the extent of
> your resources in the art, disturb too much the flow
> of the melody, and render your compositions rather
> learned exercises than songs. . . . You must throw a
> good deal more singsong into your works before you
> can expect them to succeed.
> --Thomas Moore, 1 September 1829[1]

This excerpt of a letter from the famed Irish poet to Anthony
Philip Heinrich, upon receipt of some Canzonets, is surprisingly per-
ceptive, considering that Moore was "one who has no pretensions to be
a critic in music" (from another part of the same letter). The phrase

---

1. Quoted in William Treat Upton, *Anthony Philip Heinrich: A
Nineteenth-Century Composer in America* (New York: Columbia University Press, 1939; reprint, New York: AMS Press, 1967), 103. Other
opinions, contemporary with Heinrich and more recent, are collected
in Neely Bruce, "The Piano Pieces of Anthony Philip Heinrich Contained in *The Dawning of Music in Kentucky* and *The Western
Minstrel*," chapter 2; subsequent chapters include a descriptive catalog
of the piano works and an edition of fourteen of them.

"perpetual variety" explains a large part of the style of this enigmatic composer, one who failed in achieving success during his lifetime and whose music yet resists resurrection today. The basic reason is that Heinrich's music is unlike that of any other composer--even Beethoven, in spite of the early tag "the Beethoven of America." Not only is much of the music extraordinarily difficult to perform, for vocalist or pianist, but the unique styles are also difficult to comprehend. Yet his music rivals that of Beethoven or Berlioz for its progressive experimentation. His enthusiasm for the United States, reflected in his music throughout his career, represents an early expression of Romanticism--not only in virtuosity and programmatic aspects, but also in nationalism.[2]

The most spirited proponents are often the converts, and this is the case with Heinrich. Of German descent, he was born Anton Philipp Heinrich in Bohemia (Schönbüchel, now Krásný Buk, Czechoslovakia), next to the German border. Adopted by an uncle, he inherited in 1800 a business in which he prospered for a time and which allowed trips all over Europe, and even to the United States in 1805. During his second visit in 1810 he actually became musical director--without salary, as a musical amateur--of the Southwark Theatre in Philadelphia. The following year, however, his business failed due to the economic bankruptcy of Austria.

Heinrich eventually decided to embark on a career in music, changing from amateur to professional, and he spent the years 1817-20 in Kentucky, "far from the emporiums of musical science, into the isolated wilds of nature, where he invoked his Muse, tutored only by ALMA MATER." The result was *The Dawning of Music in Kentucky, or the Pleasures of Harmony in the Solitudes of Nature*, the source of the above quotation. This "opera prima" was quickly followed by a supplement, *The Western Minstrel, a Collection of Original Moral, Patriotic, & Sentimental Songs, for the Voice & Piano Forte, Interspersed with Airs, Waltzes, &c.*, opera seconda.[3] They were both published in Philadelphia in 1820, and the composer was there for their appearance and to participate in some concerts.

While always proudly proclaiming his new origins in Kentucky, he apparently never returned there after his move to Boston in 1823 to further his new career. In Boston was published his opera terza, *The Sylviad, or Minstrelsy of Nature in the Wilds of N. America*, issued in

---

2. See the fictionalized version of Heinrich playing for Theodore Thomas his work *Rhapsodia Majestica ad Maiorem Gloriam Rei Publicae Americanae Transatlanticae*, by Josef Skvorecky in *Dvorak in Love: A Light-Hearted Dream* (New York: Alfred A. Knopf, 1987), 42-43.

3. Reprinted, together, as Earlier American Music, 10 (New York: Da Capo, 1972). For a summary of the contents, see Wolfe 3596 and 3646.

two sets, 1823 and 1825-26.[4] The dedication was to Dr. Crotch, the president of the Royal Academy of Music in London, founded in 1822, and Heinrich was hoping the dedication would pave the way to his success when he sailed for London in 1826. In spite of a number of transatlantic crossings and concert tours to Germany, Austria, Czechoslovakia, Hungary, and France, he never achieved lasting success.[5] He settled in New York City in 1837, where he died a pauper in 1861 and was buried in the Audubon family vault. Whereas his music remains almost totally unknown, it represents a striking musical parallel to the painting and literature of its time.[6]

Dawning contains three sets of variations for violin--one preceded by an Entrata for string ensemble and piano--and twenty-three songs. *Western Minstrel* has thirteen more songs. The remaining music in the two collections is for pianoforte--forty-one pieces or movements in the first and four more in the second. The predominant genre is various kinds of dances, but included is one sonata, *La Buona Mattina*, and a set of variations on Haydn's "God save the Emperor," both discussed earlier. One problem in categorizing the music in the two collections is that several of the piano works include a voice part. David Barron has determined that these are in the tradition of piano music with voice accompaniment--rather than the reverse--in which

---

4. Reprinted, with an introduction by J. Bunker Clark, in Earlier American Music, 28 (New York: Da Capo, forthcoming).

5. Vera Brodsky Lawrence, in *Strong on Music: The New York Music Scene in the Days of George Templeton Strong, 1836-1875*, vol. 1: *Resonances, 1836-1850* (New York: Oxford University Press, 1988), 121, reveals that Heinrich (unbeknownst to modern writers) also contributed music reviews to the *New York Herald*. She aptly summarizes him thus: "During his extraordinary career Heinrich traversed so great a range of extreme and contradictory adventures as to strain credulity: great wealth/destitution; big business/ivory tower creativity; life in the great world capitals/seclusion in the wilds; recognition/ridicule; success/failure; great vision/quackery; a bathetic, years-long quest for a lost (or carelessly misplaced) daughter followed by an unmemorable reunion, and on and on."

6. Wilbur Maust, "The Symphonies of Anthony Philip Heinrich Based on American Themes" (Ph.D. dissertation, Indiana University, 1973), 185, briefly cites George Catlin for painting and James Fenimore Cooper in literature. Betty E. Chmaj developed the parallels more thoroughly to Thomas Cole, Frederic Church, Asher B. Durand in painting, and William Cullen Bryant, Henry David Thoreau, and Walt Whitman in literature, in her paper "Father Heinrich as Kindred Spirit: or, How the Log House Composer Became the Beethoven of America," given to the Sonneck Society and Midcontinent American Studies Association, University of Kansas, 3 April 1982, and published in MASA's journal *American Studies* 24, no. 2 (fall 1983): 35-57.

the voice is sometimes dispensable.[7] These will be discussed individually.

Heinrich had an apparent urge to revise and refine, generally by adding more and more ornamentation. Both *Dawning* and *Western Minstrel* were revised for a second edition, characterized by the many added notes to the score--often small in size--and it is this edition that was used for the modern reprint.[8] One indication is a section of the dedication to *Sylviad*, 1823 set:

> The author has lately revised the Dawning of Music and Western Minstrel, with great care and labor, but unhappily from the want of encouragement and pecuniary means he has not been enabled to bring the corrected copy before the public.

A similar passage is also found for the second set (1825-26) of *Sylviad*. It suggests that whereas Heinrich made his revision, and had printed at least one copy, he could not afford to have more copies made for sale to the public.

Further evidence for the second edition is that on pages 55 and 167 of *Dawning* is a note that "Lord Byron's Cotillion" was "Performed as a Solo dance in the musical Melo Drama of the CHILD of the MOUNTAIN," and the cotillion "La Primavera" was "Introduced into the Melo Drama of the CHILD of the MOUNTAIN, and danced by Miss K. DURANG." *Child of the Mountain, or, the Deserted Mother*, with Heinrich's incidental music, was first performed in Philadelphia on 10 February 1821. The program also included a "National Olio, called the Columbiad intended as an Overture to . . . The Author's Night; or, the Bailiffs Outwitted," cited in *Dawning* on page 73.[9] Two songs from *Western Minstrel* (pages 4 and 17) are marked "As sung by Miss McManus," and the concert took place 7 December 1821[10]--which further restricts the time for revision.

---

7. David Barron, "The Early Vocal Works of Anthony Philip Heinrich" (Ph.D. dissertation, University of Illinois, 1972), chapter 3. Some of the songs that could be played as solo piano pieces, not discussed here, are "To My Virtuoso Friends" (pp. 150-52), "Visit to Philadelphia" (pp. 105-14), "[Prologue Song] To the Air of 'Hail to Kentucky'" (pp. 9-10), and "A Bottle Song" (pp. 41-47)--Barron, 158-66. On pp. 70-76, Barron explains that the "epitome" at the end of some of the songs are simplifications of the song, designed for the amateur to play and/or to sing. Likewise, these have not been included in this survey.

8. A comparison of one page from the two editions of *Dawning* and *Western Minstrel* is shown in Barron, 36, 38.

9. Upton, 59-63, which includes the program of the second performance of March 7.

10. Upton, 66.

Therefore, this second edition must have been prepared sometime between December 1821 and spring 1823, when he moved to Boston.

The Dawning of Music in Kentucky

Some of the piano pieces are quite complex, and often reach epic proportions. As indicated by the quotation from Thomas Moore, a related characteristic of Heinrich's style is perpetual variety.[11] Seldom is material reiterated in the same manner. Examples are cited in the following survey of piano music in *Dawning*, which commences with the simplest and nearly "normal" style found primarily in the dances.

Probably the most common use of the pianoforte from its first years in the United States was to accompany the social dance, and because of this need more dances were published than any other musical category. Dances are likewise well represented in *Dawning* and *Western Minstrel*. In spite of Heinrich's more adventuresome music-- which is not functional or popular but instead abstract and intellectual--his dances, for the most part, are usable for dancing. All are characterized by the regular four- or eight-measure phrase and part-structure associated with the genre. In addition, Heinrich often adds titles which refer to people or places, a practice in common with the many other American dances by his contemporaries and predecessors.

Two simple types of dances in *Dawning* are "A German Hopsassa Dance" and "An Allemande" (pp. 83-84). The first is binary, dominated by dotted rhythm. The second section involves a descending sequence, and the section is given a varied repeat. Heinrich has also made slight changes for the returns in the first part of "Allemande," in which the Alberti bass predominates.

Several different types of dances in *Dawning* are associated with Kentucky, and specifically Farmington, an estate of Judge John Speed located between Louisville and Bardstown, where Heinrich lived for several years beginning in 1819. "Visit to Farmington" (p. 101), "as performed in the ball rooms of Kentucky," is a cotillion. Heinrich was a performer on the violin as much as on the piano, and many of these dances may have been first conceived for the violin. One hint is the direction "spiccato" in the third section. This cotillion includes several momentary returns of material (see meas. 3-4, 27-28), and the fifth and final eight-measure section is comprised of two parallel four-measure phrases. *A Divertimento* (pp. 169-73), dedicated to Mrs. John Speed, consists of three dances associated with Judge and Mrs. Speed's estate. "Farmington Minuet" includes the performance direction "Alla Polacca," perhaps because of the emphasis on the second beat in the second measure, or because each principal phrase ends on the third beat of the measure. Each of the repeated sections is the expected eight measures long. The general style is commonplace,

---

11. Maust, 142, points out that the distinction between development, variation, and elaboration in Heinrich's music is difficult to discern.

except for a few rhythmic and harmonic complications in the trio, which is in the parallel minor. Another allemande is "Farmington Allemande," somewhat more elaborate than the isolated "Allemande" described above. This one is in 3/4 meter rather than the earlier 2/4. The key continues the G major of the minuet, and maintains it throughout. The structure consists of four succeeding eight-measure repeated sections, until the transition to the "Coda, piu vivo, quasi presto." There are no rondo-like returns, but the second section is based on the pattern set up in the first section, and likewise that in the third section becomes the accompaniment in the fourth. The coda overbalances the rest in size; sixteen measures is succeeded by a variant, then another slightly longer section. The only complexities are several added notes obviously derived from the second edition of *Dawning*.

"Farmington March," the last of *A Divertimento*, is likewise generally simple in style. The march characteristics are the dotted rhythm at the beginning, and the inclusion of a contrasting Trio ("cantabile"), especially open in texture for its first part. The overall structure (measure-lengths are underneath):

|: A :| B B' |: C C' :|: D :| D.C.
    8   8 8   4 4   8

The Farmington connection is continued with the song "From thee Eliza I must go" (pp. 175-79), probably referring to Judge Speed's daughter Elizabeth, which directly precedes the concluding "Farewell to Farmington" (p. 180), another cotillion. This dance, "arranged for the piano forte," is based on a four-measure strain which is given twice in the first section, appears in varied form at the end of the second section, and is varied again twice for the fourth section. Enrichment of the texture, added for the revised edition, is again apparent in the cadence ending the second section, and in further complications by means of the 32nd notes in the last part of the third section.

The cotillion is the most ubiquitous dance in *Dawning*, and, with only few exceptions, all are built with eight-measure units. Most have da capo markings at the end, resulting in a return to the first, or first two, sections. "Lord Byron's Cotillion" (p. 55) is further described as "an extract from 'The Fair Haïdée' a song written by that eminent English bard." No setting of such a text by Heinrich has been found, but he used the melody for the later song "Dean Swift's Receipt to Roast Mutton."[12] "Lord Byron's Cotillion," however, is followed by "Fair Haïdée's Waltz." In the cotillion, the principle of constant variation is already apparent: the second strain is succeeded by a variant, the only section without the prevailing dotted rhythm. Even here, however, Heinrich introduces sextuplet rhythm--but only for one measure. "The Fair Bohemian" (p. 81) is the simplest in construction and style of the cotillions. After the third and fourth eight-measure section (the third section being in the parallel minor mode), the da

---

12. Barron, 137.

capo marking indicates a repetition of the first and second. The Alberti accompaniment prevails.

"The Unamiable" (pp. 82-83) was humorously "composed as a counterpart to 'The Amiable,' a French air, well known and much admired in the ball-rooms of Kentucky." The style is not so simple: the Alberti bass is found in the second section, and dominates the last two of the five sections, but elsewhere there are at least five distinct accompanimental patterns. The last two sections feature the crossing of the right hand.

A possible non-piano origin for a set of "Three Cotillions" (pp. 166-68) is implied in the subtitle "composed and arranged for the piano," and confirmed by the designations in the third cotillion "Il Brillante" for "tutti," "flauti," "violino solo," and "flauto solo." Indeed, some of these passages, involving arpeggios and scale patterns in 16th and 32nd notes, seem idiomatic for those solo instruments. The da capo direction after both third and fourth sections result in the rondo form ABCADA rather than the three-part structure used in the other cotillions. Rhythmic complications are introduced in the first cotillion "Luciade" (probably referring to Miss Lucy May, of Bardstown, to whom he dedicated the preceding song in *Dawning*, "Sweet Maid"). The melody of the second section is repeated verbatim in the third, but the accompaniment is varied from 16ths to sextuplet 16ths and 32nds. Similarly, instead of the usual da capo, the fifth section consists of a varied return of the first. The "D.C." was omitted, but probably intended, after the Trio of the second of these cotillions, "La Primavera."

The last cotillions of *Dawning* are "The Sarah" (p. 192) and "The Henriade" (p. 196). The title "The Sarah" refers to Mrs. Sarah Ward Grayson of Louisville, the dedicatee of the preceding song, "Canzonet," and probably a relative of Peter W. Grayson of Bardstown, a lawyer who had furnished the poetry to several songs set to music by Heinrich. Another trait of Heinrich, a sudden borrowing from the parallel minor mode, is apparent in the cadence to the second section and in the four-measure extensions of the fourth section. The Alberti bass accompaniment, sometimes quickened to sextuplets, predominates. The minor mode is also used in the third and fourth sections of "The Henriade." The usual eight-measure first section is doubled to sixteen measures, and the extra eight measures of the fourth section consists of an elaborated dominant harmony that culminates in the da capo.

Heinrich included five waltzes in *Dawning*, some of them portions of larger works. "Fair Haïdée's Waltz" (p. 56), already mentioned as paired with the preceding "Lord Byron's Cotillion," is regular in form except that he omitted the direction "D.C." after the "Trio minore." The theme of the first section returns twice in varied format--as the second eight-measure portion of the second section, and as the "Coda Maggiore." A number of ornamental notes were added for the second edition, especially in the cadence just before the trio, and in the *ossia* left-hand part in the six measures before this cadence.

"Rondo Waltz," beginning on the next page, further illustrates Heinrich's desire for variety. There are no fewer than four varied returns of the principal theme, not including the da capo to the initial

A B A'. In the "C" section, a downward scale is presented in imitation, whereas in its second variant the "answer" rises (Ex. 8-1).

Ex. 8-1.   Heinrich, "Rondo Waltz," meas. 125-29 (*Dawning*, p. 59).

This attractive feature, however, is somewhat outweighed by clumsy parallel fifths before the second return of the main theme. "Rondo Waltz" probably lies outside the genre of dance music, in that the two varied returns of "C" are longer (19 and 30 measures) than the original sixteen measures, and because the clearly defined eight-measure phrase structure associated with dancing does not apply throughout. The overall rondo scheme:

|: A :|: B :| A' ||: C :|| D B' C' E A" C" A''' F A"" || D.C.

"Quick Step Waltz" (pp. 62-64), a part of "Kentucky March, Trio, & Quick Step Waltz," is more suitable for dancing, in spite of the rondo form. The overall scheme is A A' B A" C C' A''' A' D D' E B A"" coda. With the exception of a six-measure extension of C' and a four-measure ostinato leading to the "D" section, eight-measure phrases apply throughout. This is one of Heinrich's more rewarding simple pieces to play. Some chromatic alteration is found in the "C" section, and the "D" section emphasizes the raised second and fourth degrees of the scale. Particular effective is the manner in which the main theme returns in the left hand toward the end.

"Yankee Doodle Waltz" (pp. 74-76), with the preceding "Hail Columbia! Minuet," were "adapted by the Author as an Overture to a new Farce called the Authors Night under the title of the COLUMBIAD," that had been performed in 1821 after the *Child of the Mountain* (see above). These are in the tradition of the medley overture, with popular national tunes, performed and published at the turn of the century. "Yankee Doodle Waltz" is in the form of a rondo, but with this irregular scheme (YD = "Yankee Doodle"): A B C C' YD YD A' B' B" D coda YD. For this waltz, of course, the national tune is presented in triple rather than duple meter, and even transformed to the minor mode for its first appearance here. Although only the first two sections include repeat marks, all other material (until the end of the coda) is in eight-measure segments. One of Heinrich's favorite eccentricities, free alternation between major and minor modes, permeates the coda.

This Americana, along with a song commemorating the heroes of Tippecanoe, is succeeded by two Czech-related dances, "The Prague Waltz" and "The Fair Bohemian"--the last discussed above with the cotillions. On the surface, "Prague Waltz" is simple. It includes the rounded binary first half, and the innocuous trio beginning like a Haydn minuet, but then one discovers the persistent chromatic motive and sudden triplets in the left hand.

Probably the most extraordinary waltz of all time is "Avance et Retraite: A Military Waltz" (pp. 115-19). The title is reflected in the music, which is a palindrome. The direction to the performer at the end is "Retro, or begin at the end, and end at the beginning," similar to Machaut's famous 14th-century song "Ma fin est mon commencement et mon commencement ma fin." The direction thereby lengthens the score's 212 measures to 424. An added dimension is that the final 22 measures (meas. 191-212), in reverse order, roughly correspond in material to the first 22 measures. From then on, proceeding inwards, the relationship disappears. A number of elements recur throughout, the chief of which is the tonality of F major, maintained with only one exception of sequential material near the middle (meas. 91-103). A three-measure low trill ("alla Tamburo")--sometimes expanded to trilled chords--represents drums, and appears six times. Another military element is the fanfare material ("alla Tromba"), either on the notes of the tonic triad or in the guise of horn fifths, is placed either after--or, in the second half, before--the drum roll. Much of the remainder consists of various inventions on the harmonic pattern of alternating dominant and tonic chords. The drum trills are always four measures long, and everything else is in eight-measure phrases (exceptions: the first two and last two measures, and a passage in the middle, meas. 104-22).

The same work, in an altered version, was separately published in London about 1830 with the title "Avance et Retraite, a Military Overture, arranged for the piano forte, composed and dedicated to his esteemed friend, Mr. Richard Hughes."[13] There seems to be no significance that this was "arranged for" rather than "for" the pianoforte in *Dawning*, nor the substitution of "overture" for "waltz." The notation is made more clear in that there are clefs and accidentals facing both backwards as well as forwards. (Footnote on the first page: "The accidentals answer the same backwards as forward, in many instances they will be found marked retrograde.") The most obvious changes are the added tonic chords at the beginning (engraved backwards, on prefatory staves) and end. The first 62 measures are essentially the same in both *Dawning* and London versions, but with many minor

---

13. Ent. Sta. Hall. Pr. 2/6. London, printed & published by Clementi, Collard & Collard, 26, Cheapside. Title-page + pp. 1-7. Copy in the Heinrich scrapbook, Library of Congress, pp. 1003-11.

details changed. Several times, the drum trills are on the dominant level rather than in the tonic. Along with the many re-composed passages are a number of added sections, resulting in a total of 251--39 more than in *Dawning*. One is not better than the other--just different. This work is well worth performing.

The first of *Dawning*'s six minuets is the "Hail Columbia! Minuet" (pp. 71-73); like its mate, "Yankee Doodle Waltz," the popular tune is presented in triple meter. Two varied appearances are separated by a midsection, "alla Trio" (the tune of which was later used for the songs "La Toilette de la Cour," 1847, and "Oh Happy Land," n.d.[14]). Almost as long is the "Coda: Minuetto risoluto" with its enigmatic "Coda Trio" (the initial material does not return). Fanfare rhythms toward the end recall the "Introduzione alla trombo." There are a number of compositional surprises, such as the sudden register changes in the second treatment ("in vece del DA CAPO") of the main tune, several wide leaps--one of three octaves--in the "Coda Trio," and an introduction of chromaticism toward the end of the coda. A 16th-note scale, downwards then upwards, occurs three times during the first treatment of "Hail Columbia!" (at the marking "Minuetto"), then recurs twice in the first part of the coda. Another scale figure comes four times in the final measures of the piece.

"Five Minuets" (pp. 227-32), although scored for piano, "are more especially intended for the Violin." There are several alternate passages, specified for either violin or piano, and even a few violin fingerings. They form a section of *The Minstrel's Petition, or a Votive Wreath*, "humbly presented to Her Majesty Charlotte Augusta." The minuets are preceded by variations on "God save the Emperor," described elsewhere, and are followed by "The Austrian: A Landler," the descriptive piece "The Fair Traveller, or the Post-Ride from Prague to Vienna," and finally "Empress's March." The minuets are labeled with appropriate titles: "The Imperial," "The Royal," "The Illustrious," "The Affable," and (most important for Heinrich) "The Philanthropic." The structure is identical for all: minuet and trio, each with two repeated eight-measure sections. Heinrich briefly introduces a few rhythmic complications, such as 16th-note triplets, quintuplets, and even one sextuplet, and these minuets are not quite as simple as first appears. One display of craftsmanship is the inverted imitation beginning the trio of "The Imperial" (Ex. 8-2).

Ex. 8-2.   Heinrich, "The Imperial," beginning of trio, meas. 17-19
            (*Dawning*, p. 227).

_____

14. Barron, 136-37, 148-49.

A "Note" explains that the trio of the last minuet was modeled on music composed by a childhood friend.

"The Austrian: A Landler" that follows (pp. 232-37) is as complex in structure as the minuets are straightforward:

‖: A :‖:B :‖:A' :‖:C :‖:D :‖:E :‖: F :‖ G H A"F' F" G' I J M coda
    16 18 8   8   8   8   8   8 10 8 8 8 8 15 23 29 28

It finishes with a 28-measure coda. Actually the first section includes two different versions of the main theme, and "M" represents a triple-meter statement of Haydn's "God save the Emperor" that had begun *The Minstrel's Petition*. Further refinements are that "H" begins as a variant of the "F" section, and that sections F, G, H, F', F", and G' are based on alternating dominant and tonic harmonies. D-major tonality prevails, except for D minor in "J."

The next work of *The Minstrel's Petition* is one of the two programmatic pieces in *Dawning*: "Krásná Pocestná, a neb Gizda Postečňj z Prahÿ do Widňe (Wihlasseny Walzer) [accents thus]," with the translation given as "The Fair Traveller, or the Post-Ride from Prague to Vienna: A Descriptive Waltz" (pp. 238-45). The proper medium is not entirely clear, since after the departure the name of the first town on the descriptive journey is accompanied by the following footnote: "The following Airs are principally calculated for the Violin, as the most imitative Instrument of the Bugle or Post Horn." There are several violin fingerings and strings indicated throughout. Indeed, their first public performance was by Heinrich on solo violin, under the title "Postillion Waltzes (Concertante) written in imitation of the German Postillion Bugle airs or Post horns," 8 June 1819.[15] Nonetheless, the printed score is for pianoforte. The route was the principal one leading southeast from Prague toward Vienna:

> Introduzione alla postiglione--Bugles call, and the
>   Farewell
> The Departure--A smart trot
> Colin [now Kolín]
> Cžaslau [Cáslav]
> Böhmischbrod [Česky Brod?--if so, a backtracking;
>   perhaps Heinrich mistook this for present-day
>   Havlickov Brod, which is on the way]
> Iglau [Jihlava]
> Moravian Mountains [Česko-Moravská Vrchovina]--
>   Whipping the Horses
> Znaim [Znojmo]; Vine Hills of Austria--The inspir-
>   ing Whip again; Spurring; Kicking
> Stockerau [north-northwest of Vienna] and the
>   Danube
> Enzersdorf [Langenzersdorf, a northwestern suburb
>   of Vienna]--in full speed
> Hail Vienna!

---

15. Program in Upton, 56-57.

Zastaw w Cÿsařownè z Rakaůs--Stop at the Empress of Austria

In spite of the rapid arpeggiated flourishes in the introduction, one finger-slide, and a touch of imitative writing in the Vienna section, this is not a successful piece. "Spurring" and "kicking" are portrayed by some chromaticism, and "whipping the horses" by rolled chords. The biggest problems are that there is no relief from C major and that all of the themes are various permutations of the tonic chord, and all themes are the same eight measures in length. Heinrich, however, furnishes some element of variation when a theme returns. The musical gesture illustrating the Moravian Mountains returns in the following section with the Vine Hills of Austria--both accompanied by the whip and with right and left hand parts exchanged. There is some charm in the composer's naïve setting, and the texture and harmonies are often elaborate.

The last in the set of pieces dedicated to the Empress of Austria, "Empress's March" (pp. 245-50) is quite complex in structure, style, and even medium. In some ways, it is a rondo:

A   A' B :||: C   A" :||: D   E A'" :||: F :||: G   A'"" ext. H coda ||
8   8 14   27 8   12 11 10   8   8   10   6   8   7

Heinrich uses major and minor mode interchangeably: the first appearance of the march theme (A) is in minor, thereafter in major. Several measures with a florid right-hand part in the "B" section return within "C"--but with the mode again changed from major to minor. Sections F and G (marked "alla Trio") are likewise in minor, surrounded by the march theme in major.

The problem of medium is that section H includes a text: "May Heaven's choicest gifts descend and bless th'Empress of Austria, the Widow's stay, and the Orphan's hope! hope! hope!" Perhaps the intent is for the pianist to sing here, except that a voice range of no less than two octaves is rare for pianists. It would hardly be practical to have a separate singer for only eight measures out of a total of the thirty-two pages devoted to *The Minstrel's Petition*. Singing the text should probably be regarded as optional.

Some portions of "Empress's March" are formidable for the pianist. For example, section C becomes progressively more difficult, and its last ten measures consist of an elaborated dominant-seventh chord including a descending scale of trilled notes for the left hand, over the right, from *f'''* to *d'* (Ex. 8-3). The most demanding is section D, also based on a dominant-seventh chord, in which a rising 16th-note pattern is played in tenths--with the right hand crossed over the left.

Ex. 8-3.   Heinrich, "Empress's March," meas. 52-55 (*Dawning*, pp. 247-48).

"Empress's March" is certainly not in the tradition of the simple American march, but instead serves as a virtuoso close to a "sketch of sufferings, wrested from a convulsed heart" to "the august Mother of the land." These quotations are from the printed dedication to Empress Charlotte Augusta, which describes how Heinrich's daughter Antonio had been left in 1814 in the care of a relative near his birthplace, and his fears of never seeing her again. (When Heinrich finally reached his homeland in 1835, he found that his daughter had left to see him in the United States! They finally were reunited in New York two years later.) "I make therefore this public appeal to your Majesty, and present my helpless Infant to your throne of grace and benevolence, with the anxious hope that you will extend towards her your countenance and patronage." There is no evidence Heinrich or his daughter received the imperial patronage, but not for the lack of trying. *The Minstrel's Petition* comprises a sizeable portion of *Dawning*.

At least one march in *Dawning* is less complex than "Empress's March": his "Kentucky March, Trio, & Quick Step Waltz" (pp. 61-66). Many American marches were stately in tempo and coupled with a "quick step," but not usually with one of the character of a waltz (this waltz is discussed above). The march, however, is not the usual transcription for piano of music originally intended for a wind band. The march section includes the traditional dotted rhythm and repeated sections of its predecessors, but not the profusion of musical ideas and variety of rhythms. The formal scheme is not typical, especially the re-use of the principal themes in the trio, as seen in this summary:

```
        March                              Trio
|: A' :|: B :|| C  A' extension ||: A"  D  :|| C' || D.C.
   8     8   12 8    9                8   8+2   8
```

A striking augmented-sixth chord, on C-flat, is included in the "D" section, which also has a momentary return of the first two measures from the beginning of the march (Ex. 8-4).

Ex. 8-4.   Heinrich, "Kentucky March," meas. 54-56 (*Dawning*, p. 63).

Another pair is "Marcia di Ballo" and "Rondo Fanfare" (pp. 157-63),[16] which were "originally composed as an Overture to a Ball given by Major Smiley, of Bardstown, Kentucky, and now arranged for the Piano Forte by its Author." The only indication of an instrument is "Le Trombe" for the fanfare introduction at the beginning of the march, and the general style is not pianistic as it was for "March to Kentucky." Each section is eight or sixteen measures long, and the trio includes a contrasting section in the relative minor key.

The principal of perpetual variation again prevails for the two returns of the main theme in "Rondo Fanfare," yet one unifying factor is the rhythm 16th-16th-8th that often marks the beginning or ending of sections. The main feature of this piece, however, is the long coda, based on "Yankee Doodle"--longer than the main movement itself. The national tune is given in two variants, and after a

---

16. Recorded by Neely Bruce in *Piano Music in America*, vol. 1: *19th Century Popular Concert and Parlor Music* (Vox SVBX 5302, 1972).

contrasting section that includes some octave-work to tax the pianist, there are two more versions. The main theme, including the rhythmic motive, closes the piece. The climax comes just before the end, with a cadence to the highest keyboard note--*c''''* (Ex. 8-5).

Ex. 8-5.   Heinrich, "Rondo Fanfare," ending (*Dawning*, p. 163).

Although this is cited as part of the Allegro movement in the Overture to *Child of the Mountain*, and may have originally been intended for orchestra, the style is quite pianistic.

"March Concertante" (pp. 197-213) is only the first of a series of pieces associated with the place of Heinrich's birth and upbringing. The march itself is dedicated to the citizens of the towns where he grew up. This charming description appears on the title page: "At Schönbüchel he entered the Gamut of Life; and at Schönlinde and Georgswalde, (places which contain more than one hundred scientific musical performers,) commenced his Chromatic Variations, in the Counterpoint of human affairs." Although the first piece of this collection, the march, is dedicated to the citizens of the three towns, the others have other related dedications. The third, "Coda," is subtitled "in remembrance of the many virtues of the reigning Prince Kinsky, Lord of Kamnitz, Schönlinde, Schönbüchel, &c., &c.," and the fourth, "A Cheer!," is "in honour of the Illustrious Count Harrach, Lord of Schluckenau, Georgswalde &c. &c." The "Finalissimo" is "A Loyal Obeisance to his Imperial Majesty, Francis, II."

This collection of five pieces is balanced with *The Minstrel's Petition*, with its nine pieces, dedicated to the Empress Charlotte Augusta, immediately following in *Dawning*. Both represent a variety of media. The "March Concertante" was "adapted to the piano forte (intended for a full orchestra)." All the remaining pieces seem to be idiomatic on the pianoforte, until the last one, "A Loyal Obeisance," which (like one section in *The Minstrel's Petition*) includes a text between the staves--"Gott! erhalte Franz den Kayser!"--the same text used for Haydn's national anthem.

The first piece, "March Concertante" (spelled "Marcia" at the head of the music), includes indications for bugle, horns, fifes, and drums--the last represented by quick trills in the low register. The identical four-measure bugle call introduces both march and its trio. Everything seems able to be transferred back to an orchestral, or band, score except for a 16th-note scale passage for the left hand in the sec ond section of the march--with a range of just over two octaves.

The second piece, "Rondo Quick Step," is quite sophisticated in the varied manipulation of the basic rondo theme, as suggested in this analysis (key changes are indicated under the measure-lengths):

A	A'	B	A"	C	A'''	D	A""		A""'	A"""	A""""'	trans.
8	8	8	8	11	8	11	18		8	8+25	8	8
G				D	D-b	C-Ab	e		g			

The main rondo theme, presented in the first four measures, is already altered in the second four-measure phrase, and in the succeeding eight measures (A') is identified by its rhythmic pattern and the characteristic appoggiatura figures. The same appoggiatura motive persists in section B, and also section D--which in turn is derived from section B. The above layout may suggest that no contrasting section appears after section D, but indeed the contrast is in the differing treatment, developmental in nature. In the 25-measure passage before the final return of the main theme, both the appoggiatura figure and basic rhythmic pattern are prominent, in combination with a triplet 8th-note accompaniment. The last appearance of the rondo theme is in the left-hand tenor range. The ending transition leads to the new key of B-flat major for the "Coda," the third piece, which is marchlike in style and tempo. In the A B A' C D pattern, each section repeated, the only return of the initial theme is in the parallel minor. "A Cheer!"--the fourth piece--is a short binary movement in E-flat, also like a march in character.

The final piece, "A Loyal Obeisance," with the text "Gott! erhalte Franz den Kayser," is rather complex. First of all, Heinrich's setting seems to be a parody of the phraseology and rhythm of the setting by Haydn--which immediately follows as the first number of *The Minstrel's Petition*. For example, both begin on the second half of the measure, and both include the same musical repeat scheme (Ex. 8-6). Toward the end of his setting, however, Heinrich ventures from the original C minor into A-flat major, and then a sequence touches B-flat minor before a two-measure melisma climaxes in the cadence of the home key. A three-measure chromatic scale in the piano separates the final "unsern guten" from "Kayser Franz!" so that what otherwise would have been a 32-measure melody is extended to 34 measures-- after which is added an additional two-measure cadence. The voice range is only a tenth, f' to a''-flat. Although one could successfully play this national anthem without the voice, Heinrich undoubtedly intended that it be sung.

Ex. 8-6.   Heinrich, "A Loyal Obeisance to His Imperial Majesty
           Francis II," meas. 1-4 (*Dawning*, p. 208).

Heinrich proceeds to provide three fantasy-variations on his tune, all with a quickening of tempo to prestissimo, and a change of meter to 6/8 and mode to C major. The term "fantasy" is used here because, as in his variations to Haydn's "God save the Emperor," the original tune is sometimes difficult to trace. After the first eight measures the tune is lost in favor of an elaborated cadential trill and scale flourishes (with crossed hands). Subsequent extensions result in a variation which is nearly double the original tune in length. The second treatment begins in a similar fashion, but with the mode changed to minor; this time the 34-measure length is maintained, but the original melody and harmony is lost after seven measures. The third and final statement ("Veloce") begins like its two predecessors, but is reduced in length to only twenty measures. The final 16th-16th-8th rhythm recalls the beginning of "March Concertante," the first of this set. The 16th-note momentum is hardly relaxed during these pianistic elaborations of his tune; there are plenty of scales and arpeggios to make it a challenging and rewarding piece for the accomplished pianist.

One of the most puzzling works in *Dawning*, especially regarding the medium, is "A Serenade" (pp. 19-24). The title continues "Adapted for the Piano Forte and Dedicated to the Virtuosos of the United States by a Tyro Minstrel of Kentucky, A. P. Heinrich." The puzzle occurs in the four-measure "Serenata" at the head of the music. It is a kind of musical epigram, with text, apparently for five different voice parts.[17] It is presented in small units--one to six notes each--in a manner that later would be called *Klangfarbenmelodie* as applied to the pointillistic style of Anton Webern. The total voice range is C to g″; the text is "Vi saluto con Diffidenze ma con Amore" (I salute you with diffidence but with love). Similarly there is a four-measure

---

17. Barron, 179, suggests it could be performed by two to five voices.

appendix, or post-epigram, after the main part of the work, with the text "Bona Notte Buonissima Notte" (good night, the best night). The voice part, as distinct from the piano accompaniment, is not entirely clear, but the total range is apparently the same. The performance direction by the last measure is: "Tornando la Destra si alza a piacere per andar a Letto" (turn the right [hand] as high as wanted in order to go to bed). Perhaps this is intended for a contortionist, since the right hand plays an F-major chord under the bass staff, as the left hand likewise is notated above the treble staff.

The reason for the "good night" is the link to the following sonata *La Buona Mattina*, which includes the preface ". . . as a small Morning's Entertainment or 'BUONA MATTINA' in addition to the SERENADE or 'BUONA NOTTE,' already presented. . . ." The sonata also includes a texted voice part. Although these voice parts could be played instead of sung, perhaps a pianist should consider singing them, albeit with appropriate octave transposition when needed.

The main part of "A Serenade" is labeled "Alla marcia allegramente," for the most part based on the style and form of a march. Instead of repeated sections, however, Heinrich provides varied repeats until the trio, as seen here:

```
[March]              Alla Trio    Coda    Adagio
A ‖ A' ‖  B  B'   ‖ C ‖ C' |: D :‖:E :‖:F :‖ G
8    8       12 12+4 8     8     8     8    8    10
```

As suggested in the subtitle, this is one of Heinrich's virtuoso pieces, and some passages are quite difficult to perform. For example, in the first two measures the right hand consists of 3-octave leaps over the left hand, a feature transferred to the left hand for the beginning of the second half of section A. Two descending four-octave finger-slides in section A are balanced by one ascending slide at the end of section A'--widened to four octaves and a half (Ex. 8-7).

Ex. 8-7.   Heinrich, "A Serenade": "Alla marcia Allegramente" movement, meas. 16 (*Dawning*, p. 21).

The harmonic language of sections A and A' is restricted to the three primary chords, and not expanded until sections B and B'. In both sections A and B, the two balanced four-measure phrases form a musical period, and the added four measures in section B is given a varied repeat for the end of section B'.

The organizing principle in much of the second section (B) is an alternation of musical ideas between the two hands, especially in the second phrase (meas. 21-24). This principle becomes even more prevalent in the trio, in which the motive presented alone in the right hand is echoed no fewer than eight more times, including once inverted. During the varied repeat (C'), an additional rising 5-note scale--sometimes chromatic, sometimes extended to more than an octave--is added to the texture. Both persist in the following section D, appearing in quite different guises.

The coda sums up the principles of octave displacement and alternating a motive between the hands and keyboard registers. Not until the final "poco Adagio ma con molto Espress: e Dolc[e]" does Heinrich abandon the work's march characteristics. Although the harmonic vocabulary becomes enriched, mainly by chromaticism, its basic progression consists of repeated dominant-tonic chords--a feature also continuing in the vocal post-epigram.

The demands on the performer are not without purpose, as indicated above. The inventiveness of the composer is accompanied by an impressive understanding of how to manipulate basic ideas, in a fresh manner. If the pianist masters the difficulties of *La Buona Mattina*, prefacing it with "A Serenade" is entirely appropriate.

The last piece of *Dawning* to be discussed is the most avant-garde, yet humorous, of the collection: "A Chromatic Ramble of the Peregrine Harmonist" (pp. 135-45).[18] Although at first glance it seems to be a song, the voice part is a vocal accompaniment and can be regarded as ad libitum--especially considering the wide range of *g* to

18. Another work with the same title appears in two pages in the composer's autograph in the Heinrich collection, Library of Congress, vol. 33 no. 1. The music is different, and the text "Among the Flats and Sharps . . ." appears only at the head of the music. Immediately following is another "A Chromatic Ramble: Toccata for the Pianoforte" which contains the last two movements of "toccata grande cromatica" in *Sylviad*--see below.

e‴"-flat, nearly three octaves. David Barron[19] suggests performance by a violin, in which case the text might best be printed in a program or read to the audience. There are only two staves in the score, however, and everything is within reach of a solo pianist.[20] This is why it is included in this survey.

The text, printed between the staves in the third section, consists of a description of the music itself, which is a counterpart of "Harmonic Labyrinth," once attributed to J. S. Bach. The words begin "Among the flats and sharps a tedious journey travel," and end "Then where you set out come again, And now you're welcome home again 'A Casa'." "Home" (casa) is the key of D-flat, notated as C-sharp at the end of the last section of the piece, where printed above the staff is "Entrata a Casa" (enter the house). The many chromatic progressions and remote keys must have been especially unusual in 1820, since equal temperament was by no means common on pianos.

There are six sections, in which the text appears only in the third section. The first, "Allegrissimo agitato" (meas. 1-6), opens with a scale and written-out trill in three statements a major third apart-- D-flat, B-double-flat, F. This is the same material that introduces "The Sons of the Woods: An Indian War-Song" (p. 153), where it represents the passions of war, but the key levels are tamed to G-e-C. The chromatic harmony at the end of the section, leading from F to F-sharp, is not unlike that of Richard Strauss or Max Reger at the end of the century. Section 2, "Andantino soave" (meas. 7-16), features a florid melodic line in the middle register of the piano. The modulation from F-sharp major to C minor is accomplished with a diminished-seventh chord and two enharmonically spelled chords: a B-flat major chord spelled A-sharp, C-double-sharp, E-sharp, and a C-minor chord spelled B-sharp, D-sharp, F-double-sharp. The final four measures of the section are like an instrumental recitative, capped with a three-octave chromatic scale. For proof that Heinrich was indeed a skilled composer, able to manipulate the complexities of chromatic modulation, one need only examine these measures. Thus far, Heinrich has illustrated his upcoming text: the first section has a signature of seven flats, the second has six sharps.

The voice part ("il canto") enters for the third section, marked "Allegro assai e sempre espressivo" (meas. 17-111), the longest of the whole work and the one that vividly depicts his "chromatic ramble." The main key centers are C minor (key signature of three flats), B major (five flats), A-flat major (four flats), plus a passage with no key signature touching the keys of G minor, B-flat major, returning to C minor. The modulations are again enharmonic: from C minor to B major, with common chords spelled in C-flat and G-flat major becoming B and F-sharp major; for the next, G-sharp major becomes A-flat major of the new key. The most prominent diminished-seventh

---

19. Barron, 173.

20. A wonderful performance (without singing) by Mary Louise Boehm is available on cassette: *Center for American Music: Inaugural Concert* (Pantheon CA-PFN 2231, 1985).

chord is in the last measure of the section--a rather long measure which sets the word "Casa." A downward arpeggio pattern in the right hand, the acceleration indicated by a quickening of the note values from 8ths to 64ths, is answered in mirror by the left hand. Particularly effective text-settings are the downward gestures for "sigh," "die," "faint," succeeded by "in bliss extatic" with simple diatonic harmonies and melody, in which the duple rhythm against triplet accompaniment reminds one of Brahms. Sequential patterns are occasionally present; one involves successive broken seventh chords in the melody for a setting of "knots unravel" (meas. 39-40). Another is the gradual rise in the melodic line from *d'* to *e'''*-flat, a long passage (meas. 94-102) which even then does not complete the setting of the text "welcome home again." It is cleverly constructed so that the next higher note is reached every half-measure, for four measures, then each quarter-measure. The climax is supported by an accelerando marking.

The fourth section, marked "Allegro di molto" (meas. 112-37), has constant 16th-note motion, unlike the rhapsodic nature of the cadence immediately preceding. The basic key signature is three flats, for C minor, but after only three measures the key signature is abandoned--the practice of much 20th-century music--because of the many accidentals required for the new key of G-flat major. One "German" augmented-sixth chord (meas. 116, 118) is spelled E-double-flat, G-flat, B-double-flat, C. Toward the end, A-flat minor chords alternating with its leading-tone chords, in the manner of the trilled chords of "Avance et Retraite," are to be played "sempre accelerando e crescendo." The final D-flat major chord serves as dominant of the following section, in G-flat major.

"Alla Salterella, Prestissimo" (meas. 138-79) is the most dancelike of the movements. Except for momentary modulations to the dominant made minor (D-flat minor), the G-flat major remains clear, yet with chromatic complexities. One strange chord (meas. 165-67) is actually a "German" augmented-sixth, spelled A, D-flat, F-flat, G, except that the A and G are together in the left hand. This chord modifies the dominant-of-the-dominant, yet the chord on D-flat becomes the tonic of the following sixth and last section, "L'istesso tempo, cioè velocissimo: Furibondo." The scales and trills of the opening return, again built on descending third tonal levels, are here spelled C-sharp, A, F-sharp (comparable to the song's G-e-C)--the last a substitute for the earlier F-natural. The 16th notes of the 3/4 meter relax into triplet 8ths for a passage that may prove awkward to perform in that one hand plays in the range of the other. That this is the primary virtuoso movement can be seen by the predominance of chromatic scales in thirds or sixths--not particularly formidable for the professional pianist except that for these the composer asks that one hand be over the other. One chromatic run of three measures is topped by the final run of ten measures to which is added a six-measure double trill. The tonic C-sharp minor chord is reiterated for the "Entrata a Casa" in the final seven measures.[21]

Whereas the following song, entitled simply "A Coda," is not a part of "A Chromatic Ramble,"[22] the sentiment of the poetry seems to fit. It begins "My Harp awake! awake again, O! strike the soul inspiring strings, No more in pensive notes complain, But waft to gratitude the strain." The next song, "Supplement," dedicated "To my Virtuoso Friends," actually begins the second part of *Dawning*, and its text suggests that Heinrich realized his compositions would not attract popularity:

> My Harp that tuneless long has lain
> To blank forgetfulness a prey,
> Once more renews its humble strain
> Not for applause or smiles to gain
> But to its friends a tribute pay . . .

"A Chromatic Ramble" is the most adventuresome and progressive piece in *Dawning*, and has to be seen to be believed. Several aspects mark it as a product of Romanticism, before many of these aspects had been fully established in Europe. The virtuosity, chromatic harmony, enharmonic modulations, and remote keys bring Liszt to mind, yet Liszt was only nine when *Dawning* was published. The "program" describing the music, to be sung or presented in some other manner, predates Berlioz's programmatic *Symphonie fantastique* by ten years. Far from being a representative American--or even Czech--composer, Heinrich's fierce individualism and independent creativity mark him as the most important American musician of his time.

The contemporary review in John Rowe Parker's Boston musical journal *The Euterpeiad: or, Musical Intelligencer*,[23] for 13 April 1822 indicates some of the virtues of *Dawning*:

> Whoever has the will and ability to overstep the fence and unveil the hidden treasure, will be no less surprised than delighted with his discovery . . . the vigour of thought, variety of ideas, originality of conception, classical correctness, boldness and luxuriance of imagination, displayed throughout this voluminous work, are the more extraordinary, as the author but a few years since, was merely an amateur. . . . His genius however triumphs over every thing. There is enough in his well-stored pages to gratify

------

21. The sign Ⅺ means to hold the damper pedal. A cautionary note: the treble clef for the left hand in the last seven measures should be a bass clef.

22. Barron, 198 and 351-52.

23. Reprint of 1820-23 (New York: Da Capo, 1977).

every taste and fancy. There is versatility for the capricious, pomp for the pedant, playfulness for the amateur, pleasure for the vocalist, ingenuity for the curious, and puzzle for an academician. He seems at once to have possessed himself of the key which unlocks to him the temple of science and enables him to explore with fearless security the mysterious labyrinth of harmony. He may, therefore, justly be styled the Beethoven of America, and as such he is actually considered by the few who have taken the trouble to ascertain his merits.

Later on, in the issue for February 1823, some of the reasons for the lack of Heinrich's success are indicated:

There was, however, so much eccentricity mixed with the real merit of his compositions; so much of that *sombre* cast which betrays a protracted struggle with the evils of life, and a spirit wounded past all cure by the tragic loss of a beloved friend [a reference to his late wife]; so much more of the comet than of a regular planet; and so much laborious execution at the onset, that his voluminous works, shunned by amateurs on account of their forbidding aspect and difficulty of access, and disdained by Professors for their very originality, breaking forth in all the wildness of native grandeur, have remained a mere burthen on the shelves of music sellers in the sister-cities, where they ought to have been better known and appreciated.

Four months later, for the issue of June 1823, the *Euterpeiad*, now in a new series edited by Charles Dingley, comments on Heinrich in comparison with successful composers and musicians from Europe:

But perhaps more time is yet necessary to enable the philosopher to discover whether those fine intelligences which render the inhabitants of Middle Europe so sensible to the powers of the fine arts above their Northern and American neighbors, be the effect of physical structure or of any particular period in the progress of manners and society. . . . For ourselves, . . . we long to . . . ascertain whether it be granted to our own country to emulate them. . . . These remarks are elicited in observing the current of public taste evinced and encouragement held out to the gentleman, whose name stands at the head of this article, author of *The Dawning of Music in Kentucky,--The Western Minstrel,* &c.--works which abound in boldness, originality, science, and even sublimity; and embrace all styles of composition, from a waltz or song up to the acme of chromatic frenzy. He may be justly styled the *Beethoven of*

America, as he is actually considered by the few who
have taken the trouble to ascertain his merits.

The last sentence of two of these reviews is almost the same, but the
rejection of Heinrich's music is clear.

The Western Minstrel

In spite of the presence of relatively simple pieces in *Dawning*,
the complex styles and virtuosity is obviously directed to the professional performer. By contrast, *The Western Minstrel* seems more for
the amateur. The piano music in this op. 2 is generally simple to play.
"Philadelphia Waltz" (p. 3) is described as an extract from "Visit to
Philadelphia," a song in *Dawning* (pp. 105-14). The original material
consists of the the the first two eight-measure sections of a rather lengthy
instrumental coda to the song. In its new guise, these two sections are
followed by "Coda: Varatio"--variants of the same music plus four
measures of cadential matter. "Landler of Austria" (p. 16) is much
simpler than "The Austrian: A Landler" in *Dawning* (discussed above).
The regular four-measure phrases, in two-phrase periods, receives further unification from the almost constant return of the initial motive.
The overall form is A B A' A". A footnote explains that a Landler is
"a rustic Waltz."
  "Gipsey Dance" (p. 27) is probably the remains of some stage
show. The first part, dominated by a syncopated figure, is labeled
"Pas Seul, by the Queen"; the second is entitled "Gibberish, by the
Gipsey Corps de Ballet," and largely consists of alternating octaves.
  The last work in *Western Minstrel* is "The Minstrel's March, or
Road to Kentucky" (pp. 36-39). This is a descriptive piece, somewhat
like "The Fair Traveller, or the Post-Ride from Prague to Vienna, a
Descriptive Waltz" in *Dawning* (described above). This time, Heinrich
describes, in music, his long journey from Philadelphia to Pittsburgh--
300 miles--which he did on foot, then 400 miles further by boat on
the Ohio River to Kentucky, all in 1817.[24] This work is not
particularly interesting, largely because Heinrich seldom leaves E
major, but several techniques of description are striking. The sections
are:

> Tempo Giusto (da Filadelphia)--Post Horn--Market
>   Street hill
> Toll Gate; Schuylkill Bridge
> Turnpike
> Lancaster--stop ad lib; March
> Alleghanies [*sic*]
> Fort Pitt
> Embarkation--Salute
> Passage on the Ohio--The Rapids

---

24. Described, with imagination, in Upton, 17-28.

Standing in for Port--Casting Anchors--Side steps--
Landing and cheers
Sign of the Harp [probably a tavern]

Several musical ideas help to unify the work, among them an 8th-
16th-16th rhythm ending the posthorn call, heard again on the Turn-
pike and just before the arrival at Fort Pitt, and during the final section representing Limestone (now Maysville). Low and prolonged
measured trills represent the drums at Fort Pitt. The Allegheny
mountains are depicted by scales and arpeggios, a device again used
for the rapids on the Ohio River and the casting of the anchor at
Limestone. An amateur pianist with better-than-average ability would
be able to perform this piece after some practice.

The Sylviad, or Minstrelsy of Nature in the Wilds of N. America

As indicated earlier, *The Sylviad*, opera terza, was issued in two
sets, with identical title-pages, in 1823 and 1825-26. The title-page
indicates that the series is "presented in one hundred numbers," yet
the first set contains only seven--five piano and two vocal works--and
the second set adds twenty-seven more, including eleven for piano, a
piano arrangement of an orchestral work, and fifteen for voice.[25] The
title-page includes the dedication to the Royal Academy of Music in
Great Britain, with the following epigram:

> "It is observable in music, that the finest composi-
> tions & performances do not strike at first, but their
> beauties & their designs are elicited by repetition"

> Dr. Crotch, Pres[t].
> of the R. A. of Mus. in G. B.

The Harvard University copy has a handwritten dedication, on the
title-page, as follows:

> Presented to my whilom, faithfull, industrious and
> civil Engraver and scientific friend M[r] George Hews,

---

25. One, "The Minstrel's Catch, or Canone infinitum, a lay,
from 8 to 40 voices, more ad libitum, or a medium inbetween," was
printed both as no. 1 in the first set and as no. 8 in the second. See
Wolfe 10129-62 for a description of *Sylviad* and its individual numbers. There are only two extant copies: both sets at Harvard University and the second set at the British Library. As explained by Barron, 374, the Harvard copy of the second set is missing pp. 13-14 and
19-20 in no. 4, a song; and for no. 5, a piano duet, p. 8 is printed on
the verso of p. 10, and p. 11 is printed on the verso of p. 17. The
title-page is preceded by an added leaf which is the Heinrich entry
from Moore's *Complete Encyclopedia of Music* (Boston, 1854), copied
by hand.

> with due Apologies however, for these extravagant
> Compositions, condemned by the Author himself, as
> unworthy of the public Eye, and may perhaps only
> tell through a masterly and extraordinary perform-
> ance.
> Boston, August 1826   A. P. Heinrich

Hews was indeed the musical engraver for at least most of this
music.[26]

The copy of the second set at the British Library was presented
to Bernhard, Duke of Saxe Weimar (1792-1862), who had traveled to
the United States and wrote a book on his experience, published in
Weimar in German in 1828, and that same year in Philadelphia as
Travels through North America in the Years 1825 & 1826. The red
bookplate on a preliminary page before the *Sylviad* title-page reads
"Bernhard, Duke of Saxe Weimar," and Heinrich's handwritten dedication is:

> The Duke <u>Bernhard</u> of Saxe Weimar, the distinguished
> traveller through the United States, will deign to receive
> the homage and musical offerings of the "Western
> Minstrel." His Highness will find himself remembered in
> the freepages of the "Sylviad," by the Author
>
> A. P. Heinrich
> Boston, September, <u>1826</u>

As if disappointed because his first two opuses gained few (if
any) sales, their complexities are not continued in as many of the marches and dances of *Sylviad*. Included, however, are two of the most
difficult piano pieces Heinrich ever wrote: the two toccatas.

The second set (1825-26) has a series of songs and piano pieces
which are partly autobiographical, indicating his life in Kentucky and
the move to Boston and to England:

No. 17:	The Minstrel's March to the Woods (piano)
No. 18:	A Sylvan Scene in Kentucky, or The Barbecue Divertimento (piano)
No. 19:	The Log House (song); the title-page has a lithograph[27] showing Heinrich playing the violin in front of a log cabin and a Negro and donkey approaching from the

---

26. Hews's name as engraver appears in the second set with nos.
15, 16, 18, and 24, but J. L. Hewitt's name is on the first page of
music of the second set.

27. Wolfe, *Early American Music Engraving and Printing*, 241:
"the first dated, lithographically illustrated sheet-music cover in
America."

rear, then three small scenes underneath: 1) "Departure from Louisville," Heinrich leaving on a winged horse, 2) "Arrival in Boston," 3) "There first lov'd Minstrelsy I woo'd," with Heinrich in front of a ship flying the banner reading "For England," with a British lion pulling him toward it and an American eagle holding him back.

No. 20:   The Minstrel's Adieu (song); the poetry beginning "Alas! the minstrel, must leave this happy friendly land"

No. 21:   The Embarkation March (piano)

No. 22:   Sequel, or Farewell to My Log House, a song expressive of the anticipated feelings of the Western Minstrel during his voyage to Europe on some calm night after a heavy gale

No. 23:   The Debarkation March (piano)

No. 24:   The Western Minstrel's Musical Compliments to Mrs. Coutts (partsong for 3 voices) . . . N.B.: The fame of the patronage which Mrs. Coutts has always bestowed upon Genius, having penetrated into the forests of the New World, induced their untutored Minstrel to present to her the following wild "yager" strains from the regions of the huntsmen of Kentucky.

No. 25:   Vivat Britain's Fair! a wedding reel (piano)

No. 26:   The Western Minstrel's Recollection of the Wilderness of Kentucky, or A Vocal Fantasia, presented in addition to No. 2, "Toccata Cromatica Grande," of the "Sylviad" to the musical philosopher, the illustrious Doctor Crotch, President, and the students of song of the Royal Academy of Music in Great Britain (song)

The series does not extend to the last number, "Bohemia, a Sacred Melody." In this discussion, the piano works are described by category.

The five marches of *Sylviad* are in the second set. No. 13 relates to the dedication copy at the British Library: "Bernhard, Duke of Saxe Weimar's March, Complimentary to his arrival in the City of Boston, composed for Full Band, & therefrom arranged for the piano forte." The march is normal in comparison with those by other composers of the time, likewise published in arrangements for pianoforte. For his transcription, however, Heinrich has added several pianistic scales near the end. Three *tremolante* chords function as a transition to a short Scherzando, with a dialogue between the hands, which serves as a trio. A momentary cadenza leads back to the beginning. In one place (meas. 30), small notes were obviously added to the original engraved score to convert a quadruplet arpeggio to sextuplets. The march is succeeded by the equivalent of a quick step: "Fanfare, Quasi Presto," in 6/8 meter, climaxing in two-octave arpeggio patterns.

"Embarkation March," no. 21, is perhaps also a transcription for piano; one high part, engraved in small notes, is labeled "Fiautino." The dotted rhythm and formal structure of march & trio are representative of the genre, but some of the section lengths and key relationships are out of the ordinary. The two repeated sections that open the march are of a regular eight-measure length, but all succeeding sections are irregular. Some of the harmonic surprises are the A-major chord, dominant of the tonic D major, suddenly followed by F-sharp major (dominant of B minor) for the beginning of the third section, and the more remote relationship of the tonic D major becoming B-flat major at the beginning of the trio. For one particular passage in the second section of the trio, the mode changes from D major to D minor. A motive, presented in dialogue tossed between the hands, receives a new treatment in a style reminiscent of a Rossini opera (Ex. 8-8).

Ex. 8-8.   Heinrich, "Embarkation March," meas. 68-71 (*Sylviad* [b], no. 21, p. 4).

"The Debarkation March," no. 23 (EAKM no. 34), with a fast tempo in 6/8 meter, would seem to serve as a companion quickstep were it not for the unrelated key of C major, not to speak of the intervening song. Until the coda, all sections are of a regular eight-measure length. The material of the first two sections return in variants after the contrasting third section in F major. The subdominant F major also turns out to be the final key of the piece, in a coda based on "God save the King." This is not the first time Heinrich ended a work in a key different from the beginning.

"The Students March," no. 3 of the second set, is much more ambitious than the title suggests, and includes no marchlike characteristics. It is quite pianistic, and the structure is most like a rondo. This is the kind of work in which the returns of a principal theme are sometimes obscure, like Carr's "Fantasia on Gramachree." Therefore, perhaps a better title than "Students March" might have been "Fantasy on an Original Theme." An understanding of the piece is best accomplished by a summary chart (a double bar ends each of these sections--or subdivisions within the parentheses--except before section F, in the original score):

section	key	length	headings in score
intro.	A	12	
A	D	34 (10+8+8+8)	
B	A–D	20	
A'	D	16 (8+8)	
C	d	8	
A"	b	8	
D	b	23	
A"'	B–b	16 (8+8)	
E	d–C	16	
A""	G	8	
F	G–D	16 (8+8)	
A""'	B♭	8	
G	d	8	
	D	16	
	B	8	
	E–C	8	
	d	14	
	b–D	24	
	b♭–d–F	26	
A"""	f–d–D	16 (8+8)	
trans.	D	6	Coda d'Alliance
	D	16	A la "Yankeedoodle"
		14	"God save the King!"
coda	D	18	

This is one of Heinrich's most accessible piano works. Although there are passages challenging to the pianist, they are not as foreboding as some of the more virtuoso works. In contrast to other pieces in which one encounters a profusion of thematic ideas, often with one accompanimental pattern quickly succeeded by another, "The Students March" has many aspects of the pianistic rondos and variations by his American contemporaries such as Christopher Meineke or Charles Thibault.

Sudden key changes in some places are striking to both performer and listener. Although the main key is D major, the key signature of the introduction is that of A major, set up as a dominant of D. Yet the first chord of the piece, a D-major broken chord, sounds subdominant of A. Heinrich goes through the keys of B minor and G minor before establishing A major--but there is also a surprising B-flat used as a Neapolitan sixth.

Whereas some of the modulations, to closely related keys, are usual for the time, others are not. For example, the D minor at the end of section C (one flat) is suddenly succeeded by B minor (two sharps); the common note is D. The same common note is the link between the more remote change from D major to B-flat major at the beginning of section A"""'. Section G, the longest diversion, has many more such modulations, most a third apart if not simply a change of mode, with only one note in common. Many of these key changes are abrupt. The most remote relationship is C major to D minor--accomplished with an intermediate "German" augmented-sixth chord (meas. 225-26; p. 9, system 3).

In the traditional rondo by Haydn or Mozart, returns of the main theme are usually clear, not veiled by many changes of harmony or decoration of melody. Heinrich, by contrast, treats the returns of "Students March" almost as a concurrent set of variations, often obscuring the main rondo theme to the point that the analyst is not sure if a passage is a return or a new theme. The structure of the tune is clear: 8 + 8 measures. Just after the opening statement, however, a new 8 + 8-measure segment may be an immediate variant (since some of the harmonic and melodic characteristics may be seen), but is probably more accurately heard as the second half of the theme's most complete appearance.

Some returns of this theme are nevertheless quite clear, and have been represented in the chart. The initial descending fourth of the melody, the accompaniment, and the eight-measure structure help to distinguish them. Yet sometimes the same characteristics are discernible in the contrasting sections, such as the "C" section, so that an apparent contrast of theme is actually a variant. Similarly, the eight measures preceding the last return (last 8 meas. of p. 11) is another variant of the rondo theme, but disguised by the absence of a double bar and the use of the "wrong" key of F major. The "real" return is the one in the tonic of D major--the second half of section A""""" (p. 12, system 2).

In keeping with Heinrich's voyage from Boston to England, his "Coda d'Alliance" consists of "Yankee Doodle" and a treatment of the last half of "God save the King." Since "Students March" is in a collection dedicated to the Royal Academy of Music in London, perhaps this piece, not too demanding to perform, is the one intended as an offering from the American composer to the piano students of the Academy.

"The Minstrel's March to the Woods," no. 17, is in reality no march at all, but more allied to the category of dance. Most dances, however, have no introduction like this "Adagio quasi malinconico." In three sections, a four-measure phrase is stated twice in the first section, and a similar idea returns after a digression in the second section. The last appearance, at the end of the third section, is clearer in spite of the change from B-flat major to B-flat minor. The main part of "The Minstrel's March" is entitled "Valso Sylvano." After a sixteen-measure fanfare-related beginning, the remainder is in clearly defined sections, usually of eight-measure length: A B C D E C' F G G' H G" I J K. The same B-flat major key prevails throughout. One exception to the eight-measure lengths is section E, eighteen measures long, which largely consists of a descending five-note scale in the left hand begun in sequence on the pitches *b*-flat, *a*, *g*, *f*, *e*-flat, *d*--each statement being echoed in a different octave, sometimes placed above the right hand. The other exceptions are sections H, G", I, and J, reduced to four-measure lengths, and the last section which serves as a thirteen-measure coda. In general, because of the sameness of key, simple texture, and predictable form, this is one of Heinrich's less interesting piano works.

One other waltz in *Sylviad* is "Valsetto Triangolo," no. 4 of the first set, crowded onto one page with small musical type. It is not a simple dance, but begins that way: a four-measure introduction, then two eight-measure periods--the second a variant of the first. Basic tonic-dominant chords in E-flat are embellished with secondary chromatic notes. After a double barline a simple accompanimental pattern in the right hand, again with tonic and dominant harmonies, is laid out three times in phrases of 8, 7, and 8 measures.[28] The left hand plays in the lower register, then for the middle statement transfers above the right in a "Triangle Solo," presumably imitating the high sounds of the triangle rather than being a part for that instrument. The mode changes to minor in the third statement in which the triangle melody is transferred to the bass register. The following passage consists of an accompanimental broken-chord pattern for the right hand, then the left, in the tonic key of E-flat major. The final measures of the piece involve a striking enharmonic modulation by means of a C-flat major chord becoming B major, then to C minor, and again through G-flat major and C-flat major back to E-flat minor, made major at the end. This is a strange work, and can be regarded as one of Heinrich's short novelty pieces.

One of Heinrich's finest piano compositions, for both player and listener, is no. 18 in the second set of *Sylviad*. The full title is:

> Sylvan Scene in Kentucky, or the BARBECUE DIVERTIMENTO, Comprising the Ploughman's Grand March, and the NEGRO'S BANJO QUICK-STEP, Respectfully Dedicated as a light fancy sketch characteristic of the Western Woodlanders, to the Patrons of the Royal Academy of Music in Gt. Britain, and to all friends of harmony, by the natural harmonist, A. P. Heinrich.

It is available in a fine recording by Neely Bruce.[29] The sudden complications sometimes found in *Dawning* are not included, yet many passages are far from easy to play. For the listener, there is a multitude of catchy melodies, including one thinly disguised version of "Yankee Doodle."

What makes *Barbecue Divertimento* significant is that "The Banjo" (titled thus at the head of the second movement) predates by thirty years the well-known piece with the same title by Louis Moreau Gottschalk. The banjo is one of the few American instruments not

---

28. It seems that the left-hand triplet 8th notes of meas. 24 represent added notes, the middle ones, to originally engraved duplet 8ths.

29. *The Dawning of Music in Kentucky by Anthony Philip Heinrich* (Vanguard VSD-71178, 1973).

imported from Europe; it was apparently created by blacks from African models. The popularity of Gottschalk's piece at his time was because it represented a foreign culture in a faraway location--New Orleans--and exoticism was important in European culture in the 19th century. Among the many differences between the pieces, two are basic: 1) whereas Gottschalk's is very repetitive and based on just a few musical ideas, Heinrich's is abundant in invention, involving very few returns; 2) Gottschalk's is restricted to one key, in contrast to the many key changes in Heinrich's, some of them sudden.

One motive, however, permeates the *Barbecue Divertimento*: the "horn fifths" used by many Classical composers, especially in works often called "La Chasse." Heinrich apparently associated his "sylvan scene" with the hunt, even though there were undoubtedly no formal hunts, with horns or bugles, in Kentucky. These horn fifths open the "Ploughman's Grand March" in an introduction called "Bugle Call of the Green Mountain Boys" (Ex. 8-9).

Ex. 8-9.   Heinrich, "Ploughman's Grand March" from *Barbecue Divertimento*, meas. 1-2 (*Sylviad* [b], no. 18, p. 1).

The initial key, G major, however, is not the key of the march (titled only "La Marcia" at the head of the music), C major. The horn fifths persist in the principal theme (meas. 17-18). A rapid alternation of the tonic and dominant notes in the right hand (c''/e'' g'/d'') is also used an octave lower at the end of the introduction and as an accompanimental pattern near the beginning of the trio. The tonal stability of the march does not continue in the trio, in which a diminished-seventh passage ends in the remote key of D-flat major for four measures. The remainder is in C minor, B minor, and G minor, leading directly to the da capo of both introduction and march. One element of unity is the return of a variant of the main march theme, this time in minor, near the end of the trio.

"The Banjo" has the character and structure of a social dance, yet many aspects cause it to be impractical for dancing. Presumably Heinrich had the experience of hearing a black banjo player in Kentucky, and the kind of music such a player would perform was evidently very much like fiddle tunes, also used in social dancing. Many of the tunes are in eight-measure sections, further divided to four-measure phrases, and sometimes to two-measure cells. These sections succeed one another, sometimes with a change of mode or key, creating a composition of over 500 measures. There are no American precedents for this procedure, but it was common in Europe. Schubert, for example, wrote collections of short dances which were obviously intended to succeed one another. A string of them may be in one key, but there are modulations to related keys, and sometimes to more remote keys with only one common note connecting them (for example, his Waltzes, op. 9, German Dances, op. 33, Ländler, op. 67). An overall picture of this tradition may be apparent in the following formal chart (double lines represent heavy double barlines in the score):

meas.		*length*	*key*	*commentary*
1–20	‖	20	c–Eb–c	introduction
21–28	‖	8	C	
29–36	‖	8	C	
37–44	‖	8	E	
45–52	‖	8	E–C	second 4 meas.: variant in new key
53–62		10	C	transition
63–70	‖	8	c–C	"Yankee Doodle" in minor, then major
71–78	‖	8	C	2nd half of "Yankee Doodle"
79–86	‖	8	C	fragment of "Yankee Doodle" in l.h.
87–98		12	c–Eb	
99–106	‖	8	Eb	"dolce"
107–14	‖	8	Eb	variant of preceding
115–27	‖	12	E	
128–35	‖	8	Bb	
136–43	‖	8	Bb	
144–51	‖	8	Bb–Ab	
152–59	‖	8	Db–a–F	
160–65	‖	6	F–g–a–Bb	sequence
166–73	‖	8	Bb	
174–81	‖	8	g–Bb	
182–200	‖	19	Db–Ab–f–Ab–f	
201–10	‖	10	F	2+8-meas. structure
211–18	‖	8	F–c–Db–f	"dolce," "espressivo"
219–26	‖	8	eb	
227–34	‖	8	eb	
235–42	‖	8	C	variant of preceding
243–50	‖	8	c–C–c–Eb	
251–58	‖	8	Eb–Ab	horn fifths in l.h.
259–70	‖	12	Ab	4+8-meas. structure
271–74		4	E	"Ça ira" motive
275–82		8	C#–f#–E	
283–97		16	E	horn fifths
298–305		8	E–f#	horn fifths
306–09		4	f#	
310–30		21	d	
331–40		10	c–Db–c–db	
341–46		6	b–A–D	
347–54		8	D	4-meas. tune and its variant
355–62		8	D	2-meas. tune, plus variant, and 4 meas. of cadential material
363–72		10	d–A–C	

373-96	24	d-Db-D-Db	
397-404	8	C#-g#-B	"dolce"
405-16	12	B	
417-24 ‖	8	E	first 4 meas. like "Ça ira"
425-32	8	bb	
433-40	8	Bb	variant of preceding
441-55 ‖	15	Bb-g-eb-cb	2-meas. (one 3-meas.) sequences
456-63	8	b-D	
464-73	10	c-Bb-g-A	2-meas. sequences
474-96	23	D	more sequences and horn fifths based on "God save the King"
497-504	8	D	horn fifths
505-12	8	D	horn fifths
513-21	9	b-D	ending with a chromatic figure
522-35	14	D	beginning with chromatic figure
536-43	8	V/D	fanfare transition
544-76	13	D	"All Hail to Kentucky" "From the Dawning of Music"

The eight-measure tunes are quite dancelike, and may even be based on music Heinrich heard at dances in Kentucky.

Not all of these dance-tunes are completely separate and unrelated. One of them (Ex. 8-10) incorporates a two-note motive that permeates more than thirty measures of music, appearing in sequential passages (meas. 275 [p. 15, first meas.], 277, 279, 281, 306 [p. 16, meas. 2], 310), as well as in other guises.

Ex. 8-10. Heinrich, "The Banjo" from *Barbecue Divertimento*, meas. 298 (*Sylviad* [b], no. 18, p. 15).

But probably the most important element is the horn-fifth figure, heard throughout "The Banjo" as well as in the preceding march.

Heinrich's fondness for mixing the modes and using "foreign" scale degrees is heard in the first measures of the introduction of "The Banjo." The same alteration continues into the first tune, although the free alternation of major and minor degrees is not as obvious in later tunes. The three-note rhythmic figure 8th-16th-16th is again used in the transition to the "Yankee Doodle" section, and in the treatment of the national tune itself.

Another national tune seems to have been in Heinrich's mind for several passages: "Ça ira."[30] The characteristic four-note motive, similar to the same one just cited, first appears on different pitch-levels (meas. 271-74; p. 14 of the original score, last four meas.), shortly afterwards harmonized in horn fifths (meas. 287; 15/3/3),[31] and is inverted in one fascinating cadence (Ex. 8-11).

Ex. 8-11. Heinrich, "The Banjo" from *Barbecue Divertimento*, meas. 317-18 (*Sylviad* [b], no. 18, p. 16).

The inverted form serves as a repeated bass accompaniment (meas. 409-12), then emerges in the treble in a passage ending with the two adjacent notes quickening to a written-out trill (meas. 417-20; 19/1/5). Surprisingly, one of the tunes is almost identical to the three-16ths pattern within a duple-meter context (meas. 243-44; 14/1/1-2) that later emerged at the turn of the century as a stock figure in ragtime--specifically, "Twelfth Street Rag." "God save the King" is almost completely buried in chromatic figuration and arpeggios near the end (meas. 474-86; 21/3/1).

As indicated above, Heinrich's "The Banjo" contrasts with Gottschalk's in the frequency of key changes. Some are to related keys, involving a change of one or two accidentals in the scale, such as the modulation from E-flat major to A-flat major (meas. 254-56; 14/3/1). Others are more remote, yet involve a common note in both keys. Some key changes involve no modulations as such; instead there is a sudden leap to the new key, as exemplified in one change from E major to C major (meas. 48-49; 7/3/1-2). In another passage, the tonic note of one key (A minor) is used as the leading tone of the new one (B-flat major, meas. 127-28; 10/1/1).

There are no fewer than twenty-eight key-signature changes in the piece, some quite radical such as one move from one flat to six flats, thence to none (meas. 218-37; 13/2/1): F major, E-flat minor, C major. The relationship consists of descending major thirds in one passage of D-flat, A, then F major (meas. 152-60; 10/6/2)--here D-

---

30. The complete "Ça ira" may be seen in James Hewitt's medley *The New Federal Overture*, EAKM no. 5, and in Benjamin Carr's medley *Federal Overture*.

31. Hereafter, as an aid to finding unnumbered measures, are the beginning of locations identified by: original page number/system/measure in that system.

flat major becomes minor and the F-flat serves as the dominant note of the new key. The following modulation uses a diminished-seventh chord. In another enharmonic modulation, the tonic note of A-flat major (four flats) suddenly becomes G-sharp, the third scale degree of E major (four sharps; meas. 270-71; 14/6/1-2). Heinrich also has several passages with tonal ambiguity--sometimes sounding atonal--as in one change from D major to F-sharp minor (Ex. 8-12).

Ex. 8-12.   Heinrich, "The Banjo" from *Barbecue Divertimento*, meas. 302-06 (*Sylviad* [b], no. 18, pp. 15-16).

Another feature of "The Banjo," as seen in other piano works of Heinrich, is the repetition of music on different pitch levels--the sequence--and some of these are indicated in the formal summary above. For one particular passage, the sequence--complete with a number of writhing chromatic notes--is used to change the tonality from D-flat major, through B-flat minor, D-flat minor, and B minor, to A major (meas. 339-44; 17/2/1).

Virtuosity does not permeate "The Banjo," but there are passages to challenge the professional pianist. Among them are rapid hand-crossing (meas. 259-67; 14/4/1) such as those in *Dawning*, wide skips for one hand (meas. 118-23 and 443-45; 9/5/2 and 20/2/4), and rapid scale passages of 32nd notes (meas. 307-15 and 410-14; 16/1/3 and 19/1/last).

The succession of eight-measure tunes is gradually abandoned, especially upon the introduction of virtuoso scales, to be supplanted by freer material which eventually serves as transition to the final "All Hail to Kentucky." Some of this free material is almost developmental. Two figures beginning after a 16th-rest--one with alternating octaves, the other largely diatonic--permeate the passage (meas. 324-36; 20/5/last) before the sequences quoted above. Closer toward the end (meas. 460-90; 20/5/last), Heinrich manipulates an arpeggio motive, ranging from one to three octaves, which is often capped by two 8ths and a quarter note. The rhythm is also recalled in the final tune, in combination with the familiar horn fifths (meas. 497-500; 22/2/2).

"The Banjo," therefore, is hybrid in form and style, combining elements of a dance cycle along with the freedom of a development in a sonata movement and some of the difficulties of a virtuoso show-piece. The remaining puzzle is the question of why he began a C-major piece in G major, and why it ends in D major. The most logical explanation to the last question is the simplest: D major is the key of the original song "Hail to Kentucky" in *Dawning* (pp. 11-18, simplified on p. 9), the model for this keyboard version. The final irony is that the song, praising a then-wild area of the United States, is obviously modeled on "Hail Britannia." In spite of its eccentricities, and perhaps over-wealth of tunes and keys, Heinrich's *Barbecue Divertimento* is one of his finest piano works, and deserves wider exposure.

   A Divertimento di Ballo, which concludes the first set of *Sylviad* as no. 7, is a conglomerate of six dances. The whole is dedicated "with the Author's Respects to the Fair Sylphs of America," and includes at the head of the music a short poem:[32]

> Life's a dull dance! but step'd with you
> 'Twould move to notes of livelier measure--
> And heavy care would alter too,
> Or take the silken wings of pleasure!
>
> Seleck Osborne

   The first dance, "Cotillion per il virtuoso," the tempo marking "grazioso," is indeed more difficult for the pianist than the usual keyboard cotillion, but not beyond scales of alternating 32nd notes or two-octave arpeggios. There are nine clearly divided eight-measure phrases, of which the eighth represents a varied return of the first. Variety of key is represented by modulations from the original C major to the subdominant of F for the third and fourth phrases, then to F minor and E-flat major in the fifth, E-flat to C major in the sixth, G major in the seventh, before the return to the tonic key in the eighth. The final section is modulatory, from C minor to the E-flat major of the following dance, "Summer Step Cotillion." This quicker dance (Vivace) is likewise regular in its four eight-measure sections. The third strain acts as a midsection, in the tonic minor key; the last, in major, is a varied repeat of the first section. In the added two measures at the end is a modulation to the next dance.

   "Landler of Austria (a rustic Waltz)" has no similar returns of material at the end, but the first five of the nine sections are based on the musical idea introduced in the initial measure. The fourth section indeed represents a more faithful return, coupled with a fascinating device of composition by the gradual descent in the left hand in a scale from *b*-flat to *F'*. This dance has no unity of key, and not all sections are of the standard eight-measure length, as indicated in the following summary:

---

   32. The same poem is used with a piano scherzo, "A Valentine to the New York Philharmonic Society," copyright 1849; copy in the Heinrich collection, Library of Congress, vol. 7 no. 18.

length:	8	8	12	8	11	8	8	8	8
key:	A	A	F	D	Bb	Eb	Eb	Eb	c-a-V/C

The first three modulations are in descending thirds, then settle on a tonal center a tritone away from the beginning; those at the end prepare the key of the upcoming dance. The last few measures of the sixth section are particularly attractive in the descending four-note scales of the left hand, which begin at different places of successive measures, and in the converging scale at the end (meas. 51-55).

"The Lover's Reel" is the most regular of all dances in *A Divertimento di Ballo* thus far. All nine sections are eight measures long, divided to four-measure phrases and two-measure segments. The persistent enthusiasm of the reel is recognized in the fiddle-like 16th-note motion throughout. The accompaniment in the final measures of the preceding dance provide the thematic impetus for the beginning of "The Lover's Reel," and the same material recurs in the left hand for the first half of the sixth section. Another return takes place in the fifth section, in which the left hand plays the right-hand part of the second section. The tonic C-major key is maintained in the first five sections, except for a change to the dominant G major in the third. A modulation takes place in the sixth section from C minor to E-flat major, kept until the seven-measure transition and its return to C major for the last dance.

"Wedding Reel," concluding *A Divertimento di Ballo* and the first set of *Sylviad*, is almost identical to "Vivat Britain's Fair! a Wedding Reel," no. 25, near the end of the second set. In both there are three eight-measure sections, the last with different musical material, but in place of the first set's da capo indication, the second substitutes a coda of two more eight-measure sections--in C minor until the reversion to major at the end. This time the da capo is optional ("Da Capo a piacere"). At the head of the music in the second set is a poetic couplet:

> Ah! little needs the Minstrel's power,
> To speed the light convivial hour.

Any connection of either reel to a specific wedding remains unknown.

Completely different music is contained in a work of the same title, *A Divertimento di Ballo . . . comprising a Grand Waltz and Galopade*, published separately during the period when Heinrich was in Boston, 1823-26 (Wolfe 3597). Again, the structure is regular, and there are no extraordinary difficulties for the pianist. The "Galopade di Bravura," however, is more demanding, and the form more nearly approximates that of a rondo:

section:	A	B	C	D	A'	A"	A"'	coda
length:	32 (4x8)	17 (8+8+1)	8	8	8	10	16 (8+8)	14
key:	D	b	D	D	d	D	D	

Heinrich's typical preference for varied returns is again apparent, but the above does not account for the most faithful, least varied, return at the beginning of A"'. Although well-written, with contrast by means of two-voiced quasi-counterpoint for the second half of section B and in section A', neither of these two pieces in the independent *A Divertimento di Ballo* represents the composer at his best.[33]

In general, *Barbecue Divertimento* in the second set of *Sylviad* has a musical counterpart in the first set, no. 6: "The Minstrel's Musical Compliments to Mrs. Coutts, a Fancy Cotillon [*sic*]: Vivat Britain's Fair!" The phrase "Vivat Britain's Fair" and the couplet "Ah! little needs the Minstrel's power . . ." link this piece with the previously-discussed "Vivat Britain's Fair! a Wedding Reel" toward the end of *Sylviad*'s second set. A footnote on the first page of "Minstrel's Musical Compliments" indicates that it is based in part on the preceding partsong, for five voices, "Philanthropy: a vocal address to Mrs. Coutts, a distinguished Patroness of the Royal Academy of Music in Great Britain, and its only Constitutional Governess."[34] Section C in the following analytical summary is the theme in question. (In the score, a double barline ends each of these sections, or subdivisions indicated within the parentheses):

---

33. The Heinrich collection at the Library of Congress, vol. 15 no. 13, contains an undated six-page holograph "Divertimento di Ballo" in E major and 3/4 meter. Its texture is simple--largely with repeated chordal accompaniment in the left hand. Another related piano work is: Il Divertimento di Londra, per lo piano forte. The Grand Argyll March and Harmonic Waltz, dedicated to Thomas Welsh Esq. of the Argyll Rooms, and Harmonic Institution, by A. P. Heinrich, Performed by Mrs. Ostinelli, at the Author's Concert. Boston: published for the Author by C. Bradlee, 164 Washington St. Title-page + pp. 2-10. Plate nos. at the bottom of pp. 2-10: 1-9. Library of Congress copy, ML95.H45. This was performed in Boston by Sophia Hewitt Ostinelli in Heinrich's concert on 17 March 1832, and presumably published later that year (Upton, 122-23, 128). It lies outside the scope of this study, but demonstrates many virtuoso aspects without the idiosyncrasies of the some of the pieces in *Dawning* and *Sylviad*.

34. Mrs. Coutts's rejection of Heinrich's dedication and the music he sent her is contained in her 29 October 1826 letter (Heinrich scrapbook, Library of Congress, p. 1015), reading in part: ". . . my uniform determination is, and ever has been, never to sanction Dedications of Works to me which I have not the power to be of use too--and if Mr. Heinrich had previously intimated to me his intention of so dedicating them, he would have received my positive refusal to permit it. . . ." Heinrich's reply, dated November 6 (scrapbook, pp. 1018-19), reads in part: "About 6 Years ago, I beheld the name of Mrs. Coutts first in the papers of Kentucky in a manner as made me treasure up its recollection ever since with the highest pleasure and respect. Later I read that you had aided so generously and substantially in the establishment of the Royal Academy of Music--and what true Son of Apollo could thus withold from you his admiration, nay gratitude towards such a benefactress and patroness of the arts?"

section	key	length	commentary
intro.	e-C	4	
A	C	4	
B	C	8	Grazioso
C	C	8	16th triplets
D	F	8	
E	F	6	
F	F#	10	32nds
G	a-C	4	
H	Eb-C-e-E	6	
I	E	4	
J	e-D	8 (4+3+1)	"God save the King!"--*Fine* at end of 7th meas.
J'	D	4	"God save the King" variant
J"	Eb	7 (3+4)	variant
J"'	D	8 (4+4)	variant
K	D-b-Eb-eb	8	
L	d-A-d	8 (2+2+4)	"(con Licenza) Giga" & 2 variants--32nd triplets
C'	Bb	10 (4+5+1)	
L'	e	8	Relassamento [= Rilassamento]-- "molto commodo"--6/8
L"	c	8	variant of preceding
L"'	G	15	more variants--poco piu animato
trans.	C	5	
M	c	12 (4+4+4)	"Coda, alla Hornpipe"--2/4-- Moderato
M'	c	8	variant; melody in l.h.
trans.	B	11	the end, on B major, serves as V/e; da capo

Its relation to *The Barbecue Divertimento* is that both consist largely of one musical idea followed by another, with few thematic returns. The division into sections, usually marked by double barlines, and the apparently aimless changes of key are elements also found in "The Students March" (discussed above). This so-called cotillion is in fact no dance music at all; rather, "Fantasia ballante," the description in the footnote to the first page of music, better fits the virtuoso demands and harmonic complexities. The marking "tempo di ballo," and the Giga and "alla Hornpipe" labels point to the dance. Perhaps a better designation, in more familiar terms, might be dance fantasy.

As in "The Students March," there are some remote modulations, like the enharmonic one from F major to F-sharp major (sections E to F; 22/4/1), and a particularly chromatic one from B minor to E-flat major (within section K; see Ex. 8-13). The complexity of some sections challenge both the harmonic analyst and the performer, as in a passage at the beginning of section L" (meas. 124-27; 26/4/1). Two eccentricities of notation are the key signature for section F (which should be corrected from the original order of sharps F C G A D B), and the engraver's solution of crowding the last four measures on the last page of the piece by using a single staff, the treble part on the left, the bass on the right.

Ex. 8-13. Heinrich, "The Minstrel's Compliments to Mrs. Coutts," meas. 91-96 (*Sylviad* [a], no. 6, pp. 24-25).

This work could also serve as the second movement of a pair of movements for piano. The preceding work, "Philanthropy," has the following note at the bottom of the first page of music: "The above may be used either as a vocal Quintetto, a Solo Song, or Pianoforte movement alone, and in the latter case continue No. 6 as the Finale." The five vocal parts are printed on two staves--each voice distinguished by a differently sized or shaped notehead--making it quite suitable as a piano score. Indeed, some aspects cause its use as vocal music questionable, not the least of which is the difficulty of performing 16th-note parallel thirds and other similar passages without logical places for breathing. The cadenzas before and after the song, and an interlude before the final page, are apparently intended for the piano since they are without text, and the range, from G' to f''', is beyond the normal human voice.

Another problem of using both works as a pair is their questionable unity, one of which doubles as a song, the other being pure piano music. At least there is some relationship of key: "Philanthropy" is in D major,[35] and whereas "The Minstrel's Musical Compliments" begins in E minor the key at the Fine returns to D major.

Several other keyboard pieces in *Sylviad* are linked with piano-vocal compositions. No. 16 (second set) consists of a song, "Mary," immediately followed by a piano work, "Polly's Consolation, or a Travesty on the preceding Lament." The relationship between the two, in their details, is complex, and shows the care Heinrich typically took in his compositions, and also that his basic procedure is continual variation. Using modern terminology associated with 16th-century sacred music, "Polly's Consolation" is a parody of "Mary."

The song is preceded by a two-measure chromatic line, printed in small 32nd notes in the manner of a musical epigram. Its first measure is transferred in "Polly's Consolation" to the first four measures in the right hand, where it appears twice. It is also imitated in the left hand--canonically for two measures. This material does not reappear in the song, but the initial chromatic turn is employed during the digression of the piano piece (meas. 51-60).

"Polly's Consolation," as hinted above, is constructed as a series of variants of the song's principal theme, with a digression in the middle. Whereas "Mary" is a mournful song, marked "Adagio: Quasi malinconico," the "travesty" is marked "Molto vivace," and the contrast could hardly be greater. The same theme in the piano work first appears not only in the quicker tempo but also in halved note values. As indicated in the following chart, however, near the end the basic motion is further quickened, then restored to that of the song. None

---

35. The intent of the composer is not entirely clear. After the vocal D-major chord on the last page, the cadenza ("ad libitum") includes the direction "si riprende subito la Cadenza introdotta," meaning to return to the initial cadenza, but the cadenza ends on a dominant A-major chord. Undoubtedly the performer should repeat the first two pages of music and end on the D-major chord before the instrumental interlude.

of the thematic material is literally repeated--all returns are variants. (The theme consists of the segments a b a b c; the "c" is two measures long, the others one each. Double lines represent double barlines.)

meas.		phrase	key	commentary
5-12	‖	ababcc	G	key-signature: 1 sharp
13-16		dd	g-a	
17-20	‖	b	g	
21-24		d	c	key-signature: 2 flats
25-28	‖	abab	g	
29-32		abab	G	return to 1 sharp
33-36	‖	abab		
37-44	‖	ababcc	g	2 flats
45-50	‖	d	g-a-g	"Digressione"
51-56	‖	e	B*b*-C-D	begins with sequence
57-60		f	G	1 sharp
61-71		f	G	
72-75		abab	G	"Oggetto"
76-82		ababcd	G	note values further diminished
83-86		ab	G	note values augmented to that of the original song
87-97			g	2 flats; G pedal; coda
98-102			G	return to 1 sharp

Because of the predominance of four-measure units, sometimes made even clearer with double barlines, and the persistent rhythm, there is some resemblance--on a smaller scale--to "The Banjo." Although "Polly's Consolation" will stand alone, probably its most appropriate performance would be to follow the song "Mary."

Some of the same kind of musical organization applies to "Overture to the Fair Sylph." This is one of the least successful of Heinrich's large works (20 pages). Although written in keyboard score, a footnote reveals that it was "Intended for a full Orchestra"--yet there are no indications of instruments or orchestral textures and it seems entirely appropriate for pianoforte.

The "Overture" is the last part of no. 4 in the second set: *Overture to the Fair Sylph of America Miss Eliza Eustaphieve*, a young virtuoso, resident of Boston. The first and second parts are the songs "Original Address of the Minstrel to Miss Eliza Eustaphieve, during one of his rambles in the forests beyond the Alleghanies [*sic*]" which then goes directly to "The Stranger Friend, concludes with the following prayer for the felicity of Miss Eliza Eustaphieve." This song concludes with the direction "Segue l'overtura"; his intention, therefore, was clearly to have the whole performed as a unit.

The only thematic connection of the "Overture" to the preceding songs is that the initial rising major seventh also begins "The Stranger Friend." The "Overture" consists of a two-page introductory Andante largo, of which the A-major key is unrelated to the D minor or F major of the songs. Period structure and three-part form (a b a' at meas. 11-18, 19-26, 27-34) underlie accompanimental elaborations-- predominantly parallel thirds.

A fast chromatic descent leads to the main section, "Alla Valse: L'istesso tempo." The waltz rhythm continues to the end, and further unity is provided by the key of C major at beginning and end. The basic eight-measure phrase of the waltz is sometimes apparent, as indicated below:

meas.		theme	length	key	commentary
47–62	‖	A	8+8	C	
63–86	‖		24		
		B:			
87–102	‖	a a'	8+8	Eb	
103–18		b b'	8+8	c	
119–46			28	c–Ab	
147–54	‖	B'	8	c	
155–62	‖	B'	8	E	
163–70		B"	8	C	
171–78		B"'	8	a	
179–91			13	a–C	
192–97		(A)	6	C	trill-like figure
198–228			31	V/C	
229–33			5	a	
234–47			14	V/C	
248–53			6		
254–73		C	20	ab–E–c–C	
274–301			28	c–Ab–Db–C–a	
302–17		D	8+8	Bb–C	
318–31			14	c	
332–45		E	14	Bb–Eb	
346–53			8	C–c	
354–70			17	eb–d	
371–78		F	8	c–b	
379–89			11		
390–401		G	4+4+4	F	
402–04			3		
405–18		H	8+6	a	
419–29		I	8+3	Ab–Db–f	
430–54			25	f–C	turn-like figure
455–66			12	C–c	descending 5-note scale motive
467–75			9	c	trill-like figure
476–93			18	C	
494–531			38	C–Cb	trill-like figure
532–58			27	G–eb–Bb	two 8th-note figure on offbeats
559–624			66	Bb–c–C–f–Ab–a–c–C	
625–53			29	C	ascending 5-note scale motive
654–92			39	b–f#–c#	trill-like figure
693–715			23	C–Cb–c	chords, arpeggio
716–43			28	b–C	fanfare-like ending

There are no other important returns of earlier material after "I," except that a trill or turn-like figure, derived from the initial measures of the "Alla Valse" is employed, as indicated, often in sequential patterns. A new five-note scale--usually descending--is introduced in several sections. The general effect, however, is that this work is an unorganized succession of musical ideas and keys, unified principally only by the triple meter.

Heinrich's most ambitious work from his first ten years as composer is the first number of the second set: *Overture de la Cour*, dedicated to none other than George IV--the "first Patron of the Royal Academy of Music in Great Britain, and Protector of the Liberal Arts." This is a four-movement work. Although "Intended for the Orchestra," with some indications for specific instruments at the beginning of the second movement, nonetheless it is idiomatic for the pianoforte.

The *Overture* has some elements of the traditional sonata (in this case, perhaps symphony). The first movement is a one-page Maestoso introduction, moving from the principal key of D major to an unrelated C-sharp major. This key continues to the beginning of the second movement, Allegro con brio, but in the guise of C-sharp minor. With a reiteration of a fanfare-like phrase, the tonic D major soon reappears, and this is the key in which the second movement comes to an end.

In the meanwhile, the organization of the second movement comes as close to sonata-allegro form as any work in Heinrich's three published opuses. A first theme, marked "Quasi Tutti," is quickly succeeded by a second theme that sees a modulation from D major to the regular A major. A transition touches several other keys on the way to the D minor of the third theme, which completes a quasi-exposition. Following another transition through several other keys, the second theme returns for a developmental treatment. Where the resemblance to sonata-allegro breaks down, however, is the absence of a recapitulation. Instead, Heinrich provides a fourth theme and, following further manipulation of the sextuplets from theme 2, a fifth theme. Both of these are introduced in B-flat major, unrelated to the tonic D major. As indicated below, many of these sections are followed in the score with double barlines:

meas.		*theme*	*key*	*commentary*
1-31		intro.	C#-D	2 sharps
32-46		1	D	"Quasi Tutti"
47-59		2	D-A	
60-92	‖	trans.	A-f#-a	
93-132		3	d	1 flat
133-45	‖	trans.	d-B*b*-G*b*-g	
146-60	‖	2	b-D-a-C-E*b*-d-d*b*	2 sharps
161-69	‖	(2)	b*b*	
170-77	‖	4	B*b*	derived from theme 2; 2 flats; 8 meas.
178-93	‖	4 var.	A	16 meas.; 3 sharps
194-202			C	no sharps or flats
203-10	‖		c-g	fragment from theme 2

211-37 ‖		A	fragment from theme 2; 3 sharps
238-43 ‖	5	B*b*	2 flats
244-57 ‖	5	d	1 flat
258-70		D	2 sharps

The last two movements form a pair. "Polonoise de la Cour" consists of ten eight-measure phrases or sections, plus a five-measure coda, and each of these is marked off by double bars in the score. The first page has the principal material: the main theme (using the polonaise or polacca rhythm common at the time), a contrasting phrase, and a return in another guise (A B A'). The sixth section, with the left hand marked "Fagotto Solo" (designated in this analysis as "C"), functions in the manner of a contrasting trio. The ninth and tenth sections have varied returns of the first two sections.

The last movement, no fewer than 24 pages long, is appropriately titled "Fantasia alla Polonese" since it is a recomposition and expansion of the third movement. Indeed, the right hand of measures 3-18 are taken exactly from its model; the left hand is a bit different. The eight-measure structure still pervades, although one important change is a development-like section, marked "Espress." This structure is once more best shown in the form of a chart. (Themes labeled A, B, A', C represent variants of the first three and sixth sections from the third movement.)

meas.		*theme*	*length*	*key*	*commentary*
1-10	‖	A	10	D	
11-20	‖	B	10		
21-28	‖	A'	8		
29-44	‖		16	g-b*b*-D*b*-F	(theme "A" at meas. 33)
45-54	‖		10	d*b*-b	
55-62	‖	A	8	F	"Marcato, con Gusto"
63-70	‖	A	8	f	
71-78	‖		8	d-f	
79-86	‖	C	8	d	"Fagotto Solo"
87-94	‖		8	b-D	
95-102	‖		8	b-D	
103-10	‖	A	8	D	
111-18	‖	A'	8		"Scherzando"
119-26	‖	A	8		
127-58			32	d-D-a-b*b*-a-D	"Espress"
159-66	‖	A	8	D	"dolce"
167-74	‖	B	8		
175-82	‖		8		
183-86	‖		4		
187-94	‖	A	8		
195-98			4	d	"Tremolante"
199-206	‖	B	8		"Risoluto"

207-14	8	D	ending "Three Cheers to his Majesty!!!"
215-25	11		"God save the King: First Cheer!"
226-33	8	E*b*-e*b*-G#	
234-49	16	c#-A	
250-65	16	d-D	"Second Cheer!!"
266-81	16	D-d	"sempre crescendo"
282-306	13	D	"Third Cheer!!!"
306-15	10		

Homage to George IV is provided at the end by three well-disguised versions of the tune "God save the King" ("Cheer" with one, two, then three exclamation points), which serve as an elaborate coda.

This last movement generally follows the same plan as the preceding movement, up to the coda. Also borrowed directly are the "Fagotto Solo" from the corresponding sixth section of movement 2 (meas. 41-48; 14/4/2), marked identically in movement 3 (meas. 79-86; 22/2/1), as well as the last part of the following section (meas. 91-94; 23/2/1) from after the bassoon solo in the previous movement (meas. 53-56). Likewise, the "Scherzando" (beginning meas. 111; 24/5/2) is a variant of the third section (meas. 17-24; 13/4/2), and "Risoluto" (meas. 119-206; 32/3/1) from the penultimate section (meas. 72-79; 16/1/3) of the "Polonoise." Heinrich's typical complexity of textures and remote modulations abound, especially in the quasi-development (meas. 127-58; 26/1/2) and toward the end of the coda. The returns of the principal themes are all variants, sometimes to a point beyond easy comprehension, and there may be more such relationships not described here.[36]

In his dissertation on Heinrich's symphonic works, Wilbur Maust[37] isolates four basic formal types: 1) use of two or more contrasting themes, 2) monothematic movements with variation technique, 3) a loosely structured rondo, or 4) completely continuous or through-composed. In *Overture de la Cour*, Heinrich's first attempt at a large multi-movement work of symphonic proportions, all four types can be discerned, but the most prevalent aspect seems to be the eight-measure phrase of the dance in all except the introductory movement. Although calling for a virtuoso pianist, there is none of the extreme virtuosity required by some of the *Dawning* pieces nor by the two toccatas of *Sylviad*. *Overture de la Cour* is well-worth investigation and performance by pianists looking for challenging pieces by early Americans. .

Two pieces in *Sylviad* associated with American politics lie outside the usual musical categories. "Canone funerale, an American

---

36. Some engraving errors: p. 11, system 4, l.h., treble clef should be bass clef; p. 32, system 4, l.h., treble clef should be bass clef; and for system 5, l.h., bass clef at the beginning should be treble.

37. Maust, 88.

national dirge," no. 3 of the first set, is a short one-page musical canon for two voices. The "Leading Air" in the lower voice is imitated a beat later by the "Response" in the treble. The canon is not always exact, however; the time-values are occasionally altered (a favorite device of Josquin over three centuries earlier), a few notes are changed in the *comes*, and several notes in the bass voice are doubled at the octave. The canon ends three measures before the end, when chords begin to appear in both hands. The specific association of the piece was both Thomas Jefferson and John Adams, as explained in the note following the score:

> The above is a fragment from a Manuscript, which the Author has not been enabled yet to publish, entitled: *"The Statesman's Resignation to Death,"* set to elegiac Music, and occasioned, by reading the philosophical correspondence between *Thomas Jefferson*, and *John Adams*, Esqr's. in June 1822, respectfully dedicated to these Gentlemen, with an Address, Verses, and the Motto: "Dignum laude virum Musa vetet mori." Horace. *St. Helena*, a universal Dirge is contemplated in the series of the "Sylviad," likewise the Duke of Reichstadt's March.

Both Jefferson and Adams were to live three more years, until 4 July 1826. Neither the projected *St. Helena* nor the march ever appeared.

The same music was later used for three more funeral works. One is the "Coda Morale," for four voices and piano, at the end of "Epitaph on Joan Buff," no. 11 of the second set of *Sylviad*. In "The President's Funeral March, in memory of William Henry Harrison" (1841),[38] following a short introduction, the melody is harmonized as a march in the same key of E minor, then changed to E major. The setting as a canon is restored in another piano work, "The Cries of the Souls," the second of a diptych devoted to the North American Indian.[39] The setting, in F minor and major, is the most elaborate of

---

38. New York: author, by C. G. Christman; copies in the Heinrich collection, Library of Congress, vol. 7, no. 24, and vol. 10, no. 4.

39. The title-page reads: To Heinrich Marschner Mus. Doc., Chapel Master To His Majesty, the King of Hanover &c. &c. No. 1 The Indian Carnival, Toccata for the piano forte, theme selected from a grand orchestral Sinfonia Eratico=Fantastica, entitled "The Indians' Festival of Dreams,"* Composed by Anthony Philip Heinrich. *A Bacchanal among the North American Indians, which commonly lasts fifteen Days, and is celebrated about the end of Winter. Vide McIntosh, on the North American Indians. No. 2 "The Festival of the Dead and the Cries of the Souls." Published by the Author 75¢. nett. Also in M.S. a Concerto Grosso for the Orchestra "William Penn's Treaty with the Delawares." Entered according to Act of Congress A.D. 1849 by A. P. Heinrich in the Clerks Office of the Dist. Court of the Southn. Distr. of New York. pp. 2-9: The Indian Carnival; p. 9: The Parting Adieus; p. 10: The Festival of the Dead; pp. 11-12: The

the three; although the canon predominates there are passages with chords, and the emotional impact is heightened with tremolos.

"The Minstrel's Vote for President," no. 12 in the second set, bears some resemblance in style and form to the march, but the only specific association with the genre is the introductory fanfare. Sections of eight or four measures predominate, and the first three sections, until the change from E-flat major to minor, are quite marchlike. But then the performance suggestion "Con Grazia e Espressione" and pianistic textures--florid melodies and arpeggio figures-- quickly mitigate against this connection. The fanfare material returns before the segno at the end of the first half; at the end, leading up to the "da capo al segno" is an arrangement "Alla Yankeedoodle." No difficulties in musical language or technique await the amateur pianist in this modest work. The election Heinrich probably had in mind was the bitterly fought contest of 1824-25, finally settled by the election on 9 February 1825 of John Quincy Adams in the House of Representatives, by a majority of a single vote.

Any excesses of seriousness, virtuosity, and complexity in the piano works of Heinrich are redeemed by the light-hearted humor in one of the piano duets in the second set of *Sylviad*, "The Four Pawed Kitten Dance: A Musical Jest for the Piano Forte," no. 9. At the head of the music is the verse

> Ye nimble claws
> Stir up applause,
> Move ye with grace,
> Light is the BASE.

The secondo part consists only of a simple accompaniment, alternating dominant and tonic chords in C major, "sempre da Capo," given at the head of the music. The primo part fills the remaining five pages of score, a new idea every eight measures. The secondo part, of course, can be tiresome were it not for the challenge of playing that part while watching the score of the partner. Some relief is also achieved by a change to minor for the eighth through tenth of the twenty-two eight-measure sections, in which the top player is supposed to indicate the change of mode to the partner. The primo part is occasionally challenging, especially for several finger-slides of over two octaves, and in the rhythmic juxtaposition in one place of 8th-note triplets with alternate duple 32nds and 16ths. There may be no other duet like it in the history of piano music.[40]

Cries of the Souls. Copy in the Heinrich collection, Library of Congress, vol. 7, no. 35.

40. This work was published in a revised version by Clementi, Collard & Collard, London, ca. 1830-32 (copy in the Heinrich scrapbook, Library of Congress, pp. 993-1001) with the title-page reading as follows (emphasized type here represented by italics): "The Four-*Pawed* Kitten dance, a *Mew*-sical Jest for the Piano Forte, *Purr*-formed with e-*claw* at the *Cat*-eaton Street Assemblies, by Miss *Cat*-herine Grimalkin, and her *Talon*-ted Sister, This Capriccio, with a

The other piano duet has a rather long title:

> The Minstrel's Entertainment with his blind pupil, or
> a Divertimento for 4 hands on the Grand Piano
> Forte, Dedicated to Miss Maria Penniman, By A. P.
> Heinrich. Likewise inscribed to Master Henry &
> Miss Charlotte Graupner, as a small tribute of
> respect for their rising musical talents & exercises, in
> consonance with the established merit of their father
> & instructor G. Graupner, a name highly estimated
> in the annals of Music in New England.

His student's variations to a German waltz, "composed . . . at the age
of thirteen years," was published in 1821 when she was a pupil of
Frederick C. Schaffer in Boston, and her song "The Water Drop,"
issued in 1825, was "revised by A. P. Heinrich."[41]
    Miss Penniman must have been talented, but one wonders if she
could have memorized either part of this duet, no. 5 in the second set
of *Sylviad*. It is no small "entertainment"--the score has no fewer
than twenty-five pages and 530 measures.[42] It is a "Valso grande,"
comprising 57 sections within double barlines, including the last five
sections, a coda of duple meter. Most of the sections are eight
measures long; when the pattern is broken the purpose is usually for
modulation to a new key.
    Heinrich calls for an elaborate instrument as well. The title-
page continues:

> Nota. The Base of this piece being rather elaborate,
> requires for its proper execution a PIANO FORTE
> of short and distinct articulation. The Treble part
> should be generally played somewhat stronger than
> the Base, & will produce its full effect on an instru-

---

feline *Purr*-oration, is dedi-*cat*-ed to all *Mew*-sical *Cat*-alogues by A.
P. Heinrich." Additional puns, in the guise of performance directions,
are in sections 6 and 18: "*Purr-puss*-ly"; section 10, meas. 5, in place
of "Espress:" "Piu *Mouse-o* un *paw*-co." There is an added "*Cat*-enza
alla *cat*-alani, or feline *Purr*-oration," in which the second part is
written out, "Alla Corno di *Pussy*." The final chord, with fermata, is
marked "Paws."

    41. Heinrich's "The Green Mountain Waltz," no. 2 of "Waltzes
Pastorale" (New York: author, 1841), is also dedicated to Miss Maria
Penniman; copy in the Heinrich collection, Library of Congress, vol. 7,
no. 22.

    42. Not without some errors in the primo part, as follows: in the
21st section, p. 13, system 4, the one-measure rest should last two
measures, and the left-hand clef for the section immediately following
should have a bass rather than treble clef. In the 42nd section, p. 19,
system 2, one of the measures of rest should be ignored.

ment reaching to the highest F: & having a variety of pedals, such as are marked according to a Vienna Piano Forte.

The variety of pedals includes (in order of appearance): soft pedal, closed or open pedal (presumably the damper pedal), vibration pedal (designated in one place "Open or Vibration Pedal"--perhaps again the damper pedal), drum, bell, bassoon, and "tamborin." Other special effects are several finger-slides in the fifty-first section and (undoubtedly to foster more friendly relation among the players) several places in which the hands of the players intermingle on the keyboard.

None of the waltz tunes returns. The only quotation seems to be the two sections marked in what has become Heinrich's trademark, "alla Yankeedoodle," in the coda, where the primo plays the tune in one key in one section taken up by the secondo, in another key, immediately following.

The key changes are usually not out of the ordinary. The principal tonality is D major, but Heinrich cannot resist some avant-garde modulations. One section (pp. 6-7) stands out; tremolante chords are reinforced with the bassoon and drum/bell pedals in the succession F-sharp major, B minor, E major seventh, A major, C major, E-flat major, G-sharp diminished-seventh, then A major seventh (meas. 97-104). For another passage between sections 20 and 21 (bottom of pp. 8-9), a repeated F-major chord is suddenly followed by repeated chords in C-sharp major with a key-signature of seven sharps.

Heinrich, in his piano music, never topped the surprise, however, in the final twelve measures. After a cadence to C minor, with the next chord, on G-flat a tritone away, he continues a descent of fifths as far as B-double-flat which becomes enharmonically an A-major seventh chord in preparation to the anticipated tonic of D major. Instead he uses the leading-tone, C-sharp, enharmonically as a new tonic of D-flat--a half-step lower than expected (Ex. 8-14).

Ex. 8-14. Heinrich, "The Minstrel's Entertainment with His Blind Pupil," ending, meas. 518-30 (*Sylviad* [b], no. 5; arr. and condensed here from the original duet).

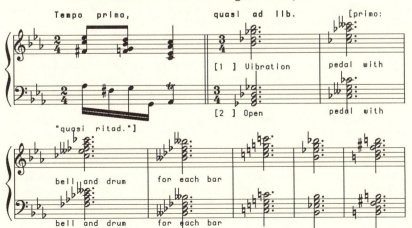

If this joke indicates something of Heinrich's personality, he must have been a very whimsical character indeed.

As indicated earlier, the full extent of Heinrich's creative imagination and pianistic virtuosity is contained in the two toccatas in *Sylviad.* "Toccatina capriciosa," no. 2 of the first set (EAKM no. 26)[43] is the shortest, but still extends eight fully packed pages in the original score. The only apparent reason for the diminutive "toccatina" is that "Toccata grande cromatica" in the second set is much longer, extending to no fewer than twenty-seven pages.

"Toccatina capriciosa" is free in form, and improvisational in style almost throughout. In keeping with some of Heinrich's other piano works, one musical idea freely follows another, and there are no easily perceived returns of any of them. The work is divided into four sections, plus coda. The principal keys of E-flat major or C minor (three flats) persist until the C major at the beginning of the coda. The final chord at the end, however, is remote--B major!

---

43. The edition can be improved and corrected by the following changes: meas. 12, r.h., add *e'* (printed small--and therefore unnoticed by your editor--in the original) to the chord with the fermata and trill; meas. 13, l.h., *F, F*-sharp, *G* are printed small as if they were last-minute additions--the *G* could be editorially sharped; meas. 30, r.h., third from last chord should read *f"*-natural, *a"*-flat, *d"'* rather than *a"*-natural, *c"'*-flat, *f"'*; meas. 31, r.h., add tie to the 2nd and 3rd *c"*; meas. 32, r.h., 4th arpeggio, the seventh note needs a ledger line to make it read *a"*; meas. 37, l.h., the top *b"'*, with fermata, could probably also use an editorial trill sign; meas. 39, l.h., *c* needs an editorial sharp and the *b'* of the r.h. an editorial natural; meas. 40, r.h., the first three G's could use editorial sharps; meas. 44, l.h., octave F should be 16ths rather than 32nds; meas. 48, l.h., the rhythm of the first three chords should be 16th 16th 8th; meas. 54, r.h., the original direction is "8va a piacere"; meas. 56, r.h., the last *c"'* appears in the original but could editorially be changed to *b"*-flat; meas. 143, l.h., add editorial flat to first *b*; meas. 158-60, l.h., add editorial sharp to all F's; meas. 165-66, l.h., the sharps in beats 2-3 are original, yet redundant.

The initial Larghetto, the most rhapsodic, seems to function as an introduction which moves from E-flat major to a long cadence preparing the C minor at the beginning of the second section. Whereas the first measures of this Adagio section emphasizes the tonic of C as a pedal point, E-flat major is established again in its seventh measure (meas. 30), and the last few measures consist of an incredible cadenza on the dominant, involving long and virtuosic chromatic scales, the hands crossing one another in one of the most impressive sights in all Heinrich's piano music. In the last measure of the section, however, the tonality deceptively changes to G major, then G-flat major and almost immediately G-flat minor, becoming enharmonically F-sharp minor for the first two measures of the succeeding section, marked "Tempo moderato alla marcia."

This third section indeed has several earmarks of the march. Although the initial subsection is an irregular eleven measures long, it bears the persistent dotted rhythm and occasional horn fifths (meas. 46-49) characteristic of the march. The following four subsections, recognized by double barlines, are each eight measures in length, also common in many marches by Heinrich and his contemporaries. Otherwise the march connection is tenuous. From the third measure onwards, E-flat major or minor persists, even through the long sequence and trilled chords that terminate the section.

The fourth section, "Listesso tempo," is the most consistent in style and texture of "Toccata capriciosa." A gentle rhythm of triplet 16th notes, generally broken chords, continues throughout, and the first few measures might pass for Schumann if it weren't for the chromaticism and constant modulations more representative of German music toward the end of the century.

The only fast section is the coda, Allegro moderato, for which the meter changes from duple to 3/4 and the key from C minor to C major. After the first thirteen measures, however, the key is unstable, progressing to C-flat minor, which enharmonically becomes the final key of B major.

As indicated earlier, "Toccata capriciosa" is full of tonal meanderings, chromatic progressions, and unusual harmonic structures, in spite of the basic adherence to E-flat major/minor until the coda. The first surprising modulation is a temporary one, from E-flat to G-flat major and back again, quite close to the beginning of the piece (meas. 5-6). Seven measures toward the end of the first section (meas. 13-19) are particularly unstable in tonality. Some of the temporary tonal levels are C-flat major, a G-major chord (but spelled A-double-flat, C-flat, E-double-flat) leading to G-flat major, suddenly landing on a D-major chord (spelled D, G-flat, A), then another enharmonic spelling of B-double-flat, D-flat, F-flat (instead of A, C-sharp, E). The remaining chords in the passage involve diminished intervals which, with the chromatic lines, are remarkable especially considering this work appeared as early as 1823. Another such passage in the second section (meas. 31-34) is almost as unsettling, and also involves ornamental arpeggios and scales, culminating in the cadenza mentioned earlier. Included in the passage is a well-established G-flat major which is suddenly abandoned in a D-major chord, which by means of a chromatic descent in the bass to B-flat, reaches the dominant of the work's principal key.

Motivic repetition is not entirely absent, but such repetition is never exact. One cannot help but admire the ingenious manner in which Heinrich is able to present a short three-note figure in the first section (meas. 11) no fewer than eight different ways. Repetition is otherwise accomplished by means of sequence. In the same section (meas. 13) a six-note motive appears three times, on higher pitch levels, followed by two successive arpeggio gestures that reappear in a different form to conclude the section. The longest sequence is toward the end of the third section (meas. 76-79), where the pattern repeats as many as thirteen times, each one a scale-step lower--this time Heinrich may be guilty of excess.

In another passage in the fourth section (meas. 91-95) each three-note member of a rising scale is accompanied similarly, but twelve repetitions in the succeeding sequential descent are not identical. The most successful sequence follows shortly (meas. 97-102): the top notes of the right-hand broken chords are *c"*, *d"*, *e"*-flat. The matching descent highlights the notes *c"*-sharp, *b'*-sharp, *b'*, *b'*-flat, accompanied by otherwise normal chords except for the free-floating tonal levels of G minor, A-flat major, C-flat major (sounding B major), F-sharp major, A major, G-sharp major, G major, thence to the main tonality of E-flat.

Although it was stated above that no easily perceived themes return in "Toccata capriciosa," a prominent three-note motive, descending by step, that occurs at the beginning of the second section, may have furnished the composer basic material for other sections in the work. In another guise, it opens the first section in the left hand, accompanied in heterophony by the right (any other explanation would need to justify the parallel octaves!), and reappears in quicker rhythm after the section's first cadence (meas. 10). Whether Heinrich considered a two-note motive later in the second section (end of meas. 31 to meas. 34) a shortened version of the basic three notes cannot be determined. Another possibility are the rising or descending three notes associated with the horn fifths in the third section (meas. 46-47, 48-49, 58-59). More likely is the cadence ending its third subsection (meas. 64-65), and the melodic line beginning the fourth section (see also meas. 97-98 and the three-note cells in meas. 91-92 and 105). Still, any such relationship is subtle, at best.

Heinrich's "Toccatina capriciosa" is one of his richest works, in spite of the difficulties for both performer and listener. Nevertheless, like the late Beethoven quartets, its mysteries are deep. There are a number of outstanding passages, among them the fourth section and the increasing difficulties leading to the end of the section. The printed quotation from Dr. Crotch on the series title-page is particularly appropriate for this work and bears repeating here:

> It is observable in Music, that the finest Compositions & performers do not strike at first, but their beauties & their designs are elicited by repetition.

The other toccata, published as the second number in the second set of *Sylviad*, is at once his most ambitious piano composition and his most uneven. In the length and seriousness of "Toccata grande cromatica" Heinrich may have had Beethoven in mind, although there is no way of knowing which works of the Viennese master Heinrich may have known. None of the four movements bears a resemblance to a specific model of Beethoven. Heinrich, as always, has created a unique work, different from those by other American composers of the time, and unlike others he had written himself.

The title appears in three versions: "Toccata grande cromatica" on its title-page, and "Gran Toccata cromatica" at the head of the score.[44] At the bottom of the first page of *A Divertimento di Ballo*, the last number of the first set, is indicated that "The above Number concludes the first mission to the Royal Academy of Music in Great Britain; the first commencement of the next offering will consist of La Toccata grande fugata, dedicated as a mark of particular respect to the musical Philosopher and Pres[t], D[r] Crotch." The main intent, therefore, seems to have been to impress Crotch with the "scientific" (according to the usage at the time, "craft" according to ours) aspects of his ability as composer.

"Toccata grande cromatica" consists of four movements, each of which could be played as separate works according to the footnote to the first page of score: "Its subdivisions may be considered collectively, or individually, for the introductory *Estravaganza*, written rather Alla *Ipocondria*, an apology is due. The same shall somewhere appear brighter." The first movement, marked "Grave," is "alla ipocondria" in that there is almost no relief from the key of E-flat major until the last thirteen measures (with a temporary modulation to G-flat major, A-flat minor, E-flat minor). The harmonic vocabulary does not often venture outside the primary I-IV-V chords. The sameness of key is the movement's greatest fault, for which an apology indeed seems appropriate.

On the other hand, the "estravaganza" aspect overcompensates by means of extremely ornate ornamentation--scales and various sequential patterns--predominantly in 64th notes, causing a measure to extend beyond the space of a single system of printed music in several instances. The climax of ornateness in this toccata, as well as in all of Heinrich's piano works, is at the bottom of the first page of score where the rhythm subdivides to 1024th notes (eight beams), with a pair of unprecedented 2048th notes (nine beams!) at the end.

Formally, this Grave introduction starts off with periodic structure. Three melodic ideas are presented in two-measure phrases, each followed by complementary variants resulting in four-measure periods.

---

44. Some of the more important editorial suggestions and corrections to the original print (page/system/meas.): "Interludio semplice," meas. 20 (6/5/2) last *g'* needs an editorial natural; meas. 46 (8/1/1) first *g* needs an editorial sharp. "Intermezzo variato," var. 2, meas. 6 (10/4/2) first *g* needs an editorial natural; var. 10, meas. 8 (13/1/1) first *g* needs an editorial flat; var. 11, meas. 2 (13/1/4) *e'* needs an editorial flat; var. 12, meas. 3 (13/3/3) *c"* needs an editorial sharp. "Finale o fantasia tripolata," meas. 14 (17/2/2) *e* needs an editorial flat; p. 20 systems 2-6, p. 21 system 1--substitute bass clef for treble; meas. 71 (23/5/1) penultimate *d* needs an editorial flat; meas. 117 (27/6/6) *f* needs an editorial sharp.

Underneath the succeeding ornamentation lies a varying return of the first (meas. 13-16; 2/5/1) and second (meas. 17-18) idea, then a clearer return of the initial two measures of the second idea (meas. 19-20; 3/4/1). Following three measures apparently unrelated to any theme, a contrasting passage (meas. 24-30) is characterized by less busy rhythmic activity and a temporary shift to C minor. The first four measures of the movement are then recapitulated. The remaining eighteen measures involve no thematic returns, but after the modulations to the other keys--previously mentioned--E-flat (alternating between minor and major modes) settles down to the tonic E-flat major at the end.

The second movement is the most disorganized in form of "Toccata grande cromatica." It is introduced by a short "Interludio semplice: Allegro moderato" beginning in E-flat major, but with a modulation to D-flat major by the end of the four measures. After a double barline, the new key of E minor is a complete surprise--there is no modulation--with the new designation "Piu vivo." The texture sounds like a fugue for four measures, subject with 16th-note countersubject, especially since the subject had just been introduced in the "Interludio semplice" (Ex. 8-15).

Ex. 8-15.   Heinrich, "Toccata grande cromatica," 2nd movement, meas. 5-8 (*Sylviad* [b], no. 2, p. 6).

Heinrich had previously provided the title "La Toccata grande fugata," as explained above. This movement, however, is no fugue: the "subject" never returns. The strongest element of unity is the basic key of E, which returns during the movement (meas. 21-29, 42-50; 6/5/3 and 7/5/3) and towards the end (meas. 60; 8/5/last). Even this key is negated at the end; just after E minor is made major comes an unexpected modulation to C, emphasized with the repeated tremolante chords for the final eight measures. Yet even here the mode ambiguously alternates between major and minor, and the final octaves of C, without harmony, never clarifies the mode. There is no discernible reason for this tonal shift, since the next movement is not in C but A major. Although a variety of keys is used between the E minor of the beginning and C at the end, no hierarchy related to either key is apparent.[45]

Neither a clear formal plan nor principal theme lends another possible aspect of unity, as if Heinrich realized he could not write a fugue and was reduced to musical gibberish. One common element that permeates the music, however, is the scale, usually diatonic and usually extending to an octave. It first appears as the "countersubject," starting with a 16th-rest and continuing in 16th-note motion, both upwards and down (meas. 5-14; see above, Ex. 8-15). Its next appearance is in quarter notes, with parallel thirds (meas. 15-17). Shortly afterwards (meas. 21-28, 33-34; 6/5/3 and 7/3/1) the scale is surrounded by sequential patterns of 16ths, each beat beginning on the next step of the scale. In the surrounding measures (29-32, 35-36; 7/1/last and 7/3/last) the scale more nearly approximates its original form. For the remainder of the movement, the scale is superseded by other figurations and patterns (meas. 37-40, 43-45, 46-47 returning in 58-59; 7/4/2, 7/6/1, 8/1/1/, 8/5/1) and a one-measure sequence appearing in differing guises (meas. 48-57; 8/1/last). The scale reappears unadorned in 8th-note sequences (meas. 61-64; 8/6/1), then, as before, with surrounding figuration (meas. 65-70; 9/1/2). (The 8th-note scale in meas. 64 is echoed in the following measures, elaborated with a kind of 16th-note figuration that returns two measures later--a rare example in his music of repetition of anything at the same tonal level.) The main method of organization, then, is the sequence, along with various forms of the scale. In summary, this movement, besides difficult for the performer, is also difficult for the listener to comprehend.

The most successful movement of "Toccata grande cromatica" is the third, marked "Intermezzo variato," a set of theme and twenty-one variations. This set of variations, and the finale, exist in the composer's manuscript as a part of "A Chromatic Ramble: Toccata for the Pianoforte"[46]--not the same as "A Chromatic Ramble of the Peregrine Harmonist" that had appeared in *Dawning* (see above). In both printed and manuscript versions, the five-measure theme is clearly presented unaccompanied by the left hand, and is discernible--albeit sometimes buried in passagework--in every variation except the twentieth. The only other set of variations by Heinrich is on Haydn's "God save the Emperor," in *The Dawning of Music in Kentucky*, and there too the tune is often buried in figuration but nonetheless can be detected by the careful ear.

---

45. Other prominent keys are established at the following measures: 8 (G), 12 (d), 15 (Bb), 19 (f#), 20 (Gb), 21 (e), 30 (b), 35 (f#), 37 (A), 41 (c#), 42 (E), 51 (G#), 57 (d#).

46. In the Heinrich collection, Library of Congress, vol. 33 no. 1. The manuscript may have been used to engrave *Sylviad*'s "Toccata grande cromatica," but there are minor differences, among them trill signs on the third beats in the "Tema" section and on the right-hand second beats for the first variation.

This movement is further unified by the principal key of A major, used in the second, fifth, and last four variations, but the "cromatica" element of the toccata is reflected in the use of many other keys for the other variations. By means of slightly altering the chromatic inflection within the theme, however, Heinrich is often able to present the theme on one pitch level while simultaneously maintaining the tonal level of another key, as summarized in the following chart--which also shows the differing lengths:

| | | tune | |
variation	length	pitch	key
Tema	5	A	A
1	5	E	E
2	8	A	A
3	5	F#	G
4	5	C#	D
5	5	C#	A
6	6	A	F
7	5	Ab	Db-eb-C#
8	5	E# (E)	C#
9	6	F	eb-gb-bbb
10	9	Eb	c-Eb
11	5	Gb	eb
12	5	A	F
13	6	A	e
14	5	A#-A	b
15	5	E	C
16	5	Eb	c-C
17	6	E	C-E
18	6	A	f#-A
19	5	C#	A
20	10	-	A
21	5	A	A
[coda]	11	-	A-a

(The tune-pitch is determined by the fourth note--the tonic in the theme--but this note is sometimes altered chromatically, creating the ambiguous account of variation 14. The tune is actually on the same pitch-level in variations 15-16; the chart represents the altered fourth note.)

Heinrich's imagination in the treatment of this theme is quite extraordinary. Of the twenty-one variations, the tune is heard as a cantus firmus--intact, or nearly so--in eight of them (variations 1, 2, 8, 10, 11, 13, 16, 17), shifted to a voice other than the top in seven (the bass in 13, 16-19, alto in 4, and tenor in 9). For the non-cantus firmus treatment, the theme is provided with melodic ornamentation (variations 4-7, 19) or buried in keyboard figuration patterns (3, 12, 14, 15, 18). The note values are quickened to 8ths and 16ths in the first measure of the last variation, and then the tune is lost as this variation changes its function to become the coda. Variations 3 and 15 are similar in that there is a pedal point in the left hand with broken-chord figuration outlining the theme in the right. This set of variations is quite unlike those by his American contemporaries of the 1820s. Several standard features are missing, among them the originality of the theme--not the usual popular melody--and the seriousness that suggests its greater suitability as a fugue subject rather than for variations. Other sets of variations of the time rarely stray from the tonic key, and normally have a slow variation in the minor mode before the increased rhythmic activity climaxes in a showy display of virtuosity at the end. By contrast, Heinrich's closing, while including a few virtuoso trills and arpeggios, surprisingly switches from A major, *forte*, to A minor, *piano*, in the final measures--a strange anticlimax. These are the only dynamic markings in "Toccata grande cromatica." Also missing are the differing tempo or character labels for each variation; "Allegro, o tempo primo" apparently applies throughout.

One of Heinrich's most prominent earmarks is his use of melodic sequence, also an important aspect of these variations beginning with the eighth one. An accompanimental pattern is often presented on new tonal levels a step apart. In variation 8, the left hand commences each measure on the pitches *c'*-sharp, *b*-sharp, *a*, *g*-sharp, *f*-sharp; for the next variation the last four measures in the right hand begin with *e'''*-flat, *d'''*-flat, *c''*-flat, *b''*-double-flat. Similar sequences are also prominent in variations 10, 12, 14, 18, and 19, and this is the main feature of variation 20, the only one without the theme. The tonic key is emphasized in the last three measures of variation 21, where a pattern begins on the descending notes of the A-major scale, *a* to *G*-sharp.

Sequences also permeate the last movement, "Finale o fantasia tripolata," the tempo marked "Giusto."[47] Taking up the final dozen pages of this 27-page toccata, the movement is a *perpetuum mobile*--not dissimilar in effect to the finale of Chopin's Sonata in B-flat minor, op. 35, also a whirlwind of notes with constantly changing keys and chromaticism. There is no relief from the persistent 16th-note triplets until the final measures. The principal key of D minor returns intermittently (meas. 15, 23, 48, 58, 86, 100; 17/3/2, 18/2/2, 21/1/2, 22/2/1, 25/2/2, 26/6/1). Other keys, when established, are usually on the flat side, such as B-flat (meas. 21, 38, 96; 18/1/2, 19/6/2, 26/3/2), A-flat (meas. 24, 69, 77; 18/3/2, 23/3/2, 24/2/2), or D-flat (meas. 8, 18, 70, 84; 16/4/2, 17/5/2, 23/4/1, 25/1/2). Of the several important keyboard patterns, the main one, established in the second measure, returns only twice during the movement--one in the tonic key (meas. 23; 18/2/2), the other in F-sharp major almost at midpoint (meas. 46-52; 20/6/1).

Many of the sequences appear on successive pitch-levels of a scale, as in the previous movement. Particularly long-lasting is one left-hand sequence beginning on *f''*-sharp, descending to *a'* (meas. 31-35; 19/2/1), accompanied by broken chords in the other hand. At its last appearance in F-sharp, just mentioned, the main pattern appears

---

47. Correction in the original engraved score: the right-hand clefs, p. 20, beginning with system 2, through the beginning of p. 21, first system, should be bass rather than treble.

thirteen times, rising from *f*-sharp to the tonic of *d"*. This is topped, however, by a shorter sequence that recurs no fewer than eighteen times (meas. 58-62; 22/2/1). It begins on all possible notes of the chromatic scale except A, the dominant, withheld until the tonic 6/4 chord at the end of the passage.

Heinrich's inventive imagination extended to the technique of mirror: one hand simultaneously duplicated in mirror by the other. In the passage following the long sequence just described, chromatic scales in each hand diverge in mirror from a sixth outwards to the triple octave (meas. 63-64; 22/5/2). In another place on the preceding page (Ex. 8-16), other mirror scales are repeated in sequence: beginning with the interval of a compound diminished-seventh, the hands converge to an augmented second before opening out to an octave.

Ex. 8-16.   Heinrich, "Toccata grande cromatica," 3rd movement, meas. 52 (*Sylviad* [b], no. 2, p. 21).

The pattern occurs five times, each a whole tone lower, contributing greatly to the instability of key in the passage.

"Toccata grande cromatica" is an ambitious undertaking, especially for someone who had acquired a serious interest in composition less than a decade earlier. Whereas the first two movements are too free and disorganized to be completely successful in performance, the set of variations is worth reviving. The last movement is especially suitable as a virtuoso showpiece for the pianist willing to invest the time to master its technical and musical difficulties. Heinrich's remark on the title-page was certainly true then: "Chromatic ears are as rare as diamonds. A.P.H." Fortunately, "chromatic ears" are less rare now, a century and a half later, and we can begin to understand what Heinrich's contemporaries could not.

Who in the United States was able to perform the virtuoso piano music Heinrich composed? One candidate is Miss Eliza Eustaphieve, the young daughter of the Russian consul in Boston, Alexis Eustaphieve, who himself was a talented violinist and a frequent contributor to Boston newspapers on various subjects including politics, literature, law, drama, and music.[48] According to John Rowe Parker's Boston journal *The Euterpeiad* for 9 September 1820, reprinted in an article on her for his *A Musical Biography* (1825),[49] "as a performer,

---

48. H. Earle Johnson, *Musical Interludes in Boston*), 148-49.

49. *A Musical Biography*, 207.

she has never yet been excelled or even equalled by any of the same age; and that in applying to her the word *prodigy*, we restore the word itself to its legitimate owner, and rescue it from the profanation to which it has so often been subjected." Heinrich dedicated a song, printed in the *Euterpeiad*, to her: "Fair Pupil of the Tuneful Muse," and in the second set of *Sylviad* two further songs: "The Sylph of Music, or Euterpe's Resignation," no. 14, and no. 4 (previously discussed):

> Overture to the Fair Sylph of America, Miss Eliza Eustaphieve, whose rising fame first reached the Wandering Minstrel on the banks of the lovely Ohio, whence he steered to hail his star of the west which diffuses such radiance around the science of music. Inscribed with feelings of admiration and gratitude for her condescension in performing the first things of the author whilst he was a stranger to her in the wilds of nature.

Indeed, according to the *Euterpeiad* for 2 September 1820, Miss Eustaphieve performed the contents of *The Dawning of Music in Kentucky* without difficulty:

> No sooner did we place this extraordinary, and to say the least, very pureling production before our young *Euterpe* (for once we must be permitted to call her so,) than she went through the whole without encountering any apparent obstruction that could for a moment stop her; and with a correctness, which, though it could not brave the ordeal of close critical inspection, a thing taken into consideration, was yet sufficient to enable us and others present to form the judgment we have just now pronounced upon its merits. This fresh proof, which surprised even us, who were already so familiar with her talents, made any longer silence on our part almost criminal. We were determined from that moment, rather to run the risk of partial offense, than to appear in the opinion of many, and in our own, guilty of apathy and indifference.

Heinrich's piano works may not be for the average amateur, but this is ample defense to the charge that it is unperformable.

The achievement of Heinrich's three collections, *The Dawning of Music in Kentucky*, op. 1, *The Western Minstrel*, op. 2, and *The Sylviad*, op. 3, are quite remarkable and unusual, and luckily copies have survived.[50] They represent strong connections with musical forms and

---

50. They are included in a printed list, "Nomenclature of Scores, Vocal and Instrumental Works, Composed by Anthony Philip Heinrich," given in Upton, 265-67. A copy annotated by the composer is in the Heinrich collection, Library of Congress, end of vol. 4,

styles popular at the time, yet almost no piece escapes Heinrich's penchant for individualism, to create music that is different. He is a unique figure in the history of American music, as important--and enigmatic--to his time as Ives was in his. To achieve as much in music could not have been possible without a stronger musical background than was available in the United States early in the century; therefore the rich musical heritage widely available in Bohemia was essential to Heinrich. Yet this background was combined with an Americanism that was more enthusiastic than demonstrated by those not born abroad. The first native-born composer to achieve international stature was Gottschalk--but he was not born until three years after Heinrich's opus 3 was completed. That Heinrich struggled for recognition without success does not indicate his musical productions were deficient; rather, that they were different. Such music could originate from no other place. Perhaps Americans are now sufficiently weaned from European musical models to recognize Heinrich's music, with all of its excesses, as a worthy manifestation of our own musical heritage.

––––––––

with the handwritten addition: "No. 76. The Washingtonian, or the Deeds of a Hero. Ouverture heroique for full Orchestra." *Dawning*, *Sylviad*, and *Western Minstrel* are nos. 71-73 of a "List of Works, together with Engraved Music Plates, lost by Fire and otherwise." *Dawning* is "out of print and lost"; *Sylviad*--412 pages--"Lost by fire in Boston"; *Western Minstrel* "likewise consumed by the flames in Boston."

BIBLIOGRAPHY

Books, Articles, Dissertations

Bakken, Howard Norman. "The Development of Organ Playing in Boston and New York, 1700-1900." D.M.A. dissertation, University of Illinois, 1975.

Barron, David Milton. "The Early Vocal Works of Anthony Philip Heinrich." Ph.D. dissertation, University of Illinois, 1972.

Benton, Rita. *Ignace Pleyel: A Thematic Catalogue of His Compositions.* New York: Pendragon, 1977.

Bigger, William George. "The Choral Music of Charles Zeuner (1795-1857), German-American Composer, with a Performing Edition of Representative Works." Ph.D. dissertation, University of Iowa, 1976.

Bio-Bibliographical Index of Musicians in the United States of America from Colonial Times. 2nd ed. Ed. Leonard Ellinwood and Keyes Porter. Washington: Music Division, Pan American Union, 1956.

Boyd, Patricia Williams. "Performers, Pedagogues and Pertinent Methodological Literature of the Pianoforte in Mid-Nineteenth Century United States, *ca.*, 1830-1880: A Socio-Cultural Study." D.A. dissertation, Ball State University, 1973.

The British Union-Catalogue of Early Music Printed before the Year 1801: A Record of the Holdings of Over One Hundred Libraries throughout the British Isles. Ed. Edith B. Schnapper. 2 vols. London: Butterworths Scientific Publications, 1957.

Bruce, Neely. "The Piano Pieces of Anthony Philip Heinrich Contained in *The Dawning of Music in Kentucky* and *The Western Minstrel.*" D.M.A. dissertation, University of Illinois, 1971.

Carden, Joy. *Music in Lexington before 1840.* Lexington: Lexington-Fayette County Historic Commission, 1980.

Chase, Gilbert. *America's Music: From the Pilgrims to the Present.* Rev. 2nd ed. New York: McGraw-Hill, 1966. Rev. 3rd ed. Urbana: University of Illinois Press, 1987.

Chmaj, Betty E. "Father Heinrich as Kindred Spirit: or, How the Log-House Composer Became the Beethoven of America." *American Studies* 24, no. 2 (fall 1983): 35-57.

Church Music and Musical Life in Pennsylvania in the Eighteenth Century. Ed. William Lichtenwanger. Publications of the Pennsylvania Society of the Colonial Dames of America, 4. Vol. 3, part 2. Lancaster, Pa.: Wickersham Printing Co., 1947.

Clark, J. Bunker. "American Musical Tributes of 1824-25 to Lafayette: A Report and Inventory." *Fontes Artis Musicae* 28, no. 1 (1979): 17-35. Reprinted in H. Earle Johnson and Bonnie Hedges, eds., *Music in America before 1825* (New York: Da Capo, forthcoming).

——. "American Organ Music before 1830: A Critical and Descriptive Survey." *Diapason*, November 1981, pp. 1, 3, 7.

——. "The Renaissance of Early American Keyboard Music: A Bibliographical Review." *Current Musicology* 18 (1974): 127-32.

——. "The Solo Piano Sonata in Early America: Hewitt to Heinrich." *American Music* 2, no. 3 (fall 1984): 27-46.

Clementi, Muzio. *Clementi's Introduction to the Art of Playing on the Piano Forte.* London, 1804. Reprint, with introduction by Sandra P. Rosenblum. New York: Da Capo, 1974.

Cole, Malcolm. "The Vogue of the Instrumental Rondo in the Late Eighteenth Century." *Journal of the American Musicological Society* 22, no. 3 (fall 1969): 425-55.

Cole, Ronald F. "Music in Portland, Maine, from Colonial Times through the Nineteenth Century." Ph.D. dissertation, Indiana University, 1975.

Complete Catalogue of Sheet Music and Musical Work Published by the Board of Music Trade of the United States of America, 1870. New York, 1871. Reprint, with introduction by Dena J. Epstein. New York: Da Capo, 1973.

Computer Catalog of Nineteenth-Century American-Imprint Sheet Music [at the University of Virginia]. Comp. Lynn T. McRae. Charlottesville: University of Virginia, 1977.

Dichter, Harry, and Elliott Shapiro. *Early American Sheet Music: Its Lure and Its Lore, 1768-1889.* New York: Bowker, 1941. Reprinted as *Handbook of Early American Sheet Music, 1768-1889.* New York: Dover, 1977.

Early American Imprints, 1639-1800. Ed. Clifford K. Shipton. Worcester, Mass.: American Antiquarian Society and Readex Microprint.

Early American Imprints, Second Series, 1801-1819. Ed. Clifford K. Shipton and James E. Mooney. Worcester, Mass.: American Antiquarian Society and Readex Microprint.

Engel, Carl. "Introducing Mr. Braun." *Musical Quarterly* 30, no. 1 (January 1944): 63-83.

Favre, Georges. *La Musique français de piano avant 1830.* Paris: Didier, 1953.

Foster, Myles Birket. *History of the Philharmonic Society of London, 1813-1912.* London: John Lane, 1912.

Fuld, James J., and Mary Wallace Davidson. *18th-Century American Secular Music Manuscripts: An Inventory.* MLA Index & Bibliography Series, 20. Philadelphia: Music Library Association, 1980.

Geil, Jean. "American Sheet Music in the Walter N. H. Harding Collection at the Bodleian Library, Oxford University." *Notes* 34, no. 4 (June 1978): 805-13.

[Gerson, Robert A.] *The Musical Fund Society of Philadelphia, Founded 1820: Its History, Charter, By-Laws, Officers and Membership Roster.* Philadelphia: Musical Fund Society, 1970.

Gerson, Robert A. *Music in Philadelphia.* Philadelphia: Theodore Presser, 1940. Reprint, Westport, Conn.: Greenwood Press, 1972.

Gillespie, John and Anna. *A Bibliography of Nineteenth-Century American Piano Music: With Location Sources and Composer Biography-Index.* Music Reference Collection, 2. Westport: Greenwood Press, 1984.

Grétry, André. *Méthode simple pour apprendre à préluder en peu de temps avec toutes les ressources de l'harmonie.* Paris, 1801/02. Reprint, Monuments of Music and Music Literature in Facsimile, series 2, vol. 102. New York: Broude Bros., 1968.

Hamm, Charles. *Music in the New World.* New York: Norton, 1983.

——. *Yesterdays: Popular Song in America.* New York: Norton, 1979.

Hastings, Thomas. *Dissertation on Musical Taste; or, General Principles of Taste Applied to the Art of Music.* Albany: Websters and Skinners, 1822. Reprint, with introduction by James E. Dooley. New York: Da Capo, 1974.

Heard, Priscilla S. *American Music, 1698-1800: An Annotated Bibliography.* Waco, Tex.: Baylor University, 1975.

Hehr, Milton Gerald. "Musical Activities in Salem, Massachusetts, 1783-1823." Ph.D. dissertation, Boston University, 1963.

Henning, Julia Elmira. "Battle Pieces for the Pianoforte Composed and Published in the United States between 1795 and 1820." D.M.A. document, Boston University, 1968.

Hindman, John Joseph. "Concert Life in Ante Bellum Charleston." Ph.D. dissertation, University of North Carolina, Chapel Hill, 1971.

Hines, James R. "Musical Activities in Norfolk, Virginia, 1680-1973." Ph.D. dissertation, University of North Carolina, Chapel Hill, 1974.

Hitchcock, H. Wiley. *Music in the United States: A Historical Introduction.* 2nd ed. Englewood Cliffs: Prentice-Hall, 1974. 3rd ed., 1988.

Hixon, Donald L. *Music in Early America: A Bibliography of Music in Evans.* Metuchen, N.J.: Scarecrow, 1970.

Hopkins, Robert Elliott. "An Edition of Four Sonatas and Two Sets of Variations for Piano by Alexander Reinagle." D.M.A. dissertation, Eastman School of Music, 1959.

Horton, Charles. "Serious Art and Concert Music for Piano in America in the 100 Years from Alexander Reinagle to Edward MacDowell." Ph.D. dissertation, University of North Carolina, Chapel Hill, 1965.

Humphries, Charles, and William C. Smith. *Music Publishing in the British Isles.* 2nd ed. Oxford: Basil Blackwell, 1970.

Johnson, H. Earle. *Hallelujah, Amen! The Story of the Handel and Haydn Society of Boston.* Boston: Bruce Humphries, 1965. Reprint, New York: Da Capo, 1981.

——. *Musical Interludes in Boston, 1795-1830.* New York: Columbia University Press, 1943. Reprint, New York: AMS Press, 1967.

Kaufman, Charles Howard. "Music in New Jersey, 1655-1860: A Study of Musical Activity and Musicians in New Jersey from Its First Settlement to the Civil War." Ph.D. dissertation, New York University, 1974. Published, with the same title, Rutherford, N.J.: Fairleigh Dickinson University Press, 1981.

Keefer, Lubov. *Baltimore's Music: The Haven of the American Composer.* Baltimore: J. H. Furst, 1962.

Kingman, Daniel. *American Music: A Panorama.* New York: Schirmer, 1979.

Kirk, Elise K. *Music at the White House: A History of the American Spirit.* Urbana: University of Illinois Press, 1986.

Krauss, Anne McClenny. "Alexander Reinagle, His Family Background and Early Professional Career." *American Music* 4, no. 4 (winter 1986): 425-56.

Krohn, Ernst C. "Alexander Reinagle as Sonatist." *Musical Quarterly* 18, no. 1 (January 1932): 140-49.

Krummel, Donald W. "Philadelphia Music Engraving and Publishing, 1800-1820: A Study in Bibliography and Cultural History." Ph.D. dissertation, University of Michigan, 1958.

——. "'Viva Tutti': The Musical Journeys of an Eighteenth-Century Part-Song." *Bulletin of the New York Public Library* 67, no. 1 (January 1963): 57-64.

Lawrence, Vera Brodsky. *Music for Patriots, Politicians, and Presidents: Harmonies and Discords of the First Hundred Years.* New York: Macmillan, 1975.

——. *Strong on Music: The New York Music Scene in the Days of George Templeton Strong, 1836-1875.* Vol. 1: *Resonances, 1836-1850.* New York: Oxford University Press, 1988.

Locke, James Eric. "Early American Piano Theme and Variations, 1790-1830: A Survey of Music and Musicians." M.A. thesis, California State University, Fullerton, 1980.

Loesser, Arthur. *Men, Women and Pianos: A Social History.* New York: Simon and Schuster, 1954.

Loveland, Karl. "The Life of Charles Zeuner, Enigmatic German-American Composer and Organist (1795-1857)." *Tracker* 30, no. 2 (2 November 1986): 19-28.

Lowens, Irving. *Haydn in America,* with "Haydn Autographs in the United States" by Otto E. Albrecht. Bibliographies in American Music, 5. Detroit: Information Coordinators, 1979.

——. *Music and Musicians in Early America.* New York: Norton, 1964.

Madeira, Louis C. *Annals of Music in Philadelphia and History of the Musical Fund Society.* Philadelphia: J. B. Lippincott, 1896. Reprint, New York: Da Capo, 1973.

Mann, Walter Edward. "Piano Making in Philadelphia before 1825." Ph.D. dissertation, University of Iowa, 1977.

Maust, Wilbur Richard. "The Symphonies of Anthony Philip Heinrich Based on American Themes." Ph.D. dissertation, Indiana University, 1973.

McKay, John. "William Selby, Musical Émigré in Colonial Boston." *Musical Quarterly* 57, no. 4 (October 1971): 609-27.

Meyer, Eve R. "Benjamin Carr's *Musical Miscellany*." *Notes* 33, no. 2 (December 1976): 253-65.

Moore, Lillian. *The Duport Mystery.* Dance Perspectives, 7. Brooklyn, 1960.

Morneweck, Evelyn Foster. *Chronicles of Stephen Foster's Family.* 2 vols. Pittsburgh: University of Pittsburgh Press, 1944.

The National Tune Index: Early American Wind and Ceremonial Music, 1636-1836. Comp. Raoul F. Camus. New York: University Music Editions, forthcoming.

The National Tune Index: 18th-Century Secular Music. Comp. Kate Van Winkle Keller and Carolyn Rabson. New York: University Music Editions, 1980.

Nelson, Robert U. *The Technique of Variation: A Study of the Instrumental Variation from Antonio de Cabezon to Max Reger.* Berkeley: University of California Press, 1949.

The New Grove Dictionary of Music and Musicians (1980). S.v. Benjamin Carr, Philip Anthony [*sic*] Corri, Joseph Gehot, Geib, Gottlieb Graupner, Peter Albrecht von Hagen, Anthony Philip Heinrich, James Hewitt, George K. Jackson, Klemm & Brother(s), Francis Linley, John Christopher Moller, Alexander Reinagle, Oliver Shaw, Raynor [*sic*] Taylor, Filippo Trajetto, George Willig.

The New Grove Dictionary of American Music (1986). Articles in addition to those revised from *New Grove* (above): Battle Music, George E. Blake, James Bremner, William Brown, Arthur Clifton, William R. Coppock, Pierre Landrin Duport, Jacob Eckhard, Sr., Denis-Germain Etienne, Charles H. Gilfert, von Hagen, Charles Hommann, James F. Hance, Francis Hopkinson, Charles Frederic Hupfield, Loud, Francesco Masi, Raymond Meetz, Christopher Meineke, Julius Metz, Peter K. Moran, Orchestral music, Organ music, Victor Pelissier, Philip Phile, Piano(forte), Piano music, Popular music II 6: popular piano music, Edward Riley, J. George Schetky, William Selby, Charles Taws, Joseph C. Taws, Charles Thibault, Peter Weldon, T. V. Wiesenthal, Joseph Willson, Charles Zeuner.

New Instructions for Playing the Harpsichord, Piano-Forte or Spinnet. London: A. Bland, ca. 1790. Reprint, Monuments of Music and Music Literature in Facsimile, series 1, vol. 15. New York: Broude Bros., 1967.

New York Public Library Music Division, Lincoln Center. *Am-1 Collection of Sheet Music to 1830.* 23 microfilm reels. LaCrosse, Wisc.: Brookhaven Press, [1980].

The Newberry Library Catalog of Early American Printed Sheet Music. Comp. Bernard E. Wilson. 3 vols. Boston: G. K. Hall, 1983.

Newman, William S. *The Sonata in the Classical Era.* Chapel Hill: University of North Carolina Press, 1963.

Norton, M. D. Herter. "Haydn in America (before 1820)." *Musical Quarterly* 18, no. 2 (April 1932): 309-37.

Ochse, Orpha. *The History of the Organ in the United States.* Bloomington: Indiana University Press, 1975.

Ogasapian, John. *Organ Building in New York City, 1700-1900.* Braintree, Mass.: Organ Literature Foundation, 1977.

Owen, Barbara. "American Organ Music and Playing from 1700." *Organ Institute Quarterly* 10, no. 3 (autumn 1963): 7-13.

——. *The Organ in New England.* Raleigh: Sunbury, 1979.

Parker, John Rowe, ed. *The Euterpeiad: or, Musical Intelligencer.* Boston, 1820-23. Reprint, with introduction by Charles E. Wunderlich. New York: Da Capo, 1977.

Parker, John Rowe. *A Musical Biography: or, Sketches of the Lives and Writings of Eminent Musical Characters, Interspersed with an Epitome of Interesting Musical Matter.* Boston: Stone & Fovell, 1825. Reprint, with introduction by Frederick Freedman. Detroit: Information Coordinators, 1975.

The Preceptor for the Piano-Forte Organ or Harpsichord. London: Preston, ca. 1785. Reprint, Monuments of Music and Music Literature in Facsimile, series 1, vol. 16. New York: Broude Bros., 1967.

Redway, Virginia Larkin. "The Carrs, American Musical Publishers." *Musical Quarterly* 18, no. 1 (January 1932): 150-77.

Ringer, Alexander L. "The Chasse as a Music Topic of the 18th Century." *Journal of the American Musicological Society* 6 (summer 1953): 148-59.

——. "The Chasse: Historical and Analytical Bibliography of a Musical Genre." Ph.D. dissertation, Columbia University, 1955.

Rogers, Delmer D. "Public Music Performers in New York City from 1800 to 1850." *Yearbook for Inter-American Musical Research* 6 (1970): 5-50.

The Scots Musical Museum. 6 vols. 1787-1803. Reprint of 4 vols., 1853, in 2 vols. Hatboro, Penn.: Folklore Associates, 1962.

Shaw, Ralph R., and Richard H. Shoemaker, comps. *American Bibliography: A Preliminary Checklist* [for 1801-19]. New York: Scarecrow, 1958-63.

Shifflet, Anne Louise. "Church Musical Life in Frederick, Maryland, 1745-1845." M.A. thesis, American University, 1971.

Shoemaker, Richard H., comp. *A Checklist of American Imprints* [for 1820-29]. New York: Scarecrow, 1964-71.

Smith, Ronnie L. "The Church Music of Benjamin Carr (1768-1831)." D.M.A. dissertation, Southwestern Baptist Theological Seminary, 1969.

Sonneck, Oscar. *A Bibliography of Early Secular American Music (18th Century).* Revised and enlarged by William Treat Upton. Washington: Library of Congress Music Division, 1945. Reprint, with preface by Irving Lowens. New York: Da Capo, 1964.

——. *Early Concert-Life in America (1731-1800).* Leipzig, 1907. Reprints, Wiesbaden: Sändy, 1969, and New York: Da Capo, 1978.

Spillane, Daniel. *History of the American Pianoforte: Its Technical Development, and the Trade.* New York: author, 1890. Reprint, with introduction by Rita Benton. New York: Da Capo, 1969.

Sprenkle, Charles A. "The Life and Works of Benjamin Carr (1768-
1831)." 2 vols. D.M.A. dissertation, Peabody Conservatory,
1970.

Stetzel, Ronald D. "John Christopher Moller (1753-1803) and His Role
in Early American Music." 2 vols. Ph.D. dissertation, University of Iowa, 1965.

Stevenson, Robert. "Música secular en Jamaica, 1688-1822." *Revista
Musical de Venezuela*, año 4, nos. 9-11 (January-December
1983): 149-50.

Tick, Judith. *American Women Composers before 1870*. Studies in
Musicology, 57. Ann Arbor: UMI Research Press, 1983.

Upton, William Treat. *Anthony Philip Heinrich: A Nineteenth-Century
Composer in America*. New York: Columbia University Press,
1939. Reprint, New York: AMS Press, 1967.

Wagner, John Waldorf. "James Hewitt: His Life and Works." Ph.D.
dissertation, Indiana University, 1969.

——. "James Hewitt, 1770-1827." *Musical Quarterly* 58, no. 2 (April
1972): 259-76.

——. "The Music of James Hewitt: A Supplement to the Sonneck-
Upton and Wolfe Bibliographies." *Notes* 29, no. 2 (December
1972): 224-27.

Waters, Edward N. "Music." *The Library of Congress Quarterly
Journal of Current Acquisitions* 16 (November 1958): 24-26.

Wilhite, Charles. "An Early American Organist: Benjamin Carr."
Clavier 12, no. 2 (February 1973): 24-31.

Wolf, Edward C. "Music in Old Zion, Philadelphia, 1750-1850."
Musical Quarterly 58, no. 3 (October 1972): 622-52.

Wolfe, Richard J. *Early American Music Engraving and Publishing: A
History of Music Publishing in America from 1787 to 1825*.
Urbana: University of Illinois Press, 1980.

——. *Secular Music in America, 1801-1825: A Bibliography*. 3 vols.
New York Public Library, 1964.

Wolverton, Byron Adams. "Keyboard Music and Musicians in the
Colonies and United States of America before 1830." Ph.D. dissertation, Indiana University, 1966.

Wright, Edith A., and Josephine A. McDevitt. "Henry Stone, Lithographer." *Antiques* 34 (July 1938): 16-19.

Wunderlich, Charles E. "A History and Bibliography of Early
American Musical Periodicals, 1782-1852." Ph.D. dissertation,
University of Michigan, 1962.

Yellin, Victor Fell. "Rayner Taylor." *American Music* 1, no. 3 (fall
1983): 48-71.

Modern and Reprint Editions of Music

Bremner, Robert. *The Harpsichord or Spinnet Miscellany*. London,
1765. Reprint, with preface by J. S. Darling. Williamsburg:
Colonial Williamsburg, 1972.

Carr, Benjamin. *Benjamin Carr's Federal Overture (1794)*. Reprint,
with introduction by Irving Lowens. Philadelphia: Musical
Americana, 1957.

——. *Selected Sacred and Secular Songs.* Ed. Eve R. Meyer. Recent Researches in American Music, 15. Madison: A-R Editions, 1986.

——, ed. *Musical Journal for the Piano Forte.* Philadelphia: Carr & Schetky, 1800-04. Reprint in 2 vols. Wilmington, Del.: Scholarly Resources, 1972.

——, ed. *Carr's Musical Miscellany in Occasional Numbers.* Baltimore and Philadelphia: Carr, 1812-25. Reprint, with introduction by Eve R. Meyer. Earlier American Music, 21. New York: Da Capo, 1982.

Clark, J. Bunker, ed. *Anthology of Early American Keyboard Music, 1787-1830.* Recent Researches in American Music, 1-2. Madison: A-R Editions, 1977.

Darling, James S., ed. *A Little Keyboard Book: Eight Tunes of Colonial Virginia.* Williamsburg: Colonial Williamsburg, 1972.

Eckhard, Jacob. *Jacob Eckhard's Choirmaster's Book of 1809.* Facsimile, with introduction by George W. Williams. Columbia: University of South Carolina Press, 1971.

Engel, Carl, comp., W. Oliver Strunk, ed. *Music from the Days of George Washington.* Washington, 1931. Reprint, New York: AMS Press, 1970.

Gillespie, John, comp. *Nineteenth-Century American Piano Music.* New York: Dover, 1978.

Gold, Edward, ed. *The Bicentennial Collection of American Keyboard Music (1790-1900).* Dayton: McAfee, 1975.

Goldman, Richard Franko, and Roger Smith. *Landmarks of Early American Music, 1760-1800: A Collection of Thirty-Two Compositions.* New York: G. Schirmer, 1943. Reprint, New York: AMS Press, 1974.

Heinrich, Anthony Philip. *The Dawning of Music in Kentucky,* op. 1, and *The Western Minstrel,* op. 2. Philadelphia, 1820. Reprint, Earlier American Music, 10. New York: Da Capo, 1972.

——. *The Sylviad, or Minstrelsy of Nature in the Wilds of N. America,* op. 3. Boston, 1823 and 1825-26. Reprint, with introduction by J. Bunker Clark. Earlier American Music, 28. New York: Da Capo, forthcoming.

Hewitt, James. *Selected Compositions.* Ed. John W. Wagner. Recent Researches in American Music, 7. Madison: A-R Editions, 1980.

Hinson, Maurice, ed. *Piano Music in Nineteenth Century America.* 2 vols. Chapel Hill: Hinshaw, 1975.

Hinson, Maurice, and Anne McClenny Krauss, with David Carr Glover, eds. *Music of the Capital City: A Collection of Keyboard Pieces and Songs Performed in Philadelphia during the Early Days of the Young Republic.* Miami, Fla.: Belwin Mills, 1987.

Hopkinson, Francis. *Seven Songs for the Harpsichord or Forte Piano.* Philadelphia, 1788. Reprint, Philadelphia: Musical Americana, 1954. 2nd reprinting, New York: Broude Bros., 1959.

——. *Francis Hopkinson's Lessons: A Facsimile Edition of Hopkinson's Personal Keyboard Book: An Anthology of Keyboard Lessons & Arrangements Copied in Hopkinson's Own Hand.* Notes by David P. McKay. Washington: C. T. Wagner, 1979.

Howard, John Tasker, ed. *The Music of George Washington's Time.* Washington, 1931.

——, ed. *A Program of Early American Piano Pieces.* New York: J. Fischer & Bro., 1931.

Keillor, Elaine, ed. *The Canadian Musical Heritage* 1: *Piano Music I.* Ottawa: Canadian Musical Heritage Society, 1983.

Krauss, Anne McClenny, and Maurice Hinson, eds. *Dances of the Young Republic.* Chapel Hill: Hinshaw, 1977.

Latrobe, Christian I. *Nine Preludes for Organ.* Ed. Karl Kroeger. Charlotte, N.C.: Brodt Music Co., 1978.

The London Pianoforte School, 1766-1860. Ed. Nicholas Temperley. Vol. 7: *Works for Pianoforte Solo by Late Georgian Composers Samuel Wesley and Contemporaries, Published from 1766 to 1830.* New York: Garland, 1985.

Marrocco, W. Thomas, and Harold Gleason, eds. *Music in America: An Anthology from the Landing of the Pilgrims to the Close of the Civil War, 1620-1865.* New York: Norton, 1964.

McClenny, Anne, and Maurice Hinson, eds. *A Collection of Early American Keyboard Music.* Cincinnati: Willis, 1971.

——, eds. *Duets of Early American Music (Level Four).* Rockville Centre, N.Y.: Belwin-Mills, 1972.

——, eds. *Early American Music (Level Four).* Rockville Centre, N.Y.: Belwin-Mills, 1972.

Miller, Carl, ed. *Marches of the Presidents, 1789-1909.* New York: Chappell & Co., 1968.

Owen, Barbara, ed. *A Century of American Organ Music.* 3 vols. Dayton: McAfee, 1975-76; Melville, N.Y.: Belwin-Mills, 1983.

Pelissier, Victor. *Pelissier's Columbian Melodies* [1812]. Ed. Karl Kroeger. Recent Researches in American Music, 13-14. Madison: A-R Editions, 1984.

Reinagle, Alexander. *Four Sonatas, Andante, Theme and Variations, and Adagio for Piano.* Ed. Sylvia Glickman. New York: Da Capo, forthcoming.

——. *The Philadelphia Sonatas.* Ed. Robert Hopkins. Recent Researches in American Music, 5. Madison: A-R Editions, 1978.

——. *Six Scots Tunes.* Ed. Maurice Hinson and Anne McClenny Krauss. Chapel Hill: Hinshaw, 1975.

——. *Thirteen Short and Easy Duets.* Ed. Anne McClenny Krauss and Maurice Hinson. Chapel Hill: Hinshaw, 1976.

——. *Twenty-Four Short and Easy Pieces.* Ed. Anne McClenny Krauss and Maurice Hinson. Chapel Hill: Hinshaw, 1975.

Selby, William. *Keyboard Music of William Selby.* Ed. Linton Powell. Boston: Boston Music Co., 1979.

——. *A Lesson for the Organ.* Ed. E. Power Biggs. New York: Associated, 1955.

——. *Two Voluntaries for Organ.* Ed. Daniel Pinkham. Boston: E. C. Schirmer, 1972.

Spong, Jon, ed. *Early American Compositions for Organ (of the 18th and 19th Centuries).* Nashville: Abingdon, 1968.

Walter, Samuel, ed. *Organ Americana: Compositions by Early American Composers.* Nashville: Abingdon, 1976.

Name Index

TITLE INDEX

(Items marked with asterisks are still listed as for sale
in the *Complete Catalogue of Sheet Music and Musical Work
Published by the Board of Music Trade of the
United States of America, 1870*)

Subject Index

About the Author

J. Bunker Clark is professor of music history at the University
of Kansas, where he has been on the faculty since 1965. He
earned three degrees at the University of Michigan, and was a
Fulbright scholar at Jesus College, Cambridge University, in
1962-63. His publications include *Transposition in Seventeenth
Century English Organ Accompaniments and the Transposing
Organ* (Detroit, 1974), *Anthology of Early American Keyboard
Music, 1787-1830* (Recent Researches in American Music, vols.
1-2, 1977), *Nathaniel Giles: Anthems* (Early English Church
Music, vol. 23, 1979), and he edited and prepared for publica-
tion Ernst C. Krohn's *Music Publishing in St. Louis* (Biblio-
graphies in American Music, vol. 11, 1988). He is also the
author of *Music at KU: A History of the University of Kansas
Music Department.* He has contributed to *Music & Letters,
Musica Disciplina, Notes, Current Musicology, Fontes Artis
Musicae, American Music,* and *The New Grove Dictionary of
American Music.* He has been active in the American Associa-
tion of University Professors, the American Musicological
Society, and the Sonneck Society. With his wife Marilyn S.
Clark, he was editor of Bibliographies in American Music, pub-
lished by Harmonie Park Press for the College Music Society, in
1975-84, has been general editor for that publisher since 1982,
and from 1985 has been the series editor of Detroit Studies in
Music Bibliography.